STUDIES IN IMPERIALISM

general editor John M. MacKenzie

When the 'Studies in Imperialism' series was founded more than twenty years ago, emphasis was laid upon the conviction that 'imperialism as a cultural phenomenon had as significant an effect on the dominant as on the subordinate societies'. With more than sixty books published, this remains the prime concern of the series. Cross-disciplinary work has indeed appeared covering the full spectrum of cultural phenomena, as well as examining aspects of gender and sex, frontiers and law, science and the environment, language and literature, migration and patriotic societies, and much else. Moreover, the series has always wished to present comparative work on European and American imperialism, and particularly welcomes the submission of books in these areas. The fascination with imperialism, in all its aspects, shows no sign of abating, and this series will continue to lead the way in encouraging the widest possible range of studies in the field. 'Studies in Imperialism' is fully organic in its development, always seeking to be at the cutting edge, responding to the latest interests of scholars and the needs of this ever-expanding area of scholarship.

Ordering Africa

MANCHESTER
1824

Manchester University Press

Ordering Africa

ANTHROPOLOGY, EUROPEAN IMPERIALISM, AND THE POLITICS OF KNOWLEDGE

Helen Tilley with Robert J. Gordon

MANCHESTER UNIVERSITY PRESS
Manchester and New York

distributed exclusively in the USA
by PALGRAVE

Published by Manchester University Press
Oxford Road, Manchester M13 9NR, UK
and Room 400, 175 Fifth Avenue, New York, NY 10010, USA
www.manchesteruniversitypress.co.uk

Distributed in the United States exclusively by
Palgrave Macmillan, 175 Fifth Avenue,
New York, NY 10010, USA

Distributed in Canada exclusively by
UBC Press, University of British Columbia, 2029 West Mall,
Vancouver, BC, Canada V6T 1Z2

British Library Cataloguing-in-Publication Data is available

Library of Congress Cataloging-in-Publication Data is available

ISBN 978 0 7190 8212 2 paperback

First published by Manchester University Press in hardback 2007

This paperback edition first published 2010

Printed by Lightning Source

CONTENTS

[v]

CONTENTS

NOTES ON CONTRIBUTORS

BRUCE BERMAN is Director and Principal Investigator of the Research Program in Ethnicity and Democratic Governance and Emeritus Professor of Political Studies at Queen's University, Canada. He is working on a book on Jomo Kenyatta and Louis Leakey with John Lonsdale and is co-editor and co-author of *Ethnicity and Democracy in Africa* (2004). He was President of the US African Studies Association in 2004–05.

JOHN CINNAMON teaches anthropology and African Studies courses at Miami University (Ohio). He has undertaken extensive research in Gabon and is currently working on the history of northern Gabonese social landscapes, the contributions of missionary ethnographers, and the biography of a late colonial spirit, Mademoiselle.

ROBERT J. GORDON is a Professor at the University of Vermont and associated with Free State University. He is author of *Bushman Myth: The Making of a Namibian Underclass* (1992) and *Picturing Bushman: the Denver African Expedition of 1925* (1997). While he has broad interests his particular concern is Namibia.

PATRICK HARRIES is Professor of African History at the University of Basel, Switzerland and author of *Work, Culture, and Identity: Migrant Labourers in Mozambique and South Africa, c. 1860–1910* (1994). He has written extensively about the politics of identity, ethnicity and slavery in Southern Africa. His latest book, *Butterflies and Barbarians: Swiss missionaries and systems of knowledge in southeast Africa*, is in press.

NANCY ROSE HUNT teaches African history at the University of Michigan. Her book, *A Colonial Lexicon: Of Birth Ritual, Medicalization, and Mobility in the Congo* (Duke, 1999), received the Herskovits Prize in 2000.

JEAN-HERVÉ JEZEQUEL defended his Ph.D. at l'Ecole des Hautes Etudes en Sciences Sociales (Paris) in 2002. His research questions the emergence and role of 'middle figures' in the French colonial system. He currently teaches African History at Emory University in Atlanta.

DOUGLAS H. JOHNSON has written extensively about the history of the Southern Sudan and North East Africa. He is the author of *Nuer Prophets* (1994), *The Root Causes of Sudan's Civil Wars* (2003), and the editor of *Governing the Nuer* (1993) and the British Documents on the End of Empire *Sudan* volume (1998).

BENOÎT DE L'ESTOILE currently holds a research fellowship from the Centre National de la Recherche Scientifique and teaches social anthropology at the Ecole Normale Supérieure, Paris. He is author of *Le goût des autres. De l'exposition coloniale aux arts premiers* (forthcoming), and coeditor of *Empires, Nations, and Natives. Anthropology and State-making* (2005). He has published widely on anthropology and empire-building in France and Britain, and on museum anthropology.

JOHN LONSDALE is Emeritus Professor of Modern African History at the University of Cambridge, England, and Fellow of Trinity College. Co-author, with Bruce Berman, of *Unhappy Valley: Conflict in Kenya and Africa* (2 vols 1992), he works on the modern history of Kenya.

SARA PUGACH was Assistant Professor of History at The Ohio State University from 2002–06, and is currently a visiting scholar at UC-Irvine. She is the author of several articles, including 'Carl Meinhof and the German Influence on Nicholas van Warmelo's Ethnological and Linguistic Writings, 1927–1935', which appeared in the December 2004 *Journal of Southern African Studies*, and 'Images of Race and Redemption: The Protestant Missionary Contribution to Carl Meinhof's *Zeitschrift für Kolonialsprachen* in the Early Twentieth Century', which was published in the December 2004 *Le Fait Missionnaire*. Professor Pugach is currently completing a manuscript on the history of African Studies in Germany and its relationship to the human sciences in South Africa during the late nineteenth and early twentieth centuries.

EMMANUELLE SIBEUD is *Maitre de Conferences* in the Histoy Department of the University of Paris VIII. She is the author of *Une science impérials pour l'Afrique? La construction des savoirs africanistes en France, 1878–1930* (Paris, 2002) and has edited, with Jean-Loup Amselle, *Maurice Delafosse. Entre orientalisme et ethnographie: l'itinéraire d'un africaniste, 1870–1926* (Paris, 1998) and with Anne Piriou, *L'africanisme en questions* (Paris, 1997).

BARBARA SÒRGONI (MA Sussex; DPhil Istituto Universitario Orientale, Naples) is Research Fellow in Cultural Anthropology at the University of Bologna. Author of *Parole e Corpi. Antropologia, Discorso Giuridico e Politiche Sessuali Interrazziali nella Colonia Eritrea, 1890–1941* (Napoli: Liguori, 1998) and *Etnografia e Colonialismo. L'Eritrea e l'Etiopia di Alberto Pollera* (Torino: Bollati Boringhieri, 2001), she has written extensively about Italian colonialism, gender and racism, and the history of Italian anthropology.

HOLGER STOECKER studied at the Humboldt University at Berlin, Germany, where he obtained a Ph.D. degree. His dissertation thesis on African Studies in Berlin will be published as *Afrikawissenschaften in Berlin von 1919 bis 1945. Zur Geschichte und Topographie eines wissenschaftlichen Netzwerkes* in 2007. He has written several articles on colonial sciences in Germany and is co-editor of *Mission und Macht im Wandel politischer Orientierungen*.

Europäische Missionsgesellschaften in politischen Spannungsfeldern in Afrika und Asien zwischen 1800 und 1945 (2005).

HELEN TILLEY is Assistant Professor in the History Department at Princeton University with affiliations to the Programs in the History of Science and African Studies. She has published a series of articles on environmental, medical and racial sciences in British Africa and is completing her first book, *Africa as a Living Laboratory: Scientific Knowledge, Imperial Development, and the Nature of British Tropical Africa.*

GARY WILDER is Associate Professor of history at Pomona College and the author of *The French Imperial Nation-State: Negritude and Colonial Humanism between the World Wars* (University of Chicago Press, 2005). His current projects include research on decolonisation and temporality and research on Francophone mercenaries and parastatal formations.

ACKNOWLEDGMENTS

Several of the chapters in this volume were first presented at a three-day conference held at Oxford University on 10–12 March 2000. Early in the planning process, I enlisted Robert J. Gordon to work with me as a collaborator. His encouragement, editorial assistance and friendship since then have been invaluable.

For their support of the conference itself, we are indebted to: Jean-Claude Vatin, then director of the Maison Française d'Oxford; Nathalie Jas, then history of science coordinator at the Maison Française; Wendy James, of the Institute of Social and Cultural Anthropology; Megan Vaughan, now Smuts Professor of Commonwealth History at Cambridge University; and William Beinart, Director of African Studies at Oxford. These individuals not only helped to secure funds for the event, but also offered many constructive suggestions about the topic itself. For their financial support our thanks to the Maison Française, the British Academy, the African Studies Program, the Institute of Social and Cultural Anthropology, the Wellcome Unit for the History of Medicine, the Inter-Faculty Committee for African Studies and the Modern History Faculty.

Among those whose work does not appear in this volume, but who formally contributed to the lively discussions that took place during the conference itself, we would like to acknowledge: Andrew Apter, Wendy James, Henrika Kuklick, Elisio Macamo, David Mills, Vinh-Kim Nguyen, Peter Pels, H. Glenn Penny, Vincent de Rooij, Lyn Schumaker, Owen Sichone, Richard Werbner, Megan Vaughan and Andrew Zimmerman. It was a particular pleasure to get to know so many of these wonderful scholars; it also seemed fitting that we had Richard Brown and Wendy James present since they were among the original contributors to Talal Asad's 1973 volume, *Anthropology and the Colonial Encounter*, which gave the event some historical continuity.

Edited volumes are sometimes a risky and almost always a lengthy undertaking and I would like to thank the contributors themselves for their patience and their willingness to revise their work. Alison Welsby, Jonathan Bevan and John MacKenzie at MUP deserve similar appreciation, particularly for their flexibility around deadlines. Princeton University's Committee on Research in the Humanities and Social Sciences and the History Department provided the funds to off-set translation and publishing expenses. Likewise, two research assistants, Matthew Fox and Jeffrey Gonda, helped me to edit and format the chapters. My time on this project was partially supported by a grant from the National Science Foundation under award number SES-0349928. (The conclusions and arguments expressed in this book are those of the authors and do not reflect the views of the NSF.) Finally we would like to thank Wolfe Schmokel, Jeanne Penvenne, and Judith Irvine for their assistance reviewing specific chapters.

[xi]

ACKNOWLEDGMENTS

Intellectual camaraderie is a marvelous thing and I was fortunate enough to be able to write the book's introduction while a visiting fellow at the Institute for Advanced Study where I was part of a superb group of colleagues including Caroline Arni, Adam Ashforth, Patricia Clough, Paulla Ebron, Duana Fullwiley, Clifford Geertz, Sarah Igo, John Mowitt, Kenda Mutongi and Joan Scott. My thanks to them all for making my time there so rewarding. Also to my friends from Princeton and Oxford for their humor and understanding, I am especially grateful to Angela Creager, Gyan Prakash, Michael Gordin, Sloan Mahone, Lotte Hughes, Michael and Judy Laffan, Christina Jimenez, Ranjani Mazumdar, Tania Munz, Ingrid Yngstrom, Cécile Fabre, Zoë Laidlaw, Damon Salesa, Peter Rainbird and James McDougall. Over the last several years, I have had some of the most interesting conversations about African history and imperialism with my mother, Susan Tilley, whose intellectual acumen and breadth never cease to amaze me. My list would not be complete without acknowledging my gratitude to her.

Helen Tilley

GENERAL EDITOR'S INTRODUCTION

The relationship between anthropology and imperialism has long been a subject of debate – at least from the years between the two world wars of the twentieth century. However, although anthropology has been seen to have its origins and development deeply implicated in the practice, performance and perceptions of imperial rule, it is far from being unique in this regard. The disciplines of Geography, Museology, Archaeology, Tropical Medicine and Agriculture, as well as many natural historical, environmental and hydrographic studies, not to mention the development of a modern western historiography, are similarly embedded in the imperial period. Indeed, Lord Hailey and his associates swept them all up into their monumental *African Survey* of 1938 (revised 1956), in so many ways an elegiac paean to the era of professionalisation and supposedly progressive studies in relation to Africa.

Yet the relationship of these disciplines with imperialism is far from unproblematic. The buzz phrase 'mutually constitutive' requires, as this volume demonstrates, many modifications and conditions imposed upon it. What is interesting for the general student of imperialism is the manner in which these anthropological analyses so well reflect developments elsewhere in the study of the pasts of so many disciplines. However much we must recognise the inequalities of power relations between imperial societies and their subjects, still a subject/object, binary relationship will not do. Both were deeply affected by the encounter. Colonised peoples never fully lost their own agency. Imperial relations were always interactive in some shape or form. Colonial systems of control, including their intellectual underpinnings, were also often hesitant, contradictory, and ineffectual. Nor were they always nationalistic. Imperial powers shared information and ideas. Scientists at least imagined that they were part of an international community. Only through 'comparative imperialism' can we fully understand the colonial urge.

This collection of essays pushes such ideas further than before. Here we have some consideration of anthropological forms in France, Germany, Italy, Switzerland (though not an imperial power, still deeply influenced by its contemporary resonances) and Britain. We have studies not only of western anthropologists, but also of the influence of their assistants and translators, both in Europe and in the wider world, of the interests of missionaries, administrators and others, of the (often fuzzy) interface between the 'amateur' and the 'professional'. Through such detailed analyses it becomes apparent that the relationship between anthropology and imperial rule was often tense and contradictory. Anthropologists could be subversive as well as supportive, their research often moving tangentially from the demands of imperial processes, their encounters in the 'field' modifying their sense of superiority and assurance. Their efforts to set up national institutions to promote the practical efficacy of their discipline seldom met with complete success; nor did their attempts to internationalise their community of scholars and knowledge. If they were indeed in the business of creating a 'cognitive architecture', it was Gaudi-esque in its complexities, ramshackle in its construction. Maybe a more monolithic restatement will come some day, but this work constitutes an important step in the establishment of imperial/intellectual diversity.

John M. MacKenzie

Introduction: Africa, imperialism, and anthropology

Helen Tilley[1]

> To the colonialist mind it was always of the utmost importance to be able to say: I know my natives, a claim which implied two things at once: (a) that the native was really quite simple and (b) that understanding him and controlling him went hand in hand – understanding being a pre-condition for control and control constituting adequate proof of understanding. (Chinua Achebe, 1975)[2]

> What do we know of Africa and its inhabitants to-day? If we sweep aside all that is hypothetical and speculative . . . what remains of solid ascertained fact? . . . The answer can be summed up in a few words: Very little as yet. Whatever department we examine the tale is much the same. We have only scratched the surface of things hitherto. (Edwin Smith, 1935)[3]

To what extent did imperial fortunes in Africa rise and fall with officials' knowledge of the people under their jurisdiction? Was it anthropologists or other kinds of experts who served as the medium for gathering, interpreting and disseminating such knowledge? How did Africans themselves take part in and shape the content of ethnographic research? What kinds of concepts preoccupied scholars and fieldworkers in colonial Africa and how did these change over time? These are but a few of the many questions that present themselves when considering the historical relationship between anthropology and empire following the Scramble for Africa.[4]

This volume follows in the tracks of those scholars who have insisted that histories of anthropology should not be limited to theoretical and methodological developments in the academy. By deliberately eschewing a Whiggish interpretation of great men and great countries (read English-speaking anthropology) this volume takes an avowedly peripheral approach in order to develop a fresh perspective. It looks instead at the institutional frameworks of anthropology, at its promoters as well as its subalterns, and shows that the colonial project to order Africa, intellectually and politically, was inevitably a messier and less comprehensive endeavor than one might expect. In this vein, Achebe's observation on the psychology of colonialism seems a fitting point of departure. If colonial rule functioned at times by constructing a self-serving myth that 'the native was really quite simple', its operations belied that myth in everyday practice. Concentrating precisely on what it meant to *know* and *control* in colonial Africa, the contributions to this volume help unpack the far from simple relationship between the two. At the crux of the stories are several questions: who took part in the goal of 'knowing the natives', how did they participate, what exactly did they want to know, and, perhaps most important, why?

The African continent has the dubious distinction of having had no fewer than seven European nations take part in its simultaneous conquest and control at the time of partition: Great Britain, France, Germany, Belgium, Portugal, Spain, and Italy.[5] A truly comprehensive history of external interventions would also include the Ottoman Empire's activities in northern Africa and the spread of Islamic influences.[6] If empires of a scholarly nature were also considered, then the place of US academics during the interwar and postwar periods would necessarily come to the fore. Wilfrid Hambly's two-volume *Source Book for African Anthropology*, published by the Field Museum of Natural History in Chicago in 1937 and nearing 1,000 pages, serves as a reminder that researchers did not require formal colonial territories to take an active anthropological interest in the continent (Hambly 1937, 1952). Yet Hambly himself noted that it was the missionary ethnographer Edwin Smith's (1935) presidential address on Africa to the Royal Anthropological Institute that inspired his compilation. Smith's speech, in which he admonished his audience that the 'best [research on Africa] we have is not good enough: does not satisfy our thirst for full, precise and accurate facts', was directed as much at British colonial officials as it was at academics (Smith 1935: 78; Tilley, 2001: 1, 12–13). Both Hambly and Smith considered anthropological research to be not solely an end in itself, but also a means of solving the political, economic and administrative problems of the continent, problems defined as often as not by the circumstances of colonialism.

The purpose of this volume is to shed light on several dimensions of these intellectual and social dynamics by considering developments in metropolitan centres in tandem with those in specific African territories. The collection derives from a conference at the University of Oxford in March 2000, which invited historians and anthropologists to reflect upon the extent to which the production and dissemination of anthropological knowledge formed a sort of *collective* imperial experience, in spite of the scholarly institutions and colonial territories' heterogeneity (Stoler and Cooper 1997: 13).[7] What sets this volume apart is its explicit effort to compare developments across five of the imperial powers active in Africa between, roughly, 1880 and 1960.[8] It is also unusual in its attention to a range of African contributions to scholarship in French, German, and British contexts. Finally, it examines the array of professionals, beyond university and museum anthropologists, who were responsible for ethnographic fieldwork: missionaries, explorers, colonial officers, research assistants, linguists, teaching assistants, physicians, informants, and doctoral candidates. This approach, we hope, will encourage scholars to pay more attention to inter-imperial and inter-African comparisons.

Africa and anthropology: historiographical and theoretical debates

Historians concerned with Africa and imperialism have, in recent years, paid increasing attention to science, technology, medicine, and the natural world. This interest has been driven, in part, by a desire to untangle the complicated web of relations between science and colonialism.[9] It has also had it origins in the aim to reinstate Africans and their environments as historical players in the unfolding drama between humans and non-human nature.[10] Further impetus stems from an ongoing need to examine the roots of contemporary African problems and perhaps to recover particular types of knowledge – whether relating to agriculture, disease control, healing, social adaptation, or environmental intervention – that could shed light on current efforts to ameliorate such problems.[11] A final prompt comes from the wish to consider how African experiences have affected wider transnational processes related to development, modernity, capital flows and state-building, to name just a few (Comaroff and Comaroff 1991, 1997; Burke 1996; Conklin 1997; Bonneuil 2000). Science and technology have arguably been integral to all these dynamics and yet we still know too little about their distinctively African dimensions and contributions.[12] The debates that emerge from this literature, not surprisingly, involve divergent interpretations of colonialism's impact and underscore the need to be sensitive to competing and possibly incommensurable epistemologies.

In taking up these questions, it is helpful to recall Steven Feierman's caution that they often derive from 'a macrohistorical narrative grounded in Europe' so that while 'the local and global interact, . . . the African is always local, and the global always originates outside Africa'

[3]

(Feierman 2001: 26).[13] This observation is not meant to undermine the legitimacy of imperial studies, but to place them in a context in which they are only one piece of a bigger puzzle.[14] Even if the point is to study interactions, the very analytic frame of colonialism tends to privilege the effects of external interventions over intrinsic dynamics. Bearing this in mind helps to keep such interpretations from obscuring the fact that 'macrohistorical narratives' can also be written about the continent of Africa itself.[15]

Anthropology and empire

One of the longest-standing threads in the historiography on science and empire revolves around critical studies of anthropology's relationship to colonialism, a literature that emerged with force in the 1960s and 1970s (Gough 1968; Asad 1973; Lewis 1973; Copans 1975; Ranger 1976). Astute observers at the time recognized that Africa's experience with colonialism served as the cornerstone for much of this analysis (Hooker 1963; Magubane 1971; Leclerc 1972; Marfleet 1973; Ojiaku 1974; Chilungu 1976; Mafeje 1976; Owusu 1978, 1979).[16] In fact, one could argue that the visceral reaction that many African intellectuals had to anthropology, and to the social sciences more broadly, not only contributed to important changes in the discipline, but also helped to galvanize historians and anthropologists to investigate its legacies. In the intervening forty years, the history of anthropology has coalesced as a sub-specialty in its own right, embracing approaches that concentrate on anthropological styles in different national contexts – especially the United States, Britain, France and Germany – as well as those that focus on the field's engagement with specific regions of the world.[17] In this latter context, studies of anthropology in Africa have begun to receive increasing attention, particularly in recent years.[18]

Critiques of anthropology grew out of African experiences largely because, as Sally Falk Moore has observed, between 1920 and 1960 'ethnographic fieldwork in Africa came into its own. And for at least the last two of those decades that very fieldwork was central to the formulation of the major theoretical perspectives of anthropology' (Moore 1994: 12). This process of professionalization coincided with rapid changes in the political status of the dependent territories and with the gradual emergence of anti-colonial and nationalist movements across the continent. The preeminence of Africanist anthropology and its perceived entanglements with colonial power structures thus made it an obvious target of analysis and criticism.

Yet studies of anthropology and empire also stemmed from concerns that social anthropology was losing its coherence and entering a period of crisis (Goddard 1969; Banaji 1970; Needham 1970; Worsley 1970). If 'anthropology was the most powerful mode of colonial discourse', as Christopher Miller and Nicholas Dirks have argued for African and Indian contexts, respectively, then perhaps colonialism's demise deprived the discipline, at least temporarily, of much of its conceptual and material unity (Miller 1990: 6).[19] Such an insight prompted contemporaries to use the occasion of decolonization to pose several practical questions. How, if at all, would anthropology continue to be relevant to newly independent states? And to what extent would other disciplines, such as economics, sociology and political science, usurp anthropology's pride-of-place in explaining African (and other cultures') social dynamics (Hooker 1963; Onwuachi and Wolfe 1966; Levi-Strauss 1966)? A principal player at the time, Georges Balandier, believed this scholarly diversification presented 'a difficult problem, a real scientific challenge, which is the *adaptation* to African conditions of disciplines unprepared to "go abroad"' (Balandier 1960: 111). Balandier recognized, astutely, that few of these other disciplines emphasized constructing knowledge *elsewhere*. Notwithstanding significant exceptions, sociologists', political scientists' and economists' epistemic frameworks and ontological evidence, in other words, were largely rooted in their home countries and were taken for granted.

While these issues could be the subject of a separate volume, I pose them here because they enable us to consider African developments in a wider geopolitical and disciplinary context. After all, anthropology was itself a field science whose practitioners considered much of the globe an appropriate realm for investigation (Kuklick 1991; Kuklick and Kohler 1996; Wolfe 1999; Penny and Bunzl 2003). Likewise, the discipline was just one among several sciences to consider questions related to the human condition and human affairs. In its jostling for disciplinary and professional supremacy in a postcolonial world, it seems clear, in hindsight, that anthropology has rarely been an undisputed victor (Owusu 1978, 1979; Said 1989; Mafeje 1998a and 1998b; Kuper 2005).

Talal Asad, one of the scholars to put studies of anthropology and empire on the map, has offered his own assessment of the relationship between the two spheres:

> The role of anthropologists in maintaining structures of imperial domination has, despite slogans to the contrary, usually been trivial; the knowledge they produced was often too esoteric for government use, and even where it was usable it was marginal in comparison to the vast body of information routinely accumulated by merchants, missionaries, and administrators. (Asad 1991: 315)

[5]

Certainly many anthropologists from the past, as well as their advocates, would confirm Asad's argument. Sir Harry Johnston, a multifaceted administrator, naturalist and amateur ethnographer, compared the resources allocated to the natural sciences in the British Empire with those going towards studies of its human inhabitants 'of every known sub-species, variety or race of mankind'. Given anthropology's alleged importance to this project, a visitor to London, wrote Johnston in 1912,

> might fairly expect to find that branch of scientific research occupying the whole of the magnificent buildings of the Imperial Institute, or endowed with the Crystal Palace, or provided with a portion of Burlington House, or a wing of the British Museum, or at any rate housed as well as are the Royal Geographical or Zoological Societies. As a matter of fact, he would discover the association for the study of anthropology squeezed into two rooms on the second-floor front of a house in Bloomsbury, having to suit its installation to its very modest income . . . [O]ut of the gigantic wealth in the metropolis of the Empire we are only able to raise two or three thousand pounds annually for the scientific study of the bodies and minds of the 400,000,000 living men and women whom fate has brought under the influence and control of the British Empire. (Johnston 1912: 2–3)

Johnston's and Asad's observations give rise to the question whether critics have been correct in their assessment of the power and pervasiveness of anthropology within imperial contexts. If we approach the problem, as Johnston did, through comparative measurements – including funding, size and stature of scientific societies, number of academic posts, number of official positions, significance in training programs, presence or absence of institutions – then it seems fair to say that anthropology's significance to colonial regimes was usually much less than that of other fields, such as the environmental or medical sciences. But if we approach our evaluation through the language and theories of anthropology, we begin to see the various ways in which the field was deeply imbricated in imperial affairs. In fact, both perspectives are necessary: anthropologists, we can safely acknowledge, never guided colonial *social* interventions to the same degree that botanists, zoologists, geographers, or even ecologists guided *natural* interventions. Nonetheless, anthropology's raison d'être was far more tailored to colonial affairs than any of these other fields, especially in the century between 1850 and 1950. To put the matter in sharp relief: anthropology needed empires far more than empires needed anthropologists. Yet even this pattern should not be exaggerated, particularly given the sometimes overlooked fact that key scientific societies at the turn of the twentieth century were as concerned to support ethnographic and folklore research about European populations as they were to encourage overseas research in colonial territories (e.g. Smith 1991; Urry 1993b; Penny and Bunzl 2003: intro).[20]

If anthropology was relatively marginal to empires when considered in a comparative disciplinary context, ethnographic knowledge was nonetheless central to the construction of colonial states. This suggests an important division of labor in the production of knowledge, a pattern that scholars have only recently begun to detail in specific colonial contexts (Pels and Salemink 1994, 1999; Thomas 1994; Dirks 2001). How then has ethnographic intelligence gathering contributed to or detracted from disciplinary formation? Critics in the 1970s made much of the fact that empire and anthropology were mutually constitutive; without colonialism and the severe disparities in political and cultural power upon which it rested, who would anthropologists have studied, where would they have gone, and how would they have developed a rationale for their work? In turn, had anthropologists and naturalists not taken up questions about human origins, racial difference, and the relationship between biology and culture, it is unlikely that imperialism could so easily have been made to seem a natural part of human evolution (Stocking 1968, 1987). However, even if these broad dynamics are historically related, there were still ways in which imperial relations and anthropological research developed independently. Teasing out these different trajectories can also reveal how both realms occasionally worked at cross-purposes.

Anthropological critiques of empire and imperial critiques of anthropology

Scholars examining the history of British social anthropology were among the first to suggest that fieldwork in Africa could sometimes generate a critical, if not openly anti-colonial, stance. Referring to anthropologists as 'reluctant imperialists', Wendy James observed that too few critics had taken into account anthropologists' political views. Noting the field's 'double ambivalence' in the interwar period – dependent as it was on colonial authorities for access to territories and equally indebted to Africans who were increasingly suspicious of anything connected to the colonial apparatus – she argued that it could still produce 'radical criticisms' of the colonial order (James 1973: 43).[21] James did not wish to deny that individuals, such as Edward Evans-Pritchard, Raymond Firth, Audrey Richards and Bronislaw Malinowski, designed their research in ways that might serve colonial needs. She simply underscored that these same individuals could also challenge colonialism's assumptions, objectives and political structures. As other scholars have since shown, these tensions were even more evident in unpublished correspondence (Mills 2002).

If anthropologists could produce criticisms of the status quo, they could also incite objections, both from administrators and from Africans themselves. A historical example will help to illuminate this pattern and its consequences.[22] In March 1934, Margery Perham, an emerging specialist in British colonial administration, gave an address on indirect rule to the Royal Society of Arts in London. In her talk she noted that indirect rule's legitimacy rested on the 'legal recognition of native institutions' (Perham 1934: 95). If administrators approached those institutions with 'faulty and incomplete' information, as she felt they often did, they were bound to make serious mistakes when they intervened (Perham 1934: 95). 'The tendency to misunderstand', she told her audience, 'and the temptation to mishandle native institutions spring from the same fact, a dissimilarity so great between the two societies in contact as to make mutual comprehension or co-operation extremely difficult' (Perham 1934: 100). Anthropologists, she argued, trained to 'recognize the forces of social cohesion which are to be found in kinship-relations, in magic, religion, economic reciprocities and other aspects of primitive life', would serve as the remedy (Perham 1934: 100).

Perham's audience included a number of luminaries in interwar British politics and African affairs, including several who commented upon the salience and inadequacies of anthropology.[23] William Macmillan, a South African historian and social critic, was particularly concerned that anthropologists had a tendency 'not merely to study, but almost to worship, African institutions' (Perham 1934: 108). This prevented them from recognizing that change could be a good thing.[24] A young lawyer from West Africa, Stella J. Thomas, concurred, explicitly rejecting Perham's recommendation, saying that she was 'not in favour of anthropologists.'[25] She continued:

> Africans were not curious to be studied in order to find out from where they came . . . They wanted to be represented and to be given training so that they would be able to express themselves. That was all they were asking for. There must be real co-operation and real understanding. At present the British were dictating to them, and the Africans had to do what they were told. They could not go against it because they had not got the power. (Perham 1934: 110)

Officials and scholars occasionally shared these sentiments, worrying that anthropology turned its research subjects into something like museum objects, a concern Perham addressed in her response to her

critics.[26] 'The new anthropologists', she replied, 'the younger generation, were no longer looking at Africans as specimens, nor seeking to
preserve the past for the convenience of their researches' (Perham
1934: 115).[27]

In spite of her reassurances, Thomas Drummond Shiels, former
Labour Under-Secretary of State for the Colonies and chair of Perham's
session, observed in his closing remarks that he 'had never been able
to feel that there was such a cleavage between the essential outlook
of Africans and ourselves as to make it necessary to delve deeply into
local superstitions and folk-lore in order to devise proper lines in
government and administration' (Perham 1934: 117). Since Perham
advocated examining the full spectrum of social dynamics, not
'superstitions' *per se*, she and Drummond Shiels were communicating
past each other, a frequent occurrence when officials and anthropologists discussed their respective roles in colonial administration.
Thomas, however, had struck at the heart of the matter: not only was
she concerned with anthropology's power to define Africans' identities, but she was also, and more deeply, troubled by colonialism's
authoritarian rule. Perhaps predictably, when anthropologists examined this dimension of colonialism (as many British and French scholars tried to do in their studies of culture contact and social
transformation), they often succeeded in putting administrators on
their guard. When they focused their research on identity and custom
(through kinship and 'tribal' studies), they ran the risk of alienating
those they studied, although admittedly few anthropologists seemed
to worry publicly about these power dynamics until the period following World War II.

Embedded within the exchange between Perham and her audience
were two incipient criticisms that surfaced at the turn of the twentieth century and developed more theoretical coherence following World
War II. The first, explored by a number of practitioners at the time,
was an *anthropological* critique of colonialism and its customary bed-
fellows, industrialization, modernization and Westernization (Kingsley 1897; Junod 1912; Malinowski 1929, 1930; Leiris 1934; Hunter
1936; Mair 1936; Balandier 1951).[28] While ethnographic research certainly had the potential to *aid* colonial ambitions and *ease* colonial
control, it also had the ability to *subvert* colonial relations, even if this
process was neither straightforward nor without ambiguities (Brown
1973; James 1973; Cocks 1995; H. Tilley 2001). The second thread,
expressed by Macmillan, Thomas and Drummond Shiels explicitly,
focused on what could be called a *colonial* critique of anthropology,
which stressed its tendency not only to objectify those it studied, but

also to exaggerate differences and highlight the exotic.[29] If one wished to 'improve' or change African conditions, as both colonial administrators and nationalists often did, then anthropological studies could sometimes be seen as either irrelevant or a hindrance. Both strands of criticism, however, may seem relatively tame when compared to analyses of colonial power relations that were flourishing in the same period among artists, political scientists, philosophers, and, of course, anti-colonial critics.[30] The key distinction, though, is that these two critical threads were a direct product of debates about the role of specialized knowledge in colonial rule, and specifically about the place of anthropology. In other words, as stakeholders discussed the appropriate relationship between science and empire, they simultaneously produced critiques that undermined and transformed both spheres.

Although later generations of scholars have often been unsatisfied with the conceptual tools of their forebears, pointing out their ideological content and perceived embrace of particular (European) value systems, studies conducted during the colonial period itself often either paved the way for more comprehensive critiques or in a sense generated them through dialectical exchange. One can see this succession most clearly in Bernard Magubane's critique of scholars working at the Rhodes-Livingstone Institute in Zambia and in some of their responses; another kind of example, also from Zambia, is Henrietta Moore and Megan Vaughan's reconstruction and extension of Audrey Richards' research on nutrition, labor and gender (Richards 1939; Magubane 1971; Moore and Vaughan 1994). The kinds of research undertaken in the first half of the twentieth century, and the multivalent debates surrounding it, thus set the stage for their postcolonial successors. Scholars rarely like to acknowledge their indebtedness to the colonial past – as Richard Brown has remarked 'each generation, it appears, must murder its immediate ancestors' – but unless they do it is virtually impossible to explain where particular points of view or angles of analysis came from (Brown 1973: 174).

Place, agency, and conceptual foundations in the production of knowledge

One of the more intriguing dimensions of recent historical research on relationships between anthropology and empire, and science and empire more broadly, is the way particular sites mattered to anthropology's content and practice. In her recent study of the history of the Rhodes-Livingstone Institute (RLI), one of the first social science institutes established in sub-Saharan Africa (outside South Africa) in the late 1930s,[31] Lyn Schumaker argues that

> The anthropology of the RLI [in Zambia] was in many respects an anthropology that had become Africanized – through the influence of research assistants, African informants, white settlers, administrators, missionaries, and others who played a role in shaping its fieldwork, and through its adaptation to the landscape of Africa itself and to the material constraints and opportunities it found there. (Schumaker 2001: 6–7)

By paying close attention to anthropologists' varied experiences in Central Africa, both during and following the colonial period, Schumaker situates a particular strand of anthropological theory that focused on social processes, networks and conflict – resting on the work of Godfrey Wilson, Max Gluckman, Elizabeth Colson, J.A. Barnes, Clyde Mitchell and A.L. Epstein – in a detailed and contingent geopolitical context.[32] While she acknowledges that ideas and concepts invariably transcend location, her work illustrates how they still depend on those places (and the people in them) for their existence. In this sense, what Schumaker really shows is not only how anthropology was *Africanized*, but also how it was *regionalized*, since there were multiple efforts across Africa following different trajectories.[33] As she reveals throughout her narrative, her protagonists' Anglo-American ties were an important dimension to the process of knowledge production since they not only shaped the concerns they brought with them to the field, but also structured how they presented their research to a wider audience. Yet, as she demonstrates, these disciplinary and professional foundations could not have developed as they did without the particular nexus of conditions generated by, among other things, the mining industries, the colonial bureaucracy and the specificity of the indigenous societies themselves. In other words, the politics and economics of colonialism in Zambia were an essential catalyst for theory formation.

To speak of the Africanization of anthropology brings two other issues to the fore: agency and epistemology. Schumaker, extending the analysis of Roger Sanjek and others, helps to resurrect the RLI's African research assistants as historical actors, complete with intentions and self-interest (Sanjek 1993). The process of 'Africanization', however, presumably goes further than bringing African actors into the frame as assistants and informants; its ultimate end is to achieve disciplinary status and authority within the continent itself.[34] Whether or not this is possible has become the subject of considerable debate, one that continues to revolve around the field's colonial legacies (Laville 1998;

Mafeje 1998a,b; Moore 1998; Nkwi 1998; Sharp 1998; Vilakazi 1998; Apter 1999; Guyer 1999). Protagonists in this debate are at odds on several points: the extent to which anthropology emerged primarily as a study of non-European 'others'; whether anthropology in Africa can ever escape the misleading and inaccurate representations produced in the colonial period; and even whether anthropology as a profession is on the wane or rise in the continent.

Although these debates will not be settled any time soon, appreciating their interlocutors' underlying concerns does help to highlight ongoing dynamics that hearken back to the age of empire. The first and most important of these patterns has to do with who produces knowledge about African societies and how their identity shapes their preoccupations.[35] As the sociologist Mazi Ojiaku observed, 'ever since the early nineteenth century when the Euro-American presence in Africa began to be noticeably felt in the interior, Africa's knowledge has increasingly ceased to be rooted in the African soil' (Ojiaku 1974: 204). This means that extra-African institutions, with their own needs and interests, continue to drive the research agenda. Such asymmetries reinforce people's perceptions that anthropology's epistemological framework and mission have not changed sufficiently since decolonization. Archie Mafeje makes this point starkly when he asks 'whether in the post-independence period there could be African Anthropology without African anthropologists' (Mafeje 1998a: 2).[36] This critique, of course, applies to a number of fields, not just anthropology. In fact, there is a growing body of literature concerning knowledge and Africa, beginning with a touchstone article by Robin Horton, which actually bridges philosophical, anthropological, historical and epistemic concerns.[37]

Moving from agency to conceptual foundations, another significant debate concentrates on how, if at all, anthropologists should deconstruct, and in turn reconceptualize, ideas and arguments developed in the colonial period and whether they can emancipate anthropology from its colonial (and, for some, bourgeois capitalist) roots. Since many may feel that this task is precisely what anthropologists and other scholars – African and non-African – have been preoccupied with over the last forty years, such a question might appear unproductive (Moore 1998; e.g. Fabian 1983, 2000; Mudimbe 1988, 1994; Appiah 1992; Comaroff and Comaroff 1992; Hountondji 2002). But for others, who feel this process has not gone far enough, the question must be posed at regular intervals. At stake is the legitimate desire to understand how forms of knowledge are implicated in and harnessed to socio-economic and political processes. A key problem for critics such as Mafeje is not that anthropologists conspired or colluded with imperial powers (although they may have done both), but that the very 'ontology of [their] thought categories' derived from and served to reinforce colonial systems (Mafeje 1976: 318). '[T]his should not mean', the sociologist Herbert Vilakazi responds, 'killing Anthropology in favor of sociology [or some other social science].' Instead it means reconstructing 'the entirety of Western scholarly and scientific imagination', so that 'the historical is digested, the old and useless discarded and the old and useful assimilated and raised to a higher level' (Vilakazi 1998: 76–77). The ultimate aim for some would thus be to transform disciplines and institutions into tools for liberation, a noble and yet still highly contested ambition (Thiong'o 1986; Harrison 1991; Wiredu 1995; Desai 2001).

Whatever one's opinion of this broader goal – and this is another debate that must be left to one side in this volume – most involved will agree that for it to succeed, it must not only rest on accurate historical analysis, but also on a theoretical framework flexible enough to account for the constant interplay that colonialism engendered among places, peoples and ideas; and for the simple fact that colonial situations were themselves never closed systems. Among other things, this would involve considering the heterogeneity of conditions and institutions across empires; the dynamism of colonial identities; the various levels at which imperial power operated and the interstitial spaces that may have escaped its reach; the dramatic shifts in dominant perceptions (scientific and otherwise) and the diversity of opinion that existed even within seemingly hegemonic ideologies; and the other political and economic forces, besides strictly colonial ones, that also shaped social dynamics. Taking these issues seriously helps scholars to avoid misleading binaries – black/white, colonized/colonizer, African/Western, and tradition/modernity being the most obvious – that have never adequately captured the interdependent and ever-changing nature of colonial worlds. This is not to say that there is no truth contained in such binaries; in fact, as a number of scholars have shown, examining how they have been constructed and deployed can be quite revealing (e.g. Said 1978). But to ground historical analysis in them is bound to lead to theoretical and empirical cul-de-sacs. While this volume was never meant to engage explicitly with debates about the place of anthropology in African societies today, it does seem appropriate to situate our historical contributions in that wider context. If nothing else, these chapters should draw attention not only to those features that were common to the different imperial powers as they engaged with both anthropology and Africa, but they also highlight the many contingent, unpredictable, and dissimilar factors that went into producing that shared experience.

Threads of inquiry: boundaries, research priorities, and colonial imaginations

Historical actors have defined anthropology in many ways, creating overlapping, intersecting and sometimes conflicting boundaries. If individuals were concerned with human origins and physical differences, for instance, then the field was encompassing enough to include archeology and prehistory as well as evolutionary and racial theories. If, on the other hand, social organization (or 'customs') was the primary concern, then anthropological studies could expand to include research in psychology, sociology, religion, economics, philology, and even philosophy. In spite of semantic distinctions that actors themselves made among, for instance, anthropology, ethnology and ethnography, which were often the root of heated controversies, scholarly societies still often managed to incorporate research across a wide spectrum of perspectives and approaches (Stocking 1971; Vermeulen 1995). Such inclusive boundaries arguably contributed to the field's growth and perceived pervasiveness. As Edwin Smith remarked in his address to the Royal Anthropological Institute, 'nothing which concerns man is alien to the anthropologist' (Smith 1935: 79).

This volume deliberately concentrates more attention on the history of social and cultural anthropology and less on the significant ethnological and biomedical work that was done in Africa on apparent somatic and psychological differences, such as questions related to racial types, blood groups, genetics, evolution, intelligence, racial immunity, demographics, and human origins (Tobias 1985; Robertshaw 1990; Dubow 1995, 1996; McCulloch 1995; Butchart 1998; Tapper 1999; El Shakry 2005; Tilley 2005).[38] This emphasis is derived from historical trends themselves, for while biological and evolutionary concerns continued to be an important element of the discipline, they were less explicitly linked to the needs of colonial states and were therefore played down by those who advocated coupling anthropological research to colonial policymaking. That said, the somatic and psychological preoccupations of anthropology are never really absent from this volume since several of the chapters consider how these concerns were often pivotal to disciplinary trends (Sibeud, Harries, Cinnamon, Sorgoni, and Wilder) as well as to the imaginative and literal work of demographic management in the colonies (Hunt). Even those authors who do not explicitly address biological and cul-

[14]

tural distinctions help to highlight how inextricably linked such concerns often were for historical actors.

Metropolitan institutions and agendas

By framing this volume as a cross-colonial examination, the aim was to encourage contributors to move beyond questions of individual or epistemological complicity in colonialism, although both remain central themes, to incorporate broader structural and institutional dynamics. In the book's first section on metropolitan agendas, for instance, the authors consider the heterogeneous roles played by specific research institutes, including one, the Deutsche Forschungsgemeinschaft (the German Research Foundation, DFG), that was established in the period *after* Germany lost its colonies.[39] Examining the political and economic fortunes of these institutions – including their promoters and opponents, their sources of funding, their changing missions, their internal conflicts and their leadership structures – helps to shift attention away from individuals and their ideas and place it more squarely on the complex relationship between disciplinary formation, on the one hand, and nation and empire building on the other. Thus we learn in Emmanuelle Sibeud's chapter that a key stimulus for French anthropologists to turn their attention to their African empire was the work of a group of 'dissident' colonial ethnographers active in French West Africa. Professionals' efforts, however, to merge what Sibeud calls the 'scientific logic of ethnography and the political logic of colonial administration' by creating a Bureau of Colonial Ethnography (p. 63) ultimately failed since they could never fully reconcile disciplinary and imperial goals. This does not mean that there was not a synergy between administrative concerns and colonial ethnographic concerns – there was, as the chapters by Sorgoni, Johnson, and Wilder demonstrate – but it does illustrate that such a synergy did not always easily translate into academic or governmental support.

A second feature that surfaces from an emphasis on metropolitan agendas is the role anthropology and its advocates played in the wider emergence of a field of African studies. Even if anthropology *per se* did not always benefit directly or substantively from being linked to colonial endeavors, it did form an ineluctable part of any strategy to investigate and understand the African continent.[40] As Sara Pugach's chapter makes clear, this process often went in tandem with support for language study. Since the publication of Johannes Fabian's landmark book *Language and Colonial Power*, it has been difficult to consider colonial administration in Africa without also paying attention to the politics of communication and to the function of a lingua franca, in Fabian's case Swahili, to imperial control (Fabian 1986). (Jan Vansina has likewise traced the complicated European theories of an original/ primordial 'Bantu' language that tended to collapse 'race', language and culture under one heading (Vansina 1979, 1980).) Scholars' attention to language in colonial contact zones has inevitably raised questions concerning translation, meaning, and even cosmology or *mentalité*, problems colonial officials often acknowledged as well (Comaroff and Comaroff 1991, 1997). Pugach's contribution helps to reveal how the study of linguistics and ethnography in imperial Germany went hand-in-glove, an institutional pursuit that was embodied quite literally by African linguistic assistants. We know all too little about translators and informants from anthropology's past. As with Schumaker's effort to historicize the research assistants of the Rhodes-Livingstone Institute, Pugach draws upon fragmentary evidence to reconstruct the social and intellectual experiences of these cultural intermediaries who operated not in the field, but in the metropole itself. At times objectified, occasionally denigrated, and always situated within social and professional hierarchies, African language assistants, Pugach argues, were nonetheless an indispensable part of the growth of a new disciplinary configuration in Germany, *Afrikanistik*, the study of African languages and cultures.[41]

An emphasis on anthropology's place in African studies also helps to explain why scholars in Germany continued to produce proposals for ethnographic research in Africa even after it lost its colonies, and why their expertise was still so sought after in collaborative ventures such as the British-based International Institute of African Languages and Cultures (IIALC/IAI).[42] From their earliest days in Africa, the Germans undertook a form of 'scientific colonial management' in an effort not to be outdone by the other imperial powers. They also pioneered a network of 'colonial research and training institutes' in Germany itself, capped by the founding in 1908 of the Colonial Institute (Kolonialinstitut) in Hamburg, which included among its thematic priorities applied ethnology (Spidle 1973). As Holger Stoecker's chapter illustrates, German ethnographers positioned their African research in the interwar period as a way to help Germany to recover its empire and remain intellectually competitive with the other imperial powers; that so many of these proposals failed to secure funding says something about the effectiveness of their rhetoric.[43] The German Research Foundation's leadership, however, obviously took such aims to heart, its inter-disciplinary patronage clearly shaping the way African studies became institutionalized in the metropole.

Imperial rivalries provided an impetus for scientific pursuits of all kinds: no nation could realistically expect another to meet its informational needs and certainly no nation would wish to depend on another during times of political conflict. Benoît de L'Estoile's parallel study of the competing approaches of French and British affiliates of the IIALC underscores this point, highlighting the challenge national-ist loyalties posed in inter-imperial ventures. That the IIALC had its headquarters in Britain and that the bulk of its funding came from the Rockefeller Foundation, which was partial to Bronislaw Malinowski's and Joseph Oldham's priorities for research, tipped the balance of power in favor of its participants in Britain. Nonetheless, to be legitimate the IIALC needed not just the support, but also the leadership of its conti-nental counterparts, and of these the French clearly had the greatest vested interest in pursuing strategies that dovetailed with their own institutional and imperial aims. These structural tensions, according to L'Estoile, help to explain why over the course of the 1930s the IIALC's executive committee split along Anglo-American and French/ continental lines with the former advocating sociological field research conducted by university-trained fellows who would produce academic monographs and the latter supporting encyclopedic ethnographic pro-jects conducted by a hierarchy of field informants (from administrators to educated Africans) and synthesized by metropolitan experts. Even if there was much on which all participants could agree, the IIALC's attempt to pursue scientific internationalism was clearly fraught by frictions that stemmed from national and imperial differences.

African ethnographers, self-expression, and modernity

A question at the core of much colonial historiography concerns how different groups of Africans – considered as a collective and as indi-viduals – responded to the multiple conditions of modernity intro-duced and consolidated via colonial processes. One facet of this subject, the role played by African ethnographers – as linguists, trans-lators, assistants, informants and scholars in their own right – forms the focus of the second section of the book, allowing us to consider the accumulating evidence amassed by Schumaker (in *Africanizing Anthropology*), Pugach, Jean-Hervé Jezequel, in his exploration of the changing roles of schoolmasters-cum-ethnographers in French West Africa, and Bruce Berman and John Lonsdale, in their study of Jomo Kenyatta's journey to produce *Facing Mount Kenya* (1938). To what extent, for instance, did increasingly literate Africans turn not to literature, religion, or philosophy for self-expression but to ethno-graphy? How were their new representations 'invented traditions' of a different sort, deriving only partially, if at all, from the needs of colonial bureaucrats and serving as a means to juggle competing social, political and ideological loyalties (Ranger 1983, 1993; Spear 2003; Peterson 2004; Kevane 2006)?[44] Ethnography for Pugach's and

Jezequel's teaching assistants was in certain respects a vehicle for self-advancement; their studies were either part of their job description or were seen as ways to provide additional remuneration. Given their structural relationships to their sponsoring institutions in Germany and French West Africa, respectively, it comes as little surprise that assistants presented their research on customs and traditions in an idiom that often resonated with their patrons' existing assumptions. In this sense, at least some ethnographic pursuits allowed their authors to express collective self-criticism even as they distanced themselves from their compatriots.

Ethnographic insight was always a double-edged sword, though, and it seems clear that for some authors, including Jomo Kenyatta and several West African schoolteachers, ethnography also served as a means to criticize what they perceived as colonizers' misunderstandings, misrepresentations and abuses of power. Again, at least some colonial officials were themselves alive to this possibility and wanted to harness African ethnographic efforts for precisely this reason: more accurate information, as Edwin Smith underscored in his 1935 speech, could potentially lead to more effective colonial administration, at least that was the hope. Most imperial powers, however, were usually unable to control the content and function of Africans' ethnographic self-expression. That was its danger. As Berman and Lonsdale make so clear in their discussion: even when there were discordant voices at play – such as Kenyatta's fellow Kikuyu commentators – auto-ethnography (i.e. ethnographic representations of one's own socio-cultural group) included an undercurrent that was trying to place command of the forces of modernity, whether economic, political or social, in the hands of Africans.[45] This made it a discursive mode that could simultaneously seem to derive from and also subvert colonial situations. The Négritude movement, pioneered in the same period – the 1930s and 1940s – by Aimé Césaire, Léopold Senghor, and Léon Damas, and influenced heavily by the writings of the German ethnologist Leo Frobenius, can in some ways be read in this tradition, but it also moved quickly beyond auto-ethnography since it did not assert insider status as its primary mark of legitimacy. It attempted, instead, to cultivate a pan-African cultural nationalism.[46] Auto-ethnography, as distinct from other ethnographic pursuits, was thus as much about taking control of one's identity and destiny as it was about achieving authentic (and in some cases valorized) representations.

It would be wrong, however, to see such efforts solely as measuring African cultures against those in Europe, although this was often integral to the process. Nor was it simply an effort to recover, reject or reconstruct traditions. As Jezequel and Berman and Lonsdale demonstrate, ethnography for the authors they examine was often a means to express a complex and sophisticated politics that concentrated on creating and sustaining new forms of political order. Kenyatta's own vision of 'conservative modernisation', Berman and Lonsdale argue, meant that he produced an ethnographic text replete with contradictions that he was fundamentally ill-equipped to confront.

While auto-ethnographic efforts often traded on perceived and real insider/outsider distinctions to establish their authenticity, individual authors were also able to escape these categories when they wished. Kenyatta, as well as several of the West African school teachers Jezequel describes, knew only too well that an ethnographer's function was to see a culture as if from the outside: by choosing to represent their own societies, they had to walk a tightrope balancing accurate representations with a desire for political and social change. No less than other anthropologists, African ethnographers' choices and interpretations reflected a range of underlying assumptions that reveal a great deal about their own ideologies as well as their ambitions.

Salvage anthropology, primordial imagination, and 'dying races'
A central motif prevalent in both colonial and metropolitan contexts from the eighteenth century onwards links the three chapters in the third section of the book: the degeneration, loss, and death that many associated with colonial and civilizing endeavors. Whether interpreted in cultural or physical terms, whether judged as a benefit or decried as a disaster, narratives of deterioration usually stood alongside, and sometimes even overshadowed, those of progress (Chamberlain and Gilman 1985). Patrick Harries' chapter on Swiss missionaries – the only example in the book of a European power without a direct vested interest in African colonies – illustrates the way 'discovery and domestication' often took place first on European soil, in his case in the Swiss Alps, before it was transferred to African soils and societies.[47] What linked this process for the intellectuals and missionaries involved was a common set of preoccupations and experiences. As Harries puts it, in their eyes, '[b]oth Alpine and African worlds were populated by uncomplicated, small-scale societies that seemed to reflect a primitive past of communitarian values, firm social hierarchies and authentic traditions' (p. 203). These 'primitive' worlds stood in stark contrast to 'modern civilization', which brought with it rampant materialism, industrial slums, prostitution, new pathologies, and even the threat of racial extinction.[48] Out of this 'primordial' imagination, according to Harries, grew a genre of 'salvage anthropology' that simultaneously recovered idealized premodern, precolonial pasts and juxtaposed them to the advances of the modern age. What got lost in this translation

was any real appreciation of what Africans, or Swiss Alpine peasants for that matter, might have wanted for their own futures.

A similar kind of primordial imagination is at work in John Cinnamon's analysis of Fang ethnographies. By concentrating on a single population, Cinnamon is able to consider those qualities that endured in ethnographic descriptions that ranged from the precolonial to the postcolonial period, culminating in an auto-ethnographic Mvet epic that some scholars see as a progenitor of Gabonese national identity. Two of the most influential of the nineteenth and early twentieth century ethnographers were Paul du Chaillu, an explorer-adventurer, and Henri Trilles, a missionary ethnographer. It was they, Cinnamon argues, who consolidated an image of Fang peoples as 'exceptional noble savages', superior to their more effete coastal counterparts who had been degraded by contact with Europeans. Fang's unique ethnographic status stemmed not only from what du Chaillu and Trilles characterized as their physical, war-like vigor, but also from their migratory zeal, which the ethnographers linked to alleged cannibalistic tendencies.

When academically trained anthropologists, Georges Balandier and James Fernandez, entered the Equatorial field after World War II much had changed. Unlike their predecessors, who tended to work comfortably within a 'tribal' paradigm, Balandier and Fernandez helped to reveal its many limitations. Nonetheless, both men still reinforced certain perceptions of Fang populations, referring to them as 'the terror of autochthonous peoples' in the nineteenth century (Fernandez) and as unemployed conquerors in the mid-twentieth (Balandier). Both, Cinnamon observes, also struggled to come to terms with competing visions of Fang people's precolonial past, oscillating between images of social cohesion, based on an analysis of clan structure and genealogy, and those of displacement and dispersal, stemming from an emphasis on long-distance migration. Ironically, Fang, like many other African populations, began to appropriate ethnographic descriptions during the colonial period itself, which was in some respects what Balandier and Fernandez were working to correct. The auto-ethnographic Mvet epic thus echoes du Chaillu and Trilles' preoccupations with Fang as a migratory, warrior people and also elaborates on Balandier and Fernandez' emphasis on clan genealogy and their more modern critique of colonial violence. Even as Fang intellectuals have transformed such characterizations, they have also remained indebted to concepts and ideas that were themselves products of a colonial imagination.

Nancy Hunt's chapter, contrasting infertility scares among the Mongo in the Belgian Congo and the Nzakara in the French Congo,

[20]

helps to underscore the fear officials associated with reproductive crises in colonial territories and brings to the fore the constant inter-action among demographic, ethnographic and biomedical pursuits that such crises prompted. Why, Hunt asks, would four Belgian protago-nists – two Flemish nationalist scholar-priests, Gustaaf Hulstaert and Edmond Boelaert, a Belgian lay ethnographer and private planter, Charles Lodewijckx, and a Belgian physician, Robert Allard – frame their concerns about 'dying races' in the Belgian Congo in terms of the psychic shock of colonialism itself? And what prompted, less than a generation later, a French doctor and anthropologist, Anne Retel-Lau-rentin, to explicitly refute their explanations and embrace a cross-cul-tural physiology that allowed Retel-Laurentin to heal infertility within a framework that bridged biomedical and Nzakara explanations of illness? Much like Harries, Hunt situates her narrative in a complex, transnational context that allows her to explore the circulation of colo-nial anxieties, the function of gender, the effects of changing discipli-nary traditions, the role of nationalism, and the place of clinical fieldwork in the construction of both scares. None of her protagonists was particularly representative of any social or professional group and all in some ways antagonized colonial rulers. Nonetheless, Hunt sees in their interaction, and particularly in the response it engendered in Retel-Laurentin herself, a form of *colonial* medical anthropology – one 'that combine[d] sustained ethnography and demography, semantics and biology' – that may have important lessons to offer contemporaries struggling with the problems of 'biosociality' and illness in Africa today.

Colonial states, applied ethnography, and policy
The final section of the book brings us full circle to consider rela-tionships among colonial intelligence gathering, amateur ethnography, and disciplinary formation. Legal frameworks established by colonial states and imperial nations in many respects served as a mediating link for these processes (Kirkby and Coleborne 2001; Benton 2002). A number of scholars have in recent years turned their attention to the nature and distinctiveness of colonial states in Africa (Lonsdale 1981; Young 1988, 1994; Vincent 1988; Berman and Lonsdale 1992; Comaroff 1997; Lewis 2000; Fairweather-Tall 2002). As John Lonsdale long ago remarked, 'European colonialism was a living denial of the ability of Africans to organize their own sovereignties' (Lonsdale 1981: 139). Paradoxically, however, once colonial rule had been imposed, admin-istrators and imperial managers were often forced to consider those judicial and social rules that had governed Africans' lives and had pre-dated colonialism. The contributions in this section, studies of Italian

Northeast Africa, the Anglo-Egyptian Sudan and French West Africa reveal the uneven ways in which ethnographic knowledge was pursued and applied in this respect.

Following Pels and Salemink's call to examine how 'ethnography, embedded in an administrative practice, was a legalist act', Barbara Sorgoni explores the changing assumptions and methods embodied in the writings of Alberto Pollera (1873–1939), an Italian colonial administrator and civil judge who went to Northeast Africa when he was only twenty-one years old and died there some forty-five years later. What makes Pollera interesting are his many atypical characteristics: few Italians settled in Northeast Africa in this period and fewer still had families with and married local women (in Pollera's case it was in that order). And, unlike his professional counterparts in Italy who remained preoccupied with physical and biological differences among human groups, Pollera concentrated, in the words of one obituary, on 'juridical, historical, social and religious aspects of Eritrean and Ethiopian populations', driven in large part by an administrative need to codify 'customary laws'. Sorgoni sees Pollera as an antecedent to Italian cultural anthropology, but one who anthropologists and historians have tended to overlook because he falls outside the realm of university hierarchies. That said, Pollera's work was obviously not negligible to professional developments since a prominent Italian anthropologist, Nello Puccioni, wrote a monograph on Somali social customs in 1937, calling it '"the brother" of Pollera's books' (p. 289).

Perhaps more intriguing than his influence on metropolitan anthropology, however, was Pollera's effect on colonial efforts to 'administer justice'. For Pollera, ethnographic knowledge could mediate between oral and literate traditions, helping to dissipate ignorance and replace it instead with sympathetic comprehension. Reason, he believed, was at the root of many Ethiopian and Eritrean practices: the task for administrator-ethnographers was to situate those reasons in their cultural and historical contexts. Despite this, even as Pollera worked to undermine stereotypes and prejudices (going so far as to privately challenge laws against the legal recognition of children of mixed marriages and to condemn 'colour phobia'), he helped to construct or reinforce others. He never abandoned a belief in the innate superiority of Italians, his marriage to an Ethiopian woman notwithstanding. He also endorsed existing beliefs in the superiority of certain African groups over others, for instance Abyssinian (Ethiopian) over Kunama populations, which led to administrative interventions that, as Sorgoni puts it, 'essentialized their alleged differences'. In the end, Pollera's story is an increasingly familiar one: an administrator whose ethnographic interests tempered more invasive interventions and replaced them with subtler policies that still caused fundamental change. And like many individuals caught between two worlds, Pollera's choices reflected the ambiguities and contradictions of his own position.

A more direct and arguably significant relationship between administrative inquiry and academic anthropology can be found in the Anglo-Egyptian Sudan according to Douglas Johnson's examination of the reciprocal influence between the *Sudan Intelligence Report* (an internal government publication) and the semi-scholarly journal *Sudan Notes and Records* (founded in 1918). Not only were Sudan's civil service officers, from 1908, taught anthropology as part of their probationary training programme, but also the territory was one of the few, in the early decades of the twentieth century, where administrative leaders were willing to support professional anthropological pursuits. In fact, the Governor-General, Sir Reginald Wingate, justified creating *Sudan Notes and Records* (SNR) because it would provide a central vehicle in which administrators and scholars alike could offer detailed information about 'the people and their mentality'. The individual who gave life to this symbiotic relationship, Johnson argues, was Edward Evans-Pritchard, whose articles in the SNR and instruction of civil service recruits helped to structure administrators' own ethnographic reporting. Even as some administrators gave credit to Evans-Pritchard's predecessor Charles Seligman, their studies often had more in common with anthropologists of Evans-Pritchard's generation, combining intensive field observation with fluency in a local language. Disciplinary parameters, in other words, gradually transformed the way a select group of administrators produced new ethnographic knowledge. Yet, as Johnson also demonstrates, these changes were never embraced wholeheartedly. The Sudan case illustrates clearly the inherent tensions that were ever-present in the desire to fuse professional anthropology and colonial intelligence gathering. Often, the skills, theories, and methods anthropologists brought with them to the field, and developed over the course of their careers, were a poor fit for the political aims of colonial administration. Likewise, some kinds of ethnographic work, such as the effort to create customary courts, relied very little on an anthropological background and depended instead on the judicial skills that administrators derived from their training in English Common Law and their experience serving as magistrates (an insight that seems applicable to Alberto Pollera as well). If anthropology provided any kind of service to the British in the Sudan, it was a feeble and inadequate one, if judged by the actual needs of the colonial state.

One can interpret the interpenetration of anthropology and administration, however, from multiple vantage points as Gary Wilder aims to show in his study of 'Colonial Ethnology and Political Rationality in French West Africa'. Setting aside certain contingencies – such as the question of whether ethnographic research received disproportionate support from the state, or why some individuals and institutions were embraced and not others – Wilder wants instead to examine the underlying logic that made ethnology and certain forms of native policy not only necessary to each other, but also to colonial statecraft. This 'circular and mutually reinforcing relationship' generated a range of preoccupations among ethnographers and policymakers – particularly concerning Africans' collective mentalities and family structures – that were in turn codified in the aims of social welfare and economic development programs. The synchronicity between governance and the production of knowledge not only retained room for disagreements among individuals, but it also seemed to depend on a critical evaluation of past colonial interventions. Wilder argues, in fact, that it was the ability of ethnographically inclined officials to see the disruptions that colonialism had produced – 'deracinated peasants, unruly veterans and resentful elites' – that enabled them to craft new governing strategies. Even so, according to Wilder, both the scholarship and the policies rested on central contradictions revolving around politics (individual versus collective representation), economics (production versus consumption), and social dynamics (stasis versus change). As a result: 'Administrators sought to promote socioeconomic individuality without creating legal and political individuals. They dreamed of colonial subjects possessed by rational self-interest, consumerist desires and a productivist ethos who were nevertheless embedded in indigenous relations of production' (p. 354).

While his chapter does not appear in this volume, it might be helpful to end with a brief discussion of the paper Elisio Macamo presented on Portugal and its activities in Mozambique.[49] Where Wilder stresses the way ethnography could legitimate incursions by the colonial state, Macamo was more interested in exploring how certain kinds of anthropology sought legitimacy by wedding themselves more closely to colonial bureaucracies. The two processes, of course, were not mutually exclusive. The lynchpin issue for Macamo was the 1899 Mozambique Native Labour Act, which he argued not only laid the foundations for Portuguese colonial rule in the twentieth century, but also structured the terms of debate for anthropological knowledge about Mozambique's populations. The Act was premised on the belief that wage labor, as well as an imperative to work, was essential to Portugal's civilizing mission. Since the African territories had been defined as 'overseas provinces' and administrators had endorsed a policy of assimilation, Africans were in theory placed on equal footing

[24]

with Portuguese. In practice, however, institutions such as the Native Affairs Board and the codification of 'native penal and civil codes' were grounded in assumptions of profound difference: if Africans were thought to have the same potential as Europeans, granting them similar roles and rights was still inconceivable. Not until their social structures and cultural norms had been fundamentally reworked, through the labor process itself, would such equality be possible.

Unlike French West Africa, where there existed multiple and comparatively powerful scientific institutions and societies, Mozambique had virtually no such infrastructure. Anthropologists' activities were, until the late 1940s, largely mediated through the Lisbon Geographical Society, which served as the umbrella group for numerous natural and social scientific activities. Italy's and Portugal's experiences with anthropology seem comparable in this respect. Macamo saw this paucity as being one factor that explained anthropologists' essentially subservient role to the colonial state's conceptual logic. Without strong institutions and a critical mass of advocates – such as existed in France, Britain and Germany – anthropological activities would necessarily remain marginal to colonial operations. Clearly, however, Portuguese scholars still initiated and embraced disciplinary shifts, reflected most obviously in the move away from physical anthropology and towards cultural anthropology following World War II. The work of António Jorge Dias stands out in this regard given his prolific writings on people in Mozambique and elsewhere, as well as his role as a professional ethnographer in various metropolitan institutions (West 2004; also Margarido 1975; Gallo 1988).[50]

Concluding thoughts

Although this volume was never intended to be the definitive word on the history of anthropology, imperialism and Africa, its findings should help to shape future inquiries. For that reason, we assembled a group of contributors whose research interests and professional training intersected with a number of fields: African history and anthropology, intellectual history and the history of science, and European and imperial history. Readers who turn to this volume wishing to gain a nation-by-nation understanding of anthropology in Africa will find themselves disappointed. So too will those who seek a new synthesis considering the effects of colonialism on metropolitan trends. Even those who understand the limits of an edited volume may still wish for a more comprehensive analysis of the different imperial powers in Africa and of the effects their ethnographic interests had on African populations. For better or worse, this volume has not tried to satisfy these aims.

The contributions to *Ordering Africa: Anthropology, European Imperialism, and the Politics of Knowledge*, however, do draw attention to certain developments that it is worth making more explicit. First is the transnational character of networks and institutions in the period under review. National systems of patronage and reward, imperial pride, funding limits, territorial boundaries, and language barriers certainly placed constraints on these links, but they never succeeded in dismantling them. Those responsible for producing new anthropological knowledge were often mobile not only within their respective nation's empire, but also beyond it. This could include joining other scientific or scholarly societies, traveling to other countries, corresponding with scholars from other nations, and reading and publishing across national boundaries. Granted most individuals, in their scholarly pursuits (i.e. fieldwork), followed paths circumscribed by nation and empire – this was particularly true of administrators, missionaries and African ethnographers – yet the effects of transnational exchange did seem to shape epistemological and administrative concerns in ways we do not yet fully understand. Limiting the analytic frame to a single imperial nation has its rewards, but it also prevents a fuller appreciation of precisely how people, ideas and materials circulated across diverse regions. Thus Hunt's study of 'infertility scares' in the Belgian and French Congo, Harries' examination of Swiss missionaries and their influence on African anthropology, de L'Estoîle's chapter on the 'internationalism' of the International Institute for African Languages and Cultures, and Cinnamon's exploration of French, North American and Gabonese treatments of Fang ethnography, all draw attention to important dimensions of this circulation.

Second, and related, is the proliferation of research institutes and scholarly 'clearinghouses' both in Europe and Africa that influenced not only anthropology, but also wider intellectual and administrative debates. This would include those institutions with an ostensibly national or territorial orientation, such as the Institut d'Ethnologie in Paris, the German Research Foundation in Berlin, or the Institut Français d'Afrique Noire (IFAN) in Dakar, as well as those with an explicitly international agenda, like the IIALC in London or the Institut Colonial International in Brussels (the latter is not discussed in this volume). If a fine-grained reading of the internal workings of these institutes reveals numerous tensions – in terms of disciplines, nations, methodologies, underlying assumptions and objectives – one could also argue that such bodies moved a wider audience towards new kinds of consensus: through training programs, publications, conferences

[26]

and research strategies. Equally significant, perhaps, is the way some of these organizations embraced a multi-disciplinary approach to African affairs, placing ethnographic concerns alongside a spectrum of others. Here, as an example, is Theodor Monod's description of IFAN's mandate under his direction:

> The science of man with its numerous divisions, properly called eth-nology, history, anthropology, linguistics, archaeology, pre-history, etc., will not exhaust [IFAN's] programme. Geography, human and physical, provides a link between the foregoing group of studies and that large group of natural sciences which include zoology and botany and implies not only simple classification but the study of form, function, and behav-iour. It [the Institute] deals, in fact, with the human being, as such, in its African environment, studied from numerous different view-points and providing material for the building up of a tropical biology, pure and applied.[51] (Monod 1944: 73)

Again, we need to know more about how anthropology (including eth-nology and ethnography) intersected with or moved against these other fields. And we need to better understand the consequences for African history of these intermixtures and institutional developments.[52]

A third pattern that emerges from the chapters is the confluence of concerns among administrators and anthropologists regarding labor, social change, culture contact, kinship and lineage networks, tradi-tions and development (or *mise en valeur*). These are issues that have become stock-in-trade among African and imperial historians, with some placing greater stress on lived experience (i.e. social history) and others on colonial policymaking. An emphasis on intellectual history helps to complete the picture, teasing out just how these preoccupa-tions surfaced, circulated, and were transformed in scholarly and offi-cial documents (and practices). While many architects of colonial rule in Africa seemed to articulate congruent 'problems' – reflecting perhaps the similarities in the situations they encountered as well as their desired goals – they nonetheless pursued different strategies to resolve these problems, underscoring the contingent and ad hoc nature of administration itself. The same can be said generally of the archi-tects of anthropology: even when there were shared concerns and prob-lems, individuals would often take these in different theoretical and empirical directions. As a number of scholars have pointed out, includ-ing several in this volume, intellectual intermediaries (explorers, mis-sionaries, administrator-ethnographers, assistants, translators) served as a bridge between these two worlds (anthropology and administra-tion), frequently helping to shore up each side. Our understanding of precisely how this worked is still incomplete, but through such cases

[27]

as Paul du Chaillu (in Cinnamon), Alberto Pollera (Sorgoni), Joseph Oldham (L'Estoile), Charles Lodewyckx (Hunt), Maurice Delafosse (Sibeud and Wilder), James Currie (Johnson), Henri Junod (Harries), and any of the numerous individuals discussed by Pugach and Jezequel, we are beginning to develop a clearer picture. The challenge, however, is to ensure that we do not lose sight of the internal workings of disciplines and professions – we ignore conceptual developments at our own peril – or of colonial regimes themselves. The apparent isomorphism that seemed to underpin patterns of administration and ethnographic research, such as Wilder describes in French West Africa, needs to be explained with care. Why there and not elsewhere? At what point, if ever, did reciprocal relations break down? What conceptual differences divided individuals even as they might have acted together? And, in turn, how could certain groups be united in their analysis and still disagree on the kinds of interventions necessary for colonial rule?

If this collection helps to highlight the institutional infrastructure and far-reaching networks that went into producing anthropological knowledge, its analysis of the field's 'cognitive architecture' could still be taken much further.[53] Not everything about anthropology's development can be explained by its socio-economic and political context. Nor should anthropological theories always be traced back to an instrumental purpose. Studies of colonialism and knowledge – with their emphases on power, application, and 'governmentality' – sometimes fall into both traps. African terrain did indeed offer anthropologists an opportunity to work out theories that remain salient even today, however much they have been criticized and modified. Classics produced in the twilight of colonial rule – such as Evans-Pritchard's *Witchcraft, Oracles, and Magic Among the Azande* (1937) and *The Nuer* (1947), Audrey Richard's *Land, Labour, and Diet in Northern Rhodesia* (1939), Meyer Fortes and Evans-Pritchard's edited collection *African Political Systems* (1940), Isaac Schapera's *Migrant Labour and Tribal Life* (1947), A.R. Radcliffe-Brown and Darryl Forde's volume *African Systems of Kinship and Marriage* (1950), and Max Gluckman's *Custom and Conflict in Africa* (1955), to name just a handful from the British tradition – offered anthropologists (and other scholars) a conceptual apparatus regarding functionalism, culture contact, stateless and segmentary societies, misfortune and healing, witchcraft and rationality, migrancy and identity, and tradition and conflict, which have had a rich shelf-life. There exists a promising opportunity for scholars who might wish to tease out the influence of these ideas in the context of anthropology at the end of empire.[54]

A final insight of this volume has to do with the nature of the questions we ask about knowledge vis-à-vis Africa. During the last two decades a burgeoning literature has emerged on science and empire that has paid less attention to the African continent than seems warranted given its centrality to late European imperialism. At the same time, studies of knowledge in and on Africa often ignore trends and developments in other parts of the world. The time has come to bridge this gap. To do so will require a certain amount of old-fashioned empirical analysis, based on archival research and sustained fieldwork, as well as a willingness to suspend judgment and consider historical events on their own terms. In certain respects, this undertaking is no less controversial today than it was in the colonial period itself: it still rests on fundamental inequalities and runs the risk of reinforcing existing relations of power. One could argue, however, that a clearer understanding of both the content and politics of knowledge in colonial Africa would shed light on postcolonial patterns and might draw attention to significant *discontinuities* that also need to be explained. While scholars will continue to analyze the colonial period in terms of complicity (i.e. whether certain theories reinforced or undermined colonial aims), new questions are also emerging that take ontology and epistemology more seriously.

The contributions to this volume should highlight the need to strike a balance between contextualizing colonial categories (including those produced by science) and assessing their veracity and impact. Infertility scares, for example, had both an imaginative and a real existence; rumors of cannibalism and migratory zeal were grounded in both true and false evidence, however partial each may have been. We should not abandon ontology even if our interest is focused more on the ways knowledge (whether accurate or inaccurate) gained currency and momentum. Likewise, if we focus only on whether theories were right or wrong – or whether, when they were applied, they succeeded or failed – we will be unable to appreciate the multiplicity of perspectives that often coexisted during the colonial era. These histories of anthropology do many things, but, above all, we hope they invite further study and discussion of Africa, imperialism, and knowledge. Edwin Smith's modest and self-critical pronouncement, 'we have only scratched the surface of things hitherto', seems a worthy one to embrace for such a complex topic.

Notes

1 For their comments on earlier drafts, I would like to thank Rob Gordon, Clifford Geertz, Henrika Kuklick and João Biehl; I alone am responsible for any shortcomings and omissions.
2 Chinua Achebe, *Morning Yet on Creation Day* (London, 1975), quoted in Ranger 1976: 117–118.

3 Edwin Smith, 'Africa: What Do We Know of It?', *Journal of the Royal Anthropological Institute*, v. 65 (1935), pp. 1–81, quotations on pp. 1–2, 77–79, 81.
4 Readers familiar with the history of anthropology will be aware that historical actors have often used different terms to designate the study of human populations. These often grew out of their respective national traditions and could reflect different objects of study. In the mid-nineteenth century, for instance, 'anthropology' would have referred primarily to biological and racial concerns (i.e. physical anthropology) while 'ethnography' would have designated predominantly cultural preoccupations. The use of the term 'ethnology' usually signaled an interest in making connections among physical, historical, and linguistic phenomena. All three terms, however, could also be used more loosely. Some actors even embraced the term 'sociology' – the Durkheimians, for instance, and even certain British functionalists. Edward Evans-Pritchard's lectureship at Oxford University was, after all, in 'African Sociology'. Nonetheless, for the purpose of this introduction I will use 'anthropology' as the umbrella term since, in the English-speaking world, it has become predominant.
5 This list reflects the main stakeholders during and following the 'scramble for Africa' and does not include those nations that colonized coastal and island areas in earlier periods.
6 Scholarly work on the human and social sciences in North Africa is beginning to flourish; see Lucas and Vatin 1975; Vatin *et al.* 1984; Berthelier 1994; Lorcin 1995; Keller 2001; El Shakry 2002.
7 This is a modified version of Stoler and Cooper's question, 'To what extent – and by what processes – did the knowledge of individual empires become a collective imperial knowledge, shared among colonizing powers?'
8 Until the very last stages of the project the volume included a chapter on anthropology in Portuguese Mozambique; for contributions on Portuguese anthropology and its connections to Africa and empire see a recent overview, Maino 2005.
9 Historical interest in each of these areas has developed unevenly; most attention has been directed to medicine (and its allied fields). For recent monographs see Jackson 2005; Hoppe 2003; Echenberg 2002; Wylie 2001; Bell 1999; Hunt 1999; Iliffe 1998; McCulloch 1995; Headrick 1994; Lyons 1992; Vaughan 1991; Packard 1989. On the environmental sciences see, for instance, Tilley 2003; Bonneuil 1999 [focused on Sénégal and the Côte d'Ivoire as well as Vietnam]; Grove 1995 [focused on the Cape of South Africa, St Helena, and Mauritius]; Osborne 1990 [focused on Algeria]; MacKenzie 1990; MacKenzie 1988.
10 African environmental history is a burgeoning field; recent noteworthy contributions, limited to those that address the history of scientific issues, include Conte 2004; Beinart 2003; Beinart 2000; Mackenzie 1998; Neumann 1998; Maddox *et al* 1996; Fairhead and Leach 1996; Leach and Mearns 1996; Moore and Vaughan 1994; Giblin 1992; Richards 1985. Two classics include Ford 1971; and Allan 1965. On the historical origins of Allan's work see Tilley 2004; on Ford's see Tilley 2001, chapter 4.
11 A diverse selection of literature falls in this category including studies of 'indigenous knowledge systems'; for some of the broad-based debates see Brokensha, Warren, and Werner 1980; Bates, Mudimbe, and O'Barr 1993; Agrawal 1995; Cooper and Packard 1997; Sillitoe 1998; Purcell 1998; Hoppers 2002.
12 This is the subject of my forthcoming book, *Africa as a Living Laboratory*, which explores the history of environmental, medical, racial and anthropological research in and on British tropical Africa between, roughly, 1860 and 1960.
13 Feierman was addressing specifically 'hybrid' colonial situations such as those discussed by the Comaroffs; his insight, however, has wider application; also see Feierman 1993.
14 Also relevant to this issue would be Frederick Cooper's discussion of 'globalization' and its relative usefulness to African history; Cooper 2001.
15 Several authors have tried to make this latter point in their work; for a recent example see Mbembe and Nuttal 2004.

16 More recently, Pels and Salemink have reiterated this point; Pels and Salemink 1999: 6–7.

17 For British anthropology see Kuper 1996 [1983]; Kuper 2005; Stocking Jr. 1987; Stocking Jr. 1995; Kuklick 1991; Urry 1993b also see Coombes 1994; and de L'Estoile 2004a [the latter two focus predominantly on Africa]; for American anthropology see Hinsley 1981; Stocking Jr. 1974; Stocking Jr. 1979; Williams 1996; Darnell 2000; and Darnell 2001; for French, German and broader European traditions see Smith 1991; Vermeulen and Roldán 1995; Blanckaert 1996; Blanckaert 2001; Amselle and Sibeud 1998; Zimmerman 2001; Sibeud 2002; Penny 2002; Penny and Bunzl 2003; L'Estoile 2004b. This is by no means a comprehensive list, but these works include more complete bibliographies.

18 Historical studies include Ranger 1976; Kuklick 1978; Thornton 1983; Zwerne-mann 1983; Gordon 1988, 1989, 1990, 1993; Miller 1990; Fardon 1990; Moore 1994; Noyes 1994; Goody 1995; Hammond-Tooke 1997; Pels 1999; Heintze 1999; Fabian 2000; L'Estoile 2000; Schumaker 2001; Sichone 2003; and Zimmerman 2006.

19 Nicholas Dirks makes the following claim for India: 'To put the matter in bold relief, after 1857, anthropology supplanted history as the principal colonial modality of knowledge and rule. By the late nineteenth century . . . the colonial state in India can be characterized as the ethnographic state' (Dirks 2001: 43).

20 For an overview of the literature, which includes over 2,000 entries, see 'Anthropology and Ethnography of Europe', which is the appended bibliography in Ripley, 1900, pp. 1–160. Urry demonstrates the administrative failure of the Ethnographic Survey of the United Kingdom, but this failure should not be read as a lack of contemporary interest.

21 Gérard Leclerc, working originally under the supervision of Georges Balandier, took a different perspective, exploring significant intersections between British functional anthropology and indirect rule, Leclerc 1972; also see Wilder, this volume, for a similar analysis of French West Africa.

22 The following discussion is taken from Tilley 2001, pp. 257–259.

23 The audience included Lord Lugard, author of The Dual Mandate in Tropical Africa; William Macmillan; Thomas Drummond Shiels, former Labour Under-Secretary of State for the Colonies; C.K. Meek, former anthropologist for S.E. Nigeria; Sir James Currie, former director of Education in the Sudan; and William McGregor Ross, former director of public works in Kenya and a vocal critic of Britain's colonial policies.

24 Macmillan reiterated and expanded upon his criticisms in Africa Emergent (Macmillan 1938: 375): anthropologists, he believed, 'end [their studies] by pronouncing in effect that whatever is essentially African is right'.

25 Stella Thomas was a Nigerian of Sierra Leone descent who received a law degree from Oxford University in the 1920s; in 1943 she became the first woman in Nigeria appointed magistrate. For details see Denzer, 1987: 446, 452.

26 For a similar postwar rebuttal countering the view that anthropologists only wanted to turn Africans into static objects, also see Audrey Richards 1944.

27 This concern had both antecedents and successors. In 1898 in one of his first ethnographic monographs Henri Junod remarked, 'An African tribe is not just an object of study like the birds, animals or insects displayed in the windows of our museums and dissected by diligent scientists. A tribe is a living thing' (Harries 1999: 27); likewise, in 1937, Frank Melland, in a chapter on 'Anthropology in Africa', observed '[W]hat are anthropologists trying to do? Primitive races are no longer studied for academic reasons, or as museum pieces, but with the desire to acquire knowledge of their past and of their present so that we can be of some assistance in their future' (Melland and Young 1937: 48–49).

28 This theme is developed further in the chapters in this volume by Sibeud, Harries, Hunt, Berman and Lonsdale, and Wilder; Kingsley is listed here for her role in transforming African and ethnographic studies in Britain; I have not included Maurice Delafosse in the list, but see Amselle and Sibeud 1998 for his role as a reformer.

29 Anthropology, of course, also had its advocates among Africans; D.D.T. Jabavu wrote in 1924, for instance, 'The science of social anthropology is in its infancy. As a line of research it is, for us, essential and practical. This country [South Africa], in particular, offers unusual opportunities for its development' (Jabavu, 'Science and the Native', quoted in Gordon 1990: 43).

30 For one strand of this critique see Fanon 1953 and Memmi 1957; also relevant is Mannoni 1950.

31 The first social science institute established in French Africa, at virtually the same time, was the Institut Français d'Afrique Noire (IFAN), founded by decree in 1936 in Dakar, Senegal.

32 On this point also see Brown 1973; Brown 1979; and Werbner 1984.

33 On the development of regional traditions in anthropology, which includes several African examples, see Richard Fardon 1990.

34 On the place of anthropology in Southern Africa today see Gordon and Spiegel 1993; LeBeau and Gordon 2002; for a discussion of place and the epistemic status of anthropology see Comaroff and Comaroff 2003.

35 For a recent discussion of the limits of identity as an analytical category see Brubaker and Cooper 2001.

36 For a thoughtful essay that responds to this point and others see Guyer 1999.

37 See, for instance, Horton 1967a, 1967b, 1982; Wiredu 1980; Hountondji 1983, 2002; Mudimbe 1994 and 1988; Appiah 1992; and Hallen 2006.

38 Historians of Africa have begun to consider the degree to which African actors shaped their own discourse related to race, genealogy, kinship, descent and heredity; for a few fascinating examples see Powell 2003; Lee 2003; Glassman 2004; earlier work on this subject was often done under the rubric of ethnicity, e.g. Young 1986.

39 I have selected only three chapters for the book's first section although almost all the contributors address metropolitan interests and priorities in their chapters; Pugach's chapter is discussed here and in the context of African ethnography.

40 For an article that explores 'the contribution of anthropology to African Studies' in the US context see Southall 1983.

41 It should be noted that both Léopold Senghor and Jomo Kenyatta while in Paris and London respectively worked as language instructors; see Berman/Lonsdale ('linguistic informant'), p. 181 and Wilder, p. 364n.26 this volume.

42 The International Institute of African Languages and Cultures, founded in 1926, took the shorter name International African Institute following World War II. It exists under this name to this day.

43 For a history of German cultural sciences between 1840 to 1920 see Smith 1991; and for two more recent studies exploring museums and the relationship between humanism and anthropology see Penny 2003; Zimmerman 2001.

44 There are presumably a large number of examples from the interwar period and onwards; for a fascinating earlier example one might consider the relationship between Sir Apolo Kagwa (1864?–1927), Katikkiro [king] of the Baganda, and John Roscoe (1861–1932) of the Church Missionary Society and former student of James Frazer. Kagwa authored several studies of the Baganda's kings, customs and clans including *Empisa Z'Abaganda* (circa 1907 and translated into English in 1934 as *Customs of the Baganda*). Using Kagwa as one of his key informants, John Roscoe then published in 1911 his *The Baganda: An Account of Their Native Customs and Beliefs*. For a preliminary discussion of their mutual influences see Rowe 1967.

45 John Cinnamon, in this volume, borrows the term auto-ethnography from the work of Mary Louise Pratt; he also refers to Pels and Salemink's discussion of the 'indigenous expert' (Pels and Salemink 1999: 20–22). In one of the first critical studies I have found on the subject, David Hayano recounts that he first heard the term used in 1966 during a seminar on structuralism taught by Raymond Firth; Firth apparently mentioned it after describing a heated exchange between Kenyatta and Louis Leakey (a Kenyan-born Kikuyu speaker of British parents) after Kenyatta presented the results of his field research (Hayano 1979: 99–100).

46 For a discussion of the relationship between 'Negritude and Anthropology' see Miller 1990: 10–21; for a wider discussion of Negritude in French colonial politics, see Wilder 2005.

47 There are several recent studies that consider the construction of ideas about 'indigenous' within Europe itself, which primarily concentrate on the eighteenth century; see Cooper 1998; and Koerner 1999.

48 For a recent study on the nineteenth-century debates on racial extinction see Brantlinger 2003.

49 Elisio Macamo, 'On the Power of Self-Fulfilling Prophecies: Portuguese Anthropology and the Regulation of Native Labour in Mozambique', draft manuscript: for a published discussion of labour in Mozambique see Macamo, 2006.

50 West's article includes a fascinating discussion of Dias' wife, Margot, who served as part of the research team when Dias was in the field and of Rafael Mwakala, one of Dias' research assistants, who conducted what West calls an 'anti-anthropology' of his own by concealing certain features of his political and social activities from the Dias team.

51 For an analysis of a similar set of research priorities in Britain established after a survey of 'science in Africa' undertaken by E.B. Worthington, who later worked with Monod in the Scientific Council for Africa South of the Sahara, see Tilley 2001.

52 Recent studies of colonial Zambia (Northern Rhodesia) and the intersections between ecological, nutritional and anthropological research provide one such case; see Moore and Vaughan 1994; Schumaker 2001; and Tilley 2004.

53 My thanks to Clifford Geertz for this phrase and for the larger point; Richard Werbner, who attended the original conference in 2000, made a similar comment during the event itself.

54 A number of anthropologists, including Benoît de L'Estoile and David Mills, have already begun this undertaking; my own work takes up some of these questions as well.

References

Agrawal, Arun. 1995. 'Dismantling the Divide between Indigenous and Scientific Knowledge'. *Development and Change* 26:413–439.

Allan, William. 1965. *The African Husbandman*. London: Oliver and Boyd.

Amselle, Jean-Loup and Sibeud, Emmanuelle (eds). 1998. *Maurice Delafosse – Entre orientalisme et ethnographie: l'itinéraire d'un africaniste (1870–1926)*. Paris: Maisonneuve.

Appiah, Kwame Anthony. 1992. *In My Father's House: Africa in the philosophy of culture*. London: Oxford University Press.

Apter, Andrew. 1999. 'Africa, Empire, and Anthropology: A Philological Exploration of Anthropology's Heart of Darkness'. *Annual Review of Anthropology* 28:577–598.

Asad, Talal (ed.). 1973. *Anthropology and the Colonial Encounter*. London: Ithaca Press.

Asad, Talal. 1991. 'From the History of Colonial Anthropology to the Anthropology of Western Hegemony'. In G. Stocking (ed.). *Colonial Situations: Essays on the Contextualization of Ethnographic Knowledge*. Madison: University of Wisconsin Press, pp. 314–324.

Balandier, Georges. 1951. 'La Situation coloniale: approche théorique'. *Cahiers internationaux de sociologie* XI:44–79.

Balandier, Georges. 1960. 'The French Tradition of African Research'. *Human Organization* 19:108–111.

Banaji, Jairus. 1970. 'The Crisis of British Anthropology'. *New Left Review* 64:71–85.

Bates, Robert H., Mudimbe, Valentin Yves and O'Barr, Jean (eds). 1993. *Africa and the Disciplines – The Contribution of Research in Africa to the Social Sciences and Humanities*. Chicago: University of Chicago Press.

Beinart, William. 2000. 'African History and Environmental History'. *African Affairs* 99:269–302.

Beinart, William. 2003. *The Rise of Conservation in South Africa: Settlers, Livestock and the Environment, 1770–1950*. Oxford: Oxford University Press.

Bell, Heather. 1999. *Frontiers of Medicine in the Anglo-Egyptian Sudan, 1899–1940*. Oxford: Clarendon Press.

Benton, Lauren. 2002. *Law and Colonial Cultures: Legal Regimes in World History, 1400–1900*. Cambridge: Cambridge University Press.

Berman, Bruce and Lonsdale, John. 1992. *Unhappy Valley: Conflict in Kenya and Africa Book One: State and Class & Book Two: Violence and Ethnicity*. Oxford: James Currey Press.

Berthelier, Robert. 1994. *L'homme Maghréban dans la Littérature Psychiatrique*. Paris: L'Harmattan.

Blanckaert, Claude (ed.). 1996. *Le terrain des sciences humaines: Instructions et enquêtes (XVIIIe–XXe siecles)*. Paris: L'Harmattan.

Blanckaert, Claude (ed.). 2001. *Les Politiques de l'Anthropologie: pratiques et applications en France (1859–1940)*. Paris: L'Harmattan.

Bonneuil, Christophe. 1999. *Mettre en ordre et discipliner les tropiques: Les sciences du végetal dans l'empire français, 1870–1940*. Paris: Edition des Archives Contemporaines.

Bonneuil, Christophe. 2000. 'Science and State Building in Late Colonial and Postcolonial Africa, 1930–1970'. In R. MacLeod (ed.). *Nature and Empire: Science and the Colonial Enterprise. Osiris 15*. Chicago: University of Chicago Press, pp. 258–281.

Brantlinger, Patrick. 2003. *Dark Vanishings: Discourse on the Extinction of Primitive Races, 1800–1930*. Ithaca: Cornell University Press.

Brokensha, David, Warren, D. M. and Werner, Oswald (eds). 1980. *Indigenous Knowledge Systems and Development*. Washington D.C.: University Press of America.

Brown, Richard. 1973. 'Anthropology and Colonial Rule: Godfrey Wilson and the Rhodes-Livingstone Institute, Northern Rhodesia'. In T. Asad (ed.). *Anthropology and the Colonial Encounter*. London: Ithaca Press, pp. 173–197.

Brown, Richard. 1979. 'Passages in the Life of a White Anthropologist: Max Gluckman in Northern Rhodesia'. *Journal of African History* 20:525–541.

Brubaker, Rogers and Cooper, Frederick. 2001. 'Beyond "Identity"'. *Theory and Society* 29:1–47.

Burke, Timothy. 1996. *Lifebuoy Men, Lux Women: Commodification, Consumption, and Cleanliness in Modern Zimbabwe*. Durham: Duke University Press.

Butchart, Alexander. 1998. *The Anatomy of Power: European Constructions of the African Body*. London: Zed Books.

Chamberlain, J. Edward and Gilman, Sander (eds). 1985. *Degeneration: The Dark Side of Progress*. New York: Columbia University Press.

Chilungu, Simeon. 1976. 'Issues in the Ethics of Research Method: An Interpretation of the Anglo-American Perspective'. *Current Anthropology* 17:457–481.

Cocks, Paul. 1995. 'The Rhetoric of Science and the Critique of Imperialism in British Social Anthropology, c. 1870–1940'. *History and Anthropology* 9:93–119.

Comaroff, John. 1997. 'Reflections on the Colonial State, in South Africa and Elsewhere: Factions, Fragments, Facts, and Fictions'. *Academia Sinica: Bulletin of the Institute of Ethnology* 83:1–50.

Comaroff, Jean and Comaroff, John. 1991. *Of Revelation and Revolution: v. 1 Christianity, colonialism, and consciousness in South Africa*. Chicago: University of Chicago Press.

Comaroff, John and Comaroff, Jean. 1992. *Ethnography and the Historical Imagination*. Boulder: Westview Press.

Comaroff, Jean and Comaroff, John. 1997. *Of Revelation and Revolution: v. 2 The Dialectics of Modernity on a South African Frontier*. Chicago: University of Chicago Press.

Comaroff, Jean and Comaroff, John. 2003. 'Ethnography on an Awkward Scale: Postcolonial Anthropology and the Violence of Abstraction'. *Ethnography* 4:147–179.

Conklin, Alice. 1997. *A Mission to Civilize: The Republican Idea of Empire in France and West Africa, 1895–1930*. Stanford: Stanford University Press.

Conte, Christopher. 2004. *Highland Sanctuary: Environmental History in Tanzania's Usambara Mountains*. Athens, Ohio: Ohio University Press.

Coombes, Annie. 1994. *Reinventing Africa: Museums, Material Culture, and Popular Imagination in Late Victorian and Edwardian England*. New Haven: Yale University Press.

Cooper, Frederick. 2001. 'What is the Concept of Globalization Good For? An African Historian's Perspective'. *African Affairs* 100:189–213.

Cooper, Frederick and Packard, Randall (eds). 1997. *International Development and the Social Sciences – Essays on the History and Politics of Knowledge*. Berkeley: University of California Press.

Cooper, Mary Alexandra. 1998. 'Inventing the Indigenous: Local Knowledge and Natural History in the Early Modern German Territories'. Harvard University: Unpublished Ph.D.

Copans, Jean (ed.). 1975. *Anthropologie et impérialisme*. Paris: François Maspero.

Darnell, Regna. 2000. *And Along Came Boas: Continuity and Revolution in Americanist Anthropology*. Philadelphia: J. Benjamins.

Darnell, Regna. 2001. *Invisible Genealogies: A History of Americanist Anthropology*. Lincoln: University of Nebraska Press.

Denzer, LeRay. 1987. 'Women in Freetown Politics, 1914–1961: A Preliminary Study'. *Africa* 54:439–456.

Desai, Gaurav. 2001. *Subject to Colonialism: African Self-Fashioning and the Colonial Library*. Durham: Duke University Press.

Dirks, Nicholas. 2001. *Castes of Mind: Colonialism and the Making of Modern India*. Princeton: Princeton University Press.

Dubow, Saul. 1995. *Scientific Racism in Modern South Africa*. Cambridge: Cambridge University Press.

Dubow, Saul. 1996. 'Human Origins, Race Typology and the Other Raymond Dart'. *African Studies* 55:1–30.

Echenberg, Myron. 2002. *Black Death, White Medicine: Bubonic Plague and the Politics of Public Health in Colonial Senegal, 1914–1945*. Portsmouth, NH: Heinemann Press.

El Shakry, Omnia. 2002. 'The Great Social Laboratory: Reformers and Utopians in Twentieth Century Egypt'. Princeton University: Unpublished Ph.D.

El Shakry, Omnia. 2005. 'Barren Lands and Fecund Bodies: The Emergence of Population Discourse in Interwar Egypt'. *International Journal of Middle East Studies* 37:351–372.

Evans-Pritchard, Edward E. 1937. *Witchcraft, Oracles, and Magic Among the Azande*. Oxford: Clarendon Press.

Evans-Pritchard, Edward E. 1940. *The Nuer: A Description of the Modes of Livelihood and Political Institutions of a Nilotic People*. Oxford: Clarendon Press.

Fabian, Johannes. 1983. *Time and the Other: How Anthropology Makes Its Object*. New York: Columbia University Press.

Fabian, Johannes. 1986. *Language and Colonial Power: The Appropriation of Swahili in the Former Belgian Congo, 1880–1938*. Berkeley: University of California Press.

Fabian, Johannes. 2000. *Out of Our Minds: Reason and Madness in the Exploration of Central Africa*. Berkeley: University of California Press.

Fairhead, James and Leach, Melissa. 1996. *Misreading the African Landscape: Society and Ecology in a Forest-Savanna Mosaic*. Cambridge: Cambridge University Press.

Fairweather-Tall, Andrew. 2002. 'From Colonial Administration to Colonial State: The Transition of Government, Education, and Labour in Nyasaland, c. 1930–1950'. Oxford University: Unpublished D-Phil.

Fanon, Frantz. 1953 [1965]. *Peau Noire, Masques Blancs*. Paris. Editions du Seuil.

Fardon, Richard (ed.). 1990. *Localizing Strategies: Regional Traditions of Ethnographic Writing*. Edinburgh: Scottish Academic Press.

Feierman, Steven. 1993. 'African Histories and the Dissolution of World History'. In R.H. Bates, V.Y. Mudimbe and J. O'Barr (eds). *Africa and the Disciplines*. Chicago: University of Chicago, pp. 167–212.

Feierman, Steven. 2001. 'The Comaroffs and the Practice of Historical Ethnography'. *Interventions* 3:24–30.

Ford, John. 1971. *The Role of the Trypanosomiases in African Ecology; a Study of the Tsetse Fly Problem*. Oxford: Clarendon Press.

Forde, Daryll. 1953. 'Applied Anthropology in Government: British Africa'. In A.L. Kroeber (ed.). *Anthropology Today: An Encyclopedic Inventory*. Chicago: University of Chicago Press, pp. 841–865.

Fortes, Meyer and Evans-Pritchard, Edward (eds). 1940. *African Political Systems*. London: Oxford University Press.

Gallo, Donato. 1988. *O Saber Português: Antropologia e Colonialismo*. Lisbon: Heptágono.

Giblin, James. 1992. *The Politics of Environmental Control in Northeastern Tanzania, 1840–1940*. Philadelphia: University of Pennsylvania Press.

Glassman, Jonathan. 2004. 'Slower than a Massacre: The Multiple Sources of Racial Thought in Colonial Africa'. *American Historical Review* 109:720–754.

Gluckman, Max. 1955. *Custom and Conflict in Africa*. Oxford: Blackwell.

Goddard, David. 1969. 'Limits of British Anthropology'. *New Left Review* n. 58:79–89.

Goody, Jack. 1995. *The Expansive Moment: Anthropology in Britain and Africa, 1918–1970*. Cambridge: Cambridge University Press.

Gordon, Robert. 1988. 'Apartheid's Anthropologists: The Genealogy of Afrikaner Anthropology'. *American Ethnologist* 15:535–553.

Gordon, Robert. 1989. 'The White Man's Burden: Ersatz Customary Law and Internal Pacification in South Africa'. *Journal of Historical Sociology* 2:41–65.

Gordon, Robert. 1990. 'Early Social Anthropology in South Africa'. *African Studies* 49:15–48.

Gordon, Robert and Spiegel, A.D. 1993. 'Southern Africa Revisted'. *Annual Review of Anthropology* 22:83–105.

Gough, Kathleen. 1968. 'Anthropology and Imperialism'. *Monthly Review* 19:12–27.

Grove, Richard. 1995. *Green Imperialism: Colonial Expansion, Tropical Island Edens and the Origins of Environmentalism, 1600–1860*. Cambridge: Cambridge University Press.

Guyer, Jane. 1999. 'Anthropology: The Study of Social and Cultural Originality'. *African Sociological Review* 3:30–53.

Hallen, Barry. 2006. *African Philosophy: The Analytic Approach*. Trenton: Africa World Press.

Hambly, Wilfrid D. 1937. *Source Book for African Anthropology*. Part I and Part II. Chicago: Field Museum of Natural History.

Hambly, Wilfrid D. 1952. *Bibliography of African Anthropology, 1937–1949, Supplement to Source Book of African Anthropology, 1937*. Chicago: Natural History Museum.

Hammond-Tooke, David. 1997. *Imperfect Interpreters: South Africa's Anthropologists, 1920–1990*. Johannesburg: Witwatersrand University Press.

Harries, Patrick. 1999. 'Field Sciences in Scientific Fields: Entomology, Botany and the Early Ethnographic Monograph in the work of H.-A. Junod'. In S. Dubow (ed.). *Science and Society in Southern Africa*. Manchester: Manchester University Press, pp. 11–41.

Harrison, Faye (ed.). 1991. *Decolonizing Anthropology: Moving Further Toward an Anthropology for Liberation*. Washington, D.C.: American Anthropological Association.

Hayano, D. 1979. 'Auto-Ethnography: Paradigms, Problems, and Prospects'. *Human Organization* 38:99–104.

Headrick, Rita. 1994. *Colonialism, Health and Illness in French Equatorial Africa, 1885–1935*. Atlanta: African Studies Association Press.

Heintze, Beatrix. 1999. 'Ethnographic Appropriations: German Exploration and Fieldwork in West-Central Africa'. *History in Africa* 26:69–128.

Hinsley, C.M. 1981. *Savages and Scientists: The Smithsonian Institute and the Development of American Anthropology, 1846–1910*. Washington, D.C.: Smithsonian Institute.

Hooker, James R. 1963. 'The Anthropologists' Frontier: The Last Phase of African Exploitation'. *The Journal of Modern African Studies* 1:455–459.

Hoppe, Kirk Arden. 2003. *Lords of the Fly: Sleeping Sickness Control in British East Africa, 1900–1960*. Westport, CT: Praeger.

Hoppers, Catherine Odora (ed.). 2002. *Indigenous Knowledge and the Integration of Knowledge Systems: Towards a Philosophy of Articulation*. Claremont, South Africa: New Africa Books.

Horton, Robin. 1967a. 'African Traditional Thought and Western Science, Part I. From Tradition to Science'. *Africa* 37:50–71.

Horton, Robin. 1967b. 'African Traditional Thought and Western Science, Part II. The "Closed" and "Open" Predicaments'. *Africa* 37:155–187.

Horton, Robin. 1982. 'Tradition and Modernity Revisited'. In M. Hollis and S. Lukes (eds). *Rationality and Relativism*. Oxford: Blackwell Press, pp. 201–260.

Hountondji, Paulin. 1983. *African Philosophy: Myth and Reality*. Bloomington, Ind: Indiana University Press.

Hountondji, Paulin. 2002. *The Struggle for Meaning: Reflections on Philosophy, Culture, and Democracy in Africa*. Translated by J. Conteh-Morgan. Athens, Ohio: Ohio University Center for International Studies.

Hunter, Monica. 1936. *Reaction to Conquest: Effects of Contact with Europeans on the Pondo of South Africa*. London: Oxford University Press.

Iliffe, John. 1998. *East African Doctors*. Cambridge: Cambridge University Press.

Hunt, Nancy. 1999. *A Colonial Lexicon: Of Birth Ritual, Medicalization, and Mobility in the Congo*. Durham: Duke University Press.

Jackson, Lynette. 2005. *Surfacing Up: Psychiatry and Social Order in Colonial Zimbabwe, 1908–1968*. Ithaca: Cornell University Press.

James, Wendy. 1973. 'The Anthropologist as Reluctant Imperialist'. In T. Asad (ed.). *Anthropology and the Colonial Encounter*. London: Ithaca Press, pp. 41–70.

Johnston, H.H. 1912. *Views and Reviews from the Outlook of an Anthropologist*. London: Williams and Norgate.

Junod, Henri. 1912. *The Life of a South African Tribe 2 vols* London: D. Nutt.

Keller, Richard. 2001. 'Action Psychologique: French Psychiatry in Colonial North Africa, 1900–1962'. Rutgers University: Unpublished Ph.D.

Kenyatta, Jomo. 1938. *Facing Mount Kenya*. London: Secker and Warburg.

Kevane, Michael. 2006. 'Dim Delobsom: French Colonialism and Local Response in Upper Volta'. *African Studies Quarterly* 8 [online]: http://web.africa.ufl.edu/asq/v8/v8:4a2.htm.

Kingsley, Mary. 1897. *Travels in West Africa: Congo Français, Corisco and Cameroons*. London: Macmillan.

Kirkby, Diane and Coleborne, Catharine (eds). 2001. *Law, History, Colonialism: The Reach of Empire*. Manchester: Manchester University Press.

Koerner, Lisbet. 1999. *Linnaeus: Nature and Nation*. Cambridge: Harvard University Press.

Kuklick, Henrika. 1978. 'The Sins of the Fathers: British Anthropology and African Colonial Administration'. *Research in Sociology of Knowledge, Sciences and Art* 1:93–119.

Kuklick, Henrika. 1991. *The Savage Within: The Social History of British Anthropology, 1885–1945*. Cambridge: Cambridge University Press.

Kuklick, Henrika and Kohler, Robert (eds). 1996. *Science in the Field. OSIRIS* 11. Chicago: University of Chicago Press.

Kuper, Adam. 1996 [1983]. *Anthropology and Anthropologists: The Modern British School*, 3rd revised and enlarged edition. London: Routledge Press.

Kuper, Adam. 2005. 'Alternative Histories of British Social Anthropology'. *Social Anthropology* 13:47–64.

Laville, Rosabelle. 1998. 'A Critical Review of "Anthropology and Independent Africans: Suicide or End of an Era?" by Archie Mafeje'. *African Sociological Review* 2:44–50.

Leach, Melissa and Mearns, Robin (eds). 1996. *The Lie of the Land: Challenging Received Wisdom on the African Environment*. Oxford: James Currey Press.

LeBeau, Debie and Gordon, Robert J. (eds). 2002. *Challenges for Anthropology in the 'African Renaissance': A Southern African Contribution*. Windhoek, Namibia: University of Namibia Press.

Leclerc, Gérard. 1972. *Anthropologie et Colonialisme: Essai sur l'histoire de l'africanisme*. Paris: Librarie Arthème Fayard.

Lee, Christopher Joonhai. 2003. 'Colonial Kinships: The British Dual Mandate, Anglo-African Status, and the Politics of Race and Ethnicity in Inter-War Nyasaland'. Stanford University: Unpublished Ph.D.

Leiris, Michel. 1934. *L'Afrique Fantôme*. Paris: Gallimard.

L'Estoile, Benoît de. 2000. 'Science de l'homme et "domination rationelle". Savoir ethnologique et politique indigène en Afrique coloniale française'. *Revue de synthèse* n. 3–4:291–323.

L'Estoile, Benoît de. 2004a. 'L'Afrique comme laboratoire. Expériences réformatrices et révolution anthropologique dans l'empire colonial britannique (1920–1950)'. L'Ecole des Hautes Etudes en Sciences Sociales: Unpublished Ph.D.

L'Estoile, Benoît de. 2004b. 'From the Colonial Exhibition to the Museum of Man: An Alternative Genealogy of French Anthropology'. *Social Anthropology* 11:341–361.

Levi-Strauss, Claude. 1966. 'Anthropology: Its Achievements and Future'. *Current Anthropology* 7:124–127.

Lewis, Diane. 1973. 'Anthropology and Colonialism'. *Current Anthropology* 14:581–602.

Lewis, Joanna. 2000. *Empire State-Building: War and Welfare in Kenya 1925–52*. Oxford: James Currey Press.

Lonsdale, John. 1981. 'States and Social Processes in Africa: A Historiographical Survey'. *African Studies Review* 24:139–225.

Lorcin, Patricia. 1995. *Imperial Identities: Stereotyping, Prejudice and Race in Colonial Algeria*. London: Taurus.

Lucas, Philippe and Vatin, Jean-Claude (eds). 1975. *L'Algerie des Anthropologues*. Paris: François Maspero.

Lyons, Maryinez. 1992. *The Colonial Disease: A Social History of Sleeping Sickness in Northern Zaire, 1900–1940*. Cambridge: Cambridge University Press.

Macamo, Elísio. 2006. 'Denying Modernity: The Regulation of Native Labor in Colonial Mozambique and Its Postcolonial Aftermath'. In E. Macamo (ed.). *Negotiating Modernity: Africa's Ambivalent Experience.* London: Zed Books.

MacKenzie, John. 1988. *The Empire of Nature: Hunting, Conservation and British Imperialism*. Manchester: University of Manchester Press.

MacKenzie, John (ed.). 1990. *Imperialism and the Natural World*. Manchester: Manchester University Press.

Mackenzie, A. Fiona. 1998. *Land, Ecology and Resistance in Kenya, 1880–1952*. Edinburgh: Edinburgh University Press.

Macmillan, William. 1938. *Africa Emergent: A Survey of Social, Political, and Economic Trends in British Africa*. London: Pelican Books.

Maddox, Gregory, Giblin, James and Kimambo, Isaria (eds). 1996. *Custodians of the Land: Ecology and Culture in the History of Tanzania*. London: James Currey Press.

Mafeje, Archie. 1976. 'The Problem of Anthropology in Historical Perspective: An Inquiry into the Growth of the Social Sciences'. *Canadian Journal of African Studies* 10:307–333.

Mafeje, Archie. 1998a. 'Anthropology and Independent Africans: Suicide or End of an Era?'. *African Sociological Review* 2:1–43.

Mafeje, Archie. 1998b. 'Conversations and Confrontations with My Reviewers'. *African Sociological Review* 2:95–107.

Magubane, B. 1971. 'A Critical Look at Indices Used in the Study of Social Change in Colonial Africa'. *Current Anthropology* 12:419–430.

Maino, Elisabetta. 2005. 'Pour une généalogie de l'africanisme portugais'. *Cahiers d'Etudes africaines* XLV:165–215.

Mair, Lucy. 1936. *Native Policies in Africa*. London: Routledge.

Malinowski, Bronislaw. 1929. 'Practical Anthropology'. *Africa* 2:22–38.

Malinowski, Bronislaw. 1930. 'Rationalization of Anthropology and Administration'. *Africa* 3:405–429.

Mannoni, Octave. 1950. *Psychologie de la Colonisation*. Paris: Éditions du Soeil.

Marfleet, Philip. 1973. 'Bibliographical Notes on the Debate'. In T. Asad (ed.). *Anthropology and the Colonial Encounter*. London: Ithaca Press, pp. 273–281.

Margarido, A. 1975. 'Le Colonialisme Portugais et l'anthropologie'. In J. Copans (ed.). *Anthropologie et impérialisme*. Paris: François Maspero, pp. 307–344.

McCulloch, Jock. 1995. *Colonial Psychiatry and 'the African Mind'*. Cambridge: Cambridge University Press.

Melland, Frank and Young, Cullen. 1937. *African Dilemma*. London: United Society for Christian Literature.

Memmi, Albert. 1957 [1965]. *The Colonizer and the Colonized*. Boston: Beacon Press.

Miller, Christopher. 1990. *Theories of Africans: Francophone Literature and Anthropology in Africa*. Chicago: University of Chicago Press.

Mills, David. 2002. 'British Anthropology at the End of Empire: the Rise and Fall of the Colonial Social Science Research Council, 1944–1962'. *Revue d'Histoire des Sciences Humaines* 6:161–188.

Monod, Th. 1944. 'The French Institute for Negro Africa (L'Institut Français d'Afrique Noire)'. Translated by H.V. Meyerowitz. *Man* 44:72–75.

Moore, Sally Falk. 1994. *Anthropology and Africa: Changing Perspectives on a Changing Scene*. Charlottesville: University of Virginia Press.

Moore, Sally Falk. 1998. 'Archie Mafeje's Prescriptions for the Academic Future'. *African Sociological Review* 2:50–57.

Moore, Henrietta and Vaughan, Megan. 1994. *Cutting Down Trees: Gender, Nutrition, and Agricultural Change in the Northern Province of Zambia, 1890–1990*. London: James Currey.

Mudimbe, V.Y. 1988. *The Invention of Africa: Gnosis, Philosophy, and the Order of Knowledge*. Bloomington, Ind: Indiana University Press.

Mudimbe, V.Y. 1994. *The Idea of Africa*. Bloomington: Indiana University Press.

Needham, Rodney. 1970. 'The Future of Social Anthropology: Disintegration or Metamorphosis?'. In *Anniversary Contributions to Anthropology: Twelve Essays*. Leiden: E.J. Brill, pp. 34–45.

Neumann, Roderick. 1998. *Imposing Wilderness: Struggles Over Livelihood and Nature Preservation in Africa*. Berkeley, Calif: University of California Press.

Nkwi, Paul Nchoji. 1998. 'The Status of Anthropology in Post-independent Africa: Some Reflections on Archie Mafeje's Perceptions'. *African Sociological Review* 2:57–66.

Noyes, John Kenneth. 1994. 'The Natives in Their Places: "Ethnographic Cartography" and the Representation of Autonomous Spaces in Ovamboland, German South West Africa'. *History and Anthropology* 8:237–264.

Ojiaku, Mazi Okoro. 1974. 'Traditional African Social Thought and Western Scholarship'. *Présence Africaine* 90:204–214.

Onwuachi, P. Chike and Wolfe, Alvin. 1966. 'The Place of Anthropology in the Future of Africa'. *Human Organization* 25:93–95.

Osborne, Michael. 1994. *Nature, the Exotic, and the Science of French Colonialism*. Bloomington, Ind: Indiana University Press.

Owusu, Maxwell. 1978. 'Ethnography of Africa: The Usefulness of the Useless'. *American Anthropologist* 80:310–334.

Owusu, Maxwell. 1979. 'Colonial and Postcolonial Anthropology of Africa: Scholarship or Sentiment'. In G. Huizer and B. Mannheim (eds). *The Politics of Anthropology: From Colonialism and Sexism Toward a View from Below*. The Hague: Mouton, pp. 145–160.

Packard, Randall. 1989. *White Plague, Black Labor: Tuberculosis and the Political Economy of Health and Disease in South Africa*. Berkeley, Calif: University of California Press.

Pels, Peter. 1999. *A Politics of Presence: Contacts between Missionaries and Waluguru in Late Colonial Tanganyika*. Amsterdam: Harwood Academic Publishers.

Pels, Peter and Salemink, Oscar. 1994. 'Introduction: Five Theses on Ethnography as Colonial Practice'. *History and Anthropology* 8:1–34.

Pels, Peter and Salemink, Oscar (eds). 1999. *Colonial Subjects: Essays on the Practical History of Anthropology*. Ann Arbor, Mich: University of Michigan.

Penny, H. Glenn. 2002. *Objects of Culture: Ethnology and Ethnographic Museums in Imperial Germany*. Chapel Hill, NC: University of North Carolina Press.

Penny, H. Glenn and Bunzl, Matti (eds). 2003. *Worldly Provincialism: German Anthropology in the Age of Empire*. Ann Arbor, Mich: University of Michigan Press.

Perham, Margery. 1934 [1967]. 'Some Problems of Indirect Rule'. In M. Perham (ed.). *Colonial Sequence, 1930 to 1949: A Chronological Commentary Upon British Colonial Policy Especially in Africa*. London: Metheun, pp. 91–118.

Peterson, Derek. 2004. *Creative Writing: Translation, Bookkeeping and the Work of Imagination in Colonial Kenya*. Portsmouth, N.H.: Heinemann.

Powell, Eve Trout. 2003. *A Different Shade of Colonialism: Egypt, Great Britain, and the Mastery of the Sudan*. Berkeley, Calif: University of California Press.

Purcell, Trevor. 1998. 'Indigenous Knowledge and Applied Anthropology: Questions of Definition and Direction'. *Human Organization* 57:258–272.

Radcliffe-Brown, A.R. and Forde, Daryll (eds). 1950. *African Systems of Kinship and Marriage*. London: Oxford University Press.

Ranger, Terence. 1976. 'From Humanism to the Science of Man: Colonialism in Africa and the Understanding of Alien Societies'. *Transactions of the Royal Historical Society* 26:115–141.

Ranger, Terence. 1983. 'The Invention of Tradition in Colonial Africa'. In E. Hobsbawm and T. Ranger (eds). *The Invention of Tradition*. Cambridge: Cambridge University Press, pp. 211–262.

Ranger, Terence. 1993. 'The Invention of Tradition Revisited: the Case of Colonial Africa'. In T. Ranger and O. Vaughan (eds). *Legitimacy and the State in Twentieth Century Africa*. Oxford: Macmillan, pp. 62–111.

Richards, Audrey. 1939. *Land, Labour, and Diet in Northern Rhodesia: An Economic Study of the Bemba Tribe*. London: Oxford University Press.

Richards, Audrey. 1944. 'Practical Anthropology in the Lifetime of the International Africa Institute'. *Africa* 14:289–301.

Richards, Paul. 1985. *Indigenous Agricultural Revolution – Ecology and Food Production in West Africa*. London: Hutchinson.

Ripley, William. 1900. *The Races of Europe: A Sociological Study*. London: Kegan Paul.

Robertshaw, Peter (ed.). 1990. *A History of African Archaeology*. London: James Currey Press.

Rowe, John. 1967. 'Roscoe's and Kagwa's Baganda'. *Journal of African History* 8:63–66.

Said, Edward. 1978. *Orientalism*. New York: Pantheon Books.

Said, Edward. 1989. 'Representing the Colonized: Anthropology's Interlocutors'. *Critical Inquiry* 15:205–225.

Sanjek, Roger. 1993. 'Anthropology's Hidden Colonialism: Assistants and Their Ethnographers'. *Anthropology Today* 9:13–18.

Schumaker, Lyn. 2001. *Africanizing Anthropology: Fieldwork, Networks, and the Making of Cultural Knowledge in Central Africa*. Durham: Duke University Press.

Schapera, Isaac. 1947. *Migrant Labour and Tribal Life: A Study of Conditions in the Bechuanaland Protectorate*. London: Oxford University Press.

Sharp, John. 1998. 'Who Speaks for Whom? A Response to Archie Mafeje's "Anthropology and Independent Africans: Suicide or End of an Era?"'. *African Sociological Review* 2:66–73.

Sibeud, Emmanuelle. 2002. *Une science impériale pour l'Afrique: la construction des savoirs africanistes en France, 1878–1930*. Paris: Éditions de l'École des hautes études en sciences sociales.

Sichone, Owen. 2003. 'The Social Sciences in Africa'. In T. Porter and D. Ross (eds). *The Cambridge History of Science, v. 7, The Modern Social Sciences*. Cambridge: Cambridge University Press, pp. 466–481.

Sillitoe, Paul. 1998. 'The Development of Indigenous Knowledge: A New Applied Anthropology'. *Current Anthropology* 39:223–252.

Smith, Edwin. 1935. 'Africa: What Do We Know of It?'. *Journal of the Royal Anthropological Institute* 65:1–81.

Smith, Woodruff D. 1991. *Politics and the Sciences of Culture in Germany 1840–1920*. Oxford: Oxford University Press.

Southall, Aidan. 1983. 'The Contribution of Anthropology to African Studies'. *African Studies Review* 26:63–76.

Spear, Thomas. 2003. 'Neo-Traditionalism and the Limits of Invention in British Colonial Africa'. *Journal of African History* 44:3–27.

Spidle, Jake W. 1973. 'Colonial Studies in Imperial Germany'. *History of Education Quarterly* 13:231–247.

Stocking Jr., George. 1968. *Race, Culture, and Evolution: Essays in the History of Anthropology*. New York: Free Press.

Stocking Jr., George. 1971. 'What's in a Name? The Origins of the Royal Anthropological Institute (1837–71)'. *Man* n.s. 6:369–390.

Stocking Jr., George (ed.). 1974. *The Shaping of American Anthropology, 1883–1911: A Franz Boas Reader*. New York: Basic Books.

Stocking Jr., George. 1979. *Anthropology at Chicago: Tradition, Discipline, Department*. Chicago, Ill: University of Chicago Press.

Stocking Jr., George. 1987. *Victorian Anthropology*. New York: Free Press.

Stocking Jr., George. 1995. *After Tylor: British Social Anthropology 1888–1951*. Madison: University of Wisconsin Press.

Stoler, Ann and Cooper, Frederick. 1997. 'Between Metropole and Colony: Rethinking a Research Agenda'. In F. Cooper and A. Stoler (eds). *Tensions of Empire: Colonial Cultures in a Bourgeois World*. Berkeley, Calif: University of California Press, pp. 1–56.

Tapper, Melbourne. 1999. 'Medical Problems with Ethnological Solutions: The Colonial Construction of Sickling in Africa'. In M. Tapper (ed.). *In the Blood: Sickle Cell Anemia and the Politics of Race*. Philadelphia, Pa: University of Pennsylvania Press, pp. 55–91.

Thiong'o, Ngugi wa. 1986. *Decolonising the Mind: The Politics of Language in African Literature*. London: James Currey Press.

Thomas, Nicholas. 1994. *Colonialism's Culture: Anthropology, Travel and Government*. Princeton: Princeton University Press.

Thornton, Robert. 1983. 'Narrative Ethnography in Africa, 1850–1920: The Creation and Capture of an Appropriate Domain for Anthropology'. *Man* 18:502–520.

Tilley, Helen. 2001. 'Africa as a "Living Laboratory": The African Research Survey and the British Colonial Empire: Consolidating Environmental, Medical, and Anthropological Debates, 1920–1940'. Oxford University: Unpublished D-Phil (Ph.D.).

Tilley, Helen. 2003. 'African Environments and Environmental Sciences: The African Research Survey, Ecological Paradigms, and British Colonial Development, 1920–1940'. In W. Beinart and J. McGregor (eds). *Social History and African Environments*. Oxford: James Currey Press, pp. 109–130.

Tilley, Helen. 2004. 'William Allan: the African Husbandman'. In W. Allan (ed.). *The African Husbandman*. Münster: LIT Verlag, pp. v–xxxix, new introduction.

Tilley, Helen. 2005. 'Ambiguities of Racial Science in Colonial Africa: The African Research Survey and the Fields of Eugenics, Social Anthropology, and Biomedicine, 1920–1940'. In B. Stutchey (ed.). *Science Across the European Empires, 1800–1950*. Oxford: Oxford University Press, pp. 245–287.

Tobias, Phillip. 1985. 'History of Physical Anthropology in Southern Africa'. *Yearbook of Physical Anthropology* 28:1–52.

Urry, James. 1993a [1984]. 'Englishmen, Celts, and Iberians: The Ethnographic Survey of the United Kingdom, 1892–1899'. In J. Urry (ed.). *Before Social Anthropology*. Philadelphia, Pa: Harwood Publishers, pp. 83–101.

Urry, James. 1993b. *Before Social Anthropology: Essays on the History of British Anthropology*. Philadelphia, Pa: Harwood Publishers.

Vansina, Jan. 1979. 'Bantu in the Crystal Ball, I'. *History in Africa* 6:287–333.

Vansina, Jan. 1980. 'Bantu in the Crystal Ball, II'. *History in Africa* 7:293–325.

Vatin, Jean-Claude, *et al.* (eds). 1984. *Connaissances du Maghreb: Sciences Sociales et Colonisation*. Paris: Centre National de la Recherche Scientifique.

Vaughan, Megan. 1991. *Curing Their Ills: Colonial Power and African Illness*. Cambridge: Polity Press.

Vermeulen, Han F. 1995. 'Origins and Institutionalization of Ethnography and Ethnology in Europe and the USA, 1771–1845'. In H.F. Vermeulen and Arturo A. Roldán (eds). *Fieldwork and Footnotes: Studies in the History of European Anthropology*. London: Routledge Press, pp. 39–59.

Vilakazi, Herbert. 1998. 'For a New Theory and Practice: Mafeje's "Anthropology and Independent Africans: Suicide or End of an Era?"'. *African Sociological Review* 2:74–84.

Vincent, Joan. 1988. 'Sovereignty, Legitimacy, and Power: Prologomena to the Study of the Colonial State'. In R. Cohen and J.D. Toland (eds). *State Formation and Political Legitimacy*. New Brunswick, NJ: Transaction Books, pp. 137–154.

Werbner, Richard. 1984. 'The Manchester School in South-Central Africa'. *Annual Review of Anthropology* 13:157–185.

West, Harry G. 2004. 'Inverting the Camel's Hump: Jorge Dias, His Wife, Their Interpreter, and I'. In R. Handler (ed.). *Significant Others: Interpersonal and Professional Commitments in Anthropology*. Madison, Wis: University of Wisconsin, pp. 51–90.

Wilder, Gary. 2005. *French Imperial Nation-State: Negritude and Colonial Humanism Between the Two World Wars*. Chicago, Ill: University of Chicago Press.

Williams, Vernon. 1996. *Rethinking Race: Franz Boas and His Contemporaries*. Lexington, Ky: University Press of Kentucky.

Wiredu, Kwasi. 1980. *Philosophy and an African Culture*. Cambridge: Cambridge University Press.

Wiredu, Kwasi. 1995. *Conceptual Decolonization in African Philosophy*. Selected and Introduced by O. Oladipo. Ibadan, Nigeria: Hope Publications.

Wolfe, Patrick. 1999. *Settler Colonialism and the Transformation of Anthropology: The Politics and Poetics of an Ethnographic Event*. London: Cassell.

Worsley, P. 1970. 'The End of Anthropology'. *Transactions of the Sixth World Congress of Sociology*: 121–129.

Wylie, Diana. 2001. *Starving on a Full Stomach: Hunger and the Triumph of Cultural Racism in Modern South Africa*. Charlottesville, Va: University of Virginia Press.

Young, Crawford. 1986. 'Nationalism, Ethnicity, and Class in Africa: a Retrospective'. *Cahiers d'Etude Africaines* 26:421–495.

Young, Crawford. 1988. 'The African Colonial State and Its Political Legacy'. In R. Rothchild and N. Chazan (eds). *The Precarious Balance: State and Society in Africa*. Boulder, Colo: Westview Press, pp. 25–66.

Young, Crawford. 1994. *The African Colonial State in Comparative Perspective*. New Haven, Conn: Yale University Press.

Zimmerman, Andrew. 2001. *Anthropology and Antihumanism in Imperial Germany*. Chicago, Ill: University of Chicago Press.

Zimmerman, Andrew. 2006. '"What do you really want in German East Africa Herr Professor?": Counterinsurgency and the Science Effect in Colonial Tanzania'. *Comparative Studies in Society and History* 48:419–461.

Zwernemann, Jürgen. 1983. *Culture History and African Anthropology: A Century of Research in Germany and Austria*. Uppsala: Almqvist and Wiksell International.

PART I

Metropolitan agendas and institutions

CHAPTER ONE

The elusive bureau of colonial ethnography in France, 1907–1925

Emmanuelle Sibeud

In an influential essay published in 1913, 'Ethnography in France and abroad', Marcel Mauss denounced the current disarray of French ethnography and pleaded for the creation of a Bureau of ethnography which might rejuvenate the discipline. He pointed out that collecting ethnographic data was a moral duty for a colonizing power 'burdened' with native souls, since it would help promote a more enlightened colonization. He was also concerned that entire segments of African cultures were silently fading out of existence and argued that the Bureau, at the least, might serve to document them. This bureau was never founded, however, and its failure provides a classic case study for the analysis of the complex connections between the exercise of French domination in colonial Africa and the reshaping of a French 'science of humanity' in the first three decades of the twentieth century.[1]

Mauss was not the sole champion for a bureau of ethnography. In fact, he was echoing claims others had made as part of a strategy to establish himself as the academic patron of a quite enthusiastic ethnographic revival. Thus he generously acknowledged the work done by colonial *amateurs*, though his criticisms of them were often harsh in reviews he wrote for *L'Année sociologique* (James 1998). He had to deal with dissenting colonial officers who claimed to be ethnographers in their own right while serving in Africa and who launched their own research institute in Paris (L'Institut ethnographique international de Paris) as early as 1910. They challenged the convenient belief that ethnography was but an auxiliary science and thereby contributed in unexpected ways to the cultural turn of French science of humanity, leading the way from Paul Broca's physical anthropology to Mauss's cultural ethnology. Discussions concerning the question of the Bureau of ethnography before World War I were a display of this subtle synergy between peripheral colonial research and epistemological change in the metropolitan center. A colonial ethnography was emerging which concentrated on Africa; its advocates chose the uneasy path of institutional dissent in order to achieve the creation of a bureau of ethnography. With the foundations first of the Institut d'ethnologie de la Sorbonne in 1925 and then of the Société des Africanistes in 1930, the 1920s seemed to follow quite a different path than the 1910s. Yet the shift was consistent with the debates of the previous decade and the 'academic turn' involved in the foundation of the Institut d'ethnologie de la Sorbonne in 1925 should be seen as a direct outcome of the failure of the earlier projected Bureau of ethnography.

The quest for a Bureau of colonial ethnography

Mauss's essay was published in the prestigious *Revue de Paris*, a major scholarly forum at the time. His critique was not new – indeed an important precursor had been Arnold van Gennep's very first review on 'ethnography and folklore', written for the more literary *Mercure de France* in 1905 (van Gennep 1905). What was novel in 1913 was the opportunity to appeal to French educated opinion, and in this regard Mauss was clearly the most authoritative voice. Since 1901 he had been teaching the 'history of the religions of uncivilized people' at the Ecole Pratique des Hautes Etudes (EPHE). Founded in 1865 by Victor Duruy, the EPHE promoted professional research patterned on German seminars and its members were learned specialists as well as teachers. The urge to copy the German model became even more insistent in the first decades of the Third Republic, when some linked the weakness of French science to the humiliating defeat of 1870. The EPHE admitted only a tiny percentage of the upcoming student population and offered peripheral degrees; nonetheless it was seen as one of the leading venues for a renewed French science.

It was also a leading place for Republican ideology: its fifth section, dedicated to the 'scientific study' of religions, suggested that religions were social and historical constructions, a position in line with current efforts to secularize French society. This positivist science of religions was part of the larger quest for a modern, secular and republican science of humanity fostered by the passionate debates surrounding the Dreyfus affair and the final split, in 1905, between the Republican State and the Catholic Church. In this context religions of 'uncivilized people' turned out to be a hotly contested topic. They were studied both by Catholic theologians and by sociologists like Emile Durkheim and his nephew Mauss. The theologians, eager to uncover signs of what they called the 'primitive revelation', had a keen interest in African pygmies, who were considered the most primitive human beings. The sociologists studied the more basic beliefs of primitive societies in order to understand religion as a whole (Durkheim 1912a). Both Catholic ethnologists and sociologists actually shared a common evolutionist framework, but the latter were growing dissatisfied with it. As ethnographic reports analysed in *L'Année sociologique*, the journal Durkheim founded in 1895, and original works by missionaries published in *Anthropos* (the Catholic international ethnological journal founded in Vienna in 1905) displayed the fascinating and disconcerting cultural variety of human societies, ordering this diversity on a single evolutionary axis was coming to seem less and less relevant. Besides, the evolutionist model relied on racialist premises that had been severely damaged by decades of anthropological controversies on the meaning of race, and which moreover were called into question for their political misuses in the Dreyfus affair (Blanckaert 2001). Dealing with human cultural diversity thus appeared as a political as well as a scientific question and all the more difficult to handle for that reason.

Mauss was adamant in his denial of racialism. In his very first lesson in 1901 he argued that there were no 'un-civilized' people. He fought for Dreyfus, wrote for the socialist newspaper *L'Humanité* and was an example of the new intellectual-as-social-figure during the Dreyfus affair (Fournier 1994). In 1913 he belonged to the influential Dreyfusist intellectual network which had been awarded prominent positions in the first decade of the twentieth century when the Sorbonne was reorganized (Charle 1990). Included in the same network was Durkheim, who was appointed to the Sorbonne in 1902 and was in charge of crucial teaching concerning educational methods. Side by side they built a comprehensive sociology designed to serve as the epistemological basis for the republican science of humanity to come. This was a long-term venture in which the issue of cultural diversity or, as Durkheim phrased it in 1912, the study of 'types of civilizations' was a major challenge (Durkheim 1912b).

Mauss and Durkheim's demanding methodology had to confront the more attractive hypothesis of diffusionism (Mucchielli 1998). Where sociologists looked for social facts distinct from the false obviousness of *prénotions* and tried to grasp universal sociological laws to explain cultural diversity, diffusionism offered historical explanations nurtured by archeological survey and illustrated by the collections of items gathered in ethnographic museums. In other words, Durkheim and Mauss were interested in ethnographic data but were at the same time afraid that these might mislead sociologists by offering them a way to escape the harder task of looking for abstract sociological laws. As a consequence they thought of ethnography as a peripheral specialty which should be organized as a 'sociological' science once sociology was strong enough, but which meanwhile should be left to amateurs (Karady 1982). Yet this cautious strategy was unexpectedly disrupted in the 1910s by what looked like a wild rebellion of amateurs, and particularly of colonial officers who claimed to be ethnographers in their own right.

This rebellion had to be answered, and in 1913 Mauss undertook the tricky task of dealing with discontented amateurs, especially with the so-called colonial ethnographers. His essay was a long plea aimed at convincing them to unite under his academic supervision. He conspicuously praised their researches and their dedication to science:

> No colonial staff is more qualified to understand natives, more intimate with them than our colonial officers and physicians. No colonial staff knows so well how to inspire natives with confidence and how to arouse their enthusiasm in order to master their shyness and changing moods. No body of scientists is so free of the prejudices so dangerous in the study of race and religion. For several years, we have listened to very good lectures and read excellent notes produced by men who, for lack of any technical training, possess the essential and incommunicable sense of social realities that makes the true ethnographer. But these well intentioned, but unaware scientists are in want of an impetus, some help and supervision. (Mauss 1913: 833–834)

To remedy this situation he called for the creation of a Bureau d'ethnographie to supervise the diverse surveys of colonial workers. He insisted that this bureau should not be another abstract research institute and argued that there was no point in launching a new chair for ethnography. Even teaching ethnography was problematic, he remarked, if it resulted merely in training more armchair ethnologists. This paradoxical disdain for proper academic objectives was both a strategy and a constraint. On the one hand, Mauss wanted to convince political authorities that founding a bureau under his supervision would be a frugal use of public subsidies, since he already held a chair and its staff could be recruited among willing colonial officers. On the other hand, he urged these authorities to postpone any other institutional creation because he feared that ethnography would escape academic control.

Actually Mauss was torn between two conflicting necessities. He was aware of the gap between his own academic circle in France and colonial officers out in the field gathering valuable data. He did not want colonial officers to surrender to the competing and attractive hypothesis of diffusionism or, worse, to get involved in the building of a racialist science of human diversity. But he was also concerned that he might hinder his own students' careers by fostering a non-professional ethnography relying solely on colonial amateurs. Despite these latent concerns, however, neither he nor his students were prepared for the task in 1913, so he used his central position at the EPHE to build up a strong if small network of well-trained academic researchers. He was in touch with the Ecole Française d'Extrême Orient in Indochina and effectively advanced the careers of a couple of colonial officers who had been his students at the EPHE. He also successfully introduced those working on North Africa to relevant Orientalist institutions. Sub-Saharan Africa, however, was out of his grasp since there was no research institution, central or local, dedicated to it. This did not discourage Mauss. In 1905 he accepted a commission from the Comité de l'Afrique Français to write an ethnographic questionnaire for the French African colonies. He also encouraged one of his most brilliant pupils, Antoine Bianconi, to specialize on West Africa. In promoting a comprehensive ethnology, the study of 'primitive' African societies could not be neglected; furthermore, since the campaign against the crimes in the Belgian (King Leopold) and the French Congo in 1905, Africa appeared to be the place where the science of humanity was most needed to enlighten colonial domination.

Yet Mauss was not the only scholar in France taking a growing interest in ethnography and Africa. His most serious rival was Arnold van Gennep. Van Gennep had completed his thesis on Malagasian totemism in 1904 under the supervision of Mauss after his first advisor, Léon Marillier, died suddenly in 1901. He published his thesis, *Tabou et totémisme à Madagascar* in 1904 (van Gennep 1904), followed shortly by *Mythes et légendes d'Australie* (van Gennep 1906) and his widely known classic *Rites de passage* (van Gennep 1909). Van Gennep was also one of the translators into French of Frazer's *Golden Bough* and a regular contributor to the *Revue de l'histoire des religions*, in which several of his important essays against the fallacies of totemistic analysis were published. He was seen as the intellectual heir to Léon Marillier and was supported by the small but quite influential group of Tylorian French anthropologists led by Salomon Reinach (Rosa 1996). It was Reinach who introduced him to prestigious international scientific networks. In short, van Gennep was qualified as a general anthropologist dealing with exotic data and in addition he had undertaken personal research in French folklore. Yet despite his credentials he had no academic position nor any realistic hope of obtaining one since Mauss, his exact contemporary, already held the post. Thus he had to try another way.

Van Gennep was a close friend of Maurice Delafosse, a dedicated ethnographer and leading figure among colonial officers serving in

Africa (Sibeud 2002). In 1907, with Delafosse's support and through his influential colonial officials, he pleaded for the creation of a 'Service of colonial ethnography' under his supervision. The proposal was quickly rejected when the Ministry of colonies realized this service would require some subsidy. Nonetheless it underscored the influence of colonial amateurs and their mounting discontent with existing scientific institutions and networks. Convinced that colonial experience allowed a privileged understanding of native people, they decided to contribute to the building of the science of humanity by founding new institutions where they could display this knowledge.

Mauss was alarmed by these developments. He was suddenly faced with not just one but a set of organized competitors arguing that they, as the only fieldworkers, were the only competent ethnographers. Their intrusion bluntly threatened Mauss's position. Ethnography was the most critical issue at stake in France in the decade before 1914. In 1906, Ernest Théodore Hamy, teacher of anthropology at the Museum of Natural History and first curator of the Musée d'ethnographie du Trocadéro, had conspicuously resigned his position in the Trocadero to protest the pitiful plight of an institution that had received the same subsidy since its foundation in 1878 (Dias 1991). Mauss immediately applied to be his successor, claiming he was Hamy's sole spiritual heir. His chief competition was the physician and anthropologist René Verneau, who had been Hamy's assistant at the Trocadero and at the Museum for several years. Trained in philosophy and philology, Mauss embodied the new generation of ethnologists more interested in the study of cultural traits than in measuring bones. In the end Verneau got the job, but Mauss had successfully qualified as the would-be patron for a comprehensive science of humanity deeply rejuvenated by its links with Durkheimian sociology. He could now wait quietly for the last remnant of the elder generation to retire. But van Gennep and Delafosse disrupted his plan. In contrast with them, Mauss looked like quite the old-style armchair ethnologist and this obviously weakened his claim to serve as patron of French ethnography, at least in the opinion of political and colonial authorities.

Mauss's (1913) article tried to strengthen his position. Yet here he provided a very loose definition of ethnography as a 'science de plein air' ('an outdoor science') and contented himself with a vague comparison of ethnographic survey to the gathering of botanical or zoological collections (Mauss 1913: 821). He addressed his appeal to colonial amateurs and was anxious not to be rejected as a scholar with an opportunistic interest in fieldwork. But he distrusted political authorities and did not want to see ethnography reduced to colonial ethnography and thus merely exploited as an applied science of domination. Besides, he had to adjust the quite positivist representation of what a sociologist should be to fit the new and disturbing experience of fieldwork. Sociologists were indeed supposed to deal with specific data, mainly repetitive and controlled social 'facts' enclosed in statistical evidence. And these social facts were as far as possible derived from the subjective narrative produced by fieldwork. Mauss was well aware that direct observation was essential, and therefore he sent his students into the field. But he was trapped, first of all, in the false and redundant analogy between the science of nature and the science of humanity and, secondly, in the still prevailing prejudice that collecting was an odd job better left to amateurs. In 1913 he did not really choose between an alliance with colonial amateurs and a more academic strategy, but instead produced a two-pronged discourse which ultimately undermined his project. While calling for a general agreement between colonial 'ethnographers' and academic 'ethnologists' in the *Revue de Paris*, he sent to the Secretary of Public Instruction a preliminary draft for a 'Bureau of ethnology' along quite different lines. He insisted that the Bureau should be part of the Sorbonne and should recruit only academically trained ethnologists (i.e., his own students), lest it became 'the preserve of colonial administrators' and 'a nursery of favorites'. His sole concession to the opposition was to acknowledge the more deserving colonial amateurs as secondary workers.

Mauss's hesitations as well as the autonomous claims of colonial amateurs were each part of the revival of French ethnography during the decade before World War I. They led to institutional failures: neither van Gennep's Service ethnographique nor Mauss's Bureau d'ethnographie were ever founded. But the ideas behind these abortive institutions were also symptoms of major epistemological changes which relied partly on colonial experience in Africa.

Voices from the field: the rise of colonial ethnography

The militant use of the words 'ethnographers' and 'ethnography' by colonial officers serving in French Africa and the unexpected resurgence of 'ethnologists' and 'ethnology' in Mauss's academic circle were meaningful events when placed within the turbulent history of the science of humanity in France. The term 'ethnography' was coined in French at the beginning of the nineteenth century around the same time as the term 'ethnology', and both immediately became competitors for the more ancient notion of 'anthropology'. The rivalry between anthropology, based on the study of the human body, and ethnography, dealing with the study of cultures, was set in 1859 by the competing foundations of the Société d'anthropologie and of the Société d'ethnographie (Blanckaert 1995a). Once brilliant and supported by key figures like Ernest Renan, the Société d'ethnographie suffered a rapid decline in the 1880s and 1890s and by 1903 had silently faded away (Chailleux 1990). The foundation of the Musée d'ethnographie du Trocadéro in 1878 paradoxically contributed to the society's marginalization. Hamy, as curator, had a keen interest in the study of cultural features but was an anthropologist belonging to the Société d'anthropologie and not to the Société d'ethnographie. He was the spiritual and institutional heir of Armand Bréau de Quatrefages, whom he succeeded at the Museum of Natural History. This also meant that Hamy happened to be the last champion of the monogenist idea that there was a cultural, if not biological, unity of the human species. But he was never given the means to train students at the Trocadero and experienced the bitter loneliness of being France's sole official ethnographer. At the beginning of the twentieth century ethnography appeared as a hollow specialty that could be occupied for political purposes.

The Trocadero was deserted by anthropologists who already had laboratories where they could measure skulls and profess a dry disdain for what they called the 'rags' of social life. But it was a popular museum among Parisians, who did care for the rags of the savages they had met first at the exhibitions of the Jardin d'acclimatation, then in the colonial sections of the universal exhibitions of 1889 and 1900, and in the colonial exhibitions of the 1890s such as the famous Dahoméens du Champ de Mars (1894). If the scientific relevance of ethnography could be contested, its political and imperial meaning was obvious. From the very beginning the Trocadero was meant to display the collections brought back first by explorers and colonial conquerors. In 1894, after the victorious and brutal campaign of Colonel Dodds, Dahomeans were exhibited on the Champ de Mars and statues of their kings displayed at the Trocadero. This allowed the young Delafosse, commissioned by Hamy, to defend the dignity of Dahomean civilization which had produced beautiful works of art. Though already occupied by imperial ideology, ethnography was not just another tool for propaganda. It was also a dynamic research practice all the more valued since the relevance of racialist analysis was more and more contested. But it was a mute practice lacking equally in rules and rulers.

A few questionnaires were available, but they were generic and obsolete. The Société de géographie de Paris and the Société d'anthropologie no longer bothered to provide travelers with detailed written instructions. The Société d'anthropologie merely advised them to report according to the *Questionnaire de sociologie et d'ethnographie* published by Charles Letourneau in 1884. It was a materialist manifesto rather than a guide for fieldwork (Blanckaert 1995b), but the society failed to convene an effective committee to reform it in 1905. Bitter comments on the lack of a French equivalent to the British *Notes and Queries* became a commonplace from 1905 onward. But even Mauss, who was in charge of providing some 'Instructions pour l'étude des populations soumises à la République dans l'Afrique occidentale et le Congo', seemed more interested in criticizing questionnaires published abroad than in writing his own. Still he dedicated one of his teaching lectures at the EPHE in 1906–07 to a discussion of it. At least two difficulties were at issue here. The table of contents of the *Année sociologique* was a schematic chart of sociology, and sociologists skillfully divided monographs into structural segments to fit its categories. However, teaching fieldworkers how to construct a thorough monograph meant stepping back from this analysis of the social structures. This was certainly more demanding than complaining about the inadequacy of existent monographs. Besides, it led to a complex question: what was going on in the field? And as Mauss's own concern in 1906 showed, the colonial situation in Africa was the case study prompting the most interest in France.

If metropolitan scholars could eventually afford to disregard ethnography as an unorganized practice, colonial officers wanting to contribute to science clung to it, especially those serving in Africa. African people were supposed to be savages without history or literacy; their study was therefore freely conceded to ethnography. The objects colonial officers sent to the Trocadero were propitiatory gifts to the sole institution displaying some, albeit weak, interest in Africa. Collecting native artifacts was encouraged by the board in control of scientific missions at the Ministry of Public Instruction as well as by the officers' own Ministry. Both had a tacit agreement at the end of the nineteenth century that colonial officers should not be given scientific missions which would distract them from their professional duties, but that they should be invited nonetheless to collect data and objects. Thus colonial officers were urged to contribute to the scientific conquest of colonial territories, which helped to legitimize political domination, but were not given a clear position in this process.

As they were prohibited from leaving their administrative district, officers could not write the thrilling and continental-scale accounts that readers of geographical journals such as *Le Tour du Monde* and of Jules Verne's marvelous travels were used to reading. Confined to what they presented as 'tiny spots' of a tamed Africa, they tried hard to have some specialist qualifications in order to get the metropolitan acknowledgement they were looking for. Collecting natural science specimens was less and less rewarding as Metropolitan specialists became reluctant to rely on partners who had no academic training (Bonneuil 1998). However, being anonymous providers of natural science inventories was hardly satisfying. Ethnography was a much better option. Colonial officers could not be accused of lacking academic training here, since none was provided in France. They were able to turn their administrative placement into an advantage if they spoke any native languages and tried to understand the populations they studied in order to control them. Last but not least, they could qualify as specialists of a particular population or set of populations without competing with any metropolitan specialists.

Still, ethnography was not simply a default choice for them. Colonial officers involved in scientific surveys gathered behind the leading figure of Delafosse. In 1901 Delafosse claimed he was a *négrologue*, a new kind of specialist of African societies qualified by his professional skills as a colonial officer (Delafosse 1901). As a close collaborator with governor François-Joseph Clozel, he contributed to Clozel's initiatives to promote an ethnographically enlightened administration. He was, for instance, the main author of *Haut-Sénégal-Niger*, commissioned in 1912 by Clozel (governor of that colony from 1908 to 1915). In 1909, Delafosse settled in Paris and taught at the Ecole Spéciale des Langues Orientales and at the Ecole coloniale. At the same time, he published a vivid portrait of the *Broussard* (bushman officer) and was elected president of a colonial officers' professional association in 1913. His professional and intellectual authority was thus as wide as his commitment to ethnography was deep. Indeed, Delafosse was an ethnographer before he joined the colonial administration in 1894, having studied museography under the supervision of Hamy. When he realized he would not get an academic position he decided to become a field colonial officer. But he kept in touch with his first mentor and was a regular contributor to Hamy's influential scientific journal, *L'Anthropologie*, where he published essays and critical reviews. When he supported van Gennep's claim for a service of colonial ethnography in 1907 Delafosse was by no means a neophyte in ethnography.

His alliance with van Gennep was based on both strategic and epistemological considerations. Both men shared a personal and somewhat bitter experience of the disarray of French ethnography, which had prevented either of them from obtaining an academic position. Both were fieldworkers who felt that their research was misunderstood, if not disregarded outright. Their marginality contributed to their project's

[58]

dismissal in 1907 as they could offer no academic guarantee for the service of colonial ethnography. But their failure encouraged them to settle down in the academic world and launch a new scientific journal, the *Revue des études ethnographiques et sociologiques (REES)*. Van Gennep was the editor and Delafosse provided the first ethnographic monograph (on the Sénoufo from the Ivory Coast), which was clearly intended as a model. The *REES* was no precarious shelter for unsuccessful scholars. Van Gennep published papers from James Frazer and from Andrew Lang in the first issues and this international bias continued in succeeding years. In 1910 they published the first French translation of William H. Rivers' important essay on genealogical method. For his part Delafosse liaised with colonial researchers who provided the journal with new and original data and he also wrote critical reviews discussing fieldwork issues. The *REES* turned out to be a long-term success. It became in 1910 the *Revue d'ethnographie et de sociologie (RES)* and reappeared from 1920 to 1929 as the *Revue d'ethnographie et des traditions populaires*. While *L'Année sociologique* was still lamenting the lapses in French ethnography, the *Revue des études ethnographiques et sociologiques* galvanized ethnographers and promoted a positive revival of ethnography.

In three years van Gennep and Delafosse gathered enough support to launch an independent research institute, the Institut ethnographique international de Paris, founded in December 1910. By 1914 the Institute had registered some 225 members, outmatching even the older Société d'anthropologie. The most dynamic members were forty colonial officers (all but one serving in French Africa) who provided more than a third of the papers presented in the Institute's monthly sessions and as many articles for the *REES*. The Institute was clearly the forum they were looking for. As an organization it represented a blend of the democratic model of learned societies and the newer model of academic research institutes which the Durkheimian team in *L'Année sociologique* were promoting. Their colonial ethnographers' republic could escape the heavy, half-blind patronage of armchair anthropologists or other metropolitan specialists. But to sustain this autonomy they had to become a consistent body of researchers carefully cross-checking data and gradually defining their collective rules. Methodological discussions sustained by van Gennep and Delafosse's extensive reviews of fieldwork accounts facilitated this difficult and critical turn of colonial ethnography. It also inaugurated the to-and-fro movement between the field and the metropolitan research institute which, eventually, invented fieldwork and provided a fresh basis on which to construct cultural anthropology. There was a flaw in this revival, however, as it maintained the separatism of nineteenth-century ethnography, an issue which had to be settled for an effective reshaping of French science of humanity.

From colonial ethnography to the Institut d'ethnologie de la Sorbonne

Mauss's call for a general reconciliation among ethnographers was indeed heeded. Colonial ethnographers wanted, not to revolutionize metropolitan science, but to stress the importance of fieldwork, and by 1913 they had made this aim clear. In 1911 Mauss, Durkheim and Verneau launched the Institut français d'anthropologie, which gathered fifty members chosen from among the most prominent specialists in all the sciences contributing to the science of humanity. This included the likes of professor Antoine Meillet for linguistics, professor Lucien Lévy-Bruhl for philosophy and Marcellin Boule for paleontology. The institute operated as a registration center for current anthropological researchers, at once acknowledging their wide diversity and providing them with a prestigious academic stamp. It was an attempt by the academic establishment to access the current revival of ethnography in order to control it; but on the whole it sought more to complement than to compete with the Institut d'ethnographie. Colonial ethnographers submitted to this willingly, as Delafosse was co-opted as a member of the Institut d'anthropologie from its inception. He owed this recognition as much to the works he had been publishing for years as to his leading position among the ethnographic dissenters. Nevertheless he welcomed this entrée to long-closed academic networks afforded by the Institut d'anthropologie not as a personal achievement but as a collective one which rewarded the scientific dedication of his fellow colonial officers and invited them to participate in a pluralistic reshaping of French science of humanity.

That metropolitan specialists and particularly social scientists were beginning to listen to fieldworkers instead of racing through their written accounts to select out 'relevant' data was indeed a crucial change. Mauss and Delafosse also teamed up to fight against the emergence of the Catholic missionary ethnology showcased in *Anthropos*. In 1912 Bishop Alexandre Le Roy, head of the important *Congrégation des Pères du Saint-Esprit*, published an essay on primitive religions mostly based on a study of the African Pygmies he had met while serving as bishop in French Gabon from 1892 to 1896 (Le Roy 1909). Using his real knowledge of some African people to assert the apologetic hypothesis of the primitive revelation, his book was a frontal attack against the laic science of religions developed at the EPHE. The separatism of Catholic ethnology, serving agendas so blatantly apologetic (in a theological sense), introduced an additional tension in the quest for a republican science of humanity. Mauss was compelled to answer, as was Delafosse who did not want Catholic dogma to interfere with the rigorous methodology he was laboriously promoting. Besides, the primitivism fostered by the primitive revelation hypothesis reinforced the hierarchical model they were trying to eradicate in order to defend the dignity of every human culture.

The growing antagonism between Catholic and secular ethnologists, whether colonial or academic, was also political. In 1905 the campaign against the crimes in the Leopoldian and in the French Congo led to a new interest in colonial matters. For years they had been settled as peripheral questions regarding the state and national greatness. Beyond the amusements of spectacular shows such as the colonial sections of universal exhibitions, public opinion was not supposed to involve itself any further with colonial issues. Thus deputies forgot colonization during election campaigns but felt free to enter the parliamentary group of the Parti Colonial as soon as they were elected. All this changed in the decade preceding World War I. The conflict between Republican principles and colonial practice was regularly stressed by the *Revue indigene* founded in 1907 by Paul Bourdarie to defend the rights of indigenous people and to fill up the anomalous gap between French citizens and their colonial subjects. Furthermore, in 1905 the Ligue des droits de l'homme engaged in a reformist fight, claiming that the mission to civilize had to be addressed and protesting against the undemocratic management of colonial matters which threatened Republican principles as well as international peace. Colonial lobbies tried to counteract this politicization by promoting propaganda in France and supposedly 'scientific' policies based on experts' reports from the colonies.

Missionaries were part of this strategy. They were considered professional specialists of the indigenous soul and were called upon as such by colonial lobbies. In French West Africa they gained the unexpected support of the governor-general, William Ponty, who commissioned a survey on the disorganization of African family structures carried out by the very Catholic Société antiesclavagiste de France. The society was actually controlled by Charles Le Myre de Vilers, a prominent figure of the decaying Parti Colonial. Le Myre de Vilers and Ponty championed the association theory and sought to impose a 'scientific' racial policy to meet the needs of economic exploitation and to refute any attempt at Republican assimilation. Le Myre de Vilers acted as the defendant of economic lobbies and Ponty was in search of a new field in which to augment his already brilliant colonial career.

Bishop Le Roy provided the questionnaire for the survey and thus appeared as its scientific and moral advisor. Colonial officers serving in French West Africa were requested by Ponty to answer it so that a synthesis could be written by Baron Joseph Du Teil, an influential member of the Société antiesclavagiste who was largely ignorant of both Africa and ethnography. The chief consequence was that colonial officers did not bother to respond, either because they were uninterested in ethnography or they resented being so blatantly reduced to odd jobs (Sibeud 1996). The failure of the survey did not prevent colonial administrators and Catholic church-based ethnologists from further collaboration. In 1913, when the Ministry of colonies relaunched the Société d'ethnographie to maintain control on ethnography, Catholic ethnology was indeed a resort of convenience, for dealing with missionaries seemed less hazardous than permitting prominent and committed intellectuals like Mauss to mingle in colonial matters.

In this regard, the position of colonial ethnographers was rather ambiguous. Not only were there no recognized intellectuals among them; they also repeatedly pointed out that the intervention of metropolitan intellectuals was clumsy because they ignored colonial realities. Yet against racialist schemes they sided with the same intellectuals in the defense of the cultural dignity of African societies. Moreover they needed academic support to be part of French science of humanity and not its fringe dissenters. They too distrusted colonial authorities and the official ethnography they suddenly promoted around the revived Société d'ethnographie. They knew that their scientific involvement offered few professional rewards and subsequently pressed for such recognition in Paris. Their Parisian tropism was urged in the 1910s by Ponty's decision to commission surveys that were overtly political, hardly scientific, and which allowed no scope for colonial ethnographers.

Thus the gap between colonial ethnographers and their metropolitan academic partners was rapidly closing, even as another one soon appeared between them and their administrative superiors. Delafosse learned this to his detriment when he returned to Africa during World War I at the behest of Clozel, who had been appointed governor-general of French West Africa when Ponty died in 1915. Clozel was dismissed as soon as 1917 and Delafosse shared his disgrace. His ethnographic expertise remained unchallenged but he was regarded as too academic to be efficient in colonial agency (Conklin 1997). Thus he was denied the function of governor in 1919 and definitively retreated into his scholarly positions.

This meant that the desire to merge the scientific logic of ethnography and the political logic of colonial administration, the raison d'être for a Bureau of ethnography, had not been successfully met. After the war, these logics resumed their separate if parallel evolutions. Delafosse succeeded brilliantly in reorganizing the Institut ethnographique, which in 1921 became the Société française d'ethnographie and was patronized by all prominent academic social scientists beginning with Mauss. Its journal, the *Revue d'ethnographie et des traditions populaires*, published the very first French essay on fieldwork methodology, written by Alfred Métraux – who claimed to be a follower of both Delafosse and Mauss (Métraux 1925). The society's effectiveness led to the foundation in 1925 of the Institut d'ethnologie de la Sorbonne where Delafosse, along with Mauss, Lévy-Bruhl and Paul Rivet, was a founding patron. Ethnography was duly replaced by academic ethnology, which received colonial subsidies but was not otherwise involved in colonial administration.

This partition between research and colonial administration was first a stopgap solution. On the one hand, Mauss and Delafosse felt ethnology should be firmly settled in the academic realm to avoid being reduced to a colonial utility. On the other hand, colonial authorities promoted their own research institutions, such as the Comité des études historiques et scientifique de l'Afrique occidentale française, founded in Dakar in 1915. These institutions were meant to control researchers: as colonial officers were all asked to contribute, metropolitan and independent researchers were superfluous. They also produced local knowledge suggesting that purely colonial artefacts such as French West Africa were relevant scientific topics. By the end of the 1930s, polyvalent learned societies had been founded in every French colony in Africa and their members were clearly amateurs who were not supposed to discuss epistemological or political matters. But these amateurs could be patronized by the new metropolitan specialists trained at the Institut d'ethnologie who chose in 1930 to become 'Africanists' when they launched the Société des Africanistes. This move signified a thorough acceptance of the partition between ethnology and the art of domination, which conveniently allowed researchers to focus on cultural matters without commenting on their colonial settings.

Not only elusive, the Bureau of ethnography was, in the end, a failure. Colonial experience in Africa played a crucial part in the reshaping of a French science of humanity as it provided what had been utterly missing: fieldwork and fieldworkers who had no other title to scientific recognition and thus clung to this still untamed qualification. Their successful dissidence in the 1910s launched an institutional revival and urged reluctant scholars to look up from their books in order to listen to the accounts of the subjective, comprehensive and somewhat disruptive experiment of studying living people. To achieve this, however, colonial ethnographers had to surrender to academic logic, thereby allowing colonial authorities to shut the door on them. Thus the liberal moment of colonial ethnography lasted only for a decade before World War I when the question of the scientific and political meaning of colonial domination was raised both by dissenting colonial ethnographers and by metropolitan social scientists. The answer was effectively postponed. Colonial authorities set up their own research structures to prevent any external inquiry, and intellectuals, for their part, wanted to believe that the civilizing mission was still attainable. This led to the confinement of French ethnology in a closed academic environment and a denial of any commitment of Africanism with colonial administration. But the real answer came at last in 1951 – in Georges Balandier's vigorous challenge to this timeless ethnology in his brilliant analysis of the colonial situation (Balandier 1951).

Note

1 The encompassing phrase 'science of humanity' will be used throughout the text as a translation of the French phrase 'la science de l'homme'.

References

Primary sources

Delafosse, Maurice. 1901. 'Les Libériens et les Baoulés: nègres dits civilisés et nègres dits sauvages'. *Les milieux et les races* avril–mai 1901:97–122, 139–149.

Durkheim, Emile. 1912a. *Les formes élémentaires de la vie religieuse*. Paris: Alcan.

Durkheim, Emile. 1912b. 'Note sur la notion de civilisation'. *L'Année sociologique* 12:47–48.

van Gennep, Arnold. 1904. *Tabou et totémisme à Madagascar*. Paris: E. Leroux Bibliothèque de l'Ecole des hautes études, sciences religieuses.

van Gennep, Arnold. 1905. 'Ethnographie, folk-lore'. *Mercure de France* 15 février 1905:608–609.

van Gennep, Arnold. 1906. *Mythes et légendes d'Australie*. Paris: E. Guilmoto.

van Gennep, Arnold. 1909. *Les rites de passage*. Paris: Emile Nourry.

Le Roy, Alexandre (ed.). 1909. *La religion des primitifs*. Paris: Beauchesne.

Mauss, Marcel. 1913. 'L'ethnographie en France et à l'étranger'. *Revue de Paris* 1913:537–560, 815–837.

Métraux, Alfred. 1925. 'De la méthode dans les recherches ethnographiques'. *Revue d'ethnographie et des traditions populaires* 1925:266–290.

Secondary sources

Balandier, George. 1951. 'La situation coloniale: approche théorique'. *Cahiers internationaux de sociologie* XI:44–79.

Blanckaert, Claude. 1995a. 'Le premesse dell'antropologia "culturale" in Francia. Il dibattito sul "Questionnaire de Sociologie et d'Ethnographie" di Charles Letourneau (1882–1883)'. *La Ricerca folklorica* 32:51–70.

Blanckaert, Claude. 1995b. 'Fondements disciplinaires de l'anthropologie française au XIXe siècle. Perspectives historiographiques'. *Politix* 29:31–54.

Blanckaert, Claude. 2001. 'La crise de l'anthropométrie: des arts anthropotechniques aux dérives militantes (1860–1920)'. In C. Blanckaert (ed.). *Les politiques de l'anthropologie: Discours et pratiques en France (1860–1940)*. Paris: L'Harmattan, pp. 95–172.

Bonneuil, Christophe. 1998. 'Le Muséum national d'histoire naturelle et l'expansion coloniale de la troisième République (1870–1914)'. *Revue française d'histoire d'outre-mer* 180:143–169.

Chailleux, Luc. 1990. 'Histoire de la Société d'Ethnographie: la Revue orientale et américaine (1858–1879). Ethnographie, orientalisme et américanisme au XIXe siècle'. *L'Ethnographie* 1990:22–46.

Charle, Christophe. 1990. *Naissance des intellectuels, 1880–1900*. Paris: Editions de Minuit.

Conklin, Alice. 1997. *A Mission to Civilize: The Republican Idea of Empire in France and West Africa, 1895–1930*. Stanford: Stanford University Press.

Dias, Nélia. 1991. *Le musée d'ethnographie du Trocadéro*. Paris: Editions du Centre national de la recherche scientifique.

Fournier, Marcel. 1994. *Marcel Mauss*. Paris: Fayard.

James, Wendy. 1998. 'The Treatment of African Ethnography in *L'Année sociologique* (I–XII)'. *L'Année sociologique* 48:193–207.

Karady, Victor. 1982. 'Le problème de la légitimité dans l'organisation historique de l'ethnologie française'. *Revue Française de Sociologie* 23:17–35.

Mucchielli, Laurent. 1998. *La découverte du social: naissance de la sociologie en France*. Paris: La Découverte.

Rosa, Federico. 1996. 'Le mouvement anthropologique français'. *Archives européennes de sociologie* 2:375–405.

Sibeud, Emmanuelle. 1996. 'Du questionnaire à la pratique: l'enquête de la Société Antiesclavagiste de France sur la famille africaine en 1910'. In C. Blanckaert (ed.). *Le terrain des sciences humaines: Instructions et enquêtes (XVIIIᵉ–XXᵉ siecles)*. Paris: L'Harmattan, pp. 329–355.

Sibeud, Emmanuelle. 2002. *Une science impériale pour l'Afrique? La construction des savoirs africanistes en France (1878–1930)*. Paris: Editions de l'EHESS.

CHAPTER TWO

The advancement of African studies in Berlin by the 'Deutsche Forschungsgemeinschaft', 1920–1945*

Holger Stoecker

The 1920s were a dramatic period for African studies in Germany. The Africanist community had to contend with the traumatic consequences of the German defeat in World War I, the loss of the German colonies, exclusion from the international scientific community, and, finally, the need to justify African studies to a German public which had become, at least in part, skeptical about colonial matters.[1] At the same time, an epistemological change was also taking place within European anthropological-ethnological studies in general, characterized primarily by a move from evolutionistic-comparative approaches to more social anthropological methods, as exemplified by the work of Bronislaw Malinowski and A.R. Radcliffe-Brown. All of these shifts, moreover, coincided with the foundation of university chairs for African languages in Hamburg and Berlin, which contributed to the academic institutionalization of German African studies in general.

Wissenschaft (that unique blend of science and scholarship) was considered one of the means to strengthen German national identity and help overcome the national crisis. After its defeat in 1918, Germany had experienced serious setbacks and losses in all of the traditional areas most important to the German sense of national identity: the military was weakened, the imperial throne had been overturned, industry and trade were failing, and science was also suffering. At this point, it looked as though only science would lend itself to the idea that, by drawing on former achievements of 'national greatness', the injured German identity could also be re-strengthened. Therefore, leading German politicians, and especially those responsible for cultural and scientific matters, felt that it was *Wissenschaft* above all which might contribute to ending the deep German national crisis.[2] To achieve this goal, however, it would first be necessary to modernize scientific infrastructures by centralizing efforts in one specific Reich authority, by promoting academic research outside the universities, and by supporting young scholars.

The newly founded Notgemeinschaft der deutschen Wissenschaften (Emergency Society for German Science) – later the Deutsche Forschungsgemeinschaft – came to fulfill this identity-building function during the interwar period by providing financial assistance to scholarly projects that its 'experts' deemed worthy. With regard to the development of African Studies in Germany, it indeed took on a number of important responsibilities. For one, the Notgemeinschaft made research possible for young Africanist scholars both within and outside academia and in so doing, assured the maintenance and cultivation of an Africanist community. Accordingly, this meant that African studies itself had an increasingly stable position among the academic disciplines. Further, if we can speak at all of a federal academic system that was regulated from a central location during the Weimar period, one which bore equal responsibilty for all German Africanists, then this body would have to be the Notgemeinschaft and its appointed African expert, even if it was not recognized as such at the time. Through the expert's activity as the leading appraiser of proposed academic projects, he not only determined the standards necessary for approval, but also shaped the content and methodological direction of the discipline as a whole. Each disciplinary representative in the Notgemeinschaft/DFG thus exerted immense power over how that discipline was moulded in the interwar period.

This chapter is therefore focused on a set of questions intended to assess how the power of the Notgemeinschaft/DFG refashioned African Studies in Germany during the interwar period. In what way and for what projects did Berlin scholars involved in African studies use the DFG, the most important German force for the promotion of science and research? What were the trends in research that can be deduced from grant applications? And more generally, how did DFG support influence the development of African studies in Berlin in the years between 1920 and 1945?

Berlin was, in the era under discussion, one of the most important centers in Germany of African studies, a field which encompassed linguistics,[3] followed by *Völkerkunde*/Ethnology/Anthropology (notions often used synonymously at the time in Germany), missionary studies, geography, and, increasingly, the natural sciences. As was so often the case with 'young' sciences, actual research tended to disregard such distinctions – quite often a scientist would be active in several different fields at once. In addition in Germany – and especially in Berlin –

African studies drew from very diverse sources, with regard to its exponents as well as its interests. The people involved came from former colonial education institutes, museum and library departments, and scientific and missionary societies, all of which formed a kind of loose scientific community that lacked a true center.[4]

The Notgemeinschaft/Deutsche Forschungsgemeinschaft

Following World War I, existing metropolitan institutions were complemented by the so-called Notgemeinschaft der Deutschen Wissenschaft, which was founded on 30 October 1920 in Berlin. In 1929 the Notgemeinschaft was renamed the Deutsche Gemeinschaft zur Erhaltung und Förderung der Forschung (Notgemeinschaft der Deutschen Wissenschaft); this title was unnofficially shortened to Deutsche Forschungsgemeinschaft or DFG. In 1935, DFG became its official name, since it did not suit the Third Reich's self-representation to have an institution that was called 'Emergency Foundation' (Mertens 1999: 58). This has remained its name up to the present day. It was the founders' intention that the Notgemeinschaft should, in the deep national crisis after World War I, promote the principal fields of German scientific research as efficiently as possible by means of scientific self-administration and legal independence (cf. Zierold 1968; Marsch 1994; Hammerstein 1999).

The Notgemeinschaft received most of its funds from the state. To a lesser degree it also obtained money from large German enterprises, private donations and foreign sources such as the United States-based Rockefeller Foundation.[5] In terms of its legal status, the Notgemeinschaft was an association registered under civil law.[6] The idea behind the creation of the Notgemeinschaft was that the problems of organizing science were best solved through scientific autonomy, in other words through scientific self-administration. And in view of the uneasy international standing of post-World War I Germany, it was quite rightly assumed that a private organization would find it easier to re-establish contacts with scientific institutions abroad than would a government agency. This was particularly relevant at a time when Germany, after its defeat in 1918, was facing a scientific boycott by other Western European countries.[7]

Because scientists – rather than state officials or private sponsors – were now deciding how to distribute research funds, the Notgemeinschaft played a fundamental role in reshaping and modernizing scientific research in Germany. This new, modern way of funding scientific research was in turn widely accepted throughout the scientific community, because the Notgemeinschaft quickly became integrated into existing academic networks.

The Notgemeinschaft counted fifty-seven members, all exclusively scientific institutions. Among these organizations were all the German academies of sciences in Berlin, Göttingen, Heidelberg, Leipzig and Munich, all twenty-three universities and eleven technical colleges in Germany, as well as the 'Kaiser-Wilhelm-Gesellschaft zur Förderung der Wissenschaften' (Kaiser Wilhelm Society for the Advancement of Sciences, which was renamed the Max Planck Society after World War II) and several scientific federations.[8]

The Notgemeinschaft had originally been founded with the intention that it should collect and coordinate the remaining financial resources – which were very limited after World War I – that were available to science, in order to promote effective scholarship. It met its task by a) underwriting research scholarships for single projects, preferably to individual candidates[9]; b) financially assisting publications (doctoral theses excluded); c) acquiring and lending scientific equipment; d) paying for research assistants' work in exceptional cases; and e) partially funding expeditions and scientific excavations.[10]

According to its guidelines, applications for grants had to be handed in directly to the Notgemeinschaft, which then sent them on to the respective experts' sub-committees for a specialist's evaluation (Zierold 1968: 60f.). The main board's task consisted primarily in 'keeping an even balance between the different branches of science'[11] that received support from the DFG. The main board was elected by the members of the Notgemeinschaft, and it consisted almost exclusively of eminent academic experts, as well as of three scholars who served as MPs in the Reichstag (House of Commons): Otto Hoetzsch (DNVP; national conservative German National People's Party), a specialist on the history of Eastern Europe, Gustav Radbruch (SPD; Social Democrats), a lawyer, and Georg Schreiber (Catholic Center Party), a theologian and prelate. Usually, they simply sanctioned the 'main board lists' in accordance with the recommendations put before them. If they ever ventured to give an opinion of their own, it seems that they only did so on applications related to their own special fields of knowledge (BK, R 73–119 to 136). Similarly, the confirmation of the 'main board lists' by the supervising Reich Ministry of the Interior (Home Office) was a pure formality (BK, R 73–107 to 118).

The final decision on an application was given by the Notgemeinschaft's main board, usually also in accordance with the recommendations handed in by the various sub-committees. Occasionally though, Friedrich Schmidt-Ott (1860–1947) – president of the Notgemeinschaft until 1934, and well known for his autocratic ways and an insistence upon having the last word on the allocation of means – might, at the last moment, reject an already recommended application. Nonetheless, it is not surprising that under these circumstances the evaluation-writing expert of each sub-committee became the most decisive authority. Usually he was a widely respected holder of a professorial chair, and his opinions were almost always accepted by the main board of the Notgemeinschaft. If on the other hand, he advocated against an application, it almost never stood a chance of getting through.

On the main board Georg Thilenius (1868–1937), an ethnologist, was the scholar most closely related to African studies. Since 1904, Thilenius had been director of the Ethnological Museum in Hamburg, as well as professor of Ethnology at the University of Hamburg founded in 1919. At that time, he was recognized as an eminent authority in German ethnology. As the university's rector he had also been involved in the founding negotiations of the Notgemeinschaft (Fischer 1990: 27 ff.).

The 'Sub-Committee for Ethnology'

When the Notgemeinschaft was founded, *Wissenschaft* had been divided into at first twenty, then later into twenty-one sub-committees. Initially, there was hardly any consideration given to the research of non-European cultures. In a first draft on the division of scientific fields, the responsibility for linguistic research on 'African language' [*sic!*] was assigned to the sub-committee for 'Ancient and Oriental Philology', and the responsibility for 'Ethnology (Anthropogeography and Anthropology)' to the sub-committee for 'Mineralogy, Geography, Geology'.[12] It was only on Thilenius's insistence that a special 'Sub-Committee on Ethnology, Anthropology, Folklore, Pre-History, and Native Languages' was formed. This somewhat awkward-sounding 'bundling' of disciplines, which may seem strange to us today, followed a then fairly common understanding of academic fields, which we can also see in the name of the long-established Berlin Society for Anthropology, Ethnology and Pre-History (Zimmerman 2001). In addition to having very fluid boundaries, for Thilenius these disciplines were also linked by a shared commitment to using natural-scientific methods when examining cultural phenomena (Thilenius 1930: 389, 399).

Regarding the prospective staff members of the expert sub-committees, it was suggested that they ought to be elected by the whole body of scholars employed at universities and other scientific institutions (Marsch 1994: 99 f.). Scientific federations possessed the (not binding) right to nominate the candidates.[13] All German

professors and lecturers at universities, polytechnics, scientific academies and the Kaiser Wilhelm Institutes were entitled to vote. If a
sub-committee proposed it, franchise could also be extended to
independent scholars. The elected members of a sub-committee then
voted on a chairman, whom they chose from among their own ranks.

The first and as yet provisional assembly of the Ethnology sub-committee members was supposed to take place under the auspices of the
Deutscher Hochschulverband (Union of German Universities), but it
was in fact Thilenius who nominated the experts. They were Rudolf
Martin (Munich) for anthropology, Karl Weule (Leipzig) for ethnography, Hans Seger (Breslau) for prehistory, Otto Laufer (Hamburg) for
folklore and Carl Meinhof (Hamburg) for 'native' languages.[14] Shortly
afterwards they were joined by the 'racial' anthropologist Eugen
Fischer, then at Freiburg. For the sub-committee's chairmanship Thilenius suggested Meinhof, his colleague from Hamburg, because 'Among
the above-mentioned members he disposes of the broadest connections
with related fields, in particular anthropology, folklore and ethnology,
and therefore he seems in my opinion best suited for the chairmanship.'[15] So it was, of all things, an Africanist, i.e. a representative of a
young discipline still struggling for academic recognition, who was
asked to take a prominent position within the head organization of
German science's self-administration. The eventual confirmation of
the nominees – in perfect accordance with Thilenius's suggestions –
by the Union of German Universities was a pure formality.

Up to 1934/35 hardly any changes took place within the sub-
committee of Ethnology, and its structure – in contrast with that of
other sub-committees – remained stable. There were some changes in
membership; after the first election to the sub-committee in 1922,
Fischer, Lauffer and Seger resigned. The latter were replaced by the
folklorist John Meier (Freiburg i. Br.), and the prehistorian Carl Schuch-
hardt (Berlin) (BK, R 73–123). When Martin died in 1925, he was
replaced by Eugen Fischer,[16] who was nominated by Meinhof.[17] After
the death of Karl Weule in 1926, he was replaced, on the suggestion
of the presidency of the Notgemeinschaft, by Thilenius himself.[18] He
was to act from 1928 onwards as the vice-chairman of the sub-
committee.[19] The elections to the sub-committees held in 1929 and
1933 simply reconfirmed the assemblage of the Ethnology sub-
committee (BK, R 73–129, 136). The longest permanent presence on
the sub-committee was that of Meinhof, who had acted as its chairman since 1921 and continued to write expert evaluations even after
the voluntary *Gleichschaltung* ('streamlining' or 'syncronizing'
according to Nazi policy) of the DFG in 1934.[20] Meinhof thus remained
in control at a time when the 'former practice of expert evaluation

through professorial experts in the committees' (Mertens 1999: 60) had already been abolished, and when many other experts had already retreated from their committee duties.

Admission into the scientific sub-committees gave the referees a great deal of prestige as eminent exponents of their particular fields. Furthermore, because the sub-committees changed so little in composition, these experts retained lasting power over the inner workings of German science (Zierold 1968: 61).

Africa-related applications

The DFG has left a considerable amount of archival material on its activities with regard to African studies. The files of Africa-related applications to the DFG contain important and detailed data on the subjects of the proposals, as well as on the financial aspects of the applications. Moreover, it is possible to gain information about the scientific and political networks in which the advisors and the applicants were involved, or which the applicants tried to join. It needs to be emphasized, though, that these materials provide evidence only about the proposals and not about the realization of the research projects. The DFG did not demand progress reports or even final reports, and thus such reports were seldom submitted. While the largely unordered archival sources do not yet allow for any precise figures, it can be safely assumed that between 1920 and 1945 more than 7,000 applications from all scientific fields were made to the DFG.[21] Among the over 200 Africa-related research applications, those of an ethnological or linguistic nature submitted by Berlin scholars form a clear majority.

More than half of these Africa-related applications were handed in between 1925 and 1933. This upsurge went along with a newly topical debate on colonial policies during this period. In the mid-1920s propaganda by the German colonial movement demanding that the former German colonies in Africa be returned by the Allies (the *Entente*) gained new force. This 'mobilization' campaign included, among other things, a meeting of the German Colonial Congress at Berlin University in September 1924. This congress was organized by the Koloniale Reichsarbeitsgemeinschaft (KORAG, Colonial Reich Syndicate), an umbrella federation made up of numerous colonial organizations, and held on the fortieth anniversary of the beginnings of German colonial politics.[22] There followed other events that found sizeable public resonance, such as the Berlin Colonial Week and various Colonial exhibitions.[23]

In terms of Germany's foreign politics, the colonial movement saw the Locarno conference of 1925 as an ideal opportunity to extract colonial concessions from the Allies. In return for agreeing to Germany's joining the League of Nations and for the conclusion of a European security pact (a wish of the Allies), they hoped to gain formal exoneration from the accusations of German 'colonial offenses', as well as concessions about the claims for colonial mandates (Rüger 1995: 459ff.).

The question of colonial politics linked to these national and international events – all of which stirred German political opinion in the mid-1920s – directly affected the situation of African studies in Berlin. In the wake of this revisionist colonial campaign, and in order to strengthen the claims for the lost colonies through 'scientific competence', the chair for East African languages at the Berlin Seminar for Oriental languages, which had stood vacant since the end of the war, was revived and given to Martin Heepe (1887–1961). On the instigation of the same colonial circles, Diedrich Westermann was promoted to the rank of full university professor for African Languages in 1925. For the first time in history, African studies in Berlin received a regular professorial chair (see Stoecker 2002: 120f.).

The marked increase in Africa-related applications to the Notgemeinschaft (quite frequently emphasizing their relevance to colonial politics) that occurred from the mid-1920s onwards did, however, also lead to criticism and was not always sympathetically regarded. The economic historian Bruno Kuske (1876–1964), who was a member of the Notgemeinschaft's main board, complained in light of enduring financial difficulties in 1930 that 'if we indeed can hardly make ends meet, some applications should be laid aside for the time being, especially if they relate to less than pressing matters and give the impression that they belong to a certain "fashion". In regard to my own field of research and work, I have already pointed out that there has been an exaggerated specialization on research concerning our former colonies.' Kuske continued to remark that, precisely in this area, 'the Notgemeinschaft has been approached in a particularly striking way, well into the very latest [main board] lists'.[24] Kuske's objections against this 'fashion' for colonial sciences in the applications to the Notgemeinschaft suggest that – despite the strong revisionist colonial propaganda – some sections of the German public as well as of the scientific community considered the colonial period to be a closed chapter in German history.[25]

The upswing of Africa-related applications also points to the emergence of a 'second generation' of German Africanists which followed the 'founders' generation' of Carl Meinhof (1857–1944) and Diedrich Westermann (1875–1956). This 'second generation' characteristically obtained their university degrees mostly after World War I, and began trying to make their way in academia from the second half of the 1920s onward.

Nearly two-thirds of the Africa-related applications were handed to the Fachausschuss für Völkerkunde, one of the ten committees responsible for humanities within the Notgemeinschaft/DFG. Due to his position in the Notgemeinschaft, Meinhof's influence on the development of German African studies during the Weimar Republic period surpassed that of anyone else. There were but a handful of other possibilities for German Africanists to obtain financial assistance for their studies. These other means were granted mainly by the state, for example by the Prussian Ministry of Culture or the Reich Foreign and Interior ministries, and were therefore more immediately subject to short-term political and budgetary considerations. Private sources such as the Baessler Foundation or wealthy private patrons like Baron Eduard von der Heydt could at best assist selectively, and to a decidedly lesser extent. The same applies to the International Institute of African Cultures and Languages (IIALC) in London, which helped – through the mediation of Westermann – about a dozen German Africanists with research scholarships and publication funds through the outbreak of World War II.

From the end of the 1920s there was almost no contact concerning the Notgemeinschaft between Westermann and his former mentor and sponsor, Meinhof. Meinhof was the undisputed expert for all things African on the sub-committee for Ethnology. This meant that he was, for one, able to finance the *Zeitschrift für Eingeborenensprachen* (of which he was the editor) year after year out of funds from the Notgemeinschaft (*Berichte der Notgemeinschaft*; BB, R 1501–126777, 126778). His assistants in Hamburg – as well as Meinhof himself – were repeatedly granted subsidies by the Notgemeinschaft.[26] Westermann, on the other hand, managed to establish himself as a co-director of the London IIALC, a position that endowed him with Europe-wide strategic influence on scientific research, money, and an excellent periodical for publication, *Africa*. This dissociation of their fields of activity and their financial sources was reflected in the personal relationship between Meinhof and Westermann, which was clearly cooling off in the late 1920s, even though it never came to public conflict. The split was partly caused by Meinhof's scientific objections to Westermann's practically-oriented methods for a standard orthography for African languages, but also to Westermann's open readiness to cooperate with Africanists from the Allied countries, especially Great Britain.[27] Not surprisingly, Westermann's (rare) applications were turned down by the Notgemeinschaft.[28] This was to change only in 1937, with Meinhof's retirement (at the age of 80) and his subsequent loss of influence in the DFG.

Applications to the Notgemeinschaft had a good chance of being recommended by Meinhof if they complied with his view of *Afrikanistik* as a discipline which deal first and foremost with language. The linguistic competence of an applicant was thus a very important criterion. Meinhof's scientific interests as an African linguist lay in the traditions of German nineteenth-century philology, and were directed mainly at the search for 'original forms . . . which for the great literary languages of Europe and Asia are a thing of the long vanished past' (Meinhof 1928: 128, 131 ff.). The same views also influenced the fate of anthropological applications. During Meinhof's chairmanship, the decisions of the sub-committee experts were therefore rather hostile towards new ideas, and skeptical about foreign methodological approaches.

Two types of reasoning were especially prevalent in the Africa-related applications to the DFG. On the one hand, the applicants emphasized the deep insights to be gained for 'German (colonial) interests' by the research project. On the other hand, they tended to hint more or less openly at the rival African studies of other colonial powers, mainly Great Britain's. These lines of reasoning are telling, but are perhaps more indicative of the attitudes of the experts than those of the applicants. To present an international scientific competition in the light of a 'colonial contest' with other nations seems to have been a particularly successful strategy of communication between the neophyte applicants and the expert 'establishment'. The Berlin African Studies coterie of the interwar years must, therefore, still be understood in the context of a German movement aimed at revoking the loss of the colonies. Colonial revisionism was *the* commonly agreed-upon political stance among the entire German African scientific community.[29]

The following examples show that DFG advisors assessed the potential benefit of each project in terms of German colonial interests. In 1933, for instance, Thilenius supported an application, despite it being for a comparatively large sum, for the printing of a book on the Bafia in Cameroon. Moreover, Thilenius overrode professional objections to the project, which had been submitted by the Berlin ethnologist and private scholar Günther Tessmann (1884–1969) for 'political reasons' (Tessmann 1934). Thilenius noted that the monograph was based upon an expedition undertaken in 1913–15, when Cameroon was still German territory. The close interdependence between colonial political interests and the practice of granting subsidies to scientists became especially clear in Thilenius's note regarding the project, which was intended for internal use only: 'Renewed colonial activity means that the German inability to colonize must be proven untrue. To this end, good monographs on colonial peoples are indispensable.'[30]

To cite another example, in 1935 Berlin anthropologist and art historian Eckart von Sydow (1885–1942) applied for a small subsidy to support a journey to British West Africa, where he wanted to study the Benin bronzes. Thilenius rejected the application, stating that the IIALC in London (which Thilenius saw as an agency run by the British Colonial Office) should cover the expenses, since it was the British, not the Germans, who would profit from the results.[31] Equally negative was Meinhof's decision on Berlin anthropologist Richard Thurnwald's application to finance *Psychological Research on the Question of the Adaptation to European Cultural Influences by the Native Population in former German East Africa*, a project that Thurnwald had planned in 1930 in the wake of an expedition financed by the IIALC.[32] Meinhof's note for internal use reads: 'It is not so much science as the English Colonial Government which is interested in this journey.'[33]

The DFG's support also favored a general process of professionalization, bringing African studies into the realm of the academy. In the colonial era, practical, personal field experience of Africa and colonial contexts were considered prerequisites for admission into the African 'knowledge community'. Beginning in the early 1920s, this proto-academic network underwent an increasing process of scientific professionalization. The first two university chairs specifically for African languages were established: first in 1919 in Hamburg and then in 1921 in Berlin. Those members who were to join the Africanist scientific community after World War I usually had a university background.[34] Native Africans, however, were still accepted into minor, dependent positions at best (see Pugach, this volume).

Academic professionalization also became apparent in the practice of the DFG. While academic degrees were not a formal prerequisite, increasingly the applicants whom the DFG supported possessed them. Applications were refused if they seemed not quite fully mature, if the candidates did not appear qualified to guarantee an adherence to scientific standards, or if the application did not serve explicitly scientific goals. 'Scientific goals' meant primarily the publication of the results, usually in the form of a scientific essay or a monograph. As far as the files show, photo or movie equipment for scholars travelling to Africa was sponsored by the Notgemeinschaft/DFG only on the condition that photos or films played but a secondary role in the realization of the project.[35] Producers of popular documentaries or 'culture films' such as Hans Schomburgk were not assisted by the DFG.[36] Applications for expedition funding, if results were to be published in a more popular, journalistic form, were also rejected.

The way the DFG managed its grants greatly influenced the integration of African studies into academia. This was undoubtedly also a consequence of the loss of the German colonies, insofar as the educated younger generations were no longer able to get non-academic jobs in the colonies or at colonial establishments in the metropole. Scientific or academic careers therefore became viable options and, partly due to the subsidies of the DFG, such careers also became fairly realistic options.

The amount of the subsidies varied greatly. Allocations for field expeditions, publications, or the acquiring of equipment and materials, were generally based on actual costs, but could be readjusted if additional financial means could be procured from a third party. Assistance to scientists in the form of a research scholarship (limited in time) could vary between 120 and 460 marks per month. The amount depended mostly on the scientific reputation of the beneficiary, even though social circumstances (for example, the family situation) played a certain part as well. The payment for scientific assistants out of DFG means, for which the holder of a university chair would apply, varied as a rule between fifty and seventy marks. This meant that the assistants remained dependent on an additional income.[37]

The epistemological change in European anthropology which led from evolutionistic-comparative approaches to an interest in applicable, practically-minded colonial knowledge – a change linked chiefly to Bronislaw Malinowski (1884–1942) – found only weak resonance in the Africa-related applications to the DFG. The trends in German research that can be gleaned from these applications point instead to a seemingly strong adherence to traditional pre-war approaches. It was only in the mid-1930s that projects of a clearly functionalist type could be realized, such as Reinhold Schober's *Modern Native Policies in Cameroon*, or Peter von Werder's *Types of Social Organisation in Western Africa*.[38] This confirms the view that in Germany functionalists enjoyed a certain success in the second half of the 1930s, but that against the resistance of the established school of ethnology they were not able to form a school of their own or arrive at a consistent method of teaching (Mischek 1996: 141).

For their part, Schober and von Werder were pupils of Diedrich Westermann, the professor for African languages at the University of Berlin. Westermann was also the co-director of the IIALC in London, and therefore far more open to British anthropological methods. From 1937 on, Westermann also began to play an increasingly important and eventually leading role in the field of colonial sciences at the DFG.

Africa-related research projects and Nazi colonial sciences

The advent of the Third Reich led to deep changes within the DFG. In particular, it meant the end of institutional independence (cf. Mertens 1996: 119ff.; Hammerstein 1999). The certainly questionable but nonetheless important attempt to maintain political impartiality and institutional independence in the allocation of grants came to an end with the demise of the Weimar Republic. After 1934, reports were drawn up on the political attitudes and characters of all applicants, in both their private and professional capacities, in order to ensure the success of the intended 'new direction' of the allocation policy.[39] In 1937 a parallel, state-run institution, the Reichsforschungsrat (Reich Research Council), was introduced with similar structures to the DFG. Its political task was to make use of all the scientific resources for Wehrforschung (military research). In practical terms, the two institutions soon merged.

The files on the DFG between 1936 and 1939 show a marked decrease in Africa-related applications. This can very likely be attributed in part to the fact that Johannes Stark, president of the DFG from 1934 to 1937, often decided on applications on his own and circumvented the sub-committees, which means that there is no written evidence about the fate of many applications during this period (Mertens 1999: 61ff.). Once the *Führerprinzip* (leader principle) had been introduced to the DFG in 1934, the work of the whole organization was extremely dependent on its leading personality. As a representative of the so-called Deutsche Physik (German physics), Stark's autocratic decisions on applications led to a very strong preference for natural sciences (Mertens 2001: 52f., 62ff., 2002: 235ff.).

No doubt more relevant, however, is the fact that in those years the scientific politics of the Nazis were concentrated on the centralization of universities, major scientific institutions, and the allocation of research subsidies, so that they could be controlled through the newly founded Reich Ministry of Education (Fischer et al. 2000: 549). Correspondingly, the majority of the Africa-related applications in the years 1937–39 were to form – for the first time ever – parts of a larger whole, namely, of a centrally coordinated, multidisciplinary 'Overarching Project' concerning 'African Research After the World War'. This project was headed by Breslau geographer Erich Obst, and it aimed at creating a comprehensive survey of the entire post-World War I literature on Africa, in the shape of a 'Universal Colonial Bibliography' (BK, R 73–13449).

The reorganization of scientific institutions – usually accompanied by chaotic feuds between rival party and state agencies about the significance of their own ideas for scientific policies – led in the end to the establishment of the Kolonialwissenschaftliche Abteilung (KWA, Department of Colonial Sciences) in September 1940. In terms of its institutional structure, the KWA was a joint venture of the Reichs-forschungsrat and the NSDAP's own Kolonialpolitische Abteilung (Department of Colonial Policy). The Kolonialpolitische Abteilung was headed by general Franz Xaver Ritter von Epp (1868–1946), and it was considered the nucleus of a future Reich Colonial Ministry (cf. Schmokel 1967: 145; Lakowski 1986: 400; Mosen 1991: 116ff.; Mischek 2000b: 129–147). The funds for the KWA were provided by the DFG. The driving force behind its foundation was Konrad Meyer (1901–73), head of the special department of 'Agricultural Sciences and General Biology' at the Reichsforschungsrat. Meyer, who was to play a leading role in the establishment of the notorious 'Generalplan Ost' (Master Plan East) in July 1941 for the 'restructuring' of the German-occupied territories in Eastern Europe (cf. Rössler 1990; Aly and Heim 1993: 394ff.), had in 1939 insisted on an increase in colonial research in the natural sciences: 'The repeated demands voiced by the Führer over the last years that the colonies be handed back make the question of realizing certain research projects in colonial sciences, and of the education of qualified young scholars in colonial sciences – especially in the fields of agriculture and natural sciences – appear all the more pressing.'[40] Precisely what other persons and offices in the state and the party – besides those already mentioned – had been involved in the founding of the KWA can no longer be reconstructed in detail (Mischek 2000b: 137).

Meyer's longstanding assistant, the agriculturalist Günter Wolff (b. 1907) who had in the summer of 1940 just returned from a field trip to western Africa, was designated head of the KWA. With ambitious determination, Wolff tried to turn the KWA into the Third Reich's central colonial agency, an institution which was to offer an interdisciplinary research program in colonial sciences in close coordination with the Department for Colonial Politics of the NSDAP. In this new context, ethnology lost the dominant role it had enjoyed within the Notgemeinschaft's 'Sub-committee for Ethnology' in the years before 1933. However, ethnology was to keep its authority in questions concerning population politics and work organization (Streck 2000: 16).

From 1940 until the end of the war in May 1945, the KWA was in every practical respect solely responsible for the coordination of

African studies in Germany. This department consisted of twenty-nine 'Colonial Sub-committees', each of which covered different fields of the 'colonial' humanities, natural sciences and geography, economy, medicine, technology and so on. In terms of specialization, the department thus went significantly further than the Notgemeinschaft ever had. Head of the new Fachgruppe Koloniale Völkerkunde (sub-committee for 'Colonial Anthropology') was the Jena ethnologist Bernhard Struck,[41] while Diedrich Westermann was head of the Fachgruppe Koloniale Sprachforschung (sub-committee for 'Colonial Language Research'). To the section of humanities were to belong, in addition, the sub-committees for Colonial Social Questions (headed by Oskar Karstedt, Berlin), Colonial Race Research (Eugen Fischer, Berlin), Colonial Law Research (Wilhelm Wengler, Berlin), Colonial Religion Research (in particular Islam, Richard Hartmann, Berlin), and Colonial History (Egmont Zechlin, Berlin) (Wolff 1941: 1 ff.). These colonial sub-committees – in contrast to the sub-committees of the Notgemeinschaft which had been concerned mainly with evaluating applications – were meant to assume 'the shape of informal assemblies of scientists uniting different special fields' as 'representatives of the colonial research of the future'.[42]

The new Kolonialwissenschaftliche Abteilung was in charge of the allocation of resources for 'colonial' research.[43] The department was equally empowered to develop and to formulate the conceptual aims of colonial scientific research.[44] This dual capacity led to the end of the former practice of providing expert evaluations on applications, and it also meant that now the very same eminent experts who worked at the Department for Colonial Sciences were granted very generous subsidies.

Westermann, for instance, managed to obtain no fewer than fifteen successful proposals between 1940 and 1945, including projects like his *Handbook of African Tribes* (1942), *The Expansion and Significance of Islam in Western Africa* (1942–43) and the revision of his *Ewe Dictionary* (1943–45).[45] Another successful candidate was the colonial historian Egmont Zechlin (1896–1992), at this time professor for Colonial and Overseas History at the University of Berlin and head of the Fachgruppe Koloniale Geschichte in the *KWA*. In April 1943, at a moment when the prospects of the German military forces in Northern Africa began to look rather bleak, Zechlin submitted the project *Northern Africa as a Historical-Political Theater of Destiny*. Nine assistants were assigned to do research for a year on 'activities of German colonial pioneers in the Northern African area . . . seen in a general political context'. 'Due to the military events in Northern Africa' it had become necessary, according to Zechlin, to 'adapt previous study matters to such scientific tasks as are now required by the war' (BK, R 73–15918). The board of the DFG judged Zechlin's project to be of high importance to the war effort, and consequently granted him 16,950 marks, the highest sum ever given to a single project in the colonial sciences.

The war also meant that German scholars could no longer carry out research in Africa, and therefore had to turn to archives (Zechlin[46]), museum depositories (Schachtzabel[47]) or libraries (Westermann). At the conference of the sub-committee for Colonial Language research in March 1941, all the participants complained that travel to Africa had now become virtually impossible. To those scholars whose papers on East and West African languages had been discussed at the conference raised the prospect that this deficiency might be compensated through field studies conducted at prisoner-of-war camps interning African soldiers. Wolff assured the participants that the KWA would provide financial assistance for such research.[48] By now POW camps offered the only possibility of getting in touch with Africans. Accordingly, the DFG granted a project submitted by Westermann in March 1941 to 'make recordings of important African languages in prisoner of war camps' (BK, R 73–15646) in occupied France, which was approved within five days. Evaluation by the KWA was deemed unnecessary in this case, 'since this concerns Professor Westermann himself, generally known to be the leading German expert in this field'.[49] Westermann delegated the trip to the south of France and the voice recordings to the younger linguists Johannes Lukas and Heinz Sölken. It is not quite clear why Westermann chose this detour via southern France for his linguistic research, instead of working with the approximately 4,000 French colonial soldiers of African origin who had been interned as POWs near Luckenwalde, close to Berlin, since June 1940. Westermann's decision not to visit the Luckenwalde detainees appears doubly surprising, considering that the High Command of the Wehrmacht (OKW) had suggested to the Hamburg Colonial Institute that they were free to select suitable language assistants from among the POWs, on condition that 'under no circumstances were they (the POWs) to come into contact with civilian life'.[50]

In Westermann's eyes, every colonial science was to be concerned as closely as possible with practical matters. In a speech given in 1941 on 'Language Research and Anthropology as a Colonial Task' Westermann argued forcefully that no colonial policies could possibly succeed unless they were guided by science (Westermann 1942; Mischek 2000a: 75f.). In a sense he was simply reiterating arguments already made by his former colleaguages at the IIALC. After the outbreak of the war, the heads of the IIALC in London were interested in learning about the present attitude of the much-admired Westermann – now in enemy Germany – towards the London institute and the so far mutually shared opinions on Africa. The Secretary-general of the IIALC, Hanns Vischer, who had read about the contents of Westermann's speech in the press, was to declare with obvious relief: 'Evidently our Director has not changed his views, and one would like to know what he thinks of the official view that Africans are only half apes.'[51]

Vischer's opinion on Westermann would no doubt have been less sympathetic had he known that since spring 1941 Wolff was – together with Westermann – preparing the way for a European Colonial Academy to be opened in Berlin. Its aim was to promote the co-operation of experts on colonial sciences from France, Belgium, the Netherlands, Finland, Spain, Switzerland, Serbia, Denmark, Romania, Sweden and Italy.[52] There were, moreover, even plans to attach the IIALC to this Academy, thereby bringing it under German control (BB, R 4901–3101, p. 47 ff.). Even though in 1941–42 some international co-operation actually took place, mainly with French experts on Africa (Henri Labouret and Louis Reteaud,[53] among others), the projects for the Academy had to be dropped relatively quickly, due to the intervention of the Reich Foreign Ministry in the summer of 1942.[54] Soon almost all the activities in the colonial sciences would come to an end anyway, since 'colonial preparatory work' in general was stopped at the beginning of 1943. Only some minor residue was left to survive. After the military defeats in Stalingrad and in northern Africa, retaking the colonies was no longer among the more important German war aims (Schmokel 1967: 150).

The political and ideological program that the KWA presented to the Africanist scientific community still maintained, however, that Germany would regain a colonial empire in Africa in the very near future – German military victory was, indeed, taken for granted through at least 1942–43. This conviction that a new German colonial empire was imminent suited the revisionist attitudes that the German Africanists had clung to since 1919. If one understands this continuity as a 'disposition' in the sense of a long-term history of mentality (Oexle 1999: 53), it is also easier to understand why most German Africanists – together with the majority of German scientists – experienced Hitler's coming to power in 1933 as something far less significant than the events of 1918/19. After all, the very foundation of the DFG had been a reaction to the Versailles Treaty.

There was another event that took place in 1933 that was to have far-reaching consequences. The so-called 'Law to Restructure the Civil Service' of 7 April 1933 heralded the expulsion of 'non-Aryans' and political opponents of National Socialism from public institutions. Jewish scientists and academics were expelled from the universities and other scientific establishments. In order to apply to the DFG, scholars now had to present a 'Proof of Aryan Descent', which was supposedly a complete documentation of the 'Aryan' background of their parents and all grandparents.[55] This meant that Jewish scholars were no longer allowed to apply to the DFG. Among them were Berlin anthropologists such as Leonhard Adam[56] (ethnology of law) and Erich von Hornbostel[57] (ethnology of music), as well as other scientists in African studies like the economist Charlotte Leubuscher[58] and the orientalist Eugen Mittwoch.[59] The behavior of the predominantly nationalistic-orientated Africanist scientific community in Germany was almost always passive toward the expulsion of scientists of Jewish ancestry.

The dependence of Africa-related colonial studies on DFG support contributed to their professionalization during the interwar years. In the early 1920s German and Berlin African studies, in particular anthropology, were still dominated by a few 'experts' following their own individual interests. The sub-committee of Ethnology of the DFG was a first step towards a nationwide coordination of Africanist research. Closely linked to the colonial plans of Nazi Germany, a centralized scientific apparatus, housed in Berlin, emerged in the late 1930s within the structures of the DFG – an apparatus which was to direct colonial African studies until 1945.

If someone were to examine African studies in Germany in terms of support lent by the DFG only, they would get the impression that the whole field was working exclusively on a national German project, and that no thought was given to international co-operation and exchange. But it should not be forgotten that prior to 1939 a fairly substantial number of German and Berlin Africanists had also won scholarships from the IIALC in London, and that these scholars were taking part in an international discourse on colonial science. Part of this co-operation arose simply for pragmatic reasons, but Germans were also involved in the general internationalization of the sciences after World War I.

After World War II all hopes for retrieving Germany's colonial possessions in Africa were forever buried. Due to their close involvement with Nazi politics, many German institutions that had conducted research on Africa were shut down, among them the Reichs-forschungsrat and the Kolonialwissenschaftliche Abteilung. On both a national and international level German African studies lost most of their former relevance.

Notes

* *Deutsche Forschungsgemeinschaft* can be translated as 'German Research Council/Society/Foundation'. Because *DFG* is a well-known proper name in the German context, I will use the abbreviation throughout the paper. I want to express my thanks to Christoph Lademann and Sara Pugach for their considerable help with the translation of this article.

1 At the end of the 1920s only about one per cent of Germans took an interest in the 'colonial question', cf. Pogge von Strandmann 2002: 236; also Schröder-Gudehus 1966: 111 ff.; Gothsch 1983: 247 ff.

2 Cf. Adolf von Harnack: 'Memorandum to the German National Assembly', February 1920, cited in Hammerstein 1999: 33.

3 *Afrikanistik* in a stricter sense.

4 It is difficult to give precise figures on the number of members of the German Africanist community in the interwar period. Exclusively Africanist associations whose membership numbers might be consulted did not exist until after the Second World War. Perhaps the number of members (comprising both individuals and institutions) of the International Institute of African Cultures and Languages (IIALC) in London may give a better idea of the size of the African community in Germany. From 1930–38 its numbers varied between fifty-five and sixty-seven, about half of whom were from Berlin (cf. Lists of Members, in: LSE-IAI, 14/3). But in this case, too, it must be taken into account that not all of these members were active as scientists, and only a minority of German Africanists were members of the IIALC.

5 Cf. Schulze 1995: 30 ff. On donations from the Rockefeller Foundation cf. Marsch 1994: 51 ff., 130. In the United States, the anthropologist Franz Boas was heavily engaged in raising funds for the German *Notgemeinschaft* during the early 1920s. Boas was President of the 'Emergency Society for German and Austrian Science and Art' in New York, which collected 50,000 marks from Germans living in the United States. This money was handed over at the foundation celebration of the *Notgemeinschaft* on October 30, 1920. Boas also offered further fund-raising, as well as his support for single scientific projects and help with the distribution of scientific periodicals in the USA (cf. Confidential Information of F. Schmidt-Ott to the members of the General Committee and chairmans of the Sub-Committees, 28.2.1921, in: UH-IAÄ, file Notgemeinschaft – Allgemeines). Through 1922 the New York 'Emergency Society' contributed almost 1.7 million marks (Marsch 1994: 129). See also *Vierter Bericht der Notgemeinschaft der Deutschen Wissenschaft umfassend ihre Tätigkeit vom 1. April 1924 bis zum 31.* Marsch 1994, Wittenberg 1925, p. 15 ff.

6 Cf. Marsch 1994: 76 f. The private status of the *Notgemeinschaft*, combined with largely public funding, came to be accepted as an efficient form of promoting schol-arship, and today the *DFG* still works along these same lines.

7 Cf. Schreiber 1926: 215. On the international relations of German science in post-World War I years cf. Schroeder-Gudehus 1990: 858–885.

8 Cf. § 3 of the statutes of the *Notgemeinschaft der Deutschen Wissenschaft* dated October 30, 1920, in: Zierold 1968: 544.

9 The promotion of individual research was of special significance to the president of the *Notgemeinschaft*, Friedrich Schmidt-Ott, who said that 'The base and the primary aim of its activities must lie in the assistance of the German scholar, and not of institutes or state agencies. And research subsidies for young scientists in

the shape of research scholarships were granted to them directly, not to their academic mentors. . . . It had to be in the *Notgemeinschaft*'s very own interest to produce capable young scientists in the greatest possible number' (Schmidt-Ott 1952: 182).

10 Statutes, cipher 9 (cited in Zierold 1968: 67).

11 Statutes of the Notgemeinschaft, dated 1920, § 5, section 1 (Zierold 1968: 543–547).

12 Verteilung der wissenschaftlichen Fächer auf die Fachausschüsse (draft, October 1920), in: BK, R 73–119.

13 Cf. Zierold 1968: 59. For the election to the sub-committee of Ethnology in 1922 these federations were: the *Association of German Ethnological Museums*, the *German Society for Anthropology, Ethnology, and Pre-History*, the *Professional Association of Pre-Historians*, and the *Union of German Associations of Volkskunde* (cf. BK, R 73–132). For the elections in the spring of 1933, they were the *Professional Association of Pre-Historians*, the *Society for German Pre-History*, and the *German Anthropological Society* (cf. ibid., R 73–133).

14 Thilenius to Schenk (President of the Union of German Universities), 26.11.1920, in: BK, R 73–119.

15 Ibid.

16 Eugen Fischer (1874–1967) was the leading German 'racial' anthropologist in the first half of the twentieth century. At the beginning of his career, Fischer published his major work on the *Rehobother Bastards und das Bastardisierungsproblem beim Menschen* ('The Rehoboth Bastards and the Problem of Bastardization among Humans') (Jena 1913), which was based on field research in the then-colony of German Southwest Africa. In the manuscript, he attempted to prove the feasibility of the Mendelian laws of inheritance among people. Later he came forth with work concerning human genetics and racial hygiene, which were at the time welcomed by racist political movements which gave him the respectfully-meant title of 'Race-Fischer.' In 1927 Fischer became a professor of physical anthropology at Berlin University. Concurrently, he took over the directorship of the 'Kaiser-Wilhelm Institute for Physical Anthropology, Human Genetics, and Eugenics' in Berlin. During the Third Reich he advanced to become the most significant racial biologist, who was, despite sometimes disagreeing with parts of the Nazi leadership, active in the implementation of Nazi racial laws (cf. Roller 2002: 132 f.). After completing the *Rehobother Bastards*, Fischer conducted no further studies on sub-Saharan Africa. On Fischer's role in eugenics and race anthropology, see Lösch 1997.

17 Circular from Schmidt-Ott to the members of the main board, 1.10.1925, in: BK, R 73–120.

18 Circular from Schmidt-Ott to the members of the main board, 6.7.1926, in: ibid.

19 On the membership of the sub-committees cf. the yearly *Berichte der Notgemeinschaft der Deutschen Wissenschaft (Deutsche Forschungsgemeinschaft)*, 1922–33. Cf. also Schmidt-Ott to Meinhof, 21.1.1921, in: UH-IAÄ, file Notgemeinschaft – Allgemeines. Thilenius' simultaneous membership of the evaluating sub-committee after 1926 as well as the main board which decided on the applications was a clear breach of a resolution once taken by the *Notgemeinschaft*'s main board itself (cf. ibid., circular from Schmidt-Ott, 29.11.1920).

20 When it came to the election of referees, Meinhof always nominated in the field of 'Native Languages' his own pupils and friendly colleagues as electors: in 1922 Maria von Tiling, August Klingenheben (both assistants of Meinhof at the Seminar for African and South Sea Languages of the university of Hamburg), and the missionary Karl Röhl, who since the early 1920s had worked on a Swahili translation of the Bible on behalf of the Berlin, Leipzig, and Bethel missionary societies. In 1933 Meinhof nominated Maria Klingenheben (née von Tiling), Walter Aichele (assistant to Meinhof in Hamburg), the Neuendettelsau missionary Christian Keysser (an expert on the Kate language and ethnology of New Guinea), and Erwin Stresemann from the institute for Zoology at Berlin University (cf. BK, R 73–123, 135).

21 The private papers of the *DFG* 1920–1945 held at the Bundesarchiv Koblenz contain 6,882 files with applications from across the disciplines (cf. BK, R 73, finding aid). Every file contains the documents of one applicant. In a few cases several files belonged to one applicant. Up to now there has been no comprehensive overview of all the applications within this collection. Since quite a number of scholars applied for several projects, I estimate that at least 7,000 applications were handed in to the *Notgemeinschaft/DFG* between 1920 and 1945.

22 Besides former colonial officials, directors of missionary societies and government officials, some scientists also attended the Colonial Congress. Carl Meinhof, for instance, gave a lecture on 'The actual state of research in African linguistics' (cf. BB, R 1001–7009).

23 Cf. Pogge von Strandmann 2002: 234 f. For colonial revisionism in Germany see e.g. Schmokel 1967; Hildebrandt 1969; Pogge von Strandmann 1986: 90–119; Rüger 1986: 297–336; Gründer 1999: 312–357.

24 Bruno Kuske to the presidium of DFG, 4.11.1930, in: BB, R 1501–126774.

25 On skeptical attitudes towards colonialism in the Weimar Republic cf. the opinion poll *Soll Deutschland Kolonialpolitik treiben? Eine Umfrage*, 1927. The opinion poll was organized by the 'Institute for Foreign Politics' in Hamburg in the context of Germany's admission into the League of Nations' Mandatory Commission on 6 July 1927, and of the revived colonial discussion caused by this admission. Nearly 200 representatives of German public opinion (politicians, members of parliament, scholars, writers, newspaper editors, former colonial governors etc.) were asked three questions: Should Germany attempt to have colonies, and if so, should they be administered as mandatory territories, or should Germany restrict herself to gaining equal rights of access to the colonies of other powers? Only two Africanist scholars were among the people interviewed: the Frankfurt cultural morphologist Leo Frobenius (1873–1938), and the director of the World Economic Archives in Hamburg, Franz Stuhlmann (1863–1928), whose answers, however, were not published (cf. BB, R 1001–4608, p. 12). The Berlin economist Moritz Julius Bonn (1873–1965) said with regard to the post-World War I situation that it could not be Germany's mission to 'support an already dying system with her insufficient means; she had rather be the spokesman of those peoples threatened by colonialisation and that she ought, as the leader of the nations without colonies, to do her best to help along a smooth transition from the Colonial age into the age of Counter-Colonialisation' (Europäische Gespräche, V, 1927, H. 12, p. 617). In this context Bonn was to introduce the term of 'de-colonialisation' into the political debate (Bonn 1926: 24).

26 E.g., August Klingenheben obtained 2,000 marks for linguistic research in Western Africa (BB, R 1501–126775). In 1934 Meinhof made it a condition that his assistant Paul Berger was to join the expedition as a linguist before he agreed to support the application for a field expedition handed in by the anthropologist Ludwig Kohl-Larsen (BK, R 73–118). For Meinhof's own travel to Eastern and South Africa in 1927/28 the *Notgemeinschaft* granted him 9,000 marks (BB, R 1501–126775).

27 After the outbreak of World War I, Meinhof refused to continue carrying his title of Doctor of Laws h.c., LL.D., obtained from Edinburgh University in 1910, and deeply resented Westermann's 'anglomania' (oral communication, 1998, with Ernst Dammann, a pupil and close assistant of Meinhof; cf. Dammann 1999: 29, 99 ff.).

28 An application for 'Research on the language of the Fante tribe of the Gold Coast' in 1933 and for a research scholarship for Günter Tessmann for the work on a 'Manual for Practical Ethnology' (cf. UH-IAÄ, file Briefjournal Notgemeinschaft der deutschen Wissenschaft – Prof. Meinhof).

29 Cf. Gothsch 1983: 210; Fischer 1990: 104 ff.; Stoecker 2001. For the case of Alfred Schachtzabel, a leading anthropologist at the Berlin Ethnological Museum, see Heintze 1995: 15–21.

30 Cf. UH-IAÄ, file Briefjournal Notgemeinschaft der deutschen Wissenschaft – Prof. Meinhof.

31 Cf. ibid.

32 Cf. ibid. Ever since 1925, Thurnwald had found himself in a rather insecure and badly paid position as an extraordinary professor for Ethnology and Psychology of People at the university in Berlin. He probably expected to gain an advancement in his university position from this expedition to Eastern Africa – his first African project (cf. Correspondence between Thurnwald and the Prussian Ministry of Culture, June/July 1929, in Geheimes Staatsarchiv Preußischer Kulturbesitz Berlin, I. HA Rep. 76 Va Sektion II Titel IV, Nr. 51, p. 180 ff.). His promotion, however, did not go through until after World War II. For the expedition, on which he was accompanied by his wife Hilde, the IIALC granted £ 1.000 out of means provided by the Carnegie Corporation (cf. Documents presented to the Seventh Meeting of the Executive Council, 28./29.11.1929, in: LSE-IAI, 1/12). The *Notgemeinschaft* granted a reduced assistance of 4.000 marks, after Westermann had, as the German IIALC representative, strongly advocated future co-operation between the IIALC and the *Notgemeinschaft* (cf. BB, R 1501–126778). To my knowledge this was to remain the only instance of a co-operation between the *Notgemeinschaft/DFG* and the IIALC. As the result of the expedition, Richard Thurnwald published – with the help of the IIALC – *Black and White in East Africa* (Thurnwald and Thurnwald 1935), while Hilde Thurnwald produced *Die schwarze Frau im Wandel Afrikas* (Thurnwald 1935).

33 Cf. UH-IAÄ, file Briefjournal Notgemeinschaft der deutschen Wissenschaft – Prof. Meinhof.

34 This suggested academisation of German African studies may be confirmed by the fact that the younger German members of the IIALC were (with very few exceptions) all in possession of a university degree (cf. Lists of Members, in: LSE-IAI, 14/3).

35 For instance, linguist Hans J. Melzian, who travelled to Southern Nigeria in 1937 for language studies, received a standard-film camera (cf. BK, R 73–13057). The application of the young Berlin ethnologist Gulla Pfeffer, on the other hand, who went on a field trip to Cameroon together with the expedition film-maker Friedrich Dalsheim in 1928, was rejected (cf. BK, R 73–109).

36 Expedition film-makers acted almost like free entrepreneurs on a commercial cultural market. This could not be reconciled with the assistance statutes of the *DFG*. On Hans Schomburgk cf. Waz 1997, Oksiloff 2001: 85–92.

37 In comparison: As a regular university professor Westermann had in 1934 an annual income of 11,600 marks without additional perks (cf. BB, R 21–10.022, p. 10403). In present day currency, one Reichsmark would equal 10 Euro.

38 Cf. UH-IAÄ, file Briefjournal Notgemeinschaft der deutschen Wissenschaft – Prof. Meinhof. The results of this project were Schober 1937 and Werder 1938.

39 Mertens 1997: 202 ff. The reports are now kept at the Hoover Institution Archives, Stanford/USA. Among the 1,140 candidates on whom reports were made were four young Africanists: Johannes Lukas (Hamburg 1935), Erwin Mai (Berlin 1934), Reinhold Schober (Berlin 1936), and Peter von Werder (Berlin 1935). The four were judged to be worthy of assistance by the *NSD-Dozentenbund* (NSDAP-lecturers' union) and by their scientific mentors (cf. Hoover Institution Archives, Collection: Germany Forschungsgemeinschaft, Box 3, Fo 6883; Box 4, Fo 5550; Box 5, Sch/1/03/2; Box 6, Fo 6364).

40 Meyer to the President of the Reichsforschungsrat, General Karl Becker, beginning of 1939, cited in Hammerstein 1999: 217.

41 Bernhard Struck (1888–1971), anthropologist and linguist, worked from 1913 to 1933 at the Ethnological Museum in Dresden, and from then until 1953 as a professor for Ethnology at the University of Jena. He was also a founding member of the IIALC and of its Executive Council 1926–1933.

42 Günter Wolff: Reichsforschungsrat und Kolonialforschung, internal memo, 31.3.1941, in: BB, R 1001–8687/1, p. 161.

43 The *KWA* received 700,000 marks from the *Reichsforschungsrat* in the fiscal year 1941/42 alone (cf. Kolonialpolitisches Amt der NSDAP. Tätigkeitsbericht der Reichsleitung vom 1.7.1942, in: BB, NS 26–266).
44 Cf. ibid., pp. 156–158.
45 Cf. BK, R 73–15646. For the Ewe dictionary Westermann was granted a last allocation of 1,500 marks on April 9, 1945. The revision was published after the Nazi period as *Wörterbuch der Ewe-Sprache* (Westermann 1954).
46 Zechlin looked after research projects on the history of the German protectorates at the Reich Archives in Potsdam (cf. BK, R 73–15918).
47 Cf. BK, R 73–14191; Heintze 1995: 14.
48 Cf. Protocol of the first conference of the sub-committee for Colonial Language research of the *Reichsforschungsrat* March 7, 1941, 24.3.1941, in: BB, R 1001–8687/1, p. 205.
49 Wolff to the President of the DFG Rudolf Mentzel, 15.3.1941, in: BK, R 73–15646.
50 Cf. Mai 1999: 147–56; Letter from the OKW of 25.1.1941, in: UH-IAÄ, Afr (S) D(x), cited in Bechhaus-Gerst 1997: 30.
51 Hanns Vischer to Lord Lugard, 22.8.1941, in: LSE-IAI, 42/65; *Das Vertrauen der Kolonialvölker. Die Leibniz-Sitzung der Preußischen Akademie der Wissenschaften*, in Frankfurter Zeitung, 5.7.1941. With the term 'half-apes', Vischer alluded to a degrading statement of Hitler's, one that he had used in Mein Kampf to suggest that Africans were 'half-apes' who did not deserve to be educated or otherwise uplifted by Europeans.
52 There were plans to found the European Colonial Academy during the First European Colonial Scientific Conference in Berlin in July 1942 (cf. List of invitations, in: BB, R 4901–2882, pp. 37–67.
53 Cf. report on the visit of Labouret in Germany, 26.2.1942, in: BB, R 4901–3101, p. 62; cf. the invitation to Reteaud in: BK, R 73–13926.
54 It was feared that this might upset the Italian allies, who had their own plans to found an international Colonial Academy (BB, R 4901–3101, p. 94).
55 Mertens (1997: 208 ff.) gives some impressive examples for marking off of Jewish scientists from *DFG*-subsidies. See also Hammerstein 1999: 91; Mertens 1999: 64.
56 Leonhard Adam (1891–1969), legal ethnologist, since 1917 editor of the '*Zeitschrift für vergleichende Rechtswissenschaft einschließlich der ethnologischen Rechtsforschung*'. In 1933 Adam was forced into retirement for racial reasons. His application to the *DFG* for the contribution for the printing of his periodical, which before had been granted year after year, was rejected in 1935 on grounds that the candidate was a 'half-Jew' (cf. BK, R 73–15987). In 1938 Adam emigrated to England, and later to Australia.
57 Erich Moritz von Hornbostel (1877–1935), music ethnologist, since 1905 head of the Berlin Phonogramme Archives, in 1933 emigration to England, professor at the New School for Social Research in New York (cf. Klotz (ed.) 1998).
58 Charlotte Leubuscher (1888–1961), political economist, from 1929 professor extraordinary at Berlin University. At first the *Notgemeinschaft* rejected a request to assist her fieldwork in South Africa on the grounds that there were doubts about her qualifications. It was only after the Reichstag deputy Marie Lüders, who was very active in women's rights, exerted strong political pressure, that the *Notgemeinschaft* agreed to pay a fraction of the estimated costs (cf. BK, R 73–108; BB, R 1501–126777). In 1931 Leubuscher published her research results in the monograph *Der südafrikanische Eingeborene als Industriearbeiter und als Stadtbewohner* ('The South African Native as Industrial Worker and City Dweller') (Leubuscher 1931). In 1933 she emigrated to England and worked at Girton College, Cambridge. She worked with Margery Perham, among others, and was a co-author of Lord Hailey's *An African survey; a study of problems arising in Africa south of the Sahara* (Hailey 1938).
59 Eugen Mittwoch (1876–1942), orientalist and expert on Ethiopian languages, 1920–33 director of the Seminar for Oriental Languages in Berlin, 1935 emigration

to England. Mittwoch was the only German who was involved in the activities of the IIALC during the war (cf. Minutes of a Special Meeting of the Linguistic Advisory Committee held on 16th December 1941, in: LSE-IAI, 6/1).

References

Aly, Götz and Heim, Susanne. 1993. *Vordenker der Vernichtung: Auschwitz und die deutschen Pläne für eine europäische Ordnung*. Frankfurt am Main: Fischer Taschenbuch.

Bechhaus-Gerst, Marianne. 1997. 'Afrikaner in Deutschland 1933–1945'. *1999. Zeitschrift für Sozialgeschichte des 20. und 21. Jahrhunderts* 4:10–31.

Berichte der Notgemeinschaft der Deutschen Wissenschaft (Deutsche Forschungsgemeinschaft) über ihre Tätigkeit, 1, 1922 to 12, 1933. Wittenberg: Herrosé & Ziemsen.

Bonn, Moritz J. 1926. *Das Schicksal des deutschen Kapitalismus*. Berlin: S. Fischer.

Dammann, Ernst. 1999. *70 Jahre erlebte Afrikanistik: ein Beitrag zur Wissenschaftsgeschichte*. Berlin: D. Reimer.

'Das Vertrauen der Kolonialvölker. *Die Leibniz-Sitzung der Preußischen Akademie der Wissenschaften*', in Frankfurter Zeitung, Reichsausgabe, 5.7.1941.

Fischer, Eugen. 1913. *Rehobother Bastards und das Bastardisierungsproblem beim Menschen*. Jena: Fischer.

Fischer, Hans. 1990. *Völkerkunde im Nationalsozialismus. Aspekte der Anpassung, Affinität und Behauptung einer wissenschaftlichen Disziplin*. Berlin/Hamburg: D. Reimer.

Fischer, Wolfram, Hohlfeld, Rainer and Nötzold, Peter. 2000. 'Die Berliner Akademie in Republik und Diktatur'. In F. Wolfram, R. Hohlfeld and P. Nötzold (eds). *Die Preußische Akademie der Wissenschaften zu Berlin 1914–1945*. Berlin: Akademie Verlag, pp. 517–566.

Gothsch, Manfred. 1983. *Die deutsche Völkerkunde und ihr Verhältnis zum Kolonialismus: ein Beitrag zur kolonialideologischen und kolonialpraktischen Bedeutung der deutschen Völkerkunde in der Zeit von 1870 bis 1975*. Baden-Baden: Nomos.

Gründer, Horst. 1999. '. . . da und dort ein junges Deutschland gründen': Rassismus, Kolonien und kolonialer Gedanke vom 16. bis zum 20. Jahrhundert*. München: Deutscher Taschenbuch Verlag.

Hailey, William Malcolm. 1938. *An African Survey: A Study of Problems Arising in Africa South of the Sahara*. London: Oxford University Press.

Hammerstein, Notker. 1999. *Die deutsche Forschungsgemeinschaft in der Weimarer Republik und im Dritten Reich 1920–1945*. München: C.H. Beck.

Heintze, Beatrix. 1995. *Alfred Schachtzabels Reise nach Angola 1913–1914 und seine Sammlungen für das Museum für Völkerkunde in Berlin*. Köln: R. Köppe.

Hildebrandt, Klaus. 1969. *Vom Reich zum Weltreich. Hitler, NSDAP und koloniale Frage 1919–1945*. München: W. Fink.

Klotz, Sebastian (ed.). 1998. *'Vom tönenden Wirbel menschlichen Tuns': Erich M. von Hornbostel als Gestaltpsychologe, Archivar und Musikwissenschaftler; Studien und Dokumente*. Berlin: Schibri.

Lakowski, Richard. 1986. 'The Second World War'. In Helmuth Stoecker (ed.). 1986. *German Imperialism in Africa: From the Beginning until the Second World War*. London: C. Hurst, pp. 379–418.

Leubuscher, Charlotte. 1931. *Der südafrikanische Eingeborene als Industriearbeiter und als Stadtbewohner; mit einem einleitenden Überblick über die afrikanische Eingeborenenfrage im allgemeinen*. Jena: G. Fischer.

Lösch, Niels C. 1997. *Rasse als Konstrukt. Leben und Werk Eugen Fischers*. Frankfurt am Main: Lang.

Mai, Uwe. 1999. *Kriegsgefangen in Brandenburg: Stalag III A in Luckenwalde 1939–1945*. Berlin: Metropol.

Marsch, Ulrich. 1994. *Notgemeinschaft der Deutschen Wissenschaft. Gründung und frühe Geschichte 1920–1925*. Frankfurt am Main: Lang.

Meinhof, Carl. 1928. 'Die Erforschung schriftloser Sprachen', *Deutsche Forschung. Aus der Arbeit der Notgemeinschaft der Deutschen Wissenschaft (Deutsche Forschungsgemeinschaft)*, Heft 5: *Völkerzusammenhänge und Ausgrabungen*: 122–133.

Mertens, Lothar. 1996. 'Forschungsförderung im Dritten Reich'. *Zeitschrift für Geschichtswissenschaft* 44:119–126.

Mertens, Lothar. 1997. 'Der 'neue Geist' an den deutschen Hochschulen 1934–1936. Gutachten und Stellungnahmen über Stipendiumsanwärter der DFG'. In *Jahrbuch für Antisemitismusforschung*, vol. 6. Frankfurt am Main/New York: Campus, pp. 203–217.

Mertens, Lothar. 1999. 'Die Forschungsförderung der DFG im Dritten Reich 1933–1937'. In *Jahrbuch für Universitätsgeschichte*, vol. 2. Stuttgart: F. Steiner, pp. 58–74.

Mertens, Lothar. 2001. 'Das Führerprinzip in der Forschungsförderung. Der politische Einfluss auf die Notgemeinschaft der deutschen Wissenschaft/Deutsche Forschungsgemeinschaft im Dritten Reich 1933–1937'. In L. Mertens (ed.). *Politischer Systemumbruch als irreversibler Faktor von Modernisierung in der Wissenschaft?* Berlin: Duncker & Humblot, pp. 33–72.

Mertens, Lothar. 2002. 'Einige Anmerkungen zur NS-Wissenschafts- und Forschungspolitik'. In Rüdiger vom Bruch and Brigitte Kaderas (eds). *Wissenschaften und Wissenschaftspolitik. Bestandsaufnahmen zu Formationen, Brüchen und Kontinuitäten im Deutschland des 20. Jahrhunderts*. Stuttgart: F. Steiner, pp. 225–240.

Mischek, Udo. 1996. 'Der Funktionalismus und die nationalsozialistische Kolonialpolitik in Afrika: Günter Wagner und Diedrich Westermann'. *Paideuma* 42:141–150.

Mischek, Udo. 2000a. 'Autorität außerhalb des Fachs: Diedrich Westermann und Eugen Fischer'. In B. Streck (ed.) *Ethnologie und Nationalsozialismus*. Gehren: Escher, pp. 69–83.

Mischek, Udo. 2000b. 'Der Weg zu einer Planungs- und Verfügungswissenschaft für den kolonialen Raum'. In B. Streck (ed.) *Ethnologie und Nationalsozialismus*. Gehren: Escher, pp. 129–147.

Mosen, Markus. 1991. *Der koloniale Traum: Angewandte Ethnologie im Nationalsozialismus*. Bonn: Holos.

Oexle, Otto Gerhard. 1999. 'Die Fragen der Emigranten'. In W. Schulze and O.G. Oexle (eds). *Deutsche Historiker im Nationalsozialismus*. Frankfurt am Main: Fischer Taschenbuch, pp. 51–62.

Oksiloff, Ossenka. 2001. *Picturing the Primitive: Visual Culture, Ethnography, and Early German Cinema*. New York: Palgrave.

Pogge von Strandmann, Hartmut. 1986. 'Imperialism and Revisionism in Interwar Germany'. In W.J. Mommsen and J. Osterhammel (eds). *Imperialism and After: Continuities and Discontinuities*. London/Boston: Allen & Unwin, pp. 90–119.

Pogge von Strandmann, Hartmut. 2002. '"Deutsches Land in fremder Hand" – Der Kolonialrevisionismus'. In Ulrich van der Heyden and Joachim Zeller (eds). 2002. *Kolonialmetropole Berlin: eine Spurensuche*. Berlin: Berlin Edition. pp. 232–239.

Roller, Kathrin. 2002. 'Der Rassenbiologe Eugen Fischer'. In Ulrich van der Heyden and Joachim Zeller (eds). 2002. *Kolonialmetropole Berlin: eine Spurensuche*. Berlin: Berlin Edition, pp. 130–133.

Rössler, Mechthild. 1990. *Wissenschaft und Lebensraum: geographische Ostforschung im Nationalsozialismus: ein Beitrag zur Disziplingeschichte der Geographie*. Berlin: D. Reimer.

Rüger, Adolf. 1986. 'The Colonial Aims of the Weimar Republik'. In Helmuth Stoecker (ed.). 1986. *German Imperialism in Africa: From the Beginning until the Second World War*. London: C. Hurst pp. 297–336.

Rüger, Adolf. 1995. 'Richtlinien und Richtungen deutscher Kolonialpolitik 1923–1926'. In P. Heine and Ulrich van der Heyden (eds). *Studien zur Geschichte des deutschen Kolonialismus in Afrika. Festschrift zum 60. Geburtstag von Peter Sebald*. Pfaffenweiler: Centaurus, pp. 453–465.

Schmidt-Ott, Friedrich. 1952. *Erlebtes und Erstrebtes 1860–1950*. Wiesbaden: F. Steiner.

Schmokel, Wolfe W. 1967. *Der Traum vom Reich: Der deutsche Kolonialismus zwischen 1919 und 1945*. Gütersloh: Sigbert Mohn.

Schober, Reinhold. 1937. *Kamerun. Neuzeitliche Verwaltungsprobleme einer tropischen Kolonie*. Berlin: E.S. Mittler & Sohn.

Schreiber, Georg. 1926. *Deutsches Reich und deutsche Medizin*. Leipzig: J.A. Barth.

Schröder-Gudehus, Brigitte. 1966. *Deutsche Wissenschaft und internationale Zusammenarbeit 1914–1928. Ein Beitrag zum Studium kultureller Beziehungen in Krisenzeiten*. Genève: Impr. Dumaret & Golay.

Schroeder-Gudehus, Brigitte. 1990. 'Internationale Wissenschaftsbeziehungen und auswärtige Kulturpolitik 1919–1933. Vom Boykott und Gegen-Boykott zu ihrer Wiederaufnahme'. In R. Vierhaus and B. vom Brocke (eds). *Forschung im Spannungsfeld von Politik und Gesellschaft: Geschichte und Struktur der Kaiser-Wilhelm-/Max-Planck-Gesellschaft*. Stuttgart: Deutsche Verlags-Anstalt, pp. 858–885.

Schulze, Wilfried. 1995. *Der Stifterverband für die Deutsche Wissenschaft 1920–1995*. Berlin: Akademie Verlag.

'Soll Deutschland Kolonialpolitik treiben? Eine Umfrage'. *Europäische Gespräche. Hamburger Monatshefte für Auswärtige Politik*, V, 1927, H. 12:609–676.

Stoecker, Holger. 2001. '"Was all the Work in Vain?" Two Responses to the German Question after the First World War'. Unpublished paper delivered at conference 'Czekanowski and his contemporaries. German and Polish research on Africa, 1900–1950,' Leipzig, 26–27 October 2001.

Stoecker, Holger. 2002. 'Das Seminar für Orientalische Sprachen'. In Ulrich van der Heyden and Joachim Zeller (eds). *Kolonialmetropole Berlin*. Berlin: Berlin Edition, pp. 115–122.

Streck, Bernhard. 2000. 'Einführung'. In B. Streck (ed.). *Ethnologie und Nationalsozialismus*. Gehren: Escher, pp. 7–21.

Tessmann, Günther. 1934. *Die Bafia und die Kultur der Mittelkamerun-Bantu*. Stuttgart: Strecker und Schröder.

Thilenius, Georg. 1930. 'Völkerkunde'. In G. Abb (ed.). *Aus fünfzig Jahren Deutscher Wissenschaft. Festschrift für Friedrich Schmidt-Ott*. Berlin: W. de Gruyter, pp. 384–399.

Thurnwald, Hilde. 1935. *Die schwarze Frau im Wandel Afrikas; eine soziologische Studie unter ostafrikanischen Stämmen*. Stuttgart: W. Kohlhammer.

Thurnwald, Richard and Thurnwald, Hilde. 1935. *Black and White in East Africa. The Fabric of a New Civilization: A Study in Social Contact and Adaptation of Life in East Africa*. London: G. Routledge & Sons.

Waz, Gerlinde. 1997. 'Auf der Suche nach dem letzten Paradies: der Afrikaforscher und Regisseur Hans Schomburgk'. In J. Schöning (ed.). *Triviale Tropen: Exotische Reise- und Abenteuerfilme aus Deutschland 1919–1939*. München: Text + Kritik, pp. 95–109.

Werder, Peter von. 1938. *Staatsgefüge in Westafrika: eine ethnosoziologische Untersuchung über Hochformen der sozialen und staatlichen Organisation im Westsudan*. Stuttgart: F. Enke.

Westermann, Diedrich. 1942. 'Sprachen- und Völkerforschung als koloniale Aufgabe. Festvortrag auf der öffentlichen Sitzung zur Feier des Leibniztages am 3. Juli 1941'. In *Jahrbuch der Preußischen Akademie der Wissenschaften*, vol. 3. Berlin: Akademie der Wissenschaften, pp. 234–246.

Westermann, Diedrich. 1954. *Wörterbuch der Ewe-Sprache*. Berlin: Akademie-Verlag.

Wolff, Günter. 1941. 'Reichsforschungsrat und Kolonialforschung'. *Afrika-Rundschau* 7, H. 8:1–4.

Zierold, Kurt. 1968. *Forschungsförderung in drei Epochen. Deutsche Forschungsgemeinschaft. Geschichte – Arbeitsweise – Kommentar*. Wiesbaden: F. Steiner.

Zimmerman, Andrew. 2001. *Anthropology and Antihumanism in Imperial Germany*. Chicago: University of Chicago Press.

Abbreviations

BB	Bundesarchiv Berlin
BK	Bundesarchiv Koblenz
LSE-IAI	London School of Economics, Library, International African Institute Manuscript Collection (formerly International Institute for African Languages and Cultures, IIALC)
UH-IAÄ	Universität Hamburg, Institut für Afrikanistik und Athiopistik, Archives (recently transferred to Staatsarchiv Hamburg)

CHAPTER THREE

Internationalization and 'scientific nationalism': the International Institute of African Languages and Cultures between the wars

Benoît de L'Estoile

I would ask that the programmes of study for each colony be presented by the English as regards English territories, by the French regarding French territories, and so forth for Italian, Belgian and Portuguese colonies. These national propositions would then be integrated in the international frame of the Institute. (Professor De Jonghe 1933)[1]

In June 1926 an international conference in London officially founded the International Institute of African Languages and Cultures (IIALC).[2] Its chairman was British (the colonial pundit Lord Lugard), while its two directors, Maurice Delafosse and Dietrich Westermann, were respectively French and German, and its General Secretary Swiss (Hanns Vischer). This line-up was to advertise clearly, a few years after the end of the Great War, the international flavor of an institution that was meant to be 'a *coordinating agency*, a central bureau and a clearing-house for information' (Lugard 1928: 3) between all those interested in Africa. Indeed the IIALC's journal, *Africa*, published from 1928, included articles in three languages (English, French, German), and swiftly established itself as a leading international forum for African studies.[3]

In this chapter, I argue that the IIALC offers a privileged opportunity to look at the tension between the drives of international cooperation and 'scientific nationalism'. I try to account for two things: first, the IIALC's failure to create an international consensus on how to approach African cultures and societies, as idealized by scientific internationalism; and, second, the fact that national (and imperial) boundaries also constituted epistemological boundaries, as strikingly formulated in 1933 by professor De Jonghe, a former magistrate in the

Belgian Congo, in the opening quotation. My particular focus is the growing divergence within the IIALC between anthropological research programs developed by the French and those developed by the British.

One can sum up briefly the contrasting developments within anthropology in France and Britain in the interwar period as follows. The dominant features of the British scene included a revolution in the division of labor, which increasingly required theoretical training and intensive fieldwork for anthropological qualification, and the redefinition of anthropology as 'social anthropology', mainly focused on the social institutions in native societies. Knowledge of African societies and cultures largely became the monopoly of what was being asserted as an academic discipline, social anthropology, which increasingly excluded both colonial residents and educated Africans. In France, by contrast, the dominant effort in the 1930s was to build up, through the creation of a network of local correspondents, scientific societies and local centers, a highly integrated structure for research, culminating in the new Museum of Man (Musée de l'Homme), inaugurated in 1937. The emphasis on the collection of 'data' (including artifacts) – the accumulation of which would progressively furnish the basis for later 'synthesis' – implied mobilizing vast numbers of 'collaborators', amateur ethnographers, colonial administrators and educated Africans, working together to collectively produce an ethnographic encyclopedia of the continent.

I cannot dwell here at length on the central issue of the links between the framing of colonial policy and the production of knowledge on subaltern groups, which I have addressed elsewhere (L'Estoile 1997a, 2004, 2005a,b), but these are certainly crucial for explaining the striking differences between French and British developments, of which I can here just offer a brief outline. In France in the 1930s, a new conception of a plurality of cultures within a common mankind challenged universalist and evolutionist assumptions that underlined the previously hegemonic assimilationist ideal, and tended to shape both the colonial and ethnological agendas. The will to display 'races, that are not unequal, but different' thus was a motto that ran from the 1931 Paris Colonial Exhibition to the founding of the Musée de l'Homme in 1937. At the same time, a number of colonial officials appeared ready to support the establishment of a distinctively French school of 'ethnologie', not least because of a need to demonstrate, in a context of international competition, that France was not falling behind other colonial powers in this respect (L'Estoile 2005b). In Britain, social anthropology offered a language for a redefinition in cultural terms of Indirect Rule, a political philosophy that from the 1920s onwards set the tone for most British colonial administrations. Concern about what was perceived as the growing disintegration of African societies, especially in Southern and East Africa, became a central issue among colonial reformers, thus fostering an interest in understanding the changes happening in Africa, in order to control them better. Social anthropologists around Bronislaw Malinowski played an active part in the 1930s in the reformulation of colonial policy in terms of social development that led to the passing of the Colonial Development and Welfare Act of 1940 (L'Estoile 1997a; L'Estoile 2004). The Colonial Office actively supported social anthropology's increasing autonomy in relation to the old inclusive Science of Man, in the hope that it would help to clarify colonial problems (L'Estoile 2004: Chapter 10).

Examining the discussions within the IIALC allows one to understand how a number of issues were framed differently in various national contexts. Should, for instance, the production of knowledge about African societies and cultures rely on a network of experienced colonials, or on academically trained specialists? Were Africans to be only passive 'objects' for study, or would they be granted an active role in the process of knowing? What should be the focus of study: the recording of a rapidly disappearing past, or the study of the dramatic changes happening in Africa?

The interests in internationalization

Reflecting back on the work of the Institute at the start of a new European war, Sir Hanns Vischer,[4] General Secretary of the Institute, affirmed his belief in its 'international spirit' in a letter to its chairman, who was also an old friend, Lord Lugard:

> The international character of our work has been brought about and maintained with the idea that we wanted to work for all Africans, whatever nation happened to be in charge of them at the present moment and that we considered that the African problems could only be solved satisfactorily by loyal co-operation between the responsible European people as far as that can be possible at the present time ... We have been able to achieve international co-operation much more sincere and effective than any of the great international institutions about which we hear so much.[5]

The creation of the IIALC was indeed symptomatic of, and contributed to, the internationalization of the colonial debate in the interwar period.[6] One of the driving forces behind its creation was the attempt by influential American and British missionaries to build up an international network that would reinforce their position in their increasingly complex dealings with the various colonial powers in Africa, especially in the area of education, which had for a time been left almost entirely in the hands of missionaries, and where colonial powers were becoming increasingly active (Hetherington 1978). In fact, internationalization can be seen as a strategy that allowed individuals to overcome local situations of weakness by mobilizing outside networks.[7] The very creation of a body dedicated to furthering knowledge of African languages and cultures was also tightly linked to a widespread belief that a scientific approach to African problems would allow both missionaries and officials to master a shifting colonial ground and to overcome in a peaceful way conflicts between various stakeholders in African matters, especially between rival colonial powers.[8] In that sense, the IIALC partook of the 'Geneva spirit', a belief in international co-operation as a contribution to peace that was also prominent in the creation of a host of other international organizations such as the International Labour Organization.[9]

An additional factor leading up to calls to international co-operation was a growing concern about 'native reactions' against White Rule. Thus at the IIALC Conference during the 1931 Colonial Exhibition, the French Colonel Derendinger, a member of the Executive Council, stressed the political emergency of a European unified front, in the face of native claims, arguing that 'its [the IIALC] international title reminds governments that . . . they must stick together in front of the formidable social movements in preparation in Africa, and must look together for the formulas that will allow for a healthy and reasonable evolution of African populations towards welfare.'[10]

The IIALC began to emerge from 1924 on as a 'network of networks', bringing together a number of formerly weakly connected networks. The initial nucleus was Protestant missionaries organized within the International Missionary Council, whose secretary was the missionary diplomat Joseph Oldham.[11] These had linked up with British educationalists through the Advisory Committee on Education in Tropical Africa, a 'think tank' set up in 1923 largely through Oldham that was to define British educational policy (Oldham 1925); they also succeeded in attracting Catholic missionary societies (through the creation in 1926 of the Conference of Catholic Missions in Africa), American philanthropists, and academics based in museums and universities, including leading European scholars in African studies such as Maurice Delafosse, Dietrich Westermann, Lucien Lévy-Bruhl, Pater Schmidt, Paul Schebesta, Rev. Edwin W. Smith and Charles Seligman.

The very success of a body like the IIALC may indeed be taken as evidence of an 'interest to internationalization', that emerged simultaneously in various spheres, from missionaries to academics to colonial reformers, to which it promised to offer new resources and opportunities. However, internationalization was by no means a self-evident process. In 1929 Vischer warned of two dangers that threatened the international character of the Institute:

> One is the national susceptibilities of our members, which show up constantly in letters I receive . . . [T]he other matter is the fact that our work appeals most to people in this country [Britain], and in the British territories.[12]

Both these 'dangers' would remain prominent in the Institute's history during the interwar years, especially within the context of competition between the various powers in Africa, both in metropolitan and colonial fields.[13]

In fact, Britain and its colonies provided the bulk of the members of the Institute, and British colonial governments were those that contributed most to its funding. However some Colonial Office officials were reluctant to have 'foreigners' (including, for Britain, citizens of British Dominions) sent to their possessions, as is apparent in their comments about the fieldworkers sent to Africa under the Five-year plan of research:

> The above 3 foreigners [Nadel, Fortes, Hofstra] are those who are immediately ripe, for work in West Africa, but I am glad to hear from Dr Oldham that he also got a young ENGLISHMAN in view, namely Mr Godfrey Wilson.[14]

The 1930s saw increasing international tension in Europe, with Germany claiming back its former colonies and Italy engaging in an aggressive imperialist policy, reinforcing the discourse of national exclusiveness. In 1937, the Executive Council thus pondered 'whether in the present state of political tension an already complex problem should be complicated by introducing into a territory an investigator of a different nationality, and with a different cultural approach from that of the governing power'.[15] These constraints reflected international colonial rivalries. But disagreement also arose in defining the scientific program of the Institute.

Labouret's 'network method' in anthropology

Originally the Institute was concerned largely with language and education issues, but it gradually shifted its emphasis to the study of native 'cultures' and institutions, which its proponents argued were essential 'moral bonds' for African societies. The Institute's program for ethnology was initially hazy. The prominent French Africanist Maurice Delafosse, an ardent proponent of a 'native policy' (*politique indigène*) based on a careful study of native institutions and 'civilizations', was initially in charge of the ethnological program of the Institute. His death at the end of 1926 was regarded as a severe blow by the Institute; he was replaced as a Director by Henri Labouret, a former army officer and administrator in West Africa, where he had done some linguistic and ethnographic work. Labouret, then an official at the Political Affairs Section of the Ministry of Colonies, also replaced Delafosse in his teaching positions at the Ecole Coloniale (which trained colonial administrators), the Ecole des Langues Orientales, and the Institut d'Ethnologie.[16] Described as an anglophile and a sympathizer of Indirect Rule, he tried to put French colonial policy on a similar track (Labouret 1931). Compared to Delafosse, Labouret was however no match to Lugard in terms of colonial prestige and connections, nor to Westermann in scientific terms.

Labouret submitted some 'Proposals to develop the activities of the Institute in the ethnological field'[17] in which he made the case that the Institute serve as a 'Central Bureau of information' for all (educated) people interested in Africa. The primary task of the Institute was to collect, coordinate, and disseminate, on an international level, all information relative to Africa. The first step towards such a goal, he proposed, was the development of 'a general bibliography on the *nègres* and the country they inhabit'. Such a bibliography would help to identify the 'considerable *lacunae* in our knowledge of Africa', which could then be remedied. Research priorities would be defined by the Executive Committee based on the interest expressed by local colonial governments, missions, and scientists. He suggested a focus on the black African family, a topic that was of interest to all of these professionals.

His scheme was based on a conventional orthodoxy for collecting data on 'primitive' societies, based on a separation between the tasks of observation and of 'synthesis'. The division of labor, originating in Natural History museums, between a fact-gathering descriptive 'ethnography' and a theory-oriented synthetical 'anthropology' was then a standard epistemological assumption shared by all Council members. In this light, the fundamental condition for the production of scientific knowledge about Africa was a more rational organization of co-operation. The crucial issue was not the training of specialists to do 'fieldwork', but rather the building up of an international network of correspondents in Africa, enabling the more efficient use of *observers* already available, that is, the 'men on the spot'.

Labouret also devised a questionnaire on family that incorporated some of the latest developments in ethnological science (1927). He stressed that he had drawn upon existing publications and incorporated elements from Marcel Mauss's teaching at the Institut d'Ethnologie as well as advice from the Seligmans (Charles and his wife Brenda) and from the Editorial Committee of the new (1929) edition of *Notes and Queries on Anthropology*. Labouret's questionnaire can thus be said to have been state of the art, and likely to gain international consensus. His scheme also had innovative aspects: he deprecated sending questionnaires through the administrative hierarchy, as had been a standard practice before World War I (Sibeud, this volume), preferring a method of 'direct contact', through 'common acquaintanceship' with the desired collaborator. For Labouret, production of knowledge had to be built on a *personal network*, that would progressively expand through further personal links, and he suggested compiling a 'complete repertory on people that may be useful to our work'.[18]

These correspondents were to be anyone living in Africa, European or native (either belonging to traditional or new elites), who were sincere enough to be trusted and willing to follow the guidance of the Institute's specialists. No special training was required, as goodwill and accurate observational skills were enough. Labouret proposed working out two questionnaires, a basic one for untrained observers and an advanced one for people 'already accustomed to this kind of research'. These guidelines would allow 'conscientious observers' to know what to look for, thus producing data useful to the progress of science.[19] At the Council meeting however, Lugard expressed doubts concerning the feasibility of

> sending a questionnaire to people who were not acknowledged experts. In his view it was the duty of Governments, and not of the Institute to train enquirers. The Institute had to collect information from trained enquirers and did not possess the staff or resources to deal with a large mass of replies from untrained persons.[20]

Nevertheless, the Executive Council arranged to send 100 questionnaires each in English and French to the appropriate Colonial authorities requesting that only 'experts' be asked to complete the questionnaire.[21]

Later in 1927, Labouret elaborated upon his proposal for an Ethnological Department of the Institute. It was to be structured as an international pyramidal system, topped by the Institute's two Directors assisted by European experts. Below them would be a network consisting of officials of specialized departments in local colonial administrations as well as regional correspondents in each colonial territory (which thus appeared as the basic scientific unit). Each of these correspondents would in turn develop a local network of collaborators. It is noteworthy that such a scheme allowed for a participation in the scholarly endeavor not only of European administrators and missionaries, but also of 'native' Africans:

> One of the main roles of these correspondents would be to discover good collaborators, European and native, who would record without delay languages, institutions, beliefs and rites before they were transformed. Correspondents would be easy to find among civil servants and missionaries, while collaborators would be found largely among black schoolteachers and mission pupils who would provide the Institute with original documents, numerous and important both from the linguistic and ethnological point of view. As for me, I consider them as extremely precious auxiliaries.[22]

Clearly, Labouret's own network was more developed among educated Africans, whom he encouraged to write ethnographic pieces, than among French colonials.[23] The ethnographic studies promoted by Labouret were monographs aimed at recording the vastest possible range of languages, institutions, beliefs and rites before they died out. The Institute adopted Labouret's scheme and proceeded to develop a network of correspondents in the colonies.[24] Similarly, Jesuit missionary Father Dubois, secretary of the Conference of Catholic Missions in Africa, produced a list of 'specialists' in African topics among Catholic missionaries (Dubois 1928, 1932). Simultaneously, the Institute undertook to publish a complete international bibliography, based on work done in Germany, France and Britain (e.g. Westermann 1929). But for the international character of its work, the activities of the IIALC with respect to anthropology was on the whole rather close to those of the Royal Anthropological Institute or the Institut d'Ethnologie. This was to change dramatically.

'Changing Africa' and the division of scientific labor

At the close of 1928, Bronislaw Malinowski, prompted by Oldham – with whom he had come into contact through the Rockefeller Foundation – offered an alternative program. Calling upon the Institute to relinquish what he disdainfully labeled 'antiquarian anthropology', he argued that 'a new branch of anthropology must be started: the anthropology of the changing Native'. What Malinowski proposed to the Institute was no less than the creation of a new branch of anthropology, which he characterized as 'practical' (Malinowski 1929, 1930). Anthropology should occupy what Malinowski termed an 'anthropological no-man's land', by tackling 'the problems of population ... ; the study of social organizations, above all of its fundamental institutions, the family, marriage, and educational agencies ... ; law, economics and politics as we find them at work in primitive communities; ... sociological or cultural linguistics' (1929: 30). What was at stake was a re-definition of the boundaries and of the very subject matter of anthropology. In December 1928, the Executive Council endorsed Malinowski's program of 'Practical anthropology' as its official policy. The missionary-anthropologist Edwin W. Smith, who had himself converted from Frazerian to 'functional' anthropology (Smith and Dale 1920; Smith 1934a), described the radical shift in the anthropological program of the Institute from the organization of fact-collecting to the opening up of a new area for research:

> There already were in existence many strong institutions ... which were engaged in a study of anthropology in all its various forms ... But the conviction grew that the Institute should devote its energies not to ploughing fields already under cultivation, but to *hitherto unexplored ground* ... What is happening to the structure of African society under the pressure of Western Civilisation? ... Many excellent monographs have been written on African tribes, but invariably these have aimed at portraying the life of the people *as it was before* contact with Europeans affected it ... As conditions are to-day, they present only one side of the picture, and therefore are inaccurate, if not misleading. (Smith 1934b)

The significance of this shift for Labouret was dramatic, as he was virtually replaced by Malinowski as principal framer of the Institute's policy in the anthropological field.

The complex and protracted negotiations around the Institute's Five Year Plan of Research (see Stocking 1992 for an overview; and L'Estoile 2004, chapter 4), led ultimately to a program based on a convergence between Malinowski's efforts to revolutionize anthropology and the Rockefeller Foundation's objectives of promoting social welfare through scientific studies. While the Plan was designed to be sufficiently wide to incorporate many kinds of research, its focus was on the 'changing African', a critical departure from standard ethnographic studies. A crucial point discussed at length on many occasions was the issue of the division of labor. Thus, at the Congress held in Paris on 'Ethnography and linguistics applied to colonization', at the occasion of the 1931 International Colonial Exhibition, three speakers discussed the 'organisation of ethnological studies in Africa'. Colonel Derendinger, who had practiced ethnography while serving in French colonial army in Chad, endorsed the division of labor, which was then gaining new momentum in France around the Trocadero Museum of Ethnography.[25] He singled out 'Laboratory studies' in which 'scientists, specialists in ethnography, sociology, ethnology, study documents, compare them and draw laws that would guide the decisions of those whose responsibility it is to rule over these young peoples'.[26] These 'Laboratory studies' however needed to be 'fed with documents, information coming from direct sources'. With the 'disintegration of native societies taking place under our eyes', one had to rely on local sources of information for the urgent task of recording the data. He urged the Institute to provide scholarships to those who were called to serve in Africa, above all junior administrators and missionaries. Derendinger insisted on the need to develop regional centers that would ensure the circulation of information, a task for which the IIALC was well placed. Similarly, Labouret, the Congress convener, concluded that only when enough *facts* had been recorded would theoreticians be able to formulate *laws*. He thus proceeded to outline the lines along which a regional monograph should be written (Labouret 1932).

Malinowski's conception ran counter to this. Early on in his career, he had attacked the notion of ethnography as 'fact-gathering' exemplified by the *Notes and Queries in Anthropology* (Malinowski 1916). Malinowski argued then that the very separation of fact and theory, a central assumption in this epistemological model where observation was *delegated* to those living in the colonial field, was but illusory, since observation was always dependent on a theoretical framework which had to be adapted by the fieldworker. Thus, the modern anthropologist had to be both theoretically trained and a competent ethnographer. Moreover, it was precisely because he was equipped with what Malinowski would later term a 'portable theory' that he was able to produce a better ethnography. Malinowski's own proposal for the Institute was thus to send students, after a period of intensive theoretical training (ideally at the London School of Economics under Malinowski's own guidance), to do fieldwork, which would lead to the desired changes in anthropology. The final version of the Five Year Plan of Research of the Institute took up Malinowski's position (IIALC 1932). On the one hand, the Plan apparently endorsed the continuing validity of the traditional model of fact-collecting, by stating that 'everyone who is interested in the subject can make a contribution by observing the facts within the range of its own work and experience'.[27] On the other hand, the main thrust of the program was to provide funds for fieldwork through fellowships and grants, to 'specially trained investigators, who can devote the whole of their time to comprehensive studies in the light of a sociological knowledge'.[28] In addition, they were 'to make clear the best lines of study and furnish guidance to other workers'.[29]

In July 1932, the Executive Council discussed at length the 'methods of research' to be used for the Five Year Plan.[30] Malinowski managed to have his students Audrey Richards, Gordon Brown and Helena Hunter, invited to the discussion 'as they had all recently been in the field and it was felt it would be helpful to hear their accounts of how they carried on their work.' In addition to Council members, (including Labouret, Lugard, Oldham, Derendinger, Seligman, Malinowski, E.W. Smith, Schmidt, de Jonghe), anthropologist Lloyd Warner (visiting from Chicago), and Outhwaite, an ex-official of the Rockefeller Foundation, also attended. What was at stake in the meeting was the very definition of anthropological inquiry: for most participants, it went without saying that the real object of 'scientific' anthropology was the past, even if they were to some extent ready to admit the practical interest of studying 'change'. In response to Richards, advocating the application of the 'functional method of fieldwork' to the study of changing Africa, Father Dubois suggested that 'while it was important to study the present it was equally important, though more difficult, to reconstruct the past. This could be done by getting into touch with old settlers and missionaries who remembered the old conditions, but the work ought to be done before it was too late'.[31]

Labouret argued that 'methods must . . . vary according to area . . . The method to be followed must be chosen according to the country' [ambiguously referring to either the place of study or the controlling power], which meant taking official advice. 'It was essential . . . the Governments concerned and experts should be consulted in order to discover what problems they considered to be of the greatest importance and urgency . . . The governments desired that past, present and future should all be taken into consideration.' He concluded that 'a regional division of Africa should be made, and the different Governments and experts consulted as to their views. Workers would be sought for the particular studies required and if the right people could not be sought for the particular studies required, *then* the Institute was in a position to train them.'[32] Malinowski, however, disagreed with Labouret's proposal that 'the plans *should be evolved with the help of nationals* belonging to the territory concerned'.[33]

Labouret's strategy was to use his position in the French colonial world to outmaneuver Malinowski by enlisting French colonial governments, who, he repeated, had to be 'consulted' in drawing up the

Institute's programs. His position was crippled, however, by his failure to gain significant financial support from French colonial authorities, who preferred to fund national institutions, while Malinowski himself had by then acquired, mostly through the Institute, a significant network and support in British colonial circles.[34]

The rise of 'scientific nationalism'

If what Vischer called 'national susceptibilities' played an important role within the Institute from the beginning, the claims for a national-based approach to African problems steadily increased in the 1930s as Malinowski's prominence in the Institute became more evident. Other members of the Council were irritated by Malinowski's monopoly on the training of fieldworkers, and by what they perceived as London's hegemony over the Institute.[35] In a 'Plan of Research in French West Africa' drawn up for the Executive Council in June 1933, Labouret proposed to establish plans of research for each 'great region' of the continent which would have to be approved by scientists and local governments interested in these investigations.[36]

> To be fecund, the study of the main questions that arise today needs to be grounded on a solid basis, which can only be obtained *through the division of labour*. Therefore it seems opportune to divide Africa into a number of sectors for which specialists would be in charge to supply the Council with the information and elements of decision for investigations to be engaged in each part.[37]

In his proposal to undertake an inquiry,[38] Labouret pointed out the specificity of the French situation, contrasted with the British: *ethnologie*, because it did not in France lead to a career, did not attract any academic *spécialistes*. Labouret made a case against the *amateur* ethnographers who played so prominent a part in French ethnologie in the 1930s, especially at the Trocadero Museum.[39] He had, he explained, rejected applications of 'young people with a temporary interest for African ethnology, but without any intention to continue in it later'. Rather, it was better to foster 'a taste for ethnography' among young colonial administrators, as he himself did through his teaching at the Ecole Coloniale. Labouret proposed to have a young Ecole Coloniale graduate accompany him to the Cameroon, where he would teach him ethnography in the field. He had done just this the preceding year in French West Africa.[40] This would also demonstrate to French colonial administrations the importance of anthropological studies.

Discussing these proposals,[41] Father Dubois proclaimed the superiority of colonial residents, who possessed a 'real knowledge' of Africa and Africans through their life-experience, in contrast to 'outside investigators', with merely a bookish training, arguing that 'One cannot penetrate the native mind (mentalité) after a two-years' stay'. Dubois's phrasing was antithetical to the five-year-plan since he argued that guidance was to be given not by the Fellows, but by experienced European residents, who were the real repositories of knowledge.

Labouret was supported not only by his French colleagues, but also by other continental scholars, such as De Jonghe, who stated his proposal for international co-operation conceived of as an addition of nationally framed schemes. Not surprisingly, Malinowski objected to this, urging his colleagues 'not to lose sight that we are an International Institute'. Being himself a foreigner in Britain, enjoying considerable financial support from American foundations, attracting to his seminar students from Europe and the British Commonwealth, Malinowski had everything to gain by endorsing an internationalization that strengthened his leadership in anthropology. Conversely, the national argument could be invoked by his competitors in continental Europe to protect their own turf from a menacing hegemony.

Dissent extended to the type of work that was to be done in the field. Labouret had drawn up a memorandum on the theoretical and technical equipment needed for research workers.[42] First of all, they needed not only a thorough knowledge of the methods of human geography and cartography, but also photographic and design skills. He also suggested that the Fellows, whom he significantly termed 'observers' (a term associated with the traditional division of labor), should take advantage of their field study to collect various data: photographs, anthropological measurements, objects, languages, etc. Observers should therefore be provided with a basic anthropometrical apparatus to make the best of 'the possibility of their obtaining a considerable number of measurements after a very short training'. Labouret also suggested they take with them sound-recording machines and movie-cameras, 'in order to note down languages not well known and aesthetic manifestations on which we have little information.' His suggestions were modeled on what was by then the standard practice of ethnological work at the Institut d'Ethnologie and the Trocadero Museum, exemplified by the famous Griaule expedition from Dakar to Djibouti (1931–33). The measure of success of these expeditions was the amount of *data* (from measurements to artifacts to photographs) collected, and reports systematically boasted about the size of their 'booty'. Labouret's own ethnographic expeditions to West Africa in 1932 and 1934 followed the same pattern.

The reactions of the Executive Council reveal however that this paradigm was no more self-evident. While Labouret's proposal to provide photographic equipment to Fellows was approved – an indication that photography was endorsed as a standard ethnographic practice – the Council expressed reluctance to include a measuring apparatus in the standard equipment, stressing that 'physical anthropology of this type could not be regarded as part of the programme of the Institute'.[43] Controversy also arose around the collection of material culture, a prominent feature of French ethnography in the inter-war years (see Jamin 1986; L'Estoile 2005a), dominated by the rise of the Trocadero Museum. Indeed, Labouret himself was probably one of the largest single donors to the Trocadero. Significantly, the Council led by Malinowski stated that 'the spending of time on such collections should be discouraged as being incompatible with the objects for which fellowship was awarded.'[44]

The following year, Labouret argued for his new program along strictly national lines.[45] In 1934, the French members of the Executive Council met in Paris and agreed to a common program to be presented to the Council, that was explicitly delivered by Labouret as the product of a national consensus. This document is interesting as it might be read as a compromise between two contradictory demands, namely the Institute's focus on the study (deemed 'sociological' in the program) of contemporary changes in colonial Africa – an interest shared by Labouret himself[46] – and the growing pressure felt by Labouret to follow the new standard French 'ethnographic' model aimed at collecting vast bodies of descriptive data in order to produce a series of all-round monographs. However, no attempt was made to find a convergence between these conflicting goals. They were juxtaposed and presented as equally necessary. Two months later, Labouret argued that

> Each nation must be left free to decide what kind of studies and research it preferred to see carried out. It was a question whether the research to be undertaken should be proposed by *nations* who had interests in Africa or by scientists interested in certain *problems*. He insisted that the programme should be elaborated in the way in which each nation considered the problems should be treated. With the French members of the Council he had prepared a programme of research for French territories.[47]

For the first time, Labouret's argument was clothed in strictly nationalistic terms, playing up 'national' against 'scientific' interests with the former having priority over the latter. Labouret also insisted on the need to produce 'as complete a documentation as possible', in an encyclopedic endeavor of collecting empirical data for a later 'synthesis':

[108]

When such detailed information had been obtained they could proceed to works of synthesis. The first thing was to have a complete study and knowledge of all aspects of tribal society.[48]

Paul Rivet, then Professor at the Museum of Natural History, Director of the Musée d'Ethnographie du Trocadero, and the leading entrepreneur of French ethnologie in the interwar period, supported Labouret. The role of the Fellows, he felt, was to encourage missionaries and settlers to make observations. This amounted to exporting the organization of research he was fostering in France, which was founded on the division of labor and the use of an 'army of auxiliary workers' (L'Estoile, forthcoming).[49]

Controversy came to involve the very definition of Africa. Did it include Northern Africa, especially those regions under French domination? The issue arose in a discussion of an application for IIALC fellowships by two students of the Institut d'Ethnologie, to undertake a standard *ethnologique* study of folklore and physical anthropology in Algeria (Kabylie). The debate was both scientific and political. Lugard stated that Mediterranean countries of northern Africa were to be out of the survey, whereas Rivet argued that 'one must consider Africa as a whole and it was very difficult to separate the North from the South. The problems were the same everywhere and the people of the North were less influenced by Western civilisation than many in South Africa.'[50] What was at stake here was indeed a different construction of 'Africa'. For the British, Egypt was seen as part not of Africa, but the Middle East; for Rivet, what qualified these territories for inquiry was the existence of populations 'practically untouched by outside civilisation'.[51] For French ethnologists, the imperial logic thus appeared stronger than a racial one ('Black Africa').[52]

This context of heightened competition within the Institute fueled alternative projects. Labouret and Westermann had clearly lost ground to Malinowski, who through his alliance with Lugard and Oldham, and the Rockefeller Foundation's backing, controlled the allocation of Fellowships. The continentals devised another project for an Encyclopedia or Handbook of African tribes, which was in line with the initial idea of the Institute as a 'coordinating center' of knowledge produced about Africa. The proposal called for an ethnological 'mapping' of the whole of Africa, by providing an Encyclopedia of 'the tribes, tribal groups, peoples, races, languages, language groups and language families in Africa, exclusive of Egypt, but including Madagascar, in alphabetical order.'[53]

The project was to be based on a strict division of labour. The editors (probably Westermann and Labouret) would design cards that would be 'filled in by the experts (in Europe and South Africa) on the basis of their own knowledge and of the existing literature [with] the help of older students, who will, under their direct guidance, search the literature and collect the data.'

[T]he cards will be sent to the correspondent in Africa who lives in the respective area and asked to make the necessary corrections and additions, or, if necessary to re-write the card . . . After the cards have been returned they will be examined first by the experts, and then by the editors, who bear the final responsibility for their reliability.[54]

In this scheme, the Institute's Fellows in the field were only to be 'correspondents', in a position little above the 'Europeans living in Africa' and 'African natives under European guidance'. Malinowski was bitterly opposed to the project, which ran in a direction opposite to the new 'social anthropology' he was actively building, and the autonomy it gave to fieldworkers working within a range of common theoretical questions. However, it was enthusiastically endorsed by the rest of the Council, and received financial support from the Carnegie Foundation.[55] The project, however, was postponed, but kept reappearing on the agenda. An interesting footnote to this story is that this international co-operation was not completely stopped by the war. In 1941, Labouret met Westermann in Berlin to 'discuss the work that would have to be done in Africa after the war on an international basis. They also discussed the Tribal Handbook which had been planned by the Institute', according to Labouret's self-serving explanations to Vischer. However, what Labouret chose to regard as a continuing spirit of international co-operation was deemed in 1944 'collaboration with the enemy' in war circumstances, and he had to resign from all his positions, including his Directorship of the Institute.[56]

After World War II, the pendulum swung back to a more traditional version of anthropology, which gained momentum in Britain with the rapid establishment of social anthropology in universities (Stocking 1996: 427–434; L'Estoile 1997b). The project of preparing tribal handbooks was resurrected under a new guise, as the Ethnographic Survey of Africa, under the auspices of the International African Institute (IAI), the new name of the IIALC, and funded by the (British) Colonial Social Sciences Research Council.[57]

Conclusion

Scientific internationalism's ideal notwithstanding (Merton 1942), efforts to establish an international forum on African languages and cultures were complicated not only by national rivalries in the colonial field, but also by epistemological dissent arising from scientists' divergent research programs, which in many cases came to be framed as national oppositions.

The IIALC offered a meeting ground where representatives of countries that had fought one another during World War I could talk together and discuss the future of Africa, but it was fragile. The 1930s witnessed a series of oppositions in colonial policy as in anthropology, which increasingly tended to become defined in national terms and made international debate more confrontational. 'Scientific nationalism' appears not as an original state, that would progressively be overcome by the growth of an 'international spirit', but rather as a by-product of internationalization and changing equilibria (L'Estoile et al. 2005). The international consensus Labouret had hoped to achieve through his 'network method' was undermined by the developments in Britain, in which the 'fieldwork method' that revolutionized the division of labor loomed large. Malinowski, for whom Africa became, in the 1930s, the main battlefield, managed through his superior assets and strategy to 'take over' the IIALC, a move that would eventually transform both anthropology and colonial policy in Britain. This generated a reaction in which continental scholars who had once been convinced internationalists increasingly embraced the rhetoric of 'scientific nationalism'. When one is no longer able to impose one's definition of scientific activity as 'international' and the 'interest in internationalization' decreases, an alternative strategy is to restrict one's claims to a definition of science on a national basis.

This study also invites us to develop a more complex vision of 'national schools' as the outcome of both internal and international processes. There is some irony in the fact that those who were resented as 'foreigners' by the Colonial Office played a prominent part in the emergence of what came to be known as the 'British School' of anthropology, although it could indeed claim to be truly international in its recruitment. In fact, this 'modern British school' (Kuper 1973) progressively silenced dissenting voices such as Seligman's. Conversely, what had been an international standard, with an emphasis on 'complete monographs' whose accumulation might add up to constitute the 'total archives of mankind', to use Marcel Griaule's telling expression, became a significant trait of the French model of anthropology by contrast with the new British paradigm. These developments came to produce across Europe significantly different constructions of 'Africa'.

Notes

1 Cited in Minutes of the International Institute of African Languages and Cultures Meeting at Bruxelles, dated 4th July, 1933 (IAI 1/18), Archives of the International

African Institute, British Library of Political and Economic Sciences, London. Original in French. Unless otherwise mentioned, the translations are mine.

2 Many a historical study calls the IIALC the International Africa Institute (IAI), a name it would adopt only in 1945.

3 Such an international co-operation was by no means self-evident: the Institut International d'anthropologie, created in 1919, did not accept citizens from former enemy countries and it was for years unthinkable to publish a piece in German in a French journal (Zerilli, 1998: 122).

4 Hanns Vischer (1876–1945), an anglicized Swiss, had been a missionary in Northern Nigeria and later Director of Education under Lugard; he was Secretary of the Advisory Committee on Education in Tropical Africa from 1923.

5 Vischer to Lugard , 20 November 1939, IAI Archives, British Library of Political and Economic Sciences, London.

6 An important factor in the emergence of an international colonial field was the Mandates Commission set up by the League of Nations to oversee the Mandates formally given by the League over former German (and Ottoman) colonial Territories, such as (in Africa) Cameroons, Togo, South-West Africa, Burundi and Rwanda. Lugard was the British representative to this commission for much of the inter-war period.

7 The strategy 'to bring into existence such a weighty and influential body of opinion that no government can afford to disregard it' was explicitly formulated by Oldham (Oldham to E.W. Riggs, American Board of Commissioners for Foreign Missions, 6.11.1925, International Missionary Council/Conference of British. Missionary Societies (IMC/CBMS) Archives, Box 205, School of Oriental and African Studies, London). Riggs concurred in seeing as vital 'some pressure stronger than the voice of individual missionaries or even missionary organizations' (Riggs to Oldham, 12.12.1925, IMC/CBMS).

8 This belief was also instrumental in securing the support of various philanthropies, such as the Carnegie Fund or the Rockefeller Foundation.

9 The International Colonial Institute in Brussels, created at the beginning of the twentieth century, increased its activities after the war, especially in terms of colonial legislation, but, by contrast with the IIALC, it did not include countries without colonial empires.

10 Derendinger, 1933: 196.

11 See J.H. Oldham papers, Rhodes House Library (RHL), Oxford.

12 Vischer, 'Notes on the agenda, meeting 28–29/11/1929'),IMC/CBMS, Box 205.

13 Concern for 'national susceptibilities' was apparent in Vischer's own preparatory notes for Lugard. For instance, in November 1927 he noted that Professor Schachtzabel, from Berlin, had been 'elected [to the Executive Council] mainly in order to bring the number of German members up to three, that is the same as the French members', Vischer, 'Notes for chairman'. Documents Presented to Fourth Executive Council, November 1927, IAI.

14 Colonial Office minutes, 17 March 1933, CO847 2/8, Colonial Office Archives, Public Record Office. (capitals in original). Siegfried Nadel was Austrian, Soerd Hofstra Dutch and Meyer Fortes South African. Another official, Alex Fiddian, gently added: 'that would certainly be an advantage in having one Englishman in this menagerie!' (ibid.). These statements notwithstanding, the majority of the Fellows sent by the IIALC to colonial territories under British control were indeed not British.

15 'Notes on the work and future of the Institute', September 1937, 16th meeting Executive Council, IAI Archives.

16 Henri Labouret was regarded as a competent linguist and ethnographer and published works on the Lobi and the Mandingue language.

17 'Propositions en vue de developper l'activité de l'institut dans le domaine ethnologique'. Documents presented to the 3rd meeting of the Executive Council, London, June 9 & 10, 1927, IAI Archives.

18 Labouret, ibid.

19 Labouret, ibid.
20 Minutes of the Third meeting of the Executive Council. London, June 9 & 10, 1927. IAI 515.
21 In 1928, Labouret reported that 656 questionnaires had been distributed in French territories to governors and colonial officials while another hundred had been handed out by the Conference of Catholic Missions. 'Progress of work' Africa, 1928: 518.
22 Labouret, ibid.
23 Among the Africans, Labouret names Dim Delobson, Mamby Sidibé, Paul Hazoumé, all of whom would later be active in the production of ethnographic knowledge and also Dominique Taraoré [Traoré], schoolteacher and 'a black official', M. Da Costa Soarès. In the European category, he names only M. Vuillaume, of the Côte d'Ivoire Civil Service (Labouret, ibid). See Jezequel's paper this volume.
24 Lugard thus wrote to the Secretary for Southern Provinces in Nigeria, asking for the 'appointment of officers as correspondants or liaison officers', 15.2.1928, IAI 1596.
25 The Society of Africanists had been created the year before, on the eve of the Colonial Exhibition, in order to organize data-collecting (L'Estoile, 1997a).
26 Congrès de l'Institut International des Langues et des Civilisations Africaines (1933).
27 IIALC, 1932, 'A Five-Year Plan of Research in Africa', Africa 1: 3–14.
28 Ibid.
29 ibid.
30 'Appendix to minutes' (original in English), XIth Executive Council, IAI.
31 Ibid.
32 Ibid.
33 It would however be too simplistic to read this discussion in nationalist terms, as British vs. French or even British vs. Continental: Seligman, who had by then become Malinowski's rival within the London School of Economics, for instance, resolutely sided with Dubois, Labouret and Pater Schmidt against Malinowski who was also supported by Lloyd Warner.
34 In 1929, the Ministry of the Colonies thus gave 150000 Francs to the Museum of Ethnography and 166000 Francs to the Institut d'Ethnologie while it contributed only 5000 Francs to the IIALC (Labouret to Ministère des colonies, 24.1.1936. Archives IAI, O403 IMOF, and Mauss).
35 Oldham had been named Administrative Director in 1931, because the Rockefeller Foundation did not trust either a French or German Director.
36 IAI 530 (1,18).
37 Labouret, 'Plan de recherche en Afrique occidentale français', emphasis added.
38 'Rapport de M. le Professeur Labouret sur un Projet de Voyage au Cameroun', IAI 530 (1,18).
39 This has been obscured by the paradoxical fact that a number of the 'amateur' ethnographers that crowded the Trocadero Museum in the early 1930s, like Marcel Griaule, Michel Leiris, André Schaeffner, G.H.Rivière, Denise Paulme, Germaine Dieterlen, etc. did in fact later become 'professionals', so that those who are retrospectively termed 'amateurs' in today's French anthropological common-sense are the colonial officials! (see L'Estoile, forthcoming).
40 'Mission de M Labouret et de M Leca en AOF', July 1933, IAI 1/18.
41 Labouret himself, being ill, was unable to attend the meeting in Brussels in July 1933, when his memorandum was discussed; this circumstance produced a detailed recording of the discussions, in French, for Labouret's personal use (Minutes of Bruxelles Meeting, in French, 4th July, 1933 (IAI 1/18).
42 'Le travail des Fellows en Europe et sur le terrain', 8.June.1933, IAI 1/18.
43 Minutes of Bruxelles Meeting. However, it conceded that 'if a qualified man wished to devote part of his time to this work, no objection would be made'.
44 Ibid.

45 'Rapport au sujet d'un programme de recherches dans les colonies francaises', Avril 1934, Musée de l'Homme, Ms 143.
46 Keenly interested in practical problems, he was a pioneer in the study of family budgets in Africa.
47 Minutes 13th meeting. Documents presented to 13th Executive Council, London, 17–18th May, 1934, IAI 1/19 (553), emphasis added.
48 Ibid.
49 A profound believer in scientific internationalism, Rivet had been decisive in defeating the proposal to exclude German anthropologists from French scientific societies after the War (Zerilli, 1998: 125–133).
50 Ibid.
51 Fellowships were eventually granted to Thérèse Rivière and Germaine L'Henry (later Tillon) in 1934. Colonna, 1987.
52 Thus the Société des Africanistes, created in 1930, included Northern Africa in its realm.
53 Westermann, 'Encyclopedia of African Tribes', June 1933, IAI 1/18.
54 Ibid.
55 Oldham to Malinowski, 25th February 1935, Malinowski papers, BLPES, London.
56 'Report to the chairman and members of the Bureau by the Secretary General on his visit to Paris', 9th February 1945, IAI Archives.
57 If the Survey aimed to produce an ethnographic digest of most African populations, it could take on various meanings according to local settings.

References

Colonna, Fanny. 1987. *Aurès, Algérie: 1935–1936. Thérèse Rivière. . . . Elle a passé tant d'heures.* Paris: Maison des sciences de l'homme.

Derendinger, Colonel. 1933. 'Le but des études ethnologiques en Afrique'. In *Congrès de l'Institut International des Langues et des Civilisations Africaines. Comptes-rendus.* Paris: IIALC.

Dubois, Henri. 1928. *L'Institut International pour l'étude des langues et des civilisations africaines à Londres et la Conférence des Missions africaines catholiques à Rome.* Rome: Imprimerie Campitelli.

Dubois, Henri. 1932. *Le Répertoire africain.* Rome: Imprimerie Campitelli.

Hetherington, P. 1978. *British Paternalism and Africa, 1920–1940.* London: Frank Cass.

International Institute of African Languages and Cultures (IIALC). 1932. 'A Five-Year Plan of Research'. *Africa* 5:1–13.

Jamin, J. 1986. 'L'ethnographie, mode d'inemploi: de quelques rapports de l'ethnologie avec le malaise dans la civilisation'. In *Le mal et la douleur.* Neuchatel: Musée d'ethnographie.

Kuper, Adam. 1973 [revised edition 1996]. *Anthropology and Anthropologists: The Modern British School.* London: Routledge.

Labouret, H. 1928. *Recommandations pour l'étude de la famille.* Paris: IIALC.

Labouret, H. 1931. *A la recherche d'une nouvelle politique indigène dans l'Ouest Africain.* Paris: Editions du Comité de l'Afrique Française.

Labouret, H. 1932. 'Ethnologie coloniale. Un programme de recherches'. *Outre-Mer* 4:48–89.

L'Estoile, Benoît de. 1997a. 'Africanisme, Africanism: esquisse de comparasion franco-britannique'. In A. Piriou and E. Sibeud (eds). *L'Africanisme en questions*, Paris: Notes et Documents du Centre d'Etudes Africaines, EHESS, pp. 19–42.

L'Estoile, Benoît de. 1997b. 'The "Natural Preserve of Anthropologists": Social Anthropology, Scientific Planning and Development'. *Social Sciences Information* 36:343–376.

L'Estoile, Benoît de. 2004. *L'Afrique comme laboratoire. Expériences réformatrices et révolution anthropologique dans l'empire colonial britannique. (1920–1950)*. Ecole des Hautes Etudes en Sciences Sociales (EHESS): Unpublished thèse de doctorat.

L'Estoile, Benoît de. 2005a. ' "Races not Inferior, but Different". Anthropological Sciences and Imperial Policy at the Paris Colonial Exhibition (1931)'. In B. Stuchtey (ed.). *Science across the European Empires, 1800–1950*. London: Oxford University Press/German Historical Institute, pp. 215–231.

L'Estoile, Benoît de. 2005b. 'A Rationalization of Colonial Domination? Anthropology and Native Policy in French-ruled Africa'. In B. de L'Estoile, F. Neiburg and L. Sigaud (eds). *Empires, Nations and Natives. Anthropology and State-making*. Durham: Duke University Press, pp. 30–57.

L'Estoile, Benoît de. Forthcoming. *Le goût du passé. De l'exposition coloniale aux arts premiers*. Paris: Flammarion, chapters 3 and 4.

L'Estoile, Benoît de, Neiburg, F. and Sigaud, L. (eds). 2005. 'Anthropology and the Government of Natives: A Comparative Approach'. In B. de L'Estoile, F. Neiburg and L. Sigaud (eds). *Empires, Nations and Natives. Anthropology and State-making*. Durham: Duke University Press, pp. 1–30.

Lugard, Lord. 1928. 'The International Institute of African Language and Culture'. *Africa* I:1–12.

Malinowski, Bronislaw. 1916. 'Baloma, Spirits of the Dead in the Trobriand Islands'. In B. Malinowski. *Magic, Science and Religion and other essays*. Chicago: University of Chicago Press: pp. 149–274. Midway reprint.

Malinowski, Bronislaw. 1929. 'Practical Anthropology'. *Africa* 2:22–38.

Malinowski, Bronislaw. 1930. 'The Rationalization of Anthropology and Administration'. *Africa* 3:405–430.

Merton, Robert. 1942. 'The Normative Structure of Science'. In R. Merton [1972] *The Sociology of Science. Theoretical and Empirical Investigations*. Chicago: University of Chicago Press, pp. 267–278.

Oldham, J.O. 1925. 'Educational Policy of the British Government in Africa'. *International Review of Missions* 14:421–427.

Smith, Edwin W. 1934a. 'Anthropology and the Practical Man'. *Journal of the Royal Anthropological Institute of Great Britain and Ireland* 64: xiii–xxxvii.

Smith, Edwin W. 1934b. 'The Story of the Institute. A Survey of Seven Years'. *Africa* 7:1–27.

Smith, Edwin W. and Dale, A.M. 1920. *The Ila Speaking Peoples of Northern Rhodesia*. 2 vols, London: Macmillan and Company.

Stocking, George W. 1992. 'Philantropoids and Vanishing Cultures: Rockefeller Funding and the End of the Museum Era in Anglo-American Anthropology'. In G. Stocking (ed.). *The Ethnographer's Magic and Other Essays.* Madison: University of Wisconsin Press, pp. 178–211.

Stocking, George W. 1996. *After Tylor: British Social Anthropology, 1881–1951.* London: Routledge.

Westermann, Dietrich. 1929. 'Bibliography of Current Literature on African languages and Cultures [prepared with the co-operation of H. Labouret, H. Melzian (Berlin), I. Schapera (London)]'. *Africa* 2:96–104.

Zerilli, F. 1998. *Il lato escuro dell'etnologia. Il contributo dell'antropologia naturalista al processo di istituzionalizzazione degli studi etnologici in Francia.* Rome: CISU.

PART II

African ethnographers, self-expression, and modernity

CHAPTER FOUR

Of conjunctions, comportment, and clothing: the place of African teaching assistants in Berlin and Hamburg, 1889–1919

Sara Pugach

In 1885 Njo Dibone, a man from Cameroon, traveled to Pomerania to learn German with a pastor named Carl Meinhof.[1] Whatever the original aims of Dibone's travels, it is safe to say that they marked the beginning of a relationship between Dibone and Meinhof that would grow to be more than a simple student-teacher affair. While Meinhof was teaching Dibone German, Dibone began to instruct the minister in his native language, Duala, and there is little doubt that Dibone had a marked influence on Meinhof's later life. Soon after their meeting, Meinhof embarked on a new career in African linguistic and ethnographic research. Eventually, he became a co-founder of the German university discipline *Afrikanistik*, the study of African languages and cultures. Meinhof thus came to play a significant role in the discourse on scientific colonialism in Germany, both during the Wilhelmine period and well beyond it (Pugach 2001), and his participation also assured Dibone a place in its history.

Without Dibone, Meinhof would likely have made less rapid progress in his early philological studies, as there were few Africans living in Germany at the time. Indeed, for most of his career Meinhof was an armchair scholar who rarely left Germany. Consequently he was at the mercy of information supplied by others, in the first instance Africans like Dibone and, in the second, missionaries in the field who had more 'direct' access to African languages. Either way, neither Meinhof nor the missionaries could have completed their work without African assistance; during an era when few Europeans understood African languages or knew much about African history and culture, they were beholden to African assistants and informants for most of their knowledge.

Information regarding Dibone is scant. He was a nephew of the Duala king Akwa and a teenager when he first met Meinhof in the mid-1880s.[2] Nonetheless, while he was not a scholar *per se* and probably did not have any university training, Dibone had a lasting impact on the emergence and development of an entire academic subject. Dibone and others like him, who came to Germany to be teaching assistants and informants in places like Berlin's Seminar for Oriental Languages and Hamburg's Colonial Institute, therefore provided Germans with a powerful counter-image of the 'African'. These colonial subjects were quite different from what most Germans of the period might have imagined or, in some instances, even had occasion to see in encounters with African men and women who appeared in touring 'people exhibitions' (Rothfels 1994; Dittrich and Rieke-Müller 1998). African teachers, who were commonly known either as *Lektoren* or *Sprachgehilfen*,[3] did not match the carefully cultivated stereotype of the purportedly 'wild' natives who were so often put on display in Germany and elsewhere.[4] Rather, they mixed quietly with Germans in quotidian settings and had 'normal' jobs that accorded them a specific – if contested – niche in German society. African lecturers also had the opportunity to shape linguistic and anthropological discourses that were blossoming around the turn of the twentieth century, because they quite literally had the ears of some of the most well-respected Africanist scholars in Germany.

German academics thus needed their African assistants, and they were central to the process of colonial knowledge production in Imperial Germany. Yet little has been said about their contributions to ethnographic or linguistic scholarship, or about the pressures they faced living among a foreign people whose prevalent vision of Africa was still guided by notions of desolation and primitivity. *Lektoren* were not in Germany to entertain, but rather to teach, and this assured a complex relationship; they may have been despised or looked down upon because of their 'race', but it was difficult to deny their pedagogical importance.

This chapter is an attempt to bring Germany's African teaching assistants back into the history of Africanist research in that country and, more broadly, German colonial history.[5] I therefore hope to reinscribe history of the *Lektoren* into the German 'colonial library' and show how they understood their own situations and positions in the empire. Gaurav Desai has argued that such a 'colonial library' needs to be redefined to incorporate texts produced by colonial Africans with attention to how their work did not simply mirror, but contributed to shaping, colonial discourse (Desai 2001).[6] In keeping with Desai's incitement to re-examine the writings that determine present under-standings of the colonial project, I address both how *Lektoren* par-ticipated in the institutionalization of African studies in German academe and how their movements – intellectual and otherwise – were limited by a society that assigned them very specific roles. Africans did not only confirm German stereotypes of African 'civilization' and the levels it had reached; they also subverted those same stereotypes and, in some cases, used them for their own personal advantage. More-over, we also get a sense of how much agency Africans actually had with respect to intellectual projects that have usually been considered completely European. On the German side, sources show how critical African (and other non-European) assistants were to the formation of a practical linguistic discipline, which was meant to supply its stu-dents not with archaic academic theory, but with the tools necessary for foreign conquest. Germans, then, were also caught in a double-bind. Those who gave instruction in African languages, as well as the colonial civil servants, soldiers and missionaries who were required to learn them, needed African help, but they also feared giving Africans too much power.

African informants in the German colonies

The process of knowledge exchange between Germans and Africans did not begin in the metropole with expatriates like Dibone. Nineteenth-century German missionaries were often engaged in compiling African-language dictionaries and grammars for practical use by other members of their mission societies, and this usually required African assistance. While dictionary-making was not the exclusive provenance of Germans, they were overrepresented in the field, as they also were in the growing discipline of comparative philology. In Germany itself, scholars such as Wilhelm von Humboldt, Jakob Grimm, August Pott, Franz Bopp, and August Schleicher – who for the most part had no par-ticular connection to Africa – fashioned comparative descriptions of a variety of languages, in an attempt to assess how they were related (cf. Alter 1999; Benes 2001). Although German-speaking missionaries were not usually educated outside of special missionary training seminars (Haller 1904), some, such as J.L. Krapf and F.W. Kolbe, were very aware of metropolitan linguistic debates.

Because knowledge of African languages and cultures was scarce in nineteenth-century Germany, missionaries, civil servants and explor-ers who visited Africa drew heavily on linguistic and ethnographic sources supplied by natives. The balance of power between the two groups may have been unequal, but was to some extent evened out by the fact that the Africans were in comfortable, familiar surroundings while the Germans were not. The informants could also assert a specific authority connected to the knowledge that they had and that the colonists so desperately wanted.

As Heintze (2002) has also suggested, the fact that the informants did not simply disappear from historical memory with the passing of their German sponsors, and that their intellectual contributions to ethnographic and linguistic projects is still apparent, owes much to the careful documentation that Europeans took of their lives. References to African linguistic and ethnographic participation can be found in a variety of sources, such as private correspondence and published journal articles. Recently, for example, Ursula Trüper (2000) has highlighted the significance of the early nineteenth-century contributions of an African woman, Zara Schmelen, to the transcription of the Southwest African Nama language.

In another instance, during the autumn of 1889 German school teacher Theodor Christaller was working to compile a set of German-Duala and Duala-German dictionaries in Cameroon. Christaller, however confessed that he was 'not yet completely fluent in the language', and required assistance from a seventeen-year-old informant named Eleme. Also known as Konrad, Eleme had been the 'best pupil' in Christaller's colonial school, and now he wanted the student to become his teacher.[7] When Christaller traveled around the colony collecting 'new' Duala words Eleme accompanied him, and he requested that the German colonial government in Cameroon cover Eleme's travel expenses. Christaller also asked the colonial authorities to ensure that Eleme was provided with a new job once he was no longer needed for the dictionary.[8]

Eleme's experience was doubtlessly replicated by many other native informants, who remain hidden in unpublicized writings such as the Tagebücher (diaries) of German missionaries, which were read by members of the particular mission societies, but not usually by anyone else. Ethnographic data from other African informants were sometimes also printed in more public forums, such as in linguistic or ethnographic journals. Most essays that appeared in Meinhof's Zeitschrift für Kolonialsprachen (Journal of Colonial Languages), mainly devoted to linguistics and anthropology, were written by missionaries, many of whom used native informants to help them with translation and transcription. Their presence in these articles was not especially apparent, often with only perfunctory mention of who they were, accompanied by a brief word or two of thanks.

Although the linguistic and anthropological efforts of all these informants were duly noted, they were not thought of as co-authors and did not receive much praise for their labor. Their presence was palpable, but as they spoke through their German collaborators the reality of their own participation was muted. While informants were commonly absent from texts that were both about them and partially created by them, on rare occasions they did speak more directly. Missionary and anthropological journals sometimes contained 'letters' written by Africans in the colonies. Such 'letters' benefited not only the Mission Society but also the African mission station, and demonstrate that informants were not simply German pawns but active figures who had their own stakes in imparting and receiving knowledge.

It is worth noting, in conclusion, that while most of the African informants in question had either no education or only a limited one, there were some rare instances in which more educated Africans also became involved with German linguistic or ethnographic projects. Such was the case for Carl Christian Reindorf, an Akan minister from the Gold Coast who worked with German missionary J.G. Christaller during the 1870s and 1880s and was a historian in his own right. Reindorf exerted considerable influence on Christaller, and attempted unsuccessfully to control the direction of linguistic transcription and standardization for the region by promoting his native language as the one most suitable for standardization over other, surrounding and competing, tongues (Bearth 2000).

African Lektoren *and* Sprachgehilfen *in Germany: life at the margins*

The situation for Africans who lived in Germany and worked as teaching assistants in Berlin and Hamburg was quite different from that of their colleagues who remained in the colonies. Indeed, some *Lektoren* produced texts that delved not only into their national customs, but German ones as well. Teachers like Victor Toso of Togo, who worked under Meinhof at the Hamburg Colonial Institute and published articles in Meinhof's *Zeitschrift für Kolonialsprachen*, assumed prominent positions in the German metropole, where they had occasion to influence people they met and to publish their own texts in ethnographic and linguistic forums. African *Lektoren* therefore straddled two societies. They were related to the informants in the field, but because they had greater access to scholarly institutions were able to move a step beyond them.

The practice of bringing Africans to Germany started well before the foundation of either the Berlin Seminar for Oriental Languages or the Hamburg Colonial Institute. Throughout the nineteenth century, individual explorers in Africa took interpreters and guides they met on the continent back to Germany (Reed-Anderson 1997). As the century drew to a close, however, more and more Africans seemed to be making their way to the newly united *Kaiserreich*. There were many reasons behind this: Germany had officially obtained its own colonies at the Berlin Conference in 1885; *Völkerschauen* were becoming increasingly popular; and wealthier African families like the Bells in Cameroon had the wherewithal to send their children to the German metropole for education (Naranch 2001). The assistants arrived as part of this wave, some finding their way to Berlin because of connections with the colonial government, others because of ties to the Protestant mission or German businesses. Many *Lektoren* seem to have been drawn to Germany by a desire for social and financial mobility and a hope for the betterment of their own social standing at home and abroad.

All of the new visitors contributed to the development of a general image of Africa. Even so, the Africans who lived in Germany were not all viewed in the same way. While participants in the *Völkerschauen* were seen as rough and primitive, African *Lektoren* assumed a significantly higher status, albeit one that was always in question and under threat. Whereas members of people exhibitions were often treated with disdain (von Luschan and Meinhof 1906: 722), the discourse surrounding *Lektoren* was one of capability and the African potential to grow and change under European guidance. The assistants even bore the external 'marks' of European respectability. On the whole they were better educated, with some having studied at Christian mission schools and others coming from traditional Islamic schools in Zanzibar or elsewhere in the Arab world.

Additionally, the assistants almost always donned Western dress. Here, though, the vexed position of Africans in Germany was brought into sharp relief, as clothing itself was somehow considered 'un-African'. For instance, even though Meinhof had many previous African acquaintances, he was still concerned that each new assistant might arrive 'naked', or in some state of undress, in Germany.[9] There is no evidence that any of them did show up this way, and Meinhof's schizophrenic assessment of the assistants demonstrates the uneasiness with which Germans generally confronted them. On the one hand, Meinhof saw the *Lektoren* as more 'civilized' than other Africans, as they were educated and helped sustain his academic research. On the other hand, there was always fear that the assistants would revert to some prior stage of primitivity, shedding their European trappings and wreaking havoc in the streets of Berlin. It is telling that the one African assistant who was actually asked to put on 'traditional' dress for his seminars was Hassan Taufik (Tewfink), a lecturer in Egyptian Arabic.[10] While Arabs were generally understood as having 'national costumes', nudity was considered the national costume of sub-Saharan Africans. Thus while African *Lektoren* and *Sprachgehilfen* conformed outwardly to German standards of education, comportment and dress, they were never placed on a par with white Germans; instead they occupied a middle space in which cultural signs jockeyed for position with racial ones.

African assistants were, however, undeniably integral to the learning process at the Berlin Seminar and Hamburg Institute. When discussions concerning the shape the Seminar was to take were first initiated in the mid-1880s, the employment of 'native-speaking' lecturers to work with German teachers was already seen as a given. Seminar Director Eduard Sachau held that this particular approach to language training was, moreover, wholly unique to Germany, because 'at the time that the Seminar was founded, this principle was completely new and until that point, as far as is known, had not been applied in any other European countries'.[11] Whether or not this was true is difficult to ascertain; the École des Langues Orientales Vivantes in Paris used *répetiteurs* to aid French professors in the classroom.[12] There is no evidence whether these were 'natives' or not, and it seems likely that other Europeans admired the German system for imparting knowledge of 'exotic' languages.[13]

The Africans and Asians who worked for the Seminar therefore played a critical educative role in Germany, providing their students with the skills necessary to negotiate everyday life in their posts abroad. Their presence was, furthermore, not unrelated to two parallel developments in the history of comparative philology and linguistics in Germany: a shift in attention to the importance of 'living' languages, and an interest in providing more 'practical' language knowledge. Throughout the nineteenth century there had been a general move toward reforming philological and literary studies, turning away from earlier emphases on classical languages such as Latin and Greek and giving more weight to *Neusprachen* such as German, French, and English. This was in part tied to a desire to raise the respectability of national languages and literatures, and to imbue them with a significance and dignity they had earlier lacked. German itself was not the only language to be recast in terms of its importance for national identity and the creation of the *Volk* (Haenicke 1979), but it still received special attention as it gained new prominence in the curriculum of German universities (Seeba 1991).

At the same time, with Germany's increased interaction with the world and its acquisition of colonies, there was an ever greater need for German scholars and civil servants who could communicate with non-Europeans. For this reason, as a late colonial pamphlet by Berlin Seminar Arabic teacher Martin Hartmann argued, instruction should be simplified and have straightforward, practical goals rather than intellectual or literary ones.

When it came to African language training, practical considerations also outweighed academic ones. Brigitte Reineke (1990) contends that sub-Saharan African language training at the Seminar for Oriental Languages was more pragmatic in its ends than any other non-European language instruction, and was thus very closely linked to the creation of colonial power networks. But the matter was more complex; while the growth of African language and culture studies in Germany was largely dependent on its significance for the German colonies, its practitioners also believed that the discipline had enormous potential to answer age-old questions about human origins and the relationship of language to *Geist* and *Volk* (Pugach 2001).

The first African *Lektoren* to arrive in Germany and work in Berlin were affiliated with the 'practical' colonial world; they had connections with the German colonial government, and employment was sometimes arranged by mediating civil servants working in the colonies. This was the case with Suleiman bin Said, the first of the sub-Saharan African *Lektoren*, who arrived in 1889 when he was seventeen to aid Swahili teacher and former Rhenish society missionary Carl Büttner. Asked by Sachau to find a suitable assistant, a Seminar alumnus stationed in Daressalam, Karl Reinhardt, used his links with both Said and his father to negotiate a three-year contract.[14] In the contract, Said acknowledged his intent to place himself under Sachau's authority, and to 'instruct the people in the Swahili language and script and explain Arabic characters to them' for 150 Rupees – or 200 German Marks – a month, significantly less than the Chinese *Lektoren* received.[15]

Said died of unknown causes after less than two years in the German capital, yet his case reveals much about German perceptions of Africans, and the position they assumed in imperial German society. Said's ethnicity and 'race', for instance, were not as fixed or bounded as the founders of the Seminar might have liked. Said did not consider himself 'Swahili', even though he had been hired to teach that language at the Seminar.[16] It seems likely that he thought of himself as more Arab than Swahili since his father was Arab. His 'Sitten der

Sansibarleute' (Customs of the Zanzibar People) (bin Said 1894), included discussions of both Arab and Swahili traditions. Further, soon after Said's arrival, Reinhardt wrote Sachau in exasperated dismay because 'in Sleman's [sic] last letter to his father, he spoke very rudely of the situation with his salary . . . which leads me to the conclusion that Sleman [sic] has been treated as an Arab, and not as a Swahili, which he is, in other words he has been spoiled.'[17] The implication was that, as a Swahili, Said had no right to complain about his wages – which were likely the main reason he was in Germany, since he remitted cash home each month.

Non-African *Lektoren* generally assumed a higher status at the Seminar for Oriental Languages, which offered courses in Chinese, Japanese, Turkish and Hindustani, among others. Asian and North African teaching assistants were often older, and consequently more experienced. The only older African *Lektor* was fortyish Aleka Taje, who taught Amharic and Ge'ez at the Seminar from 1904 to 1907. Taje's situation was different as he was specifically chosen because of his close relationship to King Menelik and his high standing at the royal court. Moreover, the Seminar wanted to introduce Amharic expressly to improve Germany's trade relationship with Ethiopia, not to extend its own colonial power. While a business component was usually associated with most of the African languages offered in Berlin and Hamburg – Hausa, for instance, was offered because its speakers were seen as controlling the financial landscape in much of north-central Africa[18] – they were often also administrative languages in the German colonies. By contrast, Amharic could only be used to strengthen ties with another polity, and therefore Seminar leaders took extra care to ensure that Taje was well treated since complaints could sour general relations between Germany and Menelik.[19]

Non-African *Lektoren* were commonly given more responsibilities and had greater social standing. In general, African teaching assistants helped European instructors with their lectures, conducted speaking exercises with students, aided in the teaching of Arabic script, continued the work of informants in the colonies with linguistic transcription, submitted themselves to phonetic research, and related oral histories. On the surface their duties were not remarkably different from those of their Asian and North African colleagues, but it also seems that work expected of Asians and North Africans was less regulated and monitored since they were more likely to have higher educational qualifications. In addition, the Asians and North Africans had obligations outside the Seminar during their tenure. The Egyptian Arabic *Lektor* Taufik compiled a manuscript and produced several reports on life in Germany at the request of the Egyptian government.

Moreover, upon leaving the Seminar Taufik was sent to London to work for the Egyptian government there.[20] Amin Ma'arbes [sic], who taught Syrian Arabic at the Seminar for 15 years, taught three independent courses in the subjects '1001 Nights', 'Exercises in Reading and Explaining Arabic Script', and 'Newspapers and Practice in Writing'. He chose his own textbooks, even arguing with a German instructor on this issue, and was married to a German woman, Ottilie Kaatz, apparently without any objections or repercussions.[21]

While some African Lektoren also translated and annotated texts in their languages much as North Africans and Asians did, one might still contend that since they lacked the experience of their older colleagues, it was reasonable that they not undertake the same kind of work. But this stance is questionable since some African assistants remained in Germany for several years and therefore had occasion to improve their teaching abilities and garner valuable experience. Moreover, although the African assistants' physical roles were commonly more subservient than those of their Asian and Arabist colleagues, they were no less vital to the learning process. The Africans' main duties involved standing next to a German co-worker and mimicking difficult pronunciations. This was not the same as leading a class, but it was arguably of equal significance. African Lektoren were indeed just as indispensable as the Asians and Arabs, because few Germans, even those with advanced linguistic training, possessed perfect pronunciation in an African language.

Africans were, however, still not accorded the same status as Arabs or Asians, as an incident from 1912 underscores. On a visit to the Seminar für Kolonialsprachen (Seminar for Colonial Languages), Carl Meinhof's department of the Hamburg Colonial Institute, British missionary W.H.T. Gairdner commented admiringly that the African teaching assistants were like 'living phonographs', who remained 'on the (European's) side' to be 'cranked up' whenever there was need for demonstration.[22] Gairdner thus located Hamburg's Lektoren less among the German teachers, many of whom had 'professional' backgrounds in subjects such as comparative philology or medicine,[23] and more among the scattered pieces of phonetic technology that littered the Seminar.[24] The Africans assistants were not viewed as language 'experts', but rather as one of the many tools necessary for language instruction.

The African assistants' duties also extended outside of the lecture hall, and in some situations they were able to exert more individual authority. After formal courses were over, Lektoren held speaking practice for their pupils, and here they were largely – if not completely – in charge. In 1892, the Seminar for Oriental Languages compiled a list of how many students had sought out-of-class assistance from Amur bin Nasur, the man who succeeded Said as Swahili *Lektor*. Nasur did not have many visitors; he usually had only two to three guests per day, out of ten students.[25] Even so, in a smaller, primarily one-on-one environment, Nasur likely had occasion to shape his pupils' understanding of Swahili. At the same time, the Colonial Institute did not allow its assistants to teach unsupervised, and while *Lektoren* held independent language exercises at the Seminar in Berlin, they did not appear to teach their own courses either.

Assistants' lives were also proscribed in other ways, limiting their movements in and outside of the classroom. Sexual politics, for one, were governed by the notion that Africans and Germans were not to form intimate relationships. When they did, they did so at their own peril. In 1900, the Seminar for Oriental Languages decided to employ Mtoro bin Mwenyi Bakari [*sic*] as its newest Swahili assistant. Bakari, formerly a Bagamoyo tax collector, initially took the position to provide financial support for his wife and daughter in East Africa. Until 1904 his tenure was unremarkable, but then he precipitated a crisis when he became engaged to a German woman named Bertha Hilske. Moreover, another German woman had contacted the Seminar to complain that Bakari had been engaged to her as well, and had then deserted her. Bakari claimed that since his Swahili wife had been unfaithful to him he wanted a divorce, and had sent her a letter to that effect. However, neither Carl Velten, then German Swahili lecturer, nor the other Seminar officials believed that Bakari's proclamation of divorce was legal.[26]

Thereafter Bakari's situation deteriorated. Although he had been looked upon favorably and considered an excellent instructor during his first three years at the Seminar, Velten, his supervisor, now contended that Bakari's moral character was 'weak', and that he was being blatantly manipulated by Hilske and her mother, who were only interested in his salary. Velten was subscribing to the stereotype that naïve Africans were prone to being exploited by more intelligent and ingenious Germans, especially women of 'dubious' morals. Velten also contended that Bakari's work had suffered as a result of the liaison, as 'it is well known that the Negro in love is, in his mindlessness (*Stumpfsinn*), incapable of any work'. Indeed, the consequences of Bakari marrying Hilske could be dire since the liaison had the potential to throw sexual – and racial – hierarchies into jeopardy in both colony and metropole. Bakari had already 'sassed' a student by refusing to answer a question after the end of a class, exhibiting 'shocking' disrespect toward a white man.[27] Further, if he took Hilske to East Africa, Bakari's actions would be:

of the greatest disadvantage for the reputation of Europeans in general and the few German women in the colonies in particular. Such a case has still not come to light in any of our African colonies, and hopefully will never come to pass. A German girl who is capable of marrying a black will surely sink even deeper in the colonies and bring shame to all Europeans. Even if the Europeans know just what to think of such a person, in the natives' eyes she will always remain the white woman, the German woman.[28]

Fear that Bakari had transgressed the boundaries of this racial order, and would continue to do so, led to his removal from the Seminar. Although he briefly resurfaced later at the Colonial Institute, his eventual marriage to Hilske excluded him from the company of 'civilized' Africans who worked in the German academy. By not complying with the hierarchical racial order that set Africans apart from Germans, Bakari – and, for that matter, Hilske – lost their social standing and retreated to the margins of German society. Unlike the Moroccan Amin Ma'arbes, whose marriage to Ottilie Kaatz seems never to have been questioned or challenged, Bakari's union with Hilske was viewed as too dangerous to allow to progress.

Bakari's 'sin' redounds through the history of African *Lektoren* in Germany. After he was ousted, Count Adolf von Gotzen, then Governor of German East Africa, mentioned that the colonial section of the German foreign office had proclaimed that assistants should have at a maximum eighteen-month long contracts, a move that he considered desirable.[29] Furthermore, the assistants' contracts now stipulated that future Swahili *Lektoren* 'reside with a suitable vocational school teacher' during their tenure in Berlin.[30] The same requirement also held true in Hamburg, which also employed several African teaching assistants between 1909 and 1919.

Fear of rampant African sexuality also forestalled the employment of certain assistants. No South-West Africans, for instance, were in fact ever allowed to teach in the metropole. The South-West African administration expressed 'grave doubts' as to whether natives from the protectorate should be allowed to travel abroad.[31] Such natives would 'after the experience return completely spoiled for local conditions'.[32] The inhabitants of South-West Africa were depicted as more depraved than those in the other colonies. Given the opportunity to leave, it was said they would drink, have untoward relationships with loose German women, and basically carouse about town in the most immoral of fashions.[33]

There was thus anxiety that Africans, once exposed to German culture, would be unwilling to 'stay in their place', as it were, once they came back to the colony. After all, the German South-West

African government maintained that it was three natives – Friedrich Maherero, Ferdinand Zemunja and Titus Tjcamuhaha – who had participated in the Berlin Colonial Exhibition of 1896, then returned to South-West Africa and incited their countrymen to revolt in 1903, which ultimately led to the disastrous Nama-Herero war.

The realization that Europeans were not necessarily as intelligent or strong as Africans threatened German authority, and perhaps did even more than that: African power subverted fixed racial hierarchies, which clearly depicted blacks as inferior to whites, Asians and Arabs. It also undermined notions of citizenship and belonging in the relatively new German state. Lora Wildenthal has shown how mixed marriages in the German colonies precipitated heated debate over who was and who was not German. According to the citizenship laws of 1870 and 1913, citizenship was passed through the male line, so that even if someone's mother was non-European, they could still be considered German. Especially after the Nama-Herero war in South-West Africa and the Maji-Maji revolt in East Africa – which occurred around the same time that Bakari intended to marry Hilske – citizenship of even those who had white fathers was called into question (Wildenthal 2001). If mixed marriages between white men and black women were threatening, how much more so must have been unions of black men with white women, where the progeny would very decidedly not be German and the woman herself would forfeit her Germanness upon entering into the relationship?

African 'Ethnographies' of Germany and other academic projects

The assistants' roles were in a sense academic ones. *Lektoren* worked within a methodological framework that demanded the presence of a native assistant when 'exotic' languages were being taught. Since they were masters of that knowledge, despite European supervision they had leverage in determining how their languages were portrayed. This was particularly the case when they aided scholars on linguistic transcription projects.

A striking example of this kind of collaboration is Martin Heepe's *Jaunde-Texte* (Ewondo Texts). In order to complete a phonetic description of the Cameroonian language, Heepe, a Colonial Institute lecturer, wanted to address problems concerning the nature of musical tone and sentence melody with the assistance of Karl Atangana, an Ewondo chief who was Meinhof's assistant, his wife Maria Biloa, his scribe Johannes Ngumu, and his nephew Paul Messi. The group worked together for two years, with Heepe recording the words and sounds that they produced. The book that resulted was a joint effort, as all five participated in its creation and all were acknowledged in its final outcome.

Assistants occasionally received higher praise for individual contributions to linguistic study as well. In 1905, when Sachau and Velten were chastising Bakari for his relationship with Hilske, Meinhof defended him on the grounds that his personal life had not affected his performance in the classroom.[34] Victor Toso, too, was praised for his contributions to Meinhof's linguistic scholarship; indeed, Meinhof observed that, far from being unwilling to express his opinions, Toso sometimes argued fine points of grammar with him.[35]

There was, however, again a shadow side to the significance of African participation in phonetic experiments: *Lektoren* were often described more as objects of study than as academic contributors. In the section of Heepe's *Jaunde-Texte* devoted to phonetic analysis, for instance, there is a clear division between his tasks and those of the assistants; Heepe was the 'scholar' whose project this ultimately was, while the others were there to 'speak' into early phonetic transcription machines such as the kymograph and E.A. Meyer's measuring device (Heepe et al. 1919: 13–20). They were necessary to the project, but for their physical capabilities, not their mental ones.

Other Africans also participated in phonetic experiments. In 1910, Meinhof established a Phonetics Laboratory with the express purpose of studying African languages and linguistics (Meinhof 1913). Here, Africans were turned into the ultimate subjects, practically disembodied vocal chords used to produce sounds that Germans could later study. The devices used to capture African voices, along with sundry other items, were displayed at an 'exhibition' in 1912, in which members of the public were encouraged to visit the Seminar and examine the various machines used in the Laboratory, as well as the 'anatomical preparations, models of the speech organs . . . and x-rays' that were so important to the linguist's academic goals.[36] While African *Lektoren* were considered teachers, as Meinhof's assessment of Bakari's work makes evident,[37] they were also imagined as experimental subjects, which detracted from any higher status they could otherwise attain. When the Phonetics Laboratory was established in 1910, it was an arm of Meinhof's Hamburg Seminar [for Colonial Languages]. While in time other professors from across the Colonial Institute clamored to use the Laboratory for their own research, it is still telling that it was first organized only for African studies. This demonstrates that, while people of all ethnic backgrounds could be observed phonetically, Africans were considered the ideal subjects of these investigations. Unlike Asians, Arabs, or Europeans, most of their languages were unwritten. Consequently, whereas other groups provided written texts, African bodies *were* texts, ones that were best read with technological assistance.[38]

African *Lektoren* in Germany were thus trapped between two conflicting roles. In a sense they were academic peers who were sometimes given responsibilities comparable to those of graduate students today. On other occasions, though, they were equated with pieces of technical equipment, tools to help facilitate quicker German understanding of their languages. They also fulfilled another function, which reinforced their intellectual position and demonstrated how much German researchers depended on African participation. From the earliest days of the Berlin Seminar, assistants described their lives and traditions in various German publications. Suleiman bin Said, for example, compiled a list of 'Sitten der Sansibarleute' ('Customs of the Zanzibari'), which was included in the book *Lieder und Geschichten der Suaheli, Beiträge zur Volks- und Völkerkunde* ('Songs and Stories from the Swahili, Contributions to Folklore and Ethnology'). Amur bin Nasur likewise contributed the 'story of his life' to the same volume. Moreover, many other assistants – including Atangana, Messi and Toso – also wrote their own ethnographic texts or had them transcribed by Germans. All of these texts offered pre-Geertzian 'thick description' of African cultures, which were also very similar to the ethnographic essays produced by missionaries that appeared in journals like Meinhof's *Zeitschrift für Kolonialsprachen*.

From early on Njo Dibone, Meinhof's first African teacher, also assisted with anthropological and literary pursuits. While in Zizow, he compiled and published a selection of Cameroonian fables with Meinhof's first wife, Elli.[39] Further, he also helped to negotiate the collection of West African idols for her husband's colleague, Felix von Luschan. Meinhof commented to von Luschan that Dibone, in part owing to his social position as King Akwa's nephew, had been able to supply Meinhof with local literature – presumably for scholarly purposes – when no one else could. He therefore believed that Dibone would be able to procure the desired idols for Luschan and then create a catalogue with the name and functional description of each.

Many later African teaching assistants in Berlin and Hamburg also worked on the production of literary and anthropological texts in a manner not dissimilar to that of the missionaries and travelers who collected data in the colonies and then either reported it to 'armchair' scholars in the metropole or published it independently. Their motives, though, seem to have been different. Missionary anthropology, whether in specifically mission-directed journals or scholarly ones, was usually meant to bolster evangelical goals by supplying religious, social or cultural information that could prove useful in furthering the spread of Christianity. Meanwhile, Meinhof presented Dibone's interest in payment in an unflattering, racist light, complaining to von Luschan that, for all his intelligence and his intimacy with Christianity through his relationship to the Basel Mission Society, Dibone sometimes asked for financial compensation for his anthropological and linguistic efforts.[40]

The financial motives Meinhof apparently saw as 'typical' of African 'nature' were, then, attributable to an understandable desire on the part of Lektoren to improve the economic and social standings of both their families and themselves, which could be achieved by collecting ethnographic materials in the colony or leaving home to work in the metropole. Suleiman bin Said certainly had financial concerns, and part of his salary went to his father in Zanzibar;[41] his successor, Amur bin Nasur, likewise supported his family by sending a portion of his pay home (Trüper 2002). Both Said and Nasur were also involved in publishing ethnographic material, though in this instance there is not much evidence that they were doing so for economic gain.

Economics may have also spurred Lektoren to provide information about their cultures. Said's 'Customs of the Zanzibari' offered Germans a template on how to behave on the island, especially when conducting business deals. It described how various inhabitants of the island interacted with each other, and what formulae Europeans should follow to facilitate relations with both the Swahili and Arabs. Said described not only proper body language, but also specific words and correct pronunciation and went out of his way to define certain terms in minute detail, such as 'anzali', a 'rude' or 'crass' person, who was 'uneducated' and 'did not know how to speak'. Said's writings on Zanzibar were both descriptive and prescriptive. By explaining how colonists were to behave, Said was engaged in a 'practical translation' between Swahili or Arab and German culture (bin Said 1894: 144–145, 152–153).

While Said described only the Swahili and Arab customs of Zanzibar, Nasur went further, comparing the two cultures he knew best, the Swahili and the German. On the one hand, he translated Zanzibari culture for the Germans, providing his own observations on island life. On the other, he became a friendly critic of German culture, chronicling his interactions with 'locals' in Berlin in a largely positive fashion (bin Nasur 1894: 180).

In contrast to Berlin, Nasur's home city of Zanzibar was not clean or well-ordered. It was a riot of color, sound and confusion, filled with 'cannibals' who, although they 'admittedly did not eat flesh itself, consumed money' from unsuspecting tourists. Cheaters and thieves lurked all around, implying that if a German did not watch himself, he would be just as lost in Zanzibar as Nasur claimed he had been in Holland, a country that he contrasted unfavorably with Germany (ibid.: 184–185). Still, not everything in Zanzibar was unpalatable; German visitors could find quite friendly Arab and Swahili hosts[42].

Nasur also wrote a brief description of Germany, describing its people as well as their surroundings. In Nasur's text, Germany seemed silent, empty, and leeched of life, and this was a good thing; in comparison, Zanzibar was crowded and dangerous, and this was in part negative. However, even knowing about Nasur's background, we can surmise that his exultant opinions of Germany might have stemmed from the fact that he was writing for a German audience in general, and for Carl Büttner, the Swahili teacher who had helped facilitate his transition to Berlin, in particular. Nasur lavished praise on Büttner, lauding his hospitality and willingness to help the *Lektor* become acclimated to the unfamiliar surroundings (bin Nasur 1894: 170).

Yet other evidence suggests that Nasur's German experience was not quite so rosy. In his private correspondence, Nasur voiced dissatisfaction with Germany and its policies toward Africans, and also expressed longing for Zanzibar. In an 1895 letter to Sachau, Nasur complained that, although he had been working at the Seminar for four years, he had never been granted a vacation while German colonial officials who were posted overseas were given six months leave after only two years' service. This he found unacceptable, since 'in my case you should take into consideration the fact that I am in a much worse position than are the German civil servants, because I have been completely removed from the habits of my homeland, my countrymen, and fellow religious believers, and been placed in a world that was originally wholly foreign to me'.[43] Wistful for home, and especially upset about having lost several family members while in Berlin, Nasur both chastised his German employers and depicted a Zanzibar that, far from being a cheater's paradise, was a place to which he very much wanted to return.

While it is difficult to assess the assistants' exact motives in producing ethnographic texts for a German public, it is clear that for Said and Nasur race was constructed very differently than it was for scholars like Meinhof. In many of the more than 600 books and articles that he wrote in his lifetime, Meinhof struggled to define African racial hierarchies. Theoretically, as a Bantu-speaking people he considered the Swahili at the 'midpoint' of African development, between the less evolved Sudanic speakers and the more advanced Hamites (Pugach 2002). In a 1910 article, Meinhof postulated that the Bantu had arisen from a union, or mixture, of the 'light-skinned' and 'conquering' Hamites, and the weak, indigenous 'black' Sudanic speakers they had encountered in Africa (Meinhof 1910: 164). He thus set up a hierarchy that organized people according not only to their languages, but also to skin color. Meanwhile in practice – that is, in Berlin and Hamburg – neither he nor his colleagues made much distinction between Africans of separate 'races'; they were all essentially accorded the same negative treatment, and placed on a level apart from Europeans, Asians and Arabs.

In terms of this hierarchy, Said and Nasur were imagined as Africans, even though both had Arab fathers. When Said complained that his salary was too low, Sachau claimed that he had the temerity to do so because he had been spoiled and treated like an Arab, and not as a Swahili, which Sachau insisted that he was. Yet Said spoke and taught both Arabic and Swahili, and when he wrote about Zanzibar in Büttner's book described the customs of both people. Said did not, therefore, see himself as Swahili, or not *only* as Swahili; rather, he was also Arab, as was his Omani father.[44] Nasur likewise considered himself both Arab and Swahili. He came from a wealthy slave-owning family, and had shuttled back and forth between Zanzibar, Oman and the East African mainland during his youth (Trüper 2002). In his contribution to Büttner's volume, Nasur also discusses the lives of both Arab and Swahili, and it seems as if his identity was fluid, not defined exclusively in terms of either group.

The motivation for African participation in linguistic or ethnographic ventures in the metropole may often be shrouded, and in some instances based on monetary concerns; their translations and representations of African culture, too, may not have matched German expectations, in that they did not delineate neat, bounded categories. However, in other cases it was in the *Lektoren*'s self-interest to please the Germans. Atangana, for instance, was intrigued with the power that a trip to Germany could bring. As an Ewondo colonial chief who had benefited from German rule, Atangana was able to bolster his reputation among the colonizers by going to their capitals and working with their scholars. In Heepe's *Jaunde-Texte* – which was not only a phonetic guide, but also a repository of Ewondo oral literature – Atangana lavished praise on Germany and its people. From very early on,

Atangana – who was approximately twenty-seven when he collaborated with Heepe – had been taught by Germans, and for ten years had worked with or for them as an interpreter, paramedic and secretary before being installed as the 'director and chief of all Kolo, from the East to the West' (Heepe et al. 1919: 89–90). Atangana's perception of Germany was thus probably colored by his position as a colonial chief favorably disposed towards German rule (Quinn 1980). He complimented his German colleagues whenever he had the chance, claiming astonishment at the scholarship of men like Meinhof and the phonetician Giulio Panconcelli-Calzia, and admiring the strength of European women (Heepe et al. 1919: 88, 107). He also recalled the great awe he felt when seeing the German Kaiser in person at the dedication of a new lecture hall in Hamburg, exulting like any German at having a chance to meet his 'ruler' (ibid.: 87–88, 116–118).

Atangana was also very interested in proving that Africans were capable of advanced civilization, and that some had already achieved it. In a lecture that he presented at the University of Hamburg, Atangana explained that whatever 'unusual' customs and traditions it might seem that the Ewondo had, both they and the other ethnic groups in Cameroon now belonged to the German *Reich*. This had permanently changed their perspectives, in Atangana's estimation for the better. 'Heathens' who had once married '200 wives' were now Christians with one mate, just like Europeans. The land was, Atangana maintained, becoming 'civilized' under German influence, and his ethnography of it was accordingly one of progress and development (ibid.: 127). Atangana therefore stressed the idea of African transformation under the influence of Christian, German culture, echoing a theme often found in Protestant missionary ethnography of the period.[45] In some ways, though, Atangana's lecture also ran counter to German narratives of colonial progress. Instead of emphasizing the *potential* of Africans to be 'christianized' and 'civilized', Atangana suggested that many Africans were already civilized.[46] Again, he likely had a vested interest in demonstrating African ability, as the more competent Africans were considered in the eyes of his German audience, the better his chances of obtaining more power.

Atangana's nephew Messi, who survived World War I in Germany, was also impressed. Many of the texts Messi supplied Heepe were reports on German military superiority, filled with accounts of German heroism and paper-thin descriptions of the people against whom they fought (Heepe et al. 1919: 214).[47] Messi was astounded by the number of ethnic groups involved in the war with Germany, plaintively asking Atangana 'Can you even imagine how many (different) peoples they are battling?' (ibid.: 211). Just as Nasur was fascinated by

the supposed orderliness of German society, so was Messi astonished
by its largeness, the utter scale of World War I being unlike anything
he had experienced in Cameroon.

Despite Messi's largely favorable opinion of Germany, there were
undercurrents of tension in the texts he published with Heepe, which
criticized the project's 'main' author himself. While Messi was in
Hamburg, Heepe was a prisoner of war in East Africa. One of Messi's
texts, therefore, was a 'Letter to Mr. Heepe', in which the *Lektor*
poured out his feelings for the linguist. Messi, who knew few people
and felt rather alone in Germany had affection for Heepe, and said he
wanted 'so much to be with' him. Yet when Heepe undertook his
research trip among the Swahili in 1914, he did not even say goodbye
to Messi, who judged him harshly as a result. 'I said to myself: A European certainly does not know what love is. The European is namely
so: You would like to have him, yes. You would like to give him everything that there is in the world, and he does not know how to estimate what you do for him' (ibid.: 212). Messi not only admonished
Heepe, he also characterized his actions as 'typical' for Europeans. In
this sense Messi ironically made the leap of many European ethnographic texts of the period, which often depicted Africans in stereotypical fashion as 'primitive', 'childlike', and so forth; just as Germans
usually stereotyped Africans, so too had Messi developed his own
stereotype of Germans.

The ethnographic and literary texts that African teaching assistants
produced may, in sum, not necessarily have been what a German audience would have expected. They both reasserted German notions of
racial and ethnic superiority and subtly undermined them by suggesting, for instance, that Africans were more 'advanced' than Germans
supposed, or that African culture was hybrid and syncretic, and not to
be confined to static categories such as 'Bantu' or 'Arab'. Africans also
used scholarship as a way of promoting their own goals, whether these
included reaffirming loyalty to the colonial state or improving their
own economic circumstances.

Conclusion

African assistants were indispensable to German scholars. At the same
time, life for Africans in Germany was heavily proscribed by racialized knowledge, which placed Africans in a developmental hierarchy
and necessitated that they 'stay in their place'. When Africans transgressed preset boundaries they were punished, and the higher status
they had achieved as *Lektoren* suffered. While African teaching assis-

tants in Berlin and Hamburg were technically seen as 'more civilized' than the Africans who traveled with *Völkerschauen* they were still subject to the same racial regulations, and not trusted to comport themselves properly. For all of Meinhof's praise for the African assistants, he too assumed that they would possess a certain degree of primitivity. He believed most of the *Sprachgehilfen* would come to Germany with no knowledge of clothing, or at least not of European clothing, even though most of his assistants had worked with Germans from the mission or government in the past.[48]

Despite this African *Lektoren* undoubtedly had a substantial influence on the development of German *Afrikanistik*. If there was not a sense of anthropological or linguistic 'professionalism' among the assistants, there was still a feeling of educative responsibility. In *Jaunde-Texte*, for instance, Atangana describes his work at the Colonial Institute in terms of his obligation to instruct Germans in the Ewondo language (Heepe et al. 1919: 117). *Lektoren* were, furthermore, not just language instructors; rather, they translated between *cultures*, describing their communities to German audiences that knew little or nothing about them. Although these translations were mediated by German scholars and were the work of Africans who had close relations to the metropole and thus good reason to show deference to it, there were still moments when they defied German categorizations and expressed their own ambitions. It may be difficult to gain much of a sense of the texture of the lives of African *Lektoren* in Germany during the colonial period. The information we do have, however, presents us with a group of individuals who both met and subverted German ideas of what it meant to be 'African'.

Notes

1 Staatsarchiv Hamburg (hereafter known as StaH) 361–1 Hochschulwesen, Dozenten-u. Personalakten IV, 673, Meinhof, Carl, 23.7.1857, Carl Meinhof's Biographischer Bogen and Lebenslauf.
2 Staatsbibliothek zu Berlin, Nachlaß von Luschan, Briefen von Carl Meinhof, 18/12/00.
3 As a general rule the assistants were called *Lektoren* at the Seminar for Oriental Languages and *Sprachgehilfen* at the Colonial Institute, as archival material from both schools shows. There is a subtle difference: being a *Lektor* implied having the status of a lecturer, whereas the title *Sprachgehilfe* connoted relegation to the more subordinate role of 'helper'.
4 These men and women were, of course, likely also very different from how they were 'presented' to the public. Z.S. Strother's essay 'Display of the Body Hottentot' (in Lindfors 1999: 1–40, along with the rest of the collection) provides a good example of how images of Africans were created, maintained, and manipulated over

long periods of time, leading the proprietors of 'people shows' to exhibit their subjects in particular ways.

5 A few works and lectures have mentioned some of the African and European actors I discuss, including Oguntoye 1997; Reed-Anderson 1997; E. von Joeden-Forgey 2001. None of these, however, address the academic involvement of *Lektoren* and *Sprachgehilfen* in Germany, or how they might have used scholarly participation to better their own positions in the metropole and colony.

6 There is a rich literature on African participation in European anthropology, linguistics, and other intellectual enterprises: e.g., Schumaker 2001.

7 Bundesarchiv Berlin (hereafter known as BBA), R 1001 6165, Erforschung der Sprachen der eingeborenen Völkerschaften, Bd. 1, November 1889–30 November 1892, Th. Christaller to Chancellor Otto von Bismarck, September 1889.

8 BBA R 1001 6165, 1, Governor Julius Freiherr von Soden to Theodor Christaller, 30 September 1889.

9 StAH 361–5, IV W 102, I, Heft 11, *Seminar für afrikanische Sprachen*, Carl Meinhof to Max Förster, 19 May 1911, 'Einstellung eines Lektors für Ful und Haussa'; see also Meyer-Bahlburg and Wolff 1986: 87–90 et passim.

10 Geheimes Staatsarchiv Preußischer Kulturbesitz (hereafter known as GStaPKB), Rep. 208A, 39, Akte betreffend Hassan Taufik (Tewfink), Lektor des Ägyptisch-Arabischen, Contract of Hassan Taufik, 26 July 1887.

11 GStaPKB Rep 76Va Sekt. 2 Tit. X, Nr. 124 Bd. VII, Acta betreffend das Seminar für Orientalische Sprachen bei der Universität zu Berlin, vol. I, vom Juli 1907 bis Dezember 1910, correspondence from Eduard Sachau, Berlin, to Kaiserlich Russischen Botschafter in Berlin Graf von der Osten-Sacken, Berlin, 18 April 1908.

12 GStaPKB Rep 76Va Sekt. 2 Tit. 1, Nr. 28 Bd. I, Acta betreffend das Seminar für Orientalische Sprachen bei der Universität zu Berlin, vol. I, vom Februar 1885 bis Oktober 1887, Abschrift aus Blocks Dictionnaire de l'administration française, deuxième édition, Paris 1878, Art. Instruction supérieure S. 1152.

13 GStaPKB Rep 76Va Sekt. 2 Tit. 1, Nr. 28 Bd. II, Acta betreffend das Seminar für Orientalische Sprachen bei der Universität zu Berlin, vol. I, vom November 1887 bis Dezember 1892, Eduard Sachau to unknown, 27 February 1891; see also Spidle 1973 for a discussion of the popularity of German 'colonial' education abroad.

14 GStaPKB, Rep. 208A, Acta betreffend Lector Sleman bin Said, Nr. 119, Bl 1–98, 1889–1892, Eduard Sachau to Herr Minister Dr. von Goßler, director of the Ministry for Scholastic, Educational, and Medical Affairs, n.d., ca. July 1889.

15 GSTaPKB, Rep. 208, Acta betreffend Au Fung Tschii, Lektor des Südchinesischen, Contract between Au Fung Tschii and the Seminar for Oriental Languages, October 14, 1890.

16 Anonymous, 'Kunst, Wissenschaft, und Literatur', Beiblatt zu Nr. 14, *National-Zeitung*, 8 April 1891.

17 GStaPKB, Rep. 208A, Acta betreffend Lector Sleman bin Said, Nr. 119, Bl 1–98, 1889–1892, correspondence between Karl Reinhardt and Eduard Sachau, 4 March 1890.

18 GStaPKB, Rep. 108A, 76, Acta betreffend den Lektor der Haussa-Sprache, Mohammed al Boschir, Bl. 1–108, 1896–1901, Eduard Sachau to Herr Dr. Bosse, 15 June 1896.

19 GStaPKB, Rep. 208A, 28, 1–132, betr. Aleka Taje, Lektor für Amharisch u.s.w., Eduard Sachau to the German Minister of Education, 28 January 1907.

20 GStaPKB Rep. 208A, 39, Geheimes Staatsarchiv, Akte betreffend Hassan Taufik (Tewfink), Lektor des Ägyptisch-Arabischen, Vita Des Herrn Taufik, Lektor des Äegyptisc-Arabischen am Seminar für Orientalischen Sprachen, and correspondence of Sachau to Althoff, 24 August 1892.

21 GStaPKB, Rep. 208A, 40, Geheimes Staatsarchiv, Akte betreffend Maarbes, Lektor des Syrisch-Arabischen, Notice of the Death of Amin Ma'arbes by Ottilie Ma'arbes, geb. Kaatz, 3 June 1915.

22 Archiv der evangelischen Missionswerk, Basel (hereafter known as EMW), QK-4, 1, Missionsgesellschaften C. England, III Teil, Konf. Brit. Miss. Gesellsch., J.M.C., C. Zirkulare 1. Teil, Memorandum by the Rev. W.H.T. Gairdner, 'Missionary training methods on the Continent', März 1912.

23 For example, Meinhof had studied both *Germanistik* – German studies – and theology, one of his Seminar colleagues, Otto Dempwolff, was a medical doctor, and another, August Klingenheben, had concentrated on the study of Semitic languages during his university career.

24 And which are in part catalogued in 'Ausstellung des Seminars für Kolonialsprachen', *Deutsche Kolonialzeitung* Nr. 25, Berlin, 22 June 1912, 29.

25 GStaPKB, Rep. 208A, Acta betreffend Amir Bin Nasir, Lector des Suaheli, Bl. 1–53, 1891–1895, list of vistors to Amur bin Nasur's office, n.d., ca. June 1892.

26 GStaPKB, Rep. 208A, Nr. 121, Blatt 1–173, Lektoren des Suaheli, Bd. I, 1899–1909, Carl Velten to Eduard Sachau, June 16, 1904.

27 Ibid, Carl Velten, *Gutachten* (Evaluation) of Mtoro bin Mwenyi Bakari, 5 May 1905.

28 Ibid, Velten to Sachau, 16 June 1904.

29 GStaPKB Rep. 208A, Nr. 121, Blatt 1–173, Lektoren des Suaheli, Bd. I, 1899–1909, Correspondence of Count Adolf von Gotzen, Governor of East Africa, Daressalam, to Auswärtige Amt, Kolonialabteilung, 19 September 1905. Gotzen was citing the *Erlaß des Auswärtigen Amts Kolonialabteilung vom 3. August No. 783.*

30 Ibid, Contract for Swahili teaching assistants, ca. October 1905.

31 StaH 361-5, I VW Nr. 102, Band I, Heft 6, betr. Seminar für afrikanische Sprachen, Max Förster to School Inspector Professor Dr. Ahlburg, Hamburg, 16 November 1910, 'Annahme einer Witbooi-Hottentotten als Sprachgehilfen'.

32 StAH IV W 102, I, Heft 6, 15/2/11.

33 StAH IV W102, I, Heft 12, 17/1/12.

34 GStaPKB Rep. 208A, Nr. 121, Blatt 1–173, Lektoren des Suaheli, Bd. I, 1899–1909, Report by Meinhof concerning Bakari, 26 May 1905. The story of Bakari's relationship and subsequent marriage to a German woman is in itself quite interesting, and has been documented by Reed-Anderson (1997) and Oguntoye (1997).

35 Staatsbibliothek zu Berlin, Nachlaß Felix von Luschan, Meinhof to von Luschan, 24 February 1916. In this letter Meinhof lavished praise on Toso, commending him for his dependability and apprising Luschan of the help he had provided to the academic community, both in proofreading a Tschi dictionary by someone named Mohr and by supplying ethnologist Bernhard Ankermann with ample information on marriage customs in Togo.

36 'Ausstellung des Seminars für Kolonialsprachen'.

37 GStaPKB Rep. 208A, Nr. 121, Blatt 1–173, Lektoren des Suaheli, Bd. I, 1899–1909, Report by Meinhof concerning Bakari, 26 May 1905.

38 Carl Meinhof, 'Warum studiert man primitive Sprachen?', in Carl Meinhof, *Die moderne Sprachforschung in Afrika*, 1910.

39 Njo Dibone and Elli Meinhof, *Märchen aus Kamerun* (Strassburg, J.H. Ed. Heitz (Heitz und Mündel): 1889).

40 Staatsbibliothek zu Berlin, Nachlaß von Luschan, Briefen von Carl Meinhof, 18/12/00.

41 GStaPKB, Rep. 208A, Acta betreffend Lector Sleman bin Said, Nr. 119, Bl 1–98, 1889–1892, Eduard Sachau, 'Bericht über der Engagement des Suaheli-Lektors Sleman aus Zanzibar'.

42 Owing, one would suspect, to the strained relations between Zanzibaris and Comoros Islanders during this era.

43 GStaPKB, Rep. 208A Nr. 120, Acta betreffend Amir Bin Nasir, Lector des Suaheli, Bl. 1–53, 1891–1895, Amir to Sachau, 26/6/95.

44 The Omani had, indeed, a long and complex relationship with Zanzibar and the Tanganyikan mainland; see Iliffe 1979: 40ff.

45 One example of this sort of ethnography can be found in Spieth 1912.

46 See also Sanjek 1993: 15 on a similar pattern in the British case.

47 In this instance Messi notes admiringly that the Germans 'fight so, as if death were nothing special'.
48 See note 15 above.

References

Alter, Stephen. 1999. *Darwinism and the Linguistic Image: Language, Race, and Natural Theology in the Nineteenth Century*. Baltimore: Johns Hopkins University Press.

Bearth, Thomas. 2000. 'J.G. Christaller. A Holistic View of Language and Culture – and C.C. Reindorf's History'. In P. Jenkins (ed.). *The Recovery of the West African Past. African Pastors and African History in the Nineteenth Century: C.C. Reindorf and Samuel Johnson*. Basel: Basler Afrika Bibliographien, pp. 83–101.

Benes, Kveta. 2001. 'German Linguistic Nationhood, 1806–66: Philology, Cultural Translation, and Historical Identity in Preunification Germany'. University of Washington: Unpublished Ph.D.

Desai, Gaurav. 2001. *Subject to Colonialism: African Self-fashioning and the Colonial Library*. Durham: Duke University Press.

Dittrich, Lothar and Rieke-Müller, Annelore (eds). 1998. *Carl Hagenbeck (1844–1913): Tierhandel und Schaustellungen im Deutschen Kaiserreich*. New York: Peter Lang.

Haenicke, Gunta. 1979. *Zur Geschichte der Anglistik an deutschsprachigen Universitäten 1850–1925*. Augsburg: Universität Augsburg.

Haller, J. 1904. *Die Vorbildung unserer Missionare*. Basel: Basel Missionverein.

Heepe, Martin, Atangana, Karl and Messi, Paul. 1919. *Jaunde-texte von Karl Atangana und Paul Messi, nebst experimentalphonetischen Untersuchungen über die Tonhöhen im Jaunde und einer Einführung in die Jaundesprache*. Hamburg: L. Friedrichsen & co.

Heintze, Beatrix. 2002. *Afrikanische Pionieren: Trägerkarawanen im westlichen Zentralafrika*. Frankfurt: Verlag Otto Lembeck.

Iliffe, John. 1979. *A Modern History of Tanganyika*. Cambridge: Cambridge University Press.

von Joeden-Forgey, Elisa. 2001. 'From "Territorium Nullius" to "Personum Nullius": German Colonial Law and the Invention of the "Eingeborene"'. Unpublished conference paper, African Studies Association 44th Annual Meeting, 15–18 November 2001.

Lindfors, Bernth (ed.). 1999. *Africans on Stage: Studies in Ethnological Show Business*. Bloomington: Indiana University Press.

von Luschan, Felix and Meinhof, Carl. 1906. 'Über sechs Pygmäen aus Ituri und Untersuchung der Pygmäensprachen'. *Zeitschrift für Ethnologie* 38:717–731.

Meinhof, Carl. 1910. 'Sudansprachen und Hamitensprachen'. *Zeitschrift für Kolonialsprachen* I:161–166.

Meinhof, Carl. 1913. 'Die Bedeutung der experimentellen Phonetik für die Erforschung der afrikanischen Sprachen'. *Vox* 23:22–26.

Meyer-Bahlburg, Hilke and Wolff, Ekkehard. 1986. *Afrikanische Sprachen in Forschung und Lehre: 75 Jahre Afrikanistik in Hamburg (1909–1984)*. Berlin, Hamburg: Dietrich Reimer.

Naranch, Bradley D. 2001. 'Return of the Natives: Regulating the African Presence in Imperial Germany, 1884–1907'. Unpublished conference paper, Annual African Studies Association 44th Annual Meeting, Houston, TX, 15–18 November 2001.

bin Nasur, Amur. 1894. 'Leben des Herrn Amur bin Nasur'. In C. Büttner (ed.). *Lieder und Geschichte der Suaheli, Beiträge zur Volks- und Völkerkunde*, 3rd volume. Berlin: Verlag von Emil Felber, pp. 159–190.

Oguntoye, Katharina. 1997. *Eine Afro-Deutsche Geschichte: zur Lebenssituation von Afrikanern und Afro-Deutsche in Deutschland, 1884–1950*. Berlin: Hoho-Verl. Hoffmann.

Pugach, Sara. 2001. '*Afrikanistik* and Colonial Knowledge: Carl Meinhof, the Missionary Impulse, and African Language and Culture Studies in Germany, 1887–1919'. University of Chicago: Unpublished Ph.D.

Pugach, Sara. 2002. 'Theories of Language and Race in German Studies of Africa'. In A. Jones (ed.). *Jan Czekanowski: Africanist ethnographer and physical anthropologist in early twentieth century Germany and Poland*. Leipzig: Institut für Afrikanistik, pp. 63–89.

Quinn, Frederick. 1980. 'Charles Atangana of Yaoundé'. *Journal of African History* 21:485–495.

Reed-Anderson, Paulette. 1997. *Metropole, Menschen, Nahaufnahme: Afrikaner in Berlin*. Berlin: Die Ausländerbeauftragte des Senats.

Reineke, Brigitte. 1990. 'Afrikanische Sprachen am Seminar für Orientalische Sprachen'. In H. Bernhardt (ed.). *Beiträge zur Geschichte der Humboldt-Universität zu Berlin*. Berlin: Der Rektor, Humboldt-Universität zu Berlin, pp. 64–73.

Rothfels, Nigel T. 1994. 'Bring 'em Back Alive: Carl Hagenbeck and Exotic Animal and People Trades in Germany, 1848–1914'. Harvard University: Unpublished Ph.D.

bin Said, Suleiman [Sleman]. 1894. 'Sitte der Sansibarileute'. In C. Büttner (ed.). *Lieder und Geschichte der Suaheli, Beiträge zur Volks- und Völkerkunde*, 3rd volume. Berlin: Verlag von Emil Felber, pp. 139–156.

Sanjek, Roger. 1993. 'Anthropology's Hidden Colonialism: Assistants and their Ethnographers'. *Anthropology Today* 9:13–18.

Schumaker, Lyn. 2001. *Africanizing Anthropology: Fieldwork, Networks, and the Making of Cultural Knowledge in Central Africa*. Durham: Duke University Press.

Seeba, Hinrich C. 1991. 'Nationalbücher: Zur Kanonisierung nationaler Bildungsmuster in der frühen Germanistik'. In J. Fohrmann and W. Vosskamp (eds). *Wissenschaft und Nation: Zur Entstehungsgeschichte der deutschen Literaturwissenschaft*. Munich: Wilhelm Fink Verlag, pp. 57–71.

Spidle, Jake W. 1973. 'Colonial Studies in Imperial Germany'. *History of Education Quarterly* 13:231–247.

Spieth, Jakob. 1912. 'Die religiöse Veranlagung des Afrikaners'. In J.K. Vietor, C. Meinhof and J. Spieth (eds). *Der Afrikaner, seine wirtschaftliche Leistungsfähigkeit, geistige Befähigung, religiöse Veranlagung.* Bremen: Verlag der Norddeutschen Missionsgesellschaft, pp. 17–28.

Trüper, Ursula. 2000. *Die Hottentottin: Das kurze Leben der Zara Schmelen (ca. 1793–1831), Missionsgehilfin und Sprachpionierin in Südafrika.* Cologne: Rüdiger Koeppe Verlag.

Trüper, Ursula. 2002. 'Amur bin Nasur ilOmeiri – Lektor der Suahelisprache am Seminar für Orientalische Sprachen'. In U. van der Heyden and J. Zeller (eds). *Kolonialmetropole Berlin: Eine Spurensuche.* Berlin: Berlin Edition, pp. 201–206.

Wildenthal, Lora. 2001. *German Women for Empire, 1884–1945.* Durham: Duke University Press.

CHAPTER FIVE

Voices of their own? African participation in the production of colonial knowledge in French West Africa, 1910–1950

Jean-Hervé Jezequel

Ethnographic writing, in the broadest sense of the term, was a popular activity among educated West Africans as early as the 1910s.[1] Unfortunately, much of this writing remains largely unknown since it was never published and has languished in family archives or in the archives of colonial administrative districts. In French-speaking Africa, the vast majority of authors were local schoolmasters trained at the prestigious Ecole Normale William Ponty in Senegal.[2] Only a handful of these authors were officially recognized as such by either the colonial administration or the scholarly community. Thus while a few actually had careers as researchers, for the vast majority their ethnographic investigations boiled down to a few pages published in a local journal. The colonial administration actually encouraged this local scholarship, but for a long time refused to recognize these authors' credentials. Consequently, this arena of knowledge production was marked by a structural inequality between the author-participants and the colonial bureaucracy.

The history of anthropology, therefore, has rarely paid attention to these marginalized actors.[3] Indeed they are almost completely absent from both bibliographical listings and academic professional associations. Yet it would be wrong to assume that scholars have ignored this important corpus of texts altogether. Historians interested in the political and social history of colonial Africa have indeed stressed the importance of this literature either as traces of cultural nationalism (Manchuelle 1995) or as privileged sites to understand how Africans have reinvented traditions (Hobsbawm and Ranger 1983). These works, however, rarely challenge the assumption that Africans played a marginal role in the production of academic knowledge.

African authors actually wasted no time mastering the art of ethnographic writing and turning it into a vehicle to advance their own interests. While it is tempting to look at this first generation of 'indigenous ethnographers' as challenging the colonial monopoly over a discourse on African culture, the historical record is not so clear-cut. This article argues for the need to analyze the production of African ethnographic studies as a complex process, which requires close attention to the multiple contexts in which these texts were produced, read, and stored. African ethnography had a range of 'different lives' that need to be interrogated carefully.

This paper first examines the unequal organization of scholarly labor in French-speaking Africa. It stresses the subordinate relationship between European scholars and African ethnographers. However this subordination did not prevent African authors from developing their own agenda. Looking at three different contexts – the history of knowledge production, the social history of African intermediaries, and the political history of the local arenas – the following sections underscore the diverse meanings encoded within these ethnographic productions.

Organizing an unequal distribution of scholarly labor

Shortly after its founding in 1895, the colonial administration in French West Africa was preoccupied with investigating local African societies. Such knowledge, the administration thought, would permit a better understanding of native cultures as well as a better means to control them (Robinson 1992). As David Robinson argues, 'the concern for establishing custom emerged from administrators preoccupied with centralization, control and a strong paternalistic and interventionist approach to their African subjects' (Robinson 1992: 237). Professional scholars from France and colonial administrators – amateur ethnographers eager for professional respectability – were placed in charge (Sibeud 2002). In terms of the production of colonial knowledge, these Europeans acted at center stage. Yet colonial scholarly research in black Africa also made use of local informants whose role in the constitution of knowledge in African studies became preponderant, although not well documented, from the outset.[4] Indeed from 1910, the development of new research and publishing networks in French West Africa (AOF) encouraged the use not only of illiterate informants but also educated *indigènes*.[5] The emergence of 'indigenous studies' in this period was a consequence of the confluence of a new generation of colonial public servants, who have been described as humanists, and an emerging number of educated African elites.[6]

This confluence is intriguing since it goes against the usual understanding that there existed antagonistic relations between colonial administrators and African literates (L'Estoile 1997).

For the colonial public servants engaged in ethnographic studies, the aim was to have their ethnographic work recognized as scholarly rather than the product of enthusiastic amateurs (Sibeud 1994, 2002). However, to obtain the recognition they desired, they needed to make use of a network of local informants in which the local educated elite would eventually play a central role. Indeed, the goal of the Committee for Historical and Scientific Studies (Comité d'Etudes Historiques et Scientifiques de l'AOF), a central research office created in 1915 in Dakar by Governor-General Clozel, was to 'coordinate the research done under the patronage of the government-general and to centralize the results obtained'.[7] For the colonial administration, 'the knowledge of the history, ethnography, physical geography and natural history of a country will be indispensable for the proper organization and administration of the country'.[8] Faced with the need to collect data for compiling ethnographic and historical records, the administrator-ethnographers soon understood the need to use the services of educated Africans. A division of scholarly labor thus emerged in West Africa based on a network of local assistants, comprising both European administrators and indigenous public servants, who did data collection, while scholars and senior administrative officials could devote their time to producing books and articles. Thus, the nineteenth-century model of scientific institutions in Europe commissioning travelers and field officials to implement studies gave way to a model driven by questionnaires sent out to local correspondents by colonial administrations in the early twentieth century. The administration of these questionnaires was a classic example of using research assistants, including Africans.[9]

The *Bulletin de l'Enseignement de l'AOF* was the first to conduct a series of surveys that explicitly made use of African schoolmasters as informants. On the initiative of Georges Hardy, it sent out several survey questionnaires on learning, habitat and, subsequently, children and play, to its readers.[10] It also had a special section of the *Bulletin* dedicated to local stories and monographs by schoolmasters. The *Bulletin* published some responses sent by African schoolteachers, yet the bulk of these short studies constituted 'raw materials' for studies published by officials from the department of education in AOF.[11] The government-general itself used the journal to launch its own surveys, for example a survey in 1916 on 'land ownership regimes in French West Africa', which it saw as 'an excellent opportunity for native schoolmasters to occupy themselves gainfully during the holidays'.[12] Thus 'indigenous studies' were not only a way to collect important data on the Empire, but they could also help the administration avoid producing dangerous *'desoeuvrés'* (idle people).[13]

Autochthonous schoolmasters responded positively to the call for 'indigenous studies'. Like the administrator-ethnographers, they saw historical and ethnographic research as a means to gain social recognition. In the 1910s, the administration's desire to collect and centralize historical and ethnographic data through surveys found an unexpected 'ally' among educated elite who were by now increasingly receiving their education in French West Africa.[14] The administrator-ethnographers, however, believed Africans' writings were only useful in terms of the collection of raw data. In much the same way that the 'armchair scholar' required his informant, the foot soldier, to stick to the facts and provide him with neutral descriptions, these officials wanted African writers to restrict themselves to simply describing the facts and not to engage in interpretation.[15]

Yet some colonial administrators recognized in these African writers data collection skills that white researchers did not have. For example, in an address to indigenous schoolmasters, Georges Hardy admitted:

> Only you the indigenous schoolmasters are able to collect and compare these oral traditions; only you are capable of penetrating the souls of your compatriots to distinguish between the 'embellishments of the griots', like Mr. Clédor aptly describes them, and the facts as they truly are. You are therefore in a position to render a great service to your country and I will be eternally grateful to those who would share the results of their research with us.[16]

However, studies that ventured past simple reporting were severely criticized. For example, Maurice Delafosse dismissed the etymologies put forward by Abdoulaye Kane, an African colonial servant writing about Muslim traditions in Fuuta Tooro (Senegal), as a figment of Kane's imagination.[17] Delafosse's critics focused on the additional information given by Kane to supposedly clarify certain passages of his text. Delafosse actually referred the reader to his own book on the historical traditions of the Fouta Djallon, where the latter was supposed to find serious materials for comparison.

Criticism of this genre was not rare. In his introduction to Moctar Diallo's article on Islam in Rip, Paul Marty, officer-interpreter in charge of Islamic affairs in the government-general of French West Africa, considered the study interesting but regretted the author's lack of knowledge on customary law and utter misunderstanding of the relationship between social traditions and religious traditions in

Islam.[18] Implicitly, as the expert on Islam in Black Africa, Marty was serving notice that it was not enough to be an African Muslim to be able to do a scientific study on the question. In the eyes of the administrator-ethnographers, these West African educated elite still lacked certain skills that were the exclusive preserve of Western researchers, be they Islamologists like Paul Marty or ethnographers and linguists like Maurice Delafosse.

Africans' participation was thus restricted to subordinate roles, their marginalization underscoring their lack of official status. An analysis of the membership list of the Committee for Historical and Scientific Studies of French West Africa reveals that anyone who ever published an article in the Committee's *Bulletin* was accorded at a minimum the honorary status of correspondent of the Committee. Yet, in the 1910s, this privilege was not extended to Africans who had sent their research to the Committee. It was not until the late 1920s that the first African, Musa Travelé, an interpreter from Bamako, was given the modest title of correspondent of the Committee.

From this overview, we see that the 1910s marked the entry of Africans into research, albeit in subordinate positions. Without official status, these authors were no more than educated informants. The co-operation between the schoolmaster-ethnographers and the colonial administrator-cum-researcher was problematic and unequal. It depended on personal networks that brought the different protagonists together in a curious mix of friendship, paternalistic relationships, and, sometimes, cronyism.[19] It was this kind of complex relationship that linked people like Musa Travelé to Maurice Delafosse, Amadou Mapaté Diagne to Georges Hardy or Dabo Sissoko to Fernand Froger.[20] Without their 'protectors', these schoolmasters did not stand a chance of being published, or even being called upon to carry out surveys. When the principal promoters of indigenous writing, namely Hardy and Delafosse, departed for France in the early 1920s, it marked the end of an era; there was subsequently a sharp decline in the publication of articles in local journals by African authors.[21] It was not until the 1930s that the colonial authorities again displayed any interest in encouraging local scholarship.

The rebirth of indigenous studies (1930s–1940s)

In the 1930s, studies carried out by Africans began to reappear in new publications (e.g., *Outre-Mer*, *Notes Africaines*) and in the journals of scholarly societies (e.g., the Institut Française d'Afrique Noire, created in Dakar in 1936), which were actively seeking out such studies both in France and in French West Africa.[22] Beyond the re-activation of networks for the promotion of scholarly research, this rebirth was closely related to inflexions in French colonial policy in the 1930s.

The promotion of research in general, and of indigenous writing in particular, was once again encouraged by the colonial administration. In French West Africa, Governor-General Brevié, appointed in 1932, was especially sensitive to the issue of scholarly knowledge production. For example, in a circular letter concerning historical research, dated 2 May 1935, he unambiguously indicated a 'desire to awaken in both the French living in Africa and educated Africans the love of history and respect of the past' in order to 'do justice and bear testimony to all those who shaped the Africa of today'.[23] Brevié was responsible for a reinvigorated policy of promoting research that continued the tradition started by Governor-General Clozel two decades earlier. He distinguished himself, however, in his desire to give the indigenous educated elite a greater role in this process:

> In most cases, it should be possible for us to use educated indigenes for these research projects. They know both the French language and the traditions of their countries. Indigenous schoolmasters should be able to collect and transcribe the chronicles of Africa. At any rate, do not hesitate to bring to my attention the works of those who could help us better understand black Africa and its history.[24]

In the same year, the *Bulletin* of the Committee for Historical and Scientific Studies published an analysis of the Fon of Dahomey by Maximilien Quénum.[25] For the first time, the journal featured a complete study by an African author that was much longer than a simple article. To encourage the participation of Africans in ethnographic and historical studies, Brevié also created a special annual prize for indigenous research in French West Africa and introduced training in research methods in the education department to improve the collation and processing of information by African schoolmasters. In Dahomey, Paul Hazoumé, a trained schoolteacher, author of a study on sacrifices, and former intern at the Paris Musée de l'Homme, was charged with training his colleagues. Brevié also inspired other officials to use the indigenous educated elite, including Charles Béart, head of the William Ponty School, who encouraged schoolmasters to respond to the call of the administration. Under his aegis, the *Bulletin de l'Enseignement de l'AOF*, which became *Education Africaine* in 1934, published several studies conducted by non-European schoolmasters. And from 1933, the William Ponty School made the presentation of a research dissertation on local societies one of the conditions for going on to the third year of study.[26]

Nonetheless these efforts reflected more than a mere desire to re-activate networks of literate informants who would develop knowl-edge of the Empire. The conservative nature of this new policy was indeed unmistakable. By encouraging the 'elite' to study their societies of origin, the colonial authority was also determined to prevent them from becoming 'detribalized'.[27] Indeed, encouraging 'indigenous studies' was part of a broader policy to prevent the development of groups of '*déracinés*' in AOF. In 1935, in a speech opening the Ponty School's yearly party, Béart declared that 'Above all, we want them to remain Africans and to receive an education adapted to the life they would have in their country. Africa has its own individuality and it is not the mission of the school to destroy it. To the contrary, the school has to disclose this individuality to the indigenous peoples who are not always conscious of it.'[28]

The creation in 1936 of the Institut Français d'Afrique Noire (IFAN), to replace the old Committee for Historical and Scientific Studies of French West Africa, also served this policy. Following the recom-mendation of Brevié, the *Bulletin de l'IFAN* gave from the start more space to African authors.[29] From 1939, IFAN also published *Notes Africaines*, which devoted much space to short publications by edu-cated Africans. Indeed, the journal became primarily an organ to enable IFAN to keep in touch with its network of literate informants:

> *Notes Africaines* is primarily a publication designed to provide a means of contact between IFAN and its correspondents all over French West Africa. It would have achieved its objectives if it enabled the gradual con-stitution of a network of intelligent and observant informants, capable of pointing out (in particular, in the area of archaeology and prehistory) interesting discoveries that advance research.[30]

The impetus did not come from the colonial authorities alone. In France *Outre-Mer*, a journal launched in 1929, brought together a group of colonial public servants seeking to develop indigenous studies, while at the same time influence colonial policies.[31] The direc-tor of the publication was none other than Georges Hardy, who encour-aged the publication of papers by some of his former protégés in the late 1910s. For example, schoolmasters Mamby Sidibé and Amadou Mapaté Diagne, whose works had already been published when Hardy was heading the education department in AOF, were among the first African contributors to the journal.[32]

In the final analysis, the rebirth of indigenous writing in the 1930s was driven by a two-pronged agenda: the conservative policy of thwart-ing the publication efforts of detribalized Africans and the reactivation of informant networks (needed to generate knowledge of rural Africa).

Yet the increasing use of indigenous writing did not bring an end to the subordinate relationship instituted in the 1910s. Anne Piriou has aptly pointed this out in her study of the review *Outre-Mer*:

> What the ethnographic literature, in the broadest sense of the term, succeeded in doing in the early 1930s was to create a relatively autonomous social space, although one that was also subjugated and protected by the legitimating and controlling powers who laid down the standards ... The context in which these writers, simple data providers and non-intellectuals, could be heard, in the sense of de Certeau (1984), was very limited and restrictive ... And in the realm of indigenous studies, their voices could only be heard if they were responding to the needs of the colonial authorities or if their works could be used by Europeans for their own research. (Piriou 1997: 66; translated from French)

The progressive integration of African authors during the following decade in research institutions like IFAN might, however, suggest that the African researcher and intellectual was finally gaining some recognition.

At the beginning of the century, indigenous authors were supposed to be content with the role of informants and were not meant to go beyond the simple task of data gathering. From the 1930s, the idea that these authors were quite capable of more complex research work in ethnography and history began to be accepted. In Paris, by the middle of the decade, the Trocadero Museum welcomed a small number of West African students for training and research. The works of Paul Hazoumé and Maximilien Quénum, which went beyond the few pages usually associated with indigenous publications, were carried out within this framework and upon returning to Dahomey, Hazoumé was delegated by the education department to train his colleagues in research methods.

The Boisson Order of 1942 marked a significant milestone with the official creation of a scientific and technical framework accessible to both the French and colonial subjects. Naturally, there was an unmistakable barrier between the status of '*assistant*', which was in practice only open to Europeans, and those of '*preparateurs*' (preparers) and '*assistants de laboratoire*' (laboratory assistants), open to the best graduates of the federal schools of French West Africa (beginning with Ecole Normale William Ponty). However, educated Africans now had career paths open to them in the area of knowledge production. Young graduates of William Ponty and other institutions in French West Africa were thus directly integrated into the scientific and technical setup of French West Africa. By 1948, IFAN had seven '*indigenous pre-*

parers' among its local staff, excluding technical and laboratory assistants. Many of them would subsequently go on to have successful careers as researchers after their countries gained independence from France, such as Amadou Hampaté Bâ, preparer in Bamako, and Tidiani Serpos, preparer in Dahomey.[33] The late 1940s confirmed the official integration of African researchers in the scientific institutions that sprung up around IFAN from the 1930s. However this integration was still mired in ambiguity and it would be premature to believe that the era of a subordinate relationship between local researchers and their Western counterparts was over.

The colonial call for African participation can thus be interpreted as part of a progressive emergence and sedimentation of an imperial field of knowledge. This field included research and academic networks that straddled both the metropole and the colonies. African ethnographers integrated into these networks as subordinate members. The earlier evidence seems to indicate that they played a modest and marginal role in the emergence of this imperial field. Unlike their colonial nemeses – the administrator-ethnographers – none of the African ethnographers was in a position to directly influence the emergence and development of anthropology, ethnography or geography as academic disciplines in the metropole.

Yet interpreting the role these Africans played is difficult to capture not only given their subordination, but also because European scholars often needed to downplay, if not erase, signs of their presence. In order to recover these 'subaltern voices', we need to look carefully for the many small traces they left behind them. This also implies that historians of anthropology need to stop privileging an elitist perspective of their own field. If we want to recover African voices within the imperial field of knowledge, we also need to consider mundane traces of the past such as the routines of field research. In other words, we need to consider the production of academic knowledge in its mundane dimensions. The way a text was materially produced and stored might be as revealing for a history of colonial knowledge as studying an academic piece of work or the epistolary exchange between an administrator-ethnographer and a metropolitan scholar.

This project is of course beyond the scope of this article. Yet in the following sections, I want to suggest how these texts should be seen as more than marginal pieces of academic works. By questioning the motives that led African authors to embrace the ethnographic discipline, despite their evident marginalization, we begin to unveil the different contexts that give meaning to this ethnographic corpus.

*Producing an 'African Ethnography': cultural nationalism or
reproduction of colonial discourse?*

Describing African ethnographers as a subordinated group does not
allow us to understand why they enthusiastically embraced 'indigenous studies'. Why did they not choose other forms of self-expression
such as literature or philosophy? Looking at African agency in relation
to colonial dependence, Lyn Schumaker rightly suggests that 'the
model of exploitation fails to capture the assistants' own motives and
goals in taking on anthropological work' (Schumaker 2001: 12).

While indigenous authors were all employees of the colonial administration, they had different motives for engaging in ethnographic
writing. Scholars have recently shown an increasing interest in understanding these motivations and, more generally, in analyzing the
ethnography Africans produced.[34] François Manchuelle was among
the first to draw attention to the early group of West African educated
elite whose ethnographic and historical research contributed to 'the
defense and illustration of [African] heritage' (Manchuelle 1995: 337).
Manchuelle focuses particularly on the schoolmasters and educated
Africans, who following in the footsteps of the Creole precursors of
the mid-nineteenth century (Abbé Boilat, Paul Holle, etc.), published
works in the early twentieth century:

> These early ethnographic and historical writings were more than just
> precursors of the Negritude movement; they were in fact attempts at
> describing a modern African culture that preserved certain elements of
> the culture of the past, while at the same time shedding the most neg-
> ative aspects of the old society. (Manchuelle 1995: 360–361)

Representative in this regard were the efforts of Mamby Sidibé, a
schoolmaster-ethnographer who in a 1923 study on the populations
of the Banfora region (Upper Volta) protested against colonial clichés,
most notably the idea that African women were bought by their
husbands and that polygamy was driven by an unnatural appetite for
sex.[35] Instead Sidibé went to great lengths to show how polygamy
and agricultural production were closely related and how, in fact, a
strict sexual morality reigned in the Banfora region. Manchuelle
admits that Sidibé's texts also contained scathing criticisms of the
indigenous societies, but suggests that such criticisms were part of a
project of modernization that was also respectful of local customs.
Overall, Manchuelle analyzes Sidibé's text as a form of 'cultural
proto-nationalism'.

Similarly Helen Coundouriotis proposes the notion of 'resistant
history' to characterize the work of Paul Hazoumé, another West
African schoolmaster-ethnographer precursor.[36] Like Manchuelle,

Coundouriotis rightly challenges the conventional perspective of the intellectual elite as accomplices of French colonization through their desire for assimilation. She argues instead that Hazoumé's ethnographic and literary production should be seen as an attempt to portray local societies in their fullest historical dimension. In a work entitled *Le pacte de sang au Dahomey*, Hazoumé shows that sacrifice, far from reflecting a barbaric and criminal ancestral act, had a history that was closely related to the economic and political development of the Kingdom of Dahomey:

> Interpreted ahistorically, the Blood oath explains the cohesiveness of criminal gangs presenting native custom as an obstacle to the progressive program of the French. When the proper historical context is elaborated, however, it becomes clear that the blood oath has a variable meaning, and its particular evolution into criminal behavior illustrates the moral decline that sets in with the loss of sovereignty. Since in the past the blood oath helped create and sustain Dahomey as a political entity, it is obviously threatening to French authorities who need to discredit it. The colonialist perspective, therefore, authorizes the ethnographic description of the blood oath as criminal behavior that Hazoumé undermines by historicizing his description. (Coundiouriotis 1999: 93)

Hazoumé's project emerges, then, as an act of resistance against colonial knowledge: he casts in historical terms practices that the colonial world view had frozen in the name of an African authenticity that was as illusory as it was intended to be belittling.

Whether interpreting their sources as representing a cultural nationalism, a political nationalism, or 'resistant history', these works had the merit of destabilizing some of the charges of collaboration levelled against the 'assimilated elite' and drew attention to a group of neglected authors. They also analyzed these texts as African initiatives to contest the colonial monopoly over discursive production of African history and cultures. However both Manchuelle and Coundoriotis were unquestionably selective in their choices of available texts. In their desire to understand acts of resistance in early literary and scholarly works, they excluded or treated only as peripheral other texts that did not fit their argument. Yet the works they ignored are as important as any other for understanding why educated Africans of the period were both enthusiastic about and invested in ethnographic knowledge production.

In addition to these early defenders of African culture, who preceded the Negritude movement, there was also, in an opposite camp, a group of 'black detractors of the Black race'.[37] These authors wholeheartedly embraced the racist clichés promoted by colonial discourse. 'The black man is like a big child', wrote schoolmasters Oumar N'Diaye and Amadou Cissé in articles published in 1913 and 1914 respectively.[38] Some authors also parroted derogatory clichés developed by colonial historiography. In 'Notes sur le royaume mandingue de Bobo', Dominique Traoré describes the Bobo country, in western Upper Volta, as a region that suffered from anarchy and wars until the arrival of the French. His image of the founder of the local Dioula dynasty summarizes the different traits that he attributes to all of the latter's successors: 'Famagan Ouattara was, above all, a warrior with an insatiable appetite for wealth, a conqueror, a destroyer that accumulated ruins in his wake but one who lacked organizational skills, without any plans for bringing peace and providing for the wellbeing of those he administered.'[39]

It is hard to miss the resemblance here with the character of the 'negro potentate' developed in the colonial historiography to which Traoré had been exposed during his sojourn at Ecole Normale William Ponty (Jezequel 2002). Even when he acknowledges the organizational ability of Dioula conqueror Samory, Traoré attributes this to his Semitic blood: 'Ethnography teaches us that the crossing of Ouagara blacks (natives of Ghana Empire) with white Semites gave birth to the Sarakolle race, who would become the masters of the land.' Traoré then proceeds to show that Samory was of Sarakolle, not Dioula descent, which leads him to the conclusion that 'the sharp intelligence of this man, who, like Napoleon 1st, his guiding star, had immense organizational abilities, is proof that he was not of the black race'.[40] Traoré's writings reflect a racialized reading of African history that is clearly linked to Western stereotypes. Traoré was by no means exceptional. For instance Bouillagui Fadiga, another schoolmaster, accounted for the renown of Timbuktu in the following terms: 'A probable explanation for the superiority of the intellectual culture of the indigenes of Timbuktu, over the other black peoples of Sudan, resides in the very quality of their minds and blood, in the fact that they resulted from the crossing of the Songhais, whom some consider – and for good reason – as the only blacks to have attained a high degree of material civilization, with all of the immigrants or white conquerors of the country: Berbers, Arabs, Moroccans and Spaniards.'[41]

How to account for this echo of colonial stigmata in the writings of these West African authors? First, some of these stigmata reflected existing or developing endogenous oppositions. For example, some littoral societies, with longer engagement with the West, developed certain notions of superiority over more inland societies. In 1916, Alexandre R. D'Oliveira, a schoolmaster from a family of Afro-

Brazilian descent on the Dahomey coast, submitted for publication to the education inspector of Dahomey a study on the Baribas among whom he taught.[42] He described them as a 'primitive people ... [who] do not take care of their children. All they do is watch them born and grow, but they do not have the faintest idea what their responsibilities and duties to their young ones should be. It is therefore imperative to remove these children from the care of such dangerous parents and place them under a true boarding house arrangement.'[43] Nor did Bariba art find favor either: 'Griots (troubadours) produce a very monotonous bellowing sound from their primitive instruments.' Generally, the echoing of colonial stigmata constituted a discursive practice by which these schoolmasters distanced themselves from populations stamped with the indigenous label. While the colonial authorities had not accorded a special status to these educated Africans, the latter did not fail to seize any opportunity to set themselves apart and, hence, to establish their difference (Michel 1998). As one would expect, these writings contained a whole register of distancing vocabulary: *indigenes, blacks, primitive peoples*, and so forth.

Should one then conclude that the body of texts could be divided into works by authors who used writing as tool for resistance or even of a proto-nationalism and those who used it to collaborate with the colonizer? Such a view would be too simplistic. On the one hand, unresolved ambiguities persisted for African authors who reproduced colonial stigmata. For example, whereas in 1932 Traoré portrayed in typical colonial tradition the leaders of the Wattara of the Bobo Kingdom as bloodthirsty tyrants, he still traced the genealogy of these Wattara chiefs to the late eighteenth century. In so doing, he was positing the existence of an old dynasty, which went against the grain of the colonial argument of Africa being a continent without history. On the other hand, the positions held by some authors defending African cultures were more ambiguous than meets the eye. Indeed, Manchuelle has drawn attention to the favor that the ethnographic writings of the 'proto-nationalist' schoolmasters of the 1930s found with colonial officials such as Charles Béart and Georges Hardy. It turns out, as noted earlier, that the motive of such colonial officials was the creation of a 'Franco-African' culture whose conservative underpinnings cannot be denied. How then could such a conservative project encourage the expression of nationalist ideas? Even if one invoked the argument of the 'craftiness of the colonized', these texts actually supported conservative goals promoted by the French colonial administration.

We should avoid selecting only the texts that confirm the idea that African ethnography or 'auto-ethnography' enabled Africans to produce 'voices of their own'. Nor should we simply juxtapose these texts to other ethnographic research that merely reproduced colonial discourses. Instead, we should heed Frederick Cooper's warnings on the danger of analyzing African agency as an opposition between African autonomy and European domination: 'the danger lies in centering colonialism too much in people's lives, leaving them no room to see themselves in other ways and no possibility of selecting and adapting symbols or elements of European domination in calculated, instrumental ways or in acts of creative bricolage. Much is lost by reducing the life worlds of people into the category of colonized subjects' (Cooper 1996: 9). It would then be misleading to reduce African ethnography to the production of discourse on culture. As stressed by Schumaker in the case of African research assistants working for the Rhodes-Livingstone Institute (RLI), 'many [among them] sought employment with the RLI for other reasons than the study of culture, and they used their expertise in culture as means to other ends' (Schumaker 2001: 13).

It is no more possible to reduce these texts to political statements on African cultures than it is to encapsulate them as a marginal series of academic work. Once again we need to extend the context in order to allow us to better understand ethnographic production. In so doing, one begins to comprehend the diverse and quite unexpected motives that complicate the preceding interpretations.

Producing ethnography as a path toward social recognition

First we should consider the manner in which these authors interpreted their own works as researchers. Indeed, through their writings, some African authors vied for the position of 'royal advisor' and desired to achieve a higher status than mere schoolteachers. Although schoolmasters were members of the educated elite, they nevertheless constituted a relatively marginalized group in the colonial public service (Jezequel 2002). Many of them complained bitterly about the physical and professional distance that separated them from the commandant of the district, who was the source of local power. They were jealous of the commandants' preference for their own interpreters and the security guards of the colonial residences whose rudimentary French they despised. Writing therefore became a way for them to get closer to the local colonial administrators. When, in 1932, schoolmaster Mamby Sidibé embarked on his *Collection of local customs of the Kita District*, it was his intention to make it 'the new administrator's bedside book' (Sidibé 1932: 92). He even considered himself a special advisor to the colonial authority when he wrote, 'The Administrator cannot hope to know everything about his district, which would require a full dissertation, or even a doctoral thesis, to study and understand. But if he should, upon arrival in a new district, adopt as bedside book my book on local customs, he should in no time understand the basics of these customs' (Sidibé 1932: 93).

Writing in this case was clearly motivated by the thirst of the schoolmaster, who had a hard time coming to terms with his professional marginalization, for social recognition. Sidibé's declared motive was to 'help the colonial administration prevent misappropriation and manipulation within the tribunal de cercle' (district court) (Sidibé 1932: 93). As the author points out, corrupt African magistrates often manipulated colonial justice. European administrators were unable to detect or defend themselves from this manipulation because they did not understand what was going on within the court. Mamby Sidibé intended to prevent such manipulation by codifying and then fixing the Malinké customary laws: 'No more abuse should be accepted in the name of the "Whites", a name that the most dishonest men abominably soiled. "To serve France loyally" should be the motto of the natives in charge of representing the colonial Authority' (Sidibé 1932: 90). This declaration of loyalty contrasts with Machuelle's description of Sidibé as a proto-nationalist (Manchuelle 1995). In this particular context, Sidibé's position makes sense in relation to the internal rivalries and competition among different subgroups and generations of African intermediaries (Jezequel 2002).[44]

Other schoolmaster-ethnographers directly challenged the subordinate role that European scholars had assigned to them and argued that they produced more authentic knowledge than Europeans did. In his Fon study, the Dahomean Maximilien Quénum makes a case for the colonial administration to produce knowledge on the societies it administered: 'No one can deny that this is absolutely necessary. Colonizing peoples have a certain moral responsibility toward the colonized and one of the necessary conditions for civilized nations to live up to their responsibility is to know the people they are administering and thus avoid doing the wrong things' (Quénum 1935: 35). However, according to Quénum, not everyone is in a position to produce that knowledge. Rejecting existing works 'that err by mixing up the different elements that make up present day Dahomey', Quénum argues in particular that 'the majority of ethnographers have used princes and former ministers, whom they seem to take for their word. But if what these princes say is anything to go by, they would never reveal to a foreigner anything that might portray their people in bad light' and also that 'lack of knowledge of local languages and rites condemn the ethnographer to unavoidable errors' (Quénum 1935: 144–145). Unlike ethnographers who were strangers to the indigenous language and mentality, Maximilien Quénum, a native of Dahomey and graduate of the Musée de l'Homme of Paris, was well equipped to produce more authentic and, thus, more useful knowledge.

Mamby Sidibé and Maximilien Quénum were staking out the same claims, albeit in different ways. They saw themselves as knowledge intermediaries, capable of producing the information that the colonial administrators needed to do their jobs effectively. Their ethnographic production was part of a broader movement to contest the colonial monopoly over written knowledge and initiate endogenous discourses on Africa. Yet it was also – and perhaps primarily – an attempt to overcome the marginalization of the African educated class in the colonial public service. In other words, this literature makes sense in relation to a social history of colonial categories.

It is, however, difficult to measure the degree to which the schoolmasters and other educated Africans succeeded in obtaining the recognition they sought as producers of knowledge. Stories told by graduates of Ecole Normale William Ponty all point to the great suspicion that colonial administrators had of the pretensions of 'these enlightened Africans'. Although the schoolmasters had difficulties persuading local colonial administrators about the validity of their claims as producers and possessors of useful knowledge, there was no doubt about their progressive integration into local research institutions during the 1940s. Confined for a long time to subordinate roles and without any official status, indigenous authors started gaining recognition in the 1930s. I have already mentioned how these ordinary correspondents of colonial journals started to be integrated into research institutions in 1942, beginning with IFAN. However a closer examination of the careers of two of these early indigenous IFAN researchers shows that such integration did not fully reverse the unequal distribution of scholarly labor.

In a 1948 presentation of IFAN staff, the special issue of *Notes Africaines*, celebrating the tenth anniversary of the creation of the Institution, highlighted the role of schoolmasters who had been transferred to new research positions. Mamby Sidibé was the first such schoolmaster. His involvement with indigenous studies went back many years. His first articles, published in *Bulletin de l'Enseignement de l'AOF* (founded and directed by Georges Hardy), dated back to 1918. In the 1930s he published, among other important works, a collection of Kita customs as well as articles in *Outre-Mer*, directed from France by the same Georges Hardy. He even won an indigenous ethnography prize started by *Outre-Mer* in 1930. In 1944, he was sent to Dakar

IFAN for a six-month specialization training and was thereafter posted to Niger where he was charged with creating an IFAN center. He was to retire a few years later and returned to French Sudan where he started a political career. His colleague, Dominique Traoré, had an almost identical career trajectory. A teacher by training, Traoré published articles both in *Bulletin de l'Enseignement de l'AOF* and *Outre-Mer*. In 1944, he too was sent to the Dakar IFAN before being made the head of the ethnography laboratory of the Bamako center (Sudan). The 1948 special issue of *Notes Africaines* summarized his activities in Bamako as follows:

> An African member of staff of IFAN who has contributed immensely to the federal center's compilation of the directory of the peoples of French West Africa as well as other publications. Further, he has carried out numerous surveys and published comments, in particular on Peuhl poetry, indigenous pharmacopoeia, etc.[45]

Official recognition does not, however, invalidate the argument that African researchers, who could only aspire to the rank of research assistants, had an essentially subordinate role relative to their Western counterparts. Mamby Sidibé may have been charged with creating the IFAN center in Niamey, but this was because of a lack of European staff during the War. Moreover, during his directorship, the activities of the center were strictly limited to the creation of a library. No research program was started until he was replaced by a European director. Similarly, Dominique Traoré, head of the ethnography laboratory of the Bamako center, was largely marginalized at the IFAN Center. Despite his age, he wanted to continue his research and therefore asked to be given a position that allowed him to do fieldwork:

> As the one in charge of indigenous pharmacopoeia, I would very much prefer a posting to the hinterland, in the south of Sudan in order to be permanently in contact with indigenous peoples in their natural settings. I could return to the headquarters at the end of each quarter to report on my work and to deposit any samples and objects collected with the laboratory and the museum.[46]

His efforts were however neglected by the head of his center who, by all indications, did not attach much importance to his activities. For example, Traoré wrote a manuscript of 300 pages and asked the head of his center to help him have the manuscript typed; in response he was asked to retire. He had to wait fifteen years for *Présence Africaine* to publish the 647 pages of his African pharmacopoeias and works on African magic.

These itineraries thus reveal some of the strategies of professional promotion that held sway within the indigenous studies circles. It is clear that ethnographic writing only led to partial recognition of the 'African ethnographer'. Yet up to now we assumed that the relevant context to understand this textual production was an emerging field of knowledge production closely linked to and controlled by the French colonial administration.[47] African authors sought to integrate into this field as a way of developing strategies of self-promotion in the highly stratified colonial service. Eventually they also produced African voices that either reinforced or contested the colonial monopoly over the production of knowledge on and in Africa. Yet closer attention to the context in which these texts were not only produced but also read, preserved, and materially stored leads us to develop alternative interpretations.[48]

Ethnographic and historical writings in the local arena

Oumar Berté was a schoolteacher born around 1888 in Zeroula (district of Sikasso, French Sudan) who graduated from the prestigious Ponty School in Senegal. Like his colleagues Fily Dabo Sissoko, Mamby Sidibé and Bouillagui Fadiga, Oumar Berté undertook historical and ethnographic research and produced different written documents. Yet Oumar Berté did not achieve the same success as his colleagues. None of his works was ever published in any review. His texts remained in his private archives or were stored in the dusty district archives of the 'cercle du Kenedougou'. He was never integrated into the small group of educated Africans who left education to begin more prestigious careers at the IFAN. Yet despite this apparent lack of success, Berté's texts had a rich life of their own.

Berté's texts should not be evaluated solely on the basis of their limited success in the field of academic knowledge, but rather should also be viewed in relation to their potential impact in the local political arena. Indeed Oumar Berté's texts were elements of a broader strategy developed by his family in the Kenedougou district. The father of this schoolmaster, Keletigui Berté, was a former warlord of Sikasso who benefited from the support of the French just after the conquest of the city in 1898 (Rondeau 1980: 333). Keletigui was offered the headship of a large province, Kaboila, an immense fiefdom carved out from the district of Sikasso. However, before the arrival of the French, the Bertés' hold on power was not only recent but also precarious.[49] In this sense, then, the colonial system consolidated this family's authority. To seal their alliance with the colonial administration, the Bertés strengthened their legitimacy through the production of written historical and ethnographic works. The work was assigned to Oumar Berté, the second son of Keletigui and the first to receive a Western-style education. There are at least two documents that attest to the Bertés' desire to codify local history and traditions.

At the death of his father in 1915, Oumar Berté wrote a 16-page memorial document, in which he told the story of Keletigui's life as a former warlord.[50] Beyond the homage, the document further consolidated the power of the family over the chiefdom by making the founding figure of the emerging dynasty a prestigious and respected figure of the local history. The 'memorial of Keletigui' is an hagiographic document that describes the origins of the family, the ascension of Keletigui, his military successes and the respect he earned from the other leaders of the Kenedougou Kingdom. While Keletigui was a sofa leader of slave origins, the memorial gives him the same rank and functions as other prominent members of the royal lineage.[51] Interestingly the memorial finishes with a list of the 43 villages that were supposedly under Keletigui's command before the arrival of the French. In a time when the French administration was preoccupied with mapping authority and appointing African 'chiefs' to assist the new colonial administration, this kind of list was probably a useful document to assert Berté's leading position in the district. Indeed in matters of succession and chiefdoms, written documents were beginning to play an increasing role in the French Empire. For example, in a circular letter dated 26 November 1925, the Governor of Sudan, Terrasson de Fougères, asked for the family tree of each chief to be placed in the district's archives to facilitate the formulation of a policy on the appointment of chiefs. Oumar Berté's text, which was available at the archives, could only solidify his family's power over Kaboila.

In 1940, Oumar Berté wrote a second document, this time a monograph on Kaboila, the fief of the Bertés.[52] In the same year, not only was his elder brother confirmed as chief but also Kaboila was given more territory and promoted to chiefdom of extraordinary class including 105 villages.[53] Neither of the two documents produced by Oumar Berté was ever published. It is clear, however, that the goal of the author was not the recognition bestowed by colonial journals. He was more interested in penetrating a highly localized space of written productions.[54] His texts were stored in the local archives and were, therefore, available for consultation by the successive commandants of the district, who did not know much about the local societies they were supposed to administer and therefore might consult the archives for guidance. From the conquest of the town in 1898 to the abolition of the chiefdom in 1957, the Bertés were able to remain masters of a fief in which they skilfully protected and probably reinvented their legitimacy. Clearly participating in, and undertaking, ethnographic writings created a form of legitimacy that could be put to good use outside the indigenous studies circles. In their book on the invention of traditions, Terence Ranger and Eric Hobsbawm allude to the manner in which some Africans encouraged the reinvention of indigenous traditions by Europeans and then re-appropriated the benefits of the resulting codification of customs (Hobsbawm and Ranger 1983). This line of analysis has shaped the reading of the itineraries of these schoolmaster-ethnographers.

The case of Oumar Berté, schoolmaster, illustrates the role that the educated could play in legitimating their family's claim to a chiefdom. Textual production in these instances was closely linked to social and political dynamics in the local arena. The case of the Bertés was not exceptional. Consider the experience of Ibrahima Diaman Bathily, born around 1897 in Tiagou, a village in Gadiaga (in the Bakel region of Senegal).[55] His father, who worked for the French as an interpreter, spent a good part of his career in Sudan where Ibrahima was educated. Ibrahima Bathily later attended the school reserved for the children of the chiefs of Saint Louis and Ecole Normal William Ponty, where he qualified as a schoolmaster in 1917. The greater part of his career was spent in Sudan. He received a number of different postings, the last of which took him to Macina. Alongside his teaching activities, he also responded to the call of *Education Africaine* to get involved in research. According to his son (Abdoulaye Bathily)[56], he was in the habit of taking notes in school exercise books and one of his studies on the Peuhls of Macina was in fact published in 1936 but was not greeted with the same acclaim as those of some of his colleagues, e.g., Mamby Sidibé and Bouillagui Fadiga.[57] Wishing to return to his home region, he requested and was granted a transfer to Senegal in 1942. In 1944, both the colonial administration and the elders of the Bathily lineage of his village requested that he become the chief of the canton. During his tenure in this position, he initiated a series of economic and social reforms in a region that was still economically marginal (Clark 1999). At the same time, he undertook a series of historical and ethnographic studies on Gadiaga and the Bakel region ('cercle de Bakel'). While the bulk of his writings were not published during his lifetime, some were sent to the colonial administration and Bathily used them to support demands he made on the administration, in particular during the land disputes that characterized the existence of the canton.

One can therefore suggest that Bathily's writings were mostly in the service of his reform efforts. His historical research allowed him to defend the land rights of Sarakolle farmers against the herdsmen of

Mauritania, whom he accused of impoverishing Gadiaga. Conversely, his works on Sarakolle society were a scathing criticism of 'idiotic customs' that stood in the way of local development and modernization. They justified the different reform projects that accompanied his notes. However, Bathily soon fell out with the elders of the dominant lineages of Gadiaga, who violently condemned his actions. He was only half-heartedly defended by the colonial administration, which was concerned about his activism and preferred to believe the homicide and embezzlement charges brought against him by his accusers. Ibrahima Bathily took his own life with a bullet in the head on 26 June 1947, two years after taking office as district chief (chef de canton). Beyond this tragic end to his life, Ibrahima Bathily's itinerary provides insight into the place of writing in the extraordinary destiny of a man caught between two worlds, two value systems. His ethnographic work was driven by the desire to accept the invitation of the colonial administration but in the last three years of his life, he managed to turn it into a platform for his own social and economic reform projects.

Examples abound that illustrate how ethnographic writing was used to pursue fairly localized personal and family objectives. It is especially important, however, to emphasize that ethnographic writing in these instances did not necessarily emerge as acts of resistance or collaboration, but instead stemmed from a whole series of highly localized dynamics: a few autochthonous specialists resorting to the production of historical and ethnographic knowledge as a means of legitimization. The practice could, in rural settings, become a potent instrument for capturing power and influencing the colonial authorities for either personal or family ends.[58]

Conclusion

The field of scholarly research that was emerging in West Africa was founded on unequal relations that worked to the detriment of African authors. Writing about the turning point of indigenous studies in the 1930s, Anne Piriou argues that 'the conversation engaged between colonial reformers and "civilized" Africans . . . does nothing to reduce the inherent violence of the unequal relation that brought them together. It is undoubtedly one of the conditions for this relationship to continue in other forms' (Piriou 1997: 66). Similarly, in the 1940s, the integration of these 'civilized' Africans in the newly established research institutions (IFAN and, subsequently, OSTROM), despite a changed terminology, continued these inequalities.[59] The emergence in the early 1950s of a field of autonomous West African ethnographic production was only a beginning.

This chapter approached the study of these pioneer West African researchers from the standpoint of social and political history. It has sought to draw attention to a body of neglected African studies materials. It also underscored the complexity of this literature by exploring the different contexts that help to explain it. It is tempting to look at these texts as pioneer pieces introducing a disturbing African voice within the colonial monopoly over knowledge production. Yet this paper stressed the limits of such an interpretation since it tends to reduce African agency to a history of resistance and contestation. Instead the essay pays attention to different levels of interpretation (the field of knowledge production, the competing world of colonial categories, and the local arenas) that shed new light on these texts and their meanings: they could be early political discourses on African culture; they could be schoolteachers' attempts to contest the hierarchy of the colonial service; they could be part of very localized strategies aimed at manipulating the colonial presence. They could, in fact, be all these things at the same time. Yet none of these interpretations can alone explain the complex meanings of these early written productions.

This book unveils the intricate ways imperialism and anthropology in Africa shaped one another. This contribution suggests that this interpenetration took place not only in the upper echelons of scholarly research and policymaking, but also in exceedingly local debates. It is precisely at this level that African ethnographers discretely escaped their marginalization and played diverse and significant roles. Scholars generally agree that French colonial policy was not only made in the corridors of the government-general in Dakar or those of the Ministère des Colonies in Paris. Similarly French anthropology was not only produced in the academic corridors in colonial and metropolitan capitals. Both were also constructed in local arenas, in the daily production and use of knowledge to reshape colonial relations. There remains much to be done to understand the role of Africans in the production of colonial knowledge. This necessarily requires that we break away from elitist perspectives that situate these processes only in prestigious intellectual sites from which subaltern groups were de facto excluded.

Notes

1 I have located as many as 112 references of scholarly works dated between the 1920s and the late 1930s by West African authors. The majority of these articles were

seldom more than fifteen pages long. However, this number seriously underestimates the volume of work done by locals during the period in question since the great majority of these works have never been published. Some were simply kept by the colonial administration and placed in the archives of the administrative districts (see Jezequel 1998). Others were used by certain Western researchers as sources of information for their own studies.

2 As far as could be determined, in the inter-war years, of the 48 West African authors 31 were schoolmasters who had graduated from Ecole Normale William Ponty. The remainder included 7 Ponty graduates (of whom 4 were clerks, 1 a veterinarian, 1 a doctor and 1 a chartered accountant).

3 Lyn Schumaker being one of the few recent exceptions.

4 Most historical and ethnographic studies required the use of interpreters and assistance of privileged informants knowledgable about oral traditions. While it is customary to assume the existence of these local assistants, not much attention has been paid to their role in the knowledge production process. Ethnographers and historians in Africa rarely cited their informants, thus consciously or unconsciously downgrading how these assistants might have manipulated the 'data' provided the researcher, for example, by framing them in favor of local socio-political concerns.

5 On the creation of the Committee for Historical and Scientific Studies of French West Africa (*Comité d'Etudes Historiques et Scientifiques de l'AOF*) at the initiative of Governor-General Clozel, see below. The Committee's objective was to encourage research in this area as well as provide a medium for the research through the publication of *Annuaire* and, subsequently, the Committee's *Bulletin du Comité d'Etudes Scientifiques et Historiques de l'AOF* (Bulletin of the Committee for Scientific and Historical Studies of French West Africa), the forerunner of the *Bulletin de l'IFAN*. In 1914 Georges Hardy also established an educational journal, which eventually began to publish ethnographic, historical and folklore studies. On the role of illiterate informants, see Simpson 1975.

6 Before the 1910s, studies published by African authors were rare and isolated, for example those by Yoro Dyao in 1864 (Yoro Dyao in Gaden 1912). However, beginning in the 1910s, this type of publication multiplied, becoming more systematic in the following decades. '*Etudes indigènes*' (indigenous studies) was one of the terms used by the colonial administration to qualify this written work by African literates. I have chosen not to use the notion of 'auto-ethnography' (Cinnamon 1998) since a number of these authors explicitly refer to their own work as an ethnography of the other. See below for further details. On colonial public servants as humanists see Amselle and Sibeud 1998.

7 Administrative order relative to the creation of the Committee for Historical and Scientific Studies of French West Africa issued by Clozel on 10 December 1915.

8 Ibid. It bears emphasizing, though, that the colonial administration was not steadfast in its support of the research efforts of colonial public servants from the motherland.

9 However there is some danger of overestimating European initiative in the development of African ethnography. For instance, looking at relations between European researchers and African informants, Lyn Schumaker convincingly suggests that '*African assistants may have chosen their anthropologists as often as their anthropologists chose them. Anthropologists frequently took on assistants suggested by local chiefs*' (Schumaker 2001: 195). Thus African societies influenced the production of colonial knowledge before the colonial administration officially requested assistance from African literates in this domain.

10 Georges Hardy was then head of the education department of French West Africa.

11 For instance Charles Beart, head of the William Ponty school in the 1930s and the 1940s, published a study entitled 'children and play in Africa' in the 1950s. He used the result of a survey on 'jeux et jouets de l'AOF' organized by the *Bulletin de l'enseignement de l'AOF* (Bourdieu 1993). For more details on the way European researchers conceal the role and presence of African assistants in their publications, see Sanjek 1993.

12 *Bulletin de l'Enseignement de l'AOF*, 26 July 1916.
13 The colonial administration became obsessed with the idea of keeping African schoolteachers busy during their holidays. Ethnographic writing, but also census-taking, training camps, administrative work at the district constituted some of the activities designed by the administration to prevent idleness among schoolteachers.
14 As a reminder, Ecole Normale de Saint-Louis (the teachers' college in Saint Louis, Senegal) was only created in 1903. In 1915, soon after it was moved to Gorée, it became the renowned Ecole Normale William Ponty, which would train the principal African assistants of the colonial period (Jezequel 2002).
15 In his work on the Trocadero Museum, Nicolas Dias refers to the description manuals often provided by scientific institutions to people in the field (adventurers, travellers, etc.) for the scientific organization of their data collection (Dias 1991).
16 *Bulletin de l'Enseignement de l'AOF*, No. 2, 1913. Excerpts of Hardy's review of Amadou N'Diaye Clédor's book. N'Diaye was himself a former schoolteacher.
17 A. Kane, 'Histoire et origine des familles du Fouta Toro', *Annuaire et mémoires du Comité d'Etudes Historiques et Scientifiques de l'AOF*, I: 325–344.
18 Moctar Diallo, 'L'Islam dans le Rip', *Bulletin de l'enseignement de l'AOF*, 20, 1916.
19 See, for example, Piriou, 1997 on the manner in which Fily Dabo Sissoko refers to his relations with Fernand Froger in *Savane rouge* (Sissoko 1962).
20 For more details on these early figures of the African ethnography, see Piriou 1997; Jezequel 1998; and Sibeud 2002.
21 Interestingly both Hardy and Delafosse went back to France after a conflict with Blaise Diagne, the Senegalese representative at the French National Assembly. Diagne struggled against colonial officials who opposed the French assimilation policy in AOF (Bouche 1975; Michel 1998).
22 While I found less than fifteen references for the period 1910s to 1920s, the number for the 1930s was more than 70.
23 Brevié's circular letter of 2 May 1935 relative to historical and research documents, Circular No. 175, *Journal Officiel du Sénégal*, 1935, 363–364.
24 Ibid.
25 Quénum, Maximilien, 'Au pays des Fons', *Bulletin du Comité d'Etudes Historiques et Scientifiques de l'Afrique Occidentale (B.C.E.H.S.A.O.F)*, 1935.
26 This school, which was for a long time located in Gorée (Senegal), trained the local elite of schoolmasters, clerks and doctors. See Jezequel 2002.
27 Afanou and Togbe Pierre (1967).
28 Charles Béart, 'Compte-rendu de la fête de l'école William-Ponty', *L'Education Africaine*, No. 90–91, April–September 1935.
29 From 1915 to 1938 (a period of 23 years), the Bulletin of the Committee of Historical and Scientific Studies of French West Africa published only nine studies by indigenous authors whereas *Bulletin d'IFAN* published ten in eleven years (1938–1949). However, this kind of publication did not make any breakthrough since in the whole of the following decade (1950–1959), there were only thirteen contributions by African authors. The first Africans to have their works published in the series 'Mémoires de l'Institut Français d'Afrique Noire' were A. Akindele and C. Aguessy in 1953, that is fourteen years after the creation of the series. Interestingly, there were to be no others before the 1960s.
30 Excerpt of Theodore Monod's editorial for the first issue of *Notes Africaines* (No. 1, January 1939, 1).
31 See Piriou (1997) which analyzes, in particular, the reasons why the journal's publishers decided to seek out the collaboration of indigenous authors. She argues that this decision was driven by both the search for authenticity and scientific legitimization. The position taken by the *'indigénophiles'* of the 1930s concerning the participation of Africans was therefore slightly different from that of the 'administrator-humanists' of the 1910s. African ethnographic and historical writing was already playing a more important if subordinate role.

32 See Amadou Mapaté Diagne, 'Contribution à l'étude des coutumes Balantes de Sédhiou', *Outre-mer*, V(1), January–March, 1933, pp. 16–42. and M. Sidibé, 'Les sorciers mangeurs d'hommes au Soudan français', *Outre-mer*, I(1), January–March, 1929, pp. 22–31.

33 Refer to a bibliography on Serpos compiled by Samuel Decalo in his *Historical Dictionary of Dahomey* (Decalo 1987).

34 Manchuelle 1995; L'Estoile 1997; Piriou 1997; Jezequel 1998; Coundiouriotis 1999; Schumaker 2001; Peterson 2004.

35 Mamby Sidibé, 'Monographie régionale de Fada N'Gourma', *B.C.E.H.S.A.O.F.*, juin 1918.

36 paul Hazoumé, *Le pacte de sang au Dahomey* Paris, Institut d'Ethnologie 1937.

37 Reversing the title (*'Black defenders of the Black Race'*) given by Professor Elikia M'Bokolo to a series of lectures he gave at the Ecole des Hautes Etudes en Sciences Sociales in 1995–1996.

38 Oumar N'Diaye's letter on the issue of classroom motivation, *Bulletin de l'Enseignement de l'AOF*, No. 7, July 1913, p. 252; Amadou Cisse, 'Les dangers de la monoculture', *Bulletin de l'Enseignement de l'AOF* No. 11, 1914.

39 Dominique Traoré, 'Notes sur le royaume mandingue de Bobo', *Education Africaine*, No. 96, 1932, p. 59.

40 According to interviews we conducted with several members of Dominique Traoré's family in Bougouni and Sikasso, Traoré was himself a Haoussa who was taken as a slave while still a child by the rulers of Kenedougou. It is interesting to recall that Samory unsuccessfully besieged Sikasso, the capital of the Kenedougou. He left behind him the image of a merciless warrior, a myth partly developed by the French colonial administration.

41 Bouillagui Fadiga, 'La culture arabe au Soudan et à Tombouctou', *Bulletin de l'Enseignement de l'AOF*, No. 89, January–March 1935, pp. 32–33. According to an interview I had with Fadiga Bouillagui's son in Bamako in 1998, Fadiga was a Sarakolle born in Sofara in the 1890s.

42 For more information on Afro-Brazilians, see, among others, P. Verger 1968; the Baribas were people of the north of Dahomey.

43 Administrative report, Kouandé school, 1919–1920. French national Archives, AOF, J45.

44 The beginning of Amadou Hampate Ba's *Fortunes of Wangrin* is another good example of the hostility between schoolteachers and interpreters (Ba 1999).

45 *Notes Africaines*, No. 37, January 1948: 19.

46 Undated notes from personal notebook in 'Dossier personnel de Dominique Traoré' (Dominique Traoré's personal file), I c 393, National Archives of Senegal, Dakar.

47 Field in the sense defined by Pierre Bourdieu (Bourdieu, 1993).

48 In this last part of the paper, I owe a lot to Derek Peterson's work on 'creative writing' in Kenya (Peterson 2004) and Lyn Schumaker's study of African assistant researchers in Northern Rhodesia (Schumaker 2001).

49 Keletigui himself was, according to Chantal Rondeau, the son of a slave, and groom of the king of Kenedougou, Tieba Traoré. It is said he became a guard or soldier of the king and then head of the king's army as a result of his acts of bravery and victories. Rondeau points out that, although warlords in those days were quite powerful, they did not really control large territories besides the few villages around Sikasso. They were content with carrying out raids to capture slaves that they subsequently sold or settled in farming hamlets around Sikasso. Rondeau further argues that *'before Kenedugu, there were no political entities beyond the village* [in Minianka country, at least] . . . *The Kenedugus did not have true traditional chiefdoms comparable to those of Mossis kingdoms, for example'* (Rondeau 1980: 328).

50 This memorial has recently been published by Roland Colin, a former colonial administrator in Sikasso who received the document directly from its author, Oumar Berté (Colin 2004).

51 According to the document, after the death of King Tieba Traoré of Kenedougou during the French assault on Sikasso, Keletigui Berté became the first negotiator

with the French colonial administration. He took part in a plan to subdivide the Kingdom into districts (canton). Berté was appointed chief of the largest district while the power of the Traoré royal family was divided into two smaller districts.

52 In those days the colonial administration frequently placed a special order for this kind of regional monograph from an indigenous schoolmaster. For example, in the Bougouni district, adjacent to Sikasso where the Bertés lived, the colonial administration placed an order, also in 1940, with a schoolmaster from the region for a monograph on the region. It needed the document to settle a chieftaincy succession dispute (see Samaké 1984: 330). These monographs remain unpublished.

53 Interview with Amadou Berté, son of Oumar Berté, 4 March 1998, Sikasso (Mali). As a reminder, Amadou Berté was chiefdom secretary to his uncle from 1940 to 1957, when the chiefdom was abolished, a further proof of the control of the Bertés over the fief inherited from Keletigui.

54 Other producers of documents in Sikasso were colonial administrators, missionaries, and other categories of African intermediaries. While the Berté family was able to directly penetrate this discursive space through Oumar Berté, other families were able to do the same by providing oral informants to colonial administrators. In his study of the Kikuyu in Kenya, Derek Peterson stresses the tensions and rivalries surrounding the production of written documents in the local arena. Even illiterate groups were interested and participated in this production (Peterson 2004).

55 The comments that follow are from the posthumous publication of the works of Ibrahima Bathily by his son, Abdoulaye Bathily (1969).

56 Quoted by Bathily, 1969: 36.

57 Bathily, Ibrahima, 'Les Diawandos ou Diogoramés', *Education Africaine*, No. 94, 1936, pp. 173–191.

58 This is not just the case for the rural areas alone. Coundouriotis has demonstrated that the writings of Paul Hazoumé expressed a political opposition rooted in littoral towns. This opposition pitted the intelligentsia (to which Hazoumé belonged) against the old littoral bourgeoisie that made its wealth from the slave trade in the nineteenth century (Coundiouriotis 1999: 94).

59 OSTROM is the Office de la Recherche Scientifique et Technique Outre-Mer.

References

Afanou, François and Togbe Pierre, Raymond (eds). 1967. *Catalogue des 'Cahiers William Ponty'*. Dakar: IFAN.

Amselle, Jean-Loup and Sibeud, Emmanuelle (eds). 1998. *Maurice Delafosse. Entre orientalisme et ethnographie: l'itinéraire d'un africaniste (1870–1926)*. Paris: Maisonneuve & Larose.

Ba, Amadou Hampaté. 1999. *The Fortunes of Wangrin*. Bloomington: Indiana University Press.

Bathily, Abdoulaye. 1969. 'Notices socio-historiques sur l'ancien royaume soninké du Gadiaga. D'après Ibrahima Diaman Bathily (1897–1947)'. *Bulletin de l' IFAN* 41:31–105.

Bouche, Denise. 1975. 'L'enseignement dans les territoires français de l'Afrique Occidentale de 1817 à 1920. Mission civilisatrice ou formation d'une élite?'. L'Université Lille III: Thèse de doctorat.

Bourdieu, Pierre. 1993. *The Field Of Cultural Production*. New York: Columbia University Press.

Cinnamon, John M. 1998. 'The Long March of the Fang: Anthropology and History in Equatorial Africa'. Yale University: Unpublished Ph.D.

Clark, Andrew F. 1999. *From Frontier to Backwater: Economy and Society in The Upper Senegal Valley. 1850–1920.* Lanham: University Press of America.

Colin, Roland. 2004. *Kènèdougou au crépuscule de l'Afrique coloniale. Mémoires des années cinquante.* Paris: Présence africaine.

Cooper, Frederick. 1996. *Decolonization and African Society: The Labor Question in French and British* Africa. Cambridge: Cambridge University Press.

Coundiouriotis, Eleni. 1999. *Claiming History: Colonialism, Ethnography and the Novel.* New York: Columbia University Press.

Decalo, Samuel. 1987. *Historical Dictionary of Dahomey.* New York: Scarecrow.

Dias, N. 1991. *Le musée d'ethnographie du Trocadéro, 1878–1908.* Paris: Editions du C.N.R.S.

Gaden, Henri. 1912. *Légendes et coutumes sénégalaises, cahiers de Yoro Dyâo.* Paris: Leroux.

Hobsbawm, E. and Ranger, Terence (eds). 1983. *The Invention of Tradition.* Cambridge: Cambridge University Press.

Jezequel, Jean-Herve, 1998. 'Maurice Delafosse et l'émergence d'une littérature africaine à vocation scientifique'. In J.L. Amselle and E. Sibeud (eds). *Maurice Delafosse, entre Orientalisme et africanisme.* Paris: Maisonneuve et Larose, pp. 90–104.

Jezequel, Jean-Herve. 2002. 'Les "mangeurs de craies": sociohistoire d'une catégorie lettrée en Afrique Occidentale Française. Les instituteurs diplômés de l'Ecole Normale William-Ponty (c. 1900–c. 1960)'. Ecole des Hautes Etudes en Sciences Sociales: Thèse de doctorat.

L'Estoile, Benoît de. 1997. 'Au nom des "vrais africains". Les élites scolarisées de l'Afrique coloniale face à l'anthropologie (1930–1950)'. *Terrain* 28: 87–102.

Manchuelle, François. 1995. 'Assimilés ou patriotes africains? Naissance du nationalisme culturel en Afrique française (1853–1931)'. *Cahiers d'Etudes Africaines.* XXXV:333–368.

Michel, Marc. 1998. 'Maurice Delafosse et l'invention d'une africanité nègre'. In J.L. Amselle and E. Sibeud (eds). *Maurice Delafosse, entre Orientalisme et africanisme.* Paris: Maisonneuve et Larose, pp. 78–89.

Peterson, Derek R. 2004. *Creative writing. Translation, bookkeeping and the world of Imagination in Colonial Kenya.* Portsmouth: Heinemann.

Piriou, Anne. 1997. 'Indigénisme et changement social: le cas de la revue Outre-Mer (1929–1937)'. In E. Sibeud and A. Piriou (eds). *L'Africanisme en question.* Paris: Centre d'Etudes Africaines, pp. 43–70.

Quénum, Maximilien. 1935. *Au pays des Fons.* Paris: Bulletin du Comité d'études historiques et scientifiques de.

Robinson, David. 1992. 'Ethnography and Customary Law in Senegal'. *Cahiers d'Etudes Africaines* 32:221–237.

Rondeau, Chantal. 1980. 'La société senufo du sud Mali (1870–1950) de la "tradition" à la dépendance'. Ecole des Hautes Etudes en Sciences Sociales: Thèse de doctorat.

Samaké, Maximin. 1984. 'Pouvoir traditionnel et conscience politique paysanne: les Kafo de la région de Bougouni'. Ecole des Hautes Etudes en Sciences Sociales: Thèse de doctorat.

Sanjek, Roger. 1993. 'Anthropology's Hidden Colonialism: Assistants and their ethnographers'. *Anthropology Today* 9:13–18.

Schumaker, Lyn. 2001. *Africanizing Anthropology: Fieldwork, Networks, and the Making of Cultural Knowledge in Central Africa*. Durham: Duke University Press.

Sibeud, Emmanuelle. 1994. 'La naissance de l'ethnographie africaniste en France avant 1914'. *Cahiers d'Etudes Africaines* XXXXIV:659–671.

Sibeud, Emmanuelle. 2002. *Une science impériale pour l'Afrique? La construction des savoirs africanistes en France, 1878–1930*. Paris: Editions de l'EHESS.

Sidibé, Mamby. 1932. 'Coutumier du cercle de Kita'. *Bulletin du Comité d'études historiques et scientifiques de l'AOF* 15.

Simpson, Donald. 1975. *Dark Companions: The African Contribution to the European Exploration of East Africa*. London: Elek.

Sissoko, Fily Dabo. 1962. *La Savane Rouge*. Avignon: Presses Universelles.

Verger, Pierre. 1968. *Flux et reflux de la traite des nègres entre le Golfe de Bénin et Bahia de Todos os Santos, du XVIIe au XIXe siècle*. Paris: Mouton.

CHAPTER SIX

Custom, modernity, and the search for *Kihooto*: Kenyatta, Malinowski and the making of *Facing Mount Kenya*[1]

Bruce Berman and John Lonsdale

Jomo Kenyatta and Bronislaw Malinowski met in December 1934, soon after the latter had told Princess Marie Bonaparte he was to meet 'real experts' on the Kikuyu people.[2] Malinowski had spent a week in the Kikuyu area of Kenya two months previously. He shared with the princess, one of Freud's first female students, an interest in Kikuyu resistance to a missionary campaign against clitoridectomy, the surgical element in their rite of female initiation. Their land grievance against white settlers was also well known. Kenyatta, for his part, had been the London representative of the Kikuyu Central Association (KCA) for the previous five years, trying to catch the imperial government's attention. He had looked in vain for an authoritative voice – the 'unanswerable argument' that Kikuyu call *kihooto* – to force the British to pay heed to his people. His journey to London had upset his elders at home and thus far his search for helpful metropolitan patrons had been fruitless. Missionaries, liberal imperialists, Stalinists, Trotskyists, independent Marxists – all had been found wanting. In social anthropology Kenyatta hoped at last to have found a medium in which to make his people worthy of British attention, whose grievances warranted British redress.

Kenyatta and Malinowski hit it off immediately. Without benefit of even a secondary education, Kenyatta became a postgraduate student in social anthropology at the London School of Economics and held his own in seminars with the leading social scientists of the day. In under three years, with Malinowski's enthusiastically critical support, he published his revised diploma dissertation. The book, *Facing Mount Kenya*, was one of the first anthropological monographs by an African.

The relationship between the two men is rarely mentioned in histories of anthropology, and then only to illustrate the cosmopolitan character of Malinowski's students, or his use of Kenyatta to promote his functionalist social anthropology (Stocking 1992: 264, 267–268, 1995: 412–415; Goody 1995: 27, 84, 192; Kuper 1996: 114). *Facing Mount Kenya*, although a classic insider's view of African society, similarly warrants barely a footnote – with the suggestion that Kenyatta had a political agenda, seeing social anthropology as a tool of nationalism (James 1973: 61–63). His agenda, its relation to Kikuyu cultural politics, why it led him to social anthropology, and how it shaped his ethnography have been left unexplored. Here we analyze how the making of *Facing Mount Kenya* both furthered Malinowski's hopes for social anthropology, for ethnography as politics; and emerged from Kenyatta's effort to represent his people, pursuing his politics as ethnography.

Representing the Kikuyu

Johnstone Kenyatta[3] first sailed for Britain in February 1929. Delegate of the youthful, nominally Christian, KCA, he was seeking redress on behalf of all Kikuyu, who conventionally respected age and of whom not five percent were Christian. The twin aims of representation: depiction and advocacy, were therefore a challenge. Persuasive advocacy of Kikuyu claims needed, first, an authoritative portrayal of their society. Both his audiences, Kikuyu and British, doubted his credentials for that, culturally uprooted as he seemed to be. Kenyatta in any case faced an ineluctable contradiction, between the always argumentative internal politics of a cultural community and the preferably decisive external representation of group interests – or, in our terms, between moral ethnicity and political tribalism. On the one hand Africans imaginatively constructed local public spheres, ethnic discursive arenas, when renegotiating the bounds of moral community and sources of social status, in face of the changes brought by colonialism, capitalism, Christianity and new print vernaculars. Political tribalism, on the other hand, reflected the need for the unchallenged leadership of united communities against other such emergent ethnicities, made rivals by the unequal costs and benefits of colonial political economy (Lonsdale 1996a; Berman 1998). To bridge this contradiction Kenyatta had to create his authority to speak, and imagine Kikuyu as a united people who spoke with one voice: his own. His earlier experience as vernacular journalist had taught him how difficult this would be.

In 1928 Kenyatta, the KCA's general secretary, became founding editor of its monthly journal *Muigwithania*, 'the reconciler'. The title epitomized the association's hopes. Among the first Christians, a tiny minority called *athomi* or 'readers', they tried to restore their relations with other Kikuyu by advancing the general good in a vision of modernizing reform. In *Muigwithania*'s columns they claimed to be better than the unlettered majority at defending true, *karing'a*, Kikuyu culture, since only *athomi* could renew its sense of order, to cope with the disorders of modernity (Lonsdale 1996b). The plausibility of this claim depended on getting fractious Kikuyu to agree on consistent accounts both of their deep past and the recent history of their land losses to white settlers. It was the KCA's failure to achieve consensus, and their limited success in bending the ear of colonial officials, that led them to send Kenyatta to Britain, to the fury of their chiefs. In London Kenyatta had to try to establish his credibility before imperial authorities skeptical of any sophisticated statement of the 'native point of view'. They looked to European science to create practical knowledge about Africa, not to the knowledge offered by Africans, especially educated Africans, themselves (Tilley 2001).

To be unanswerable Kenyatta's argument would have to address Europeans in an idiom that was his own but which his audience would respect. The KCA had tackled this problem in the petition he took back to London on his second visit in 1931 – one that lasted for fifteen years. Unable to lay it before a parliamentary enquiry into a 'closer union' proposed for British East Africa, he presented it to the Kenya Land Commission (KLC) in the following year. The KCA's opening paragraph expounded both the humiliations of colonialism and African efforts to represent themselves in new ways:

> We are a primitive race having come in contact with what is called civilisation for not more than half-a-century and yet we are confronted with the task of having to prepare a case in a manner which should be worth the consideration of a body composed entirely of gentlemen whose methods of thinking ... are entirely alien to the community on whom they are sitting in judgment. We therefore have to borrow means and methods and ape the manner in which the case may appeal to you from your point of view and according to your standards of measuring the requirements of a people who from the alien point of view are a species of living being which was hardly known to them about fifty years ago.[4]

The KLC reported in 1934. It dismissed the KCA's claim to authority, contradicted as it was by other Kikuyu evidence. The Commission's failure to remedy Kikuyu grievance was a long-term cause of Mau Mau violence after World War II. *Facing Mount Kenya* was Kenyatta's most immediate response.

The KCA had appointed Kenyatta their secretary because of his seeming facility in English (Spencer 1985: 67). It was harder to impress London than Nairobi. Kenya's man-about-town was a metropolitan bumpkin, needing white patronage. But Kenyatta saw the remedy. Kikuyu must enter the global race to control modernity. He told *Muigwithania*'s readers at home, 'if you want us to become ... the counsellors of our country, busy yourselves with EDUCATION. For knowledge is in the forefront here; it is as though knowledge were power ... But do not think that the education I refer to is that which we are given a lick of [in mission schools]; no, it is a methodical education to open up a man's head.' Kikuyu could afford it; they had money 'lying idle' that could be used for educating '1. THE KIKUYU LAWYER; 2. THE KIKUYU TEACHER; 3. THE KIKUYU DOCTOR.' Other black people already training in London were no 'further advanced than the Kikuyu in knowledge'.[5] The search for education, as well as patronage, shaped Kenyatta's odyssey. His generation had had to justify even their 'lick of education' to their elders. They had done so with a flair and conviction that he later found hard to recover.

Searching for Kihooto: *readers and elders*

Kikuyu saw power in eloquence. They often called themselves *mbari ya atiriri*, 'the clan of "Hear this"'. Their big men were not chiefs; they exercised little formal sway, claiming that their authority rested on the force of 'unanswerable argument'. This can be glossed as proof, reason, or justice, all summed up in the word *kihooto*. Proverbially, *kihooto* was wealth; it could ford a flooded river; and while somebody defeated with a club might hit back, the man beaten by *kihooto* would never return (Wanjohi 1997: 49–55). Wealth added weight to their views. 'How can a man of one goat,' Kikuyu asked, 'speak to a man of a hundred?' Kikuyu lacked institutional hierarchy but not inequality. It was perhaps the fragility of inequality that made lineage, *mbari*, elders insist on self-discipline, *wiathi*, as the core of reputation, and made the young Christians' literacy seem so anarchic a route to discursive authority. No *Muigwithania* correspondent counted his goats before writing; women wrote too, overcoming a nervousness that must have been more crippling in speech. Print had a power of its own; it could convey *kihooto* irrespective of an author's status. Holders of oral authority – elders, official chiefs, British administrators – found that hard to accept (Lonsdale 2002a: 204–216).

Athomi succeeded to a marked extent, nonetheless. For a time district officers accepted that the KCA, with its correspondence files and ideas of 'improvement', was the voice of progress. Elders, concerned to defend their land not only against white settlers but also against neighbors, valued their educated sons' legal skills. As *athomi* said, pen had replaced spear in defense of property. But what most gave Kenyatta's generation its self-confidence was the ease with which they aligned their Christian literacy with existing ideas of social decay and renewal. Kikuyu thought about society in the tragic terms of opposition between selfishly segmentary descent and cooperative age and generation – unavoidably conflicting loyalties. They ruefully reflected that 'birds that land together fly up separately' – or, 'young men seek their fortune together as age-mates, only to be divided by household property'. But Kikuyu also held hopes of moral rebirth. A declining generation was obliged, every thirty years or so, to cede its judicial powers to its more vigorous successor, known as *irungu*, the 'straighteners' (of society). The culminating ceremony was an expensive goat-feasting rite called *ituika*. It was the genius of Kenyatta's generation to attach their innovations in religion and communication to this recurrent yearning for societal renewal (Lonsdale 1995; Peterson 2004: chap. 3).

Elders saw Christian practice, hostile to household ritual, as the main threat to order. *Muigwithania's* correspondents placed the blame elsewhere – on 'the road of wilful ways' that led, via the migrant labor market in nearby Nairobi, to shameless independence in the young, not least young women. Colonial capitalism was the problem, Christianity the solution. Rural household heads contemplated 'Nairobi Kikuyu' and their dereliction of duty to parents with something like moral panic. Christians claimed to have the answer to juvenile delinquency. They took to calling themselves prodigal sons (Luke 15: 11–32) yet also *irungu*, straighteners, a candidate generation aspiring to ritual leadership. They also imagined Kikuyu as one people, as they had not been before. They were like the children of Israel, of whose heroes *athomi* had read, in a school primer, since 1909 (Peterson 2002). The Kikuyu New Testament translated Christ's crucifixion as equivalent to the *irungu* redemption of the land from its accumulations of ill-will at *ituika*. Literacy was the new cleanser. After all, church outschools structured Kikuyu life more visibly than lineage, clan or age-set. Print enabled one to record tradition, at a time when migrant labor was breaking household cohesion and thus the thread of moral memory. All literate Kikuyu could reason together about social obligation, no matter how far away they lived, beyond the reach of any elder's voice. Contributions to *Muigwithania* often started with the invocation

Atiriri, 'Listen', to give print the force of speech. Many saw Christianity as the future unifier of Kikuyu, a ritual medium that could both domesticate an otherwise disruptive modernity and project local culture as the equal of other cultures on the world stage. Kenyatta, the readers' editor, had orchestrated this self-confident reconciliation of Kikuyu continuity and Christian, literate, renewal.[6] When he came to write *Facing Mount Kenya*, almost a decade later, he was not nearly so sure.

Searching for a voice: missionaries, liberals and communists

Kenyatta met Britain's African affairs community on his first visit to London in 1929–30. He explored its many facets over the years – missionaries, liberal imperialists, the several 'lefts', the exiled black intelligentsia – discarding one set of patrons after another. Each attached unacceptable conditions to their political assistance, substituting their own self-interested voice for his (Murray-Brown 1973: 114–179; Howe 1993: 66–67).[7]

Kenyatta broke first with the missionaries, and they with him. His rumored enjoyment of London's fleshpots and his visit to the Soviet Union with George Padmore, the Comintern's highest black official, caused a senior missionary and former friend of the KCA to feel that Kenyatta was 'making a fool of himself ... To send a boy [*sic*] like Kenyatta is worse than not sending anyone, and just makes the friends of Africa in this country sad.'[8] Kenyatta found such paternalism increasingly intolerable. His relations with the missions were also worsened by crisis in Kikuyu. This erupted when the Church of Scotland Mission (CSM) led a campaign to ban in *athomi* households the practice of clitoridectomy, female circumcision. In Kenyatta's absence the KCA had leapt to its defense. As Kenyatta looked to the Scots, his former mentors, for support, they in turn tried to enlist him against what they deplored as genital mutilation. Faced with the medical case, Kenyatta temporized. He urged that patient education, *kihooto*, would be more effective than the club of prohibition in ending an initiation rite so crucial for gender discipline. Returning to Kenya, he tried to mediate. Both mission and KCA were intransigent. The talks failed. Dr Arthur, crusading head of the CSM, denounced Kenyatta as 'a man of guile', subject to 'forces of evil'.[9]

Kenyatta and the missions severed contact. He participated little in formal religion thereafter. The tendency of older missionaries to characterize all conflicts as clashes between good and evil, with much

African custom classed as evil, had become insufferable. In Kenya, Christianity had seemed the key to modernization with social order. Not only were missionaries now attacking gender disciplines already weakened by migrant labor, in Europe Kenyatta heard modernity's many discordant voices, some of them hostile to all religion. Reconciling self-determination with modernity no longer seemed to require membership of a mission church – however much a sense of religious duty always permeated his politics (Lonsdale 2002b).

Kenyatta continued to work with liberal imperialists, like the former Kenya officials McGregor Ross and Norman Leys. They helped him to explain the KCA's aims to the educated public through such 'quality' newspapers as the *Manchester Guardian* and *The Times*. It was 'not a subversive organisation. Its object is to help the Kikuyu to improve himself as a better Mu-Kikuyu, not to "ape" the foreigner.' Kenyatta also urged the reconciling power of *kihooto*. Kikuyu wanted 'to be permitted to retain our many good tribal customs, and by means of education to elevate the minds of our people to the willing rejection of bad customs'.[10] They also enabled Kenyatta to satisfy his desire for further education. In 1931 Leys and Ross enrolled him at a Quaker college near Birmingham, with Charles Buxton, a Quaker and a Labour MP, paying the fees. Here Kenyatta's English made rapid progress. In 1932 he earned a certificate in composition. No religious demands had been made on him. But liberal imperialists could never entirely sympathize with his politics. They aspired, rather, to make the Empire live up to its civilizing claims. As paternalist as missionaries, they saw Africans as victims, too primitive to defend themselves against white greed or to build a better future. Yet they mistrusted African political initiatives. Educated Africans might well have rejected primitive society – but at the expense of their tribal ties. They were unrepresentative, impatient young men. Liberals did at least meet and sponsor people like Kenyatta, giving him more room to speak. But their stereotypes deafened them to what he said. With his interest in 'custom', he risked accusations of obscurantism, especially from a radical democrat like Leys. Advocating equal rights for Africans, Leys believed their (distant) future lay only in full Westernization (Leys 1924: chap. XII).

In 1932, still exploring models of *kihooto*, Kenyatta returned to Moscow. Marxists offered a rigorous analysis of colonialism; they did not seem overtly paternalist. In the 1930s crisis the Soviet Union appeared, even to many non-Communists, to be a beacon of progress and the only defense against fascism. Left journals welcomed a man like Kenyatta, happy to print and indeed, helpfully insert, more critical language than the mainstream press would accept. But it was the promise of higher education that led him back to Moscow, to spend an academic year at KUTVU, the University of the Toilers of the East. This taught Asian and African students political economy and propaganda 'from a Marxist point of view' (Padmore 1956: 318). Kenyatta was not impressed. He complained of poor conditions, and of his lecturers' inadequate English. The Comintern responded in kind, rejecting Kenyatta as a prospective party member. He questioned the Marxist line on class and religion. He was too well known to the British police to be trained as an agent. Despite his views on missionaries, Kenyatta told his tutors that bourgeois democracy allowed more freedom of thought than Soviet communism (McClellan 1993; Pegushev 1996: 192).

Kenyatta left Russia in 1933, after Hitler's capture of power led the Comintern to switch its support from colonial revolutions to European 'popular fronts'. It abandoned organizations like the KCA, denounced as 'bourgeois national reformists'. Kenyatta returned to London, penniless. Until mid-1934 he remained in touch with several communist groups; some probably helped him financially. He contributed to their journals. An article in *Labour Monthly* about the gold rush in Western Kenya was his first to champion people other than Kikuyu.

A short essay in the glossy anthology *Negro*, edited by Nancy Cunard, a friend of Padmore's, was Kenyatta's most interesting work at this time, and in distinguished company.[11] His piece, 'Kenya', enlivened Marxist analysis with communist invective. He appeared to welcome 'detribalization', the unwittingly progressive consequence of exploitation. The British, however, refused representation to 'detribalized natives' and, by supporting the 'backward form of social relationships', thwarted the 'national liberation movement' with 'divide and rule'. It was time for Kenya's Africans to 'unite and demand our birthright' (Kenyatta 1934). Kenyatta's political imagination had apparently been radicalized. But the absence of any mention of Kikuyu issues revealed the tension that had perhaps already distanced him, privately, from Marxism.

Like his other patrons, the Left tried to harness Kenyatta to their agenda. To them he represented oppressed colonial masses, in theory natural supporters of proletarian internationalism. Cultural nationalism smacked of backward 'tribalism' and threatened African solidarity with their socialist brethren elsewhere. Kenyatta, however, had asserted in *Muigwithania*, and would again in *Facing Mount Kenya*, a Kikuyu right to follow their own road to modernity. All ethnic groups had this right to self-determination; ethnic history taught liberty (Kenyatta 1938: 317). How could he call for a detribalized nationalism? Marxists required him to imagine a non-existent Kenyan proletarian nation, not realizing that Kikuyu consciousness was itself only now crystallizing. A socialist future would also be anathema to the prop-ertied Kikuyu self-mastery that Kenyatta fought to preserve (Lonsdale 2002b). We doubt Kenyatta wholeheartedly believed what he wrote in *Negro*. In the end, communists were as Eurocentric as missionaries. Marxism provided no 'unanswerable argument', no *kihooto*, for his cause.

By late 1934 Kenyatta had become his own man, no longer a token, a client. He was about to embark on a surge of political activity and intellectual achievement, to become a respected, if not always fully understood, figure in two different, linked, worlds – that of Britain's black intelligentsia, and of academic social anthropology.

Kenyatta, Malinowski, and anthropology

On returning from Russia Kenyatta lived mainly on his work as a lin-guistic informant at University College London. This was also his entrée to the academic world. In June 1935 he made the transition from detribalized native, with suspect Bolshevik connections, to student – in the foremost graduate course of its day in social anthropology. Mali-nowski forwarded Kenyatta's application for a London School of Eco-nomics (LSE) library card, remarking on his great 'influence among the educated Africans here and in Africa'. He would work under Mali-nowski's personal supervision.[12] Kenyatta enrolled for the three-year postgraduate diploma, for students lacking the qualifications to read for the Ph.D. Early in 1938 he presented the dissertation that would become *Facing Mount Kenya*. Before discussing this work, we must show why Malinowski and Kenyatta were attracted to each other.

Between the wars, Malinowski helped to make the LSE one of the world's leading schools of social anthropology. His fieldwork in the Tro-briand Islands in World War I and his functionalist approach to 'prim-itive' societies had transformed the discipline's practice and theory. Malinowski furnished its mythical charter and role model. His Tro-briand experience was the primal encounter with otherness, and he the archetype ethnographer (Stocking 1992: 214–219). A charismatic and complex man, he was loved and hated with equal passion by his peers. He had close and exacting relations with his students but did not demand discipleship; no Malinowski cult developed. His students – Raymond Firth, Ashley Montagu, E.E. Evans-Pritchard, Isaac Schapera, Hortense Powdermaker, Meyer Fortes, Audrey Richards, Hilda Kuper, Godfrey Wilson, Phyllis Kaberry, S.F. Nadel – became some of the most influential anthropologists of the mid-twentieth century, and pioneers of African studies.

Malinowski was increasingly turning from Melanesian and Australian aboriginal society to Africa – the main focus of British anthropology for the next forty years. He was closely involved with the International African Institute (IAI), founded in 1926 by colonial governments and mission societies, and a friend of its director. An academic entrepreneur, he helped to win the large Rockefeller Foundation grant that made the IAI the main source of African social research funding before 1940. The chairman of its executive council, the redoubtable imperialist Lord Lugard, ensured credibility with government while its academic and missionary members connected the IAI to the native rights lobbies.

Malinowski had long hoped to do research in Kenya. His only visit to Africa, however, was in 1934 as keynote speaker at a conference in South Africa on 'Educational Adaptations in a Changing Society'. On his way home he spent some weeks in East Africa. He visited several Kenyan peoples, including Kikuyu, and came home with a sheaf of field notes.[13] He had good reasons for wanting to meet a literate Kikuyu. There were deeper grounds too, important to both men.

As champion of participatory field research, Malinowski taught that total immersion in native life was the sole authority for an account of a culture 'from the native's point of view'. It was also objective, scientific knowledge, but only if practiced by trained anthropologists. Kenyatta was a native African, of political influence, who purported to speak for his people. If Malinowski could train him to express his 'native point of view' in a functionalist analysis of his own society, the validity of the new scientific anthropology would be powerfully affirmed. The native insider would have become an objective outsider, just as the scientific outsider could become an empathetic insider.

Kenyatta's politics increased his value, since Malinowski maintained that functionalist anthropology could be politically useful to colonial administrators. A liberal himself, he distrusted militant, ethnocentric nationalism and recognized that potential in Kenyatta. But if anthropology could teach colonialism a more humane form of social engineering in Africa, it might avert the threat of violent 'black bolshevism' (Stocking 1992: 194–195; Tilley 2001: 206–212). Kenyatta's experience could help to prove this case. It was also a utilitarian argument to put before men with limited funds and large imperial responsibilities.[14] Malinowski supported Kenyatta's application for a £70 IAI studentship with a note to Lugard:

> since the aim of the Institute has always been entirely non-political, the present application is of high importance. Mr. Kenyatta started his work in my department about two years ago. At that time he had a definite

political bias . . . This, I think, has almost been entirely eradicated by the constant impact of detached scientific method on his mental processes. The highly depoliticising effect of scientific anthropology has worked a remarkable change . . . Since Mr. Kenyatta has considerable influence on African students, and also on educated Africans in Kenya, the contribution will be not only towards the advancement of theoretical studies, but also towards the practical influence of anthropology.[15]

Kenyatta got his grant. Lugard, 'unconvinced of the brainwashing power of functionalist anthropology', cast the IAI's sole dissenting vote (Stocking 1995: 412).

Malinowski was increasingly critical of colonialism and came to believe that anthropologists must become 'not only the interpreter of the native, but also his champion' (1937: viii). This view was reinforced by his growing despair over Western civilization as a whole. Europe's liberalism had been replaced, as he wrote in his Introduction to *Facing Mount Kenya*, by a 'new historical demoralisation' in face of general crisis (Malinowski 1938: ix). His relationship with Kenyatta probably also informed his new conviction that educated Africans could no longer be denied equal rights.[16] While avoiding overt attacks on colonialism, Malinowski privately scorned the 'detribalised tropical European – whether he develops the pathological form of Kenya lunacy or only the ordinary idiocy of the average colonial administrator or missionary'.[17]

Despite his fame, Malinowski remained an outsider in Britain. Many in the academic establishment, he well knew, felt this émigré Pole to be uncomfortable in their society, always 'a foreigner in England' (Goody 1995: 29). He was also developing a brash new discipline, suspect to conservative academics, at a new school, the LSE, widely regarded as dangerously 'pink'. Many of his students were socially marginal too: Jews, white colonials, continental Europeans, women, and reputed leftists.[18] Malinowski could empathize with Kenyatta's social position, and did not patronize him.

Kenyatta had his own reasons for taking up this further opportunity for advanced education. Study at the LSE, a magnet for overseas students, would raise his status both in Kenya and among Britain's black intelligentsia. He would be able to deal as an equal with Oxbridge-educated colonial officials. With a better education than many white settlers, he could scarcely be dismissed as a 'semi-educated detribalized native'. In a racist Britain, where scholars still debated African educability, he wanted, as his friend Peter Mbiyu Koinange remembered, to show 'what others can do, we can do too' (Koinange 1963: 21).

Social anthropology had its own attractions. It was the only discipline that offered Kenyatta an academic qualification through study of his own people. Malinowski's functionalist approach – which saw 'primitive' peoples as living, integrated, societies, not evolutionary laggards – affirmed their human dignity and undermined racist stereotypes of Kenya's 'blank, uninteresting, brutal barbarism'.[19] Kenyatta stood in urgent need of such insights. In 1934, a year earlier, the KLC's report had rejected his (or anybody else's) claims to be a typical Kikuyu and all notion of their historically grounded, collective, interests. It recommended that they adopt modern forms of property, to farm more intensively the land that remained to them. Such a policy would eradicate the detailed history of achievement that Kikuyu associations and *mbari* elders had offered in evidence; and thus demolish the basis of Kikuyu society (Cmd 4556: 1934). Worse still, disbelief in the past as a guide to a distinctively Kikuyu future was also spreading among *athomi*. Two 'readers' known to Kenyatta published their ethnographic apologia for progress in the same year. Parmenas Mukiri, who had accompanied Kenyatta on his second visit to London and had stayed, latterly at Ruskin College, Oxford, until 1933, portrayed in English a Kikuyu past subject to the permanent revolution of youthful *ituika* against exploitation by their elders. Stanley Kiama Gathigira, an opponent of the KCA, published in Kikuyu an account that similarly praised the progressive energy of precolonial youth. Thus far they agreed with Kenyatta the journalist on the reforming potential of junior generations. But both proceeded to extend the logic of their argument into dangerous territory. Mukiri hoped modernity would bring detribalization, as the Romans had detribalized Britain. Industrial democracy, as Leys had argued, would defend African interests better than tribes (Leys 1924: 298–302). And, even after the 'female circumcision crisis', Gathigira saw no reason why Christianity should conflict with Kikuyu discipline (Gathigira 1934; Lonsdale 2002a: 239–241). Mukiri's argument was similar to that expressed by Kenyatta in Nancy Cunard's anthology. Mukiri seems to have believed it. We doubt that Kenyatta did. And while we do not know that Kenyatta read Gathigira, he was familiar with the latter's argument. It was the view of Christians who agreed to the ban on clitoridectomy.[20] To Kenyatta it would have seemed feebly compliant, unreasoned, naïve. Facing such internal subversion of the reasoned self-confidence of *muigwithania*, Kenyatta had to be doubly sure of his own 'unanswerable argument', which was that Kikuyu should be heeded as Kikuyu, not as detribalized 'Africans' nor yet as disorientated missionary 'converts'.

Every page of *Facing Mount Kenya*, makes plain that Kenyatta found in functionalist anthropology a convincing medium of representation. He could show, with scientific authority, the logic of

[184]

Kikuyu civilization and its right, therefore, to a modernity it could call its own. As for his personal advocacy, the suspect partisan was now a trained expert. Neither the KLC, Mukiri or Gathigira could make that claim. Anthropology implicitly justified this otherwise questionable conversion of personal experience into scientific observation. Such duality made the discipline. The ethnographer needed no apology for being both 'pilgrim and cartographer'. A research monograph was necessarily both 'an intimate view and a cool assessment', poised between science and fable (Geertz 1988: 4–6, 9–10). Kenyatta's marginality, between European and Kikuyu, was no longer a cause for disdain but became his core qualification to speak.

Kenyatta contributed three papers to Malinowski's seminars, on initiation – including clitoridectomy – education and land tenure; and others for Raymond Firth; the one on magic 'aroused vigorous discussion'.[21] These went into his dissertation, submitted in late 1937. His pan-Africanist colleagues, Padmore, C.L.R. James and Ras Makonnen put him in touch with Dinah Stock, an Independent Labour Party (ILP) friend, lecturer for the Workers' Education Association, co-editor of the ILP journal *The New Leader* and secretary of the British Centre Against Imperialism. She found it easy enough to turn dissertation into book, taking about three weeks. James took Kenyatta to his publisher, Frederic Warburg, an anti-communist social democrat. His firm, Secker and Warburg, published *Facing Mount Kenya* in September 1938, shortly before James's own *The Black Jacobins* (Makkonen 1973: 112–116; Warburg 1959).

Facing Mount Kenya

Functionalist anthropology's model of integrated and harmonious cultures appeared, as we have said, to suit Kenyatta's purpose, since its approach suggested that Kikuyu were not inferior to the British but different. Kenyatta repeatedly compared the two cultures; age-sets, for example, were stronger associations than the old school tie (1938: 116). His book also showed he was representative of true Kikuyu, not detribalized and out of touch; and invented the harmonious nationality that functionalism looked for in pre-industrial societies. He pictured his credentials in the frontispiece. Photographed in an off-the-shoulder monkey-fur cloak, he gazed ruminatively at the head of his spear. He represented elderhood, authority. His friend Mbiyu Koinange, whose cloak it was, remembered that they wished to give 'an elderly tone' to a book by 'an elderly Mugikuyu' (Koinange 1963: 21). Kenyatta was no longer an upstart 'reader'. An elder was equally competent in print, at home with scholarship. In the preface Kenyatta gave four other grounds for his representational authority.

First, he was his own man. He repudiated ' "professional friends of the African" who are prepared to maintain their friendship for eternity as a sacred duty, provided only that the African will continue to play the part of an ignorant savage so they can monopolise the office of interpreting his mind and speaking for him. To such people, an African who writes a study of this kind is encroaching on their preserves. He is a rabbit turned poacher', whose 'power of expression ... will very soon sweep away the patronage and repression which surround him' (Kenyatta 1938: xviii).[22] Second, he was a typical Kikuyu, schooled in tradition; initiated, he evasively claimed, according to 'custom'; and a third-grade elder, having earned by marriage and fatherhood the right to sit on judicial councils. His wealthy, well-connected family gave him a right to be heard (1938: xix). Third, he was expert in land law, as future trustee of his *mbari* land; in magic, by apprenticeship to his magician grandfather; and in the ceremonial procedures of *ituika*, the inter-generational transfer of authority. This recitation of expertise was to impress his Kikuyu constituency as much as his British audience. Fourth – and this was the point – his civic virtue qualified him as an external advocate, as *muthamaki*. An elected KCA spokesman, his 'knowledge of the outside world' made him leader of 'progressive movements among the Kikuyu' (1938: xx).

Kenyatta claimed that his anthropological training amounted to no more than the 'necessary technical knowledge for recording ... scientifically' the Kikuyu knowledge in his head. His archive of custom remained unchanged; he had learned merely how to display it to others. In becoming an external observer he had not ceased to be a participant insider. Duality carried no taint of detribalization. He was at last both representative and authority, since the ethnography was also his autobiography. His hard-earned elderhood and experience of the world epitomized his people. Pilgrim and cartographer, his career represented modern Kikuyu nationhood, integrated but extrovert. Imagining Kikuyu in print, Kenyatta invented himself. Even his new nom de plume Jomo was more 'African' than his baptismal Johnstone.[23]

Kenyatta's Kikuyu were an Arcadian republic of the elders – a democratic, rule-bound, civilized, organic community free from conflict. The internal debate that gave him his platform for reconciliation with modernity in *Muigwithania* had been silenced – and with it, one might suppose, the legitimacy of the 'progressive movements' applauded in his preface. He portrayed an indigenous democracy, true enough, but one that spoke with a single, unchanging voice – after the first, revolutionary, *ituika* had deposed its tyrant king. Kenyatta's subsequent *ituika*s, unlike those of Mukiri and Gathigira, confirmed rather than changed custom (1938: 192–195). To construct this other Eden he high-lighted some aspects of Kikuyu culture, and slurred over others. The core issue, made still more urgent by the KLC's report, was land. Alien-ated from Kikuyu to the profit of white settlers, it was the emotional bedrock of colonial inequality, conferring supremacy on whites, con-firming subordination in blacks. Land was also time: it was the past with its ancestral bones; the present resource with which the living competed for civic virtue; and the future, sustaining marriage, repro-duction, and the hope of productive labor for one's grandchildren (1938: chap. 2). Kenyatta turned this argument into poetry, even biblical text, in dedicating his work: 'To Moigoi and Wamboi and all the dispos-sessed youth of Africa: for perpetuation of communion with ancestral spirits through the fight for African freedom, and in the firm faith that the dead, the living and the unborn will unite to rebuild the destroyed shrines' (1938: v).[24] The prayer invoked both past and future in naming his parents, also re-named in his first-born children.

Kenyatta showed that land was privately held family property, con-trolled by *mbari* or sub-clan elders. It was not the 'tribal' land that the British had felt free to alienate, on the assumption that affected house-holds were disturbed rather than dispossessed, since they could always take up communal land elsewhere. Kikuyu property was also legally secure. It was created either by the civilizing toil that had cultivated undeveloped forest, or by purchase from its former owners, Ndorobo (now Okiek) hunters – not by the 'force and chicanery' of which the KLC had accused Kikuyu pioneers. This patrimonial history legit-imized the elders' authority, the rational foundation of the Arcadian republic.

In creating a harmonious society obedient to rules laid down by landed elders-in-council, Kenyatta had indeed written an 'elderly' text. The voice of an elder rich in lawful property and *kihooto* now dispar-aged the subversive voice of literate youth he had published a decade before. He had switched sides in the argument of moral ethnicity, from liberty to order. Kikuyu education, he now maintained, was integral to daily life. There was no question of 'opening up a man's head'. Like a contemporary European 'progressive education', it aimed to social-ize the young to know their proper adult place in society (1938: 98–106, 120–129, 312–314). Initiation rites, particularly clitoridectomy, were similarly functional. They trained the young for adult responsibility. Missionaries were simply ignorant in supposing initiation to be a barbarous encouragement to promiscuity (1938: 130–134).

The most striking silences in Kenyatta's account related to social and gender differentiation. The property-owning *mbaris* were, we now know, not miniature democracies but patrimonial oligarchies, supported by tenants and clients tied by various forms of dependence to their wealthy patrons (Kershaw 1997). Kenyatta had told the KLC his father had had fifteen clients. Scarcely mentioning such dependence in his book, he portrayed it as a relationship of friendly generosity (1938: 22). As to women, he treated them as a source of potential disorder except when under patriarchal control. Their admirably fruitful energy in the household was good evidence of male managerial capacity, making wealthy men self-evidently fit for leadership (1938: 9, 76, 175, 194–195, 265, 310, 315–316). Women of independent power might revert to type, as polyandrous oppressors of men (1938: 6–7). Kenyatta's chapter on marriage was lyrical in its defense of polygamy and women's subordination as the basis of social harmony (1938: chap. 8). His 'Kikuyu' were almost invariably men, however much he bridled at the missionary accusation that wives were men's chattels (1938: 165).

European intrusion into this patriarchal idyll had vandalized paradise. Colonialism was an ordeal that disrupted and demoralized Kikuyu, especially the educated young. These were no longer reconcilers or straighteners but mischief-makers, 'floundering' between two worlds (1938: 92, 110, 120–125, 249–254). While the younger Kenyatta had also seen modernity as an ordeal, he had believed Kikuyu could overcome it. Now he merely attacked, or ridiculed, the fanaticism or hypocrisy of the British bearers of modernity. He denounced missionaries – who had expertly defended Kikuyu land rights before the KLC – as 'ignorant fanatics' (1938: 135); and condemned colonial rule as treachery, in that British pioneers had abused Kikuyu hospitality (1938: 44–47; Lonsdale 1995). He satirized the KLC, in a folk tale of the generous (Kikuyu) man and the ungrateful (British) elephant. The man had offered shelter to the rain-soaked animal who then crowded him out of his home. The man protested. The elephant called an investigating commission of other 'jungle lords'. These crammed into the hut to pontificate on their 'law of the jungle' regarding property. Driven from his home, the despairing owner burnt it down with the squabbling lords inside, reflecting that 'Peace is costly, but it's worth the expense' (1938: 47–52).

In his final chapter, Kenyatta restated Kikuyu functionalism: 'It cannot be too strongly emphasised that the various sides of Gikuyu life here described are parts of an integrated culture. No single part is detachable; each has its context and is fully understandable only in relation to the whole' (1938: 309). He concluded with a ringing reiteration of his central argument, that Kikuyu and other Africans had the right and ability to preserve what was of value in their own cultures and to adopt from Europe only what was useful or desirable:

> There certainly are some progressive ideas among the Europeans. They include the ideas of material prosperity, of medicine, and hygiene, and literacy which enable people to take part in world culture. But so far the Europeans who visit Africa have not been conspicuously zealous in imparting these parts of their inheritance to Africans and seem to think the only way to do it is by police discipline and armed force . . .

> If Africans were left in peace on their own lands, Europeans would have to offer them the benefits of white civilisation in real earnest before they could obtain the African labour they want so much. They would have to offer the African a way of life which really was superior to one his fathers lived before him, and a share in the prosperity given them by their command of science. They would have to let the African choose what parts of European culture could be beneficially transplanted, and how they could be adapted (1938: 317–318).

But had Kenyatta really found in ethnography the unanswerable argument that advanced his goal – to represent the Kikuyu as a people well capable of entering modernity on their own terms, if only their disabling grievances were removed? Could *Facing Mount Kenya* indeed serve, not as a 'eulogy for a society destroyed, but a cultural call to arms to create a modern Kikuyu culture' (Shaw 1995: 136)? Not even Malinowski, his mentor, seems to have grasped Kenyatta's intention, to judge by the chief reservation he made in his introduction to Kenyatta's book. His student's functionalism, he thought, was too crudely enthusiastic in its comparisons of Kikuyu and European institutions, even referring, misleadingly, to relations between 'church and state' (1938: viii, xi–xii).[25] The comparability of the Kikuyu and the British was precisely Kenyatta's point. His version of Kikuyu history, in which his people arrived at democracy by overthrowing an ancient tyranny, provided particularly telling evidence (1938: chapter 9). But Malinowski's synchronic method had no use for history. Anthropology may have impressed Kenyatta as an armory of unanswerable argument; but anthropologists do not seem to have been so impressed with Kenyatta.

Conclusion: modernity and the contradictions of conservative reform

Functionalist anthropology had appeared to give Kenyatta the means to imagine a golden past of disciplined harmony – a fine platform from which to denounce the disruptions of colonialism. His core concern, however, as we have just seen, was the control of social change: 'They would have to let the African choose . . .'. Who should decide what change was desirable, who pioneer it, to whose benefit and at whose expense? Could so rule-bound a community as he devised exercise the freedom of conscience he advocated as the solution to the circumcision crisis (1938: 131–132)? To answer such questions with confidence and consistency Kenyatta needed a theory of social change that authorized Kikuyu self-determination. Young *athomi* had celebrated that possibility, using the indigenous social theory of generational renewal. Malinowski's anthropology was not so immediately helpful, at least as Kenyatta understood it. Functionalism offered no analysis of the colonial situations that African societies actually experienced (Kuper 1996 119–120). And Kenyatta's strict interpretation of Malinowski's model put him in a double bind. Rigid functionalism was not only ill-equipped to detect internal sources of change, it also implied that externally induced change was bound to be disruptive, if not destructive, of the previously functional order. Liberal imperialists had feared as much. The problem of how to achieve continuity by reform, without risk of deep disturbance, was by no means unique to Kenyatta. It was 'the classic dilemma of the anthropologist, the contradiction of the progressive preservationist, the radical conserver' (Goody 1995: 53). Nonetheless, other analytical approaches might have served Kenyatta better. The *athomi* he had published in *Muigwithania* had appreciated, as younger anthropologists were also coming to see in the late 1930s, that colonial political economy had not so much disrupted Kikuyu society as greatly enlarged its scale (Wilson and Wilson 1945: chapter II).[26]

Because the anthropology Kenyatta learned at the LSE had made his depiction of the Kikuyu more seamlessly coherent it made his advocacy more difficult. In giving him a theory, functionalism had weakened his politics. True, he could condemn colonialism more cogently than the young journalist of ten years before. The British had not only appropriated Kikuyu land and labor, they had disrupted an organic society. But a focus on systemic distortion rather than on popular grievance made it more difficult to sustain the next stage of his argument, which was that by denying Africans power, whites denied them the chance to decide how to rebuild a socially harmonious house of custom. For the more Kenyatta portrayed Kikuyu society as a damaged system, the harder he made the task of self-conscious reconstruction. If colonialism destroyed 'the spirit of manhood' that promoted rational choice, where then could one find the men of 'morale and courage' who might steer reform (1938: 211, 119)? In his concluding pages, it was with the club of his political conviction rather than the rational *kihooto* of social science that he insisted on the possibility of non-traumatic change, if only the British would grant more economic and political freedom.

In glorifying a social order based on the authority of wealthy *mbari* elders over juniors and the poor, Kenyatta had curtailed the potential for generational change led by the educated young. His studies had apparently made him only too conscious of the dilemma that has per-plexed dozens of other small societies confronted with the 'juggernaut' of Western modernity (Giddens 1990). Only those of their number with modern knowledge could protect tradition with selective reforms. But that educational qualification was itself disruptive. Kenyatta now agreed: 'Unless Western education in Africa can keep these bonds [of family, kin, and gendered age-sets] vital and strong it cannot be expected to mould the African in a way which will make him fit in his community on one hand and establish good relations with the outside world on the other.' Conventional Western schooling was anti-social in Kikuyu terms, linked as it was to 'social groupings which are largely determined by economic, professional and religious associa-tions' of modernity (1938: 122). Mukiri had welcomed that prospect. Kenyatta did not. But then, few elders or social scientists are able to reconcile the contradictions of *Gemeinschaft* (community) and *Gesellschaft* (civil society).

Facing Mount Kenya, in any case, failed to establish Kenyatta's representative role. Few people read it. The first edition sold only 517 copies before the rest were destroyed in an air-raid. Its audience was overwhelmingly British. Only three copies seem to have reached his Kikuyu colleagues. Reviews were few, and unenthusiastic. The main British anthropological journals, *Man* and the *Journal of the Royal Anthropological Institute*, ignored it, as did Kenyatta's former com-munist friends. On the Left, Dinah Stock, who helped edit the manu-script, reviewed it before publication for the ILP journal *The New Leader* (Stock 1938). Another ILP member, H.N. Brailsford, reviewed it for the *New Statesman and Nation* (Brailsford 1938). While both accepted Kenyatta's account of Kikuyu custom at face value, only Stock took his main point, that Africans could think and act for themselves. Brailsford took the characteristically paternalist position, despairing of the ability of Kikuyu, 'a people rapidly deteriorating', to act on their own behalf. In the *Journal of the Royal Africa Society* Cullen Young, former missionary in Malawi and amateur ethnogra-pher, praised Kenyatta's political restraint, expressed the liberal impe-rialist hope that he could be co-opted into a more progressive colonialism, and denounced the racism which made that improbable

(Young 1938). Missionaries with Kenya connections were more negative. In the IAI's journal *Africa*, A.R. Barlow (1939), one of Kenyatta's patrons, sympathized with his project but thought him out of date; missionaries were more effective Kikuyu advocates. From Kenya, Dr Philp (1938), in the CSM publication, *Kikuyu News*, accused Kenyatta of wallowing in shame and indecency; Christianity had yet to defeat the 'unfruitful works of darkness'. The business journal *East Africa and Rhodesia* did not even try to understand; in seventeen lines it thought Kenyatta's 'no doubt reliable description' was discredited by his politics (Anonymous 1938).

Facing Mount Kenya was, then, no *kihooto*. Far from an unanswerable argument, it was a political failure. It neither established Kenyatta's authority nor forced the British to heed Kikuyu grievance. And the dismissive reviews rankled. Eight years after his book's publication, at a Fabian conference on post-war policy, Kenyatta complained that 'we have published books and our friends have reviewed them more critically than the books of our enemies . . . our friends are undermining our activities'.[27] But he himself was a better argument than his book against any prophecy of the enfeebling effects of 'detribalization'. To the contrary, he embodied the conflicts of conservative modernization, living out his project's unresolved contradictions. Malinowski understood that dilemma at least. Europeans must recognize, he said in his Introduction, 'that an African who looks at things from the tribal point of view and at the same time from that of Western civilisation, experiences the tragedy of the modern world in an especially acute manner' (1938: ix). And the tragedy, he implied, was that Kenyatta's people could not enter the modern world just as Kenyatta chose.

Kenyatta's relations with both whites and the black intelligentsia reflected this ambivalence. Having finally opened up his head with education, the defender of the elders' republic was also an urbane Western intellectual. His British friends spread well beyond the African affairs community. To them he was a charming, intelligent and charismatic figure of moderate, well reasoned views – antithesis to the savage 'other'. But he also played on his flamboyant otherness, arriving for dinner at the home of his publisher, Frederic Warburg, holding a spear and wearing a leopard skin (Warburg 1959: 253). And to black colleagues like Ralph Bunche he 'expressed hatred and distrust of all whites – "use them, but don't trust them" is his advice'.[28]

Kenyatta's relations with the black intelligentsia were equally ambivalent. Most were West Indians. While wishing to bring Africa to British political attention, none except perhaps Padmore had visited the continent. Needing an African past that would counter the racist claptrap that Africans were not worth an entry in the story of civilization, they were dubious of existing indigenous societies. As Marxists they looked to an African future that would be rationalist and socialist, framed by nation states. Indigenous society seemed an unpromising foundation. Padmore and James attacked tribalism and feudalism as anachronisms; Padmore later wrote that the 'traditional African way of life needs a cataclysm to free it from its own decay. It is the newly emancipated generation of Africans with a detribalised outlook, who under the stimulus of Western political ideas and technocracy can alone bring about the necessary regeneration' (1956: 373). What, then, did they make of Kenyatta? His book's moralistic and reverential tone was quite unlike the sophistication of Padmore's Marxism or James's historiography. The pan-Africanist Makonnen dismissed Kenyatta as 'simply concerned to get certain things known about his people' (1973: 162). If his black critics did not appreciate Kenyatta's search for *kihooto*, they did recognize his political passion. James thought Kenyatta a 'simmering volcano of African nationalism'; Makonnen conceded that he was 'much more obviously marked for leadership than many of the others in England at the time' (James 1963: 301; Makkonen 1973: 162). Yet Peter Abrahams later described Kenyatta as 'the most relaxed, sophisticated and "westernised" of the lot of us' (Abrahams 1961: 55).

Finally, if *Facing Mount Kenya* did not achieve Kenyatta's political purpose or resolve the contradictions of conservative reform, it did represent the Kikuyu with more understanding than had any study since the Routledges' of thirty years before (Routledge and Routledge 1910). Kenyatta had also, with fellow *athomi* Mukiri and Gathigira, done what the Routledges could never do. He had imagined a Kikuyu community on a far wider scale than their segmentary institutions and fractious politics had previously permitted. Further, his transformation of the many Kikuyu pasts into a progressive 'national' history chartered both representative Kikuyu politics and his own leadership. He took these themes further in the last of his publications before his country's independence: two pamphlets written during his final years in Britain during World War II (Kenyatta 1942, 1945; Berman and Lonsdale 1998). They appeared to provide an agenda for his return to Kenya in September 1946. But, in the event, Kenyatta proved utterly unable to cope with the colony's post-war politics. Functionalism turned out to be no guide at all to the turbulence of nationalism and the rigors of post-war 'development', what imperialism called its latest attempt to order Africa.

Notes

1 This chapter is based on Berman 1996; Lonsdale 1996b; Berman and Lonsdale 1998. We acknowledge our continuing debt to Greet Kershaw.

2 Malinowski to Bonaparte, 6 December 1934, Malinowski Papers, Stirling Library, Yale University.

3 Born Kamau wa Ngengi, baptised Johnstone Kamau, he was nicknamed 'Kenyatta' because of his beaded belt, a *kinyata*.

4 Public Record Office: CO 822/33: Memorandum of the Kikuyu Land Board Association, 6 April, 1931; Mockerie 1934, Appendix. The Asian lawyers who helped in drafting may have overstated the problem. See below for Kenyatta's refusal to 'ape' the British.

5 Kenyatta to editor, *Muigwithania*, I, 11, April 1929, p. 6. Kenya National Archives: DC/MKS 10B/12/1.

6 This section summarises Lonsdale 1996b.

7 We discuss Kenyatta's contacts more fully in our projected book, *The House of Custom: Jomo Kenyatta, Louis Leakey, and the Making of the Modern Kikuyu*.

8 Hooper to Miss Soles, 26 September 1929, Hooper Papers, CMS Archives, Birmingham.

9 Arthur to H. S. Scott, 23 December 1930, Presbyterian Church of East Africa Archives, Nairobi. Missionaries had accepted and hospitalised male circumcision – for Kenyatta among others. Anglicans were divided on clitoridectomy, Catholics ignored it. Arthur's physician's view was, thus, extreme.

10 *Manchester Guardian*, 18 March 1930; *The Times*, 26 March 1930. Leys (1924) and Ross (1927) were well-informed critics of British rule in Kenya.

11 Contributors included Langston Hughes, W.E.B. Dubois, Arthur Schomburg, William Carlos Williams, and Melville Herskovits. Samuel Beckett translated Francophone pieces. The African section focused on art and music, with some political essays by Kenyatta, Padmore, Ben Azikiwe and others.

12 Malinowski to Dickson, 21 June 1935; Malinowski to Kenyatta, 21 June 1935: Malinowski Papers 3/539, London School of Economics (MP).

13 Africa II/555; Africa II/129: MP.

14 Malinowski thought anthropology's lack of a 'practical basis' made it unattractive to funding bodies; to use the Rockefeller money for fieldwork needed 'an almost surreptitious deviation': 'Res. Needs in Soc. and Cult. Anth.' draft memo: MP.

15 Malinowski to Lugard, 7 November 1936: Africa I/696: MP.

16 As he told white and black audiences in South Africa: Africa II/555, 1934: MP. See also Rossetti 1985; Stocking 1995: 413–415.

17 Meeting with Philip Kerr, March 1930: Africa I/495: MP.

18 Stocking 1995: 407–409. Malinowski's supposed racism has been an issue since publication of his Trobriand diaries (Malinowski 1967). Those who knew him and most historians of anthropology deny this trait, despite his private use of 'earthy ethnic language'. While yearning for students who were 'not a Jew, Dago, [or] Pole', he always defended their interests when needed, regardless of their origin or politics (Goody 1995: 26–29, 44–47; Stocking 1995: 409, 411–412).

19 Sir Charles Eliot, 1903, Commissioner of the East African Protectorate, later Kenya (Mungeam 1978: 93).

20 Gathigira won a second prize of £10 in the International African Institute's African writing competition of 1933. Kenyatta was not, apparently, the Institute's reader. Information from Derek Peterson, 6 August 2002.

21 Sir Raymond Firth to John Lonsdale, 24 July 1989.

22 He may have had Louis Leakey in mind, although, as we have seen, he had met many other ostensibly benevolent white gamekeepers. For rivalry between Kenyatta and Leakey see: Berman and Lonsdale 1991.

23 Koinange remembered that he and Kenyatta had experimentally discovered a more 'African' name (Koinange 1963). Ralph Bunche's 1937 diaries suggest Kenyatta used 'Jomo' well before the book's publication: Bunche Papers, UCLA (BP).

24 Compare Isaiah 61:4. Today the names are rendered Wambui and Muigai.

25 Kenyatta had plagiarised this terminology from the first full European account of the Kikuyu, published 30 years earlier, itself proof that Kikuyu were worthy of British notice: Routledges 1910: 227.

26 Legal history, much later, might also have made Kenyatta ask if the 'custom' he defended had not become more restrictive under colonialism, as indigenous elders and British officials colluded to protect household discipline against the economic imperatives and market freedoms that drove and enticed the young away (Chanock 1985; Moore 1986).

27 Fabian Colonial Bureau papers 365/69, File 2, 'The Relationship between the British and Colonial Peoples', April 13, 1946: Oxford, Rhodes House Library.

28 Diary, April 22, 1937: BP.

References

Abrahams, Peter. 1961. 'The Blacks'. In L. Hughes (ed.). *An African Treasury*. New York: Pyramid Books, pp. 50–62.

Anonymous. 1938. Review of *Facing Mount Kenya*. *East Africa and Rhodesia* 15 (NS), 741/1 December:368.

Barlow, A.R. 1939. Review of *Facing Mount Kenya*. *Africa* xii/1: 114–116.

Berman, Bruce. 1996. 'Ethnography as Politics, Politics as Ethnography: Kenyatta, Malinowski and the Making of Facing Mount Kenya'. *Canadian Journal of African Studies* 30:313–344.

Berman, Bruce. 1998. 'Ethnicity, Patronage and the African State: the Politics of Uncivil Nationalism'. *African Affairs* 97:305–341.

Berman, Bruce and Lonsdale, John. 1991. 'Louis Leakey's Mau Mau: A Study in the Politics of Knowledge'. *History and Anthropology*, 5:142–204.

Berman, Bruce and Lonsdale, John. 1998. 'The Labors of Muigwithania: Jomo Kenyatta as Author, 1928–1945'. *Research in African Literatures* 29:16–42.

Brailsford, H.N. 1938. 'An African on African life'. *New Statesman and Nation* XVI 395 (NS) 17 September:420.

Chanock, Martin. 1985. *Law, Custom and Social Order: The Colonial Experience in Malawi and Zambia*. Cambridge: Cambridge University Press.

Cmd 4556. 1934. *Report of the Kenya Land Commission*. London: HMSO.

Gathigira, Stanley Kiama. 1934. *Mikaiire ya Gikuyu [Kikuyu customs]*. Reprint 1986. Nairobi: Scholars Press. MS translation by James Njenga.

Geertz, Clifford. 1988. *Works and Lives: The Anthropologist as Author*. Cambridge: Cambridge University Press.

Giddens, Anthony. 1990. *The Consequences of Modernity*. Stanford/Cambridge: Stanford University Press/Polity Press.

Goody, Jack. 1995. *The Expansive Moment: Anthropology in Britain and Africa, 1918–1970*. Cambridge: Cambridge University Press.

Howe, Stephen. 1993. *Anticolonialism in British Politics: The Left and the End of Empire 1918–1964*. Oxford: Clarendon Press.

James, C.L.R. 1963. 'From Toussaint L'Overture to Fidel Castro', reprinted. In A. Grimshaw (ed.). *The C.L.R. James Reader*. Oxford: Blackwell, pp. 296–314.

James, Wendy. 1973. 'The Anthropologist as Reluctant Imperialist'. In T. Asad (ed.). *Anthropology and the Colonial Encounter*. London: Ithaca Press, pp. 41–69.

Kenyatta, Johnstone. 1934. 'Kenya'. In N. Cunard (ed.). (1934) *Negro*. London: Lawrence & Wishart, pp. 803–807.

Kenyatta, Jomo. 1938. *Facing Mount Kenya*. London: Secker & Warburg.

Kenyatta, Jomo. 1942. *My People of Kikuyu and the Life of Chief Wangombe*. London: Lutterworth Press.

Kenyatta, Jomo. 1945. *Kenya: The Land of Conflict*. London: Panaf Service.

Kershaw, Greet. 1997. *Mau Mau from below*. Oxford/Nairobi/Athens, OH: Currey/EAEP/Ohio University Press.

Koinange, Peter Mbiyu. 1963. 'Jomo: Colleague in the Struggle for Freedom and Independence'. In A. Patel (ed.). *Struggle for Release [sic] Jomo and His Colleagues*. Nairobi: New Kenya Publishers, pp. 18–34, 232.

Kuper, Adam. 1996. *Anthropology and Anthropologists: the Modern British School*, 3rd edn. London: Routledge.

Leys, Norman. 1924. *Kenya*. London: Hogarth Press.

Lonsdale, John. 1995. 'The Prayers of Waiyaki: Political Uses of the Kikuyu Past'. In D. Anderson and D. Johnson (eds). *Revealing Prophets: Prophecy in Eastern African History*. London/Athens, OH: James Currey/Ohio University Press, pp. 240–291.

Lonsdale, John. 1996a. 'Moral Ethnicity, Ethnic Nationalism and Political Tribalism: The Case of the Kikuyu'. In P. Meyns (ed.). *Staat und Gesellschaft in Afrika: Erosions- und Reformprozesse*. Hamburg: Lit Verlag, pp. 93–106.

Lonsdale, John. 1996b. 'Listen while I Read: The Orality of Christian Literacy in the Young Kenyatta's Making of the Kikuyu'. In L. de la Gorgendiere, K. King and S. Vaughan (eds). *Ethnicity in Africa: Roots, Meanings and Implications*. Edinburgh: University of Edinburgh, African Studies Centre, pp. 17–53.

Lonsdale, John. 2002a. 'Contests of Time: Kikuyu Historiographies, Old and New'. In A. Harneit-Sievers (ed.). *A Place in the World: New Local Historiographies from Africa and South Asia*. Leiden: Brill, pp. 201–254.

Lonsdale, John. 2002b. 'Jomo Kenyatta, God & the Modern World'. In J.-G. Deutsch, P. Probst and H. Schmidt (eds). *African Modernities: Entangled Meanings in Current Debate*. Oxford/Portsmouth, NH: James Currey/Heinemann, pp. 31–66.

McClellan, Woodford. 1993. 'Africans and Black Americans in the Comintern Schools, 1925–34'. *International Journal of African Historical Studies* 26:371–390.

Makkonen, Ras. 1973. *Pan Africanism From Within*. Recorded and edited by K. King. Nairobi: Oxford University Press.

Malinowski, Bronislaw. 1938. 'Introduction'. In Jomo Kenyatta. *Facing Mount Kenya*. London: Secker & Warburg, pp. vii–xiv.

Malinowski, Bronislaw. 1967. *A Diary in the Strict Sense of the Term*. Translated by N. Guterman. London: Routledge Kegan Paul.

Mockerie [sc. Mukiri], Parmenas. 1934. *An African Speaks for His People*. London: Hogarth Press.

Moore, Sally Falk. 1986. *Social Facts and Fabrications: 'Customary' Law on Kilimanjaro, 1880–1980*. Cambridge: Cambridge University Press.

Mungeam, G.H. (ed.). 1978. *Kenya: Select Historical Documents 1884–1923*. Nairobi: East African Publishing House.

Murray-Brown, Jeremy. 1973. *Kenyatta*. London: Allen & Unwin.

Padmore, George. 1956. *Pan-Africanism or Communism: the Coming Struggle for Africa*. London: Dobson.

Pegushev, Andrei. 1996. 'The Unknown Jomo Kenyatta'. *Egerton Journal* 2:172–198.

Peterson, Derek. 2004. *Creative Writing: Translation, Bookkeeping and the Work of Imagination in Colonial Kenya*. Portsmouth, N.H.: Heinemann.

Peterson, Derek. 2002. 'Introduction: Autobiography as History and Literature'. In C. Muhoro Kageri. *The Life of Charles Muhoro Kageri*. Translated by J.M. Kariuki, D. Peterson. Madison: University of Wisconsin African Studies Center.

Philp, H.R.A. 1938. 'Review of Facing Mount Kenya'. *Kikuyu News*, Sept.: 175–176.

Ross, William McGregor. 1927. *Kenya from within*. London: Allen & Unwin.

Rossetti, Carlo. 1985. 'B. Malinowski, the Sociology of "Modern Problems" in Africa and the "colonial situation"'. *Cahiers d'Études Africaines* 25/100:477–503.

Routledge, W. Scoresby and Routledge, Katherine. 1910. *With a Prehistoric People: the Akikuyu of British East Africa*. Reprint 1968. London: Cass.

Shaw, Carolyn Martin. 1995. *Colonial Inscriptions: Race, Sex, and Class in Kenya*. Minneapolis/London: University of Minnesota Press.

Spencer, John. 1985. *KAU: The Kenya African Union*. London: KPI.

Stock, Dinah. 1938. 'An African Describes His Own People'. *The New Leader*, 1 July:7.

Stocking, George Jr. 1992. *The Ethnographer's Magic and Other Essays in the History of Anthropology*. Madison: University of Wisconsin Press.

Stocking, George Jr. 1995. *After Tylor: British Social Anthropology, 1888–1951*. Madison: University of Wisconsin Press.

Tilley, Helen. 2001. 'Africa as a "Living Laboratory": The African Research Survey and the British Colonial Empire: Consolidating Environmental, Medical, and Anthropological Debates, 1920–1940'. Unpublished D.Phil. University of Oxford.

Wanjohi, Gerald Joseph. 1997. *The Wisdom and Philosophy of the Gikuyu Proverbs: the Kihooto World-view*. Nairobi: Paulines Publications.

Warburg, Frederic. 1959. *An Occupation for Gentlemen*. London: Secker & Warburg.

Wilson, Godfrey and Wilson, Monica. 1945. *The Analysis of Social Change: Based on Observations in Central Africa*. Cambridge: Cambridge University Press.

Young, Cullen. 1938. Review of *Facing Mount Kenya*. *Journal of the Royal Africa Society* 37:522–523.

PART III

Salvage anthropology, primordial imagination, and 'dying races'

CHAPTER SEVEN

From the Alps to Africa: Swiss missionaries and anthropology

Patrick Harries

Neuchâtel in western Switzerland (pop. 15,000 in 1880) produced a remarkable group of missionary anthropologists during the last decade of the nineteenth century. It included Edmond Perregaux, remembered for his Asante work, and Héli Chatelain who labored among the Ovimbundu of Angola (Péclard 1995). Two other missionary anthropologists were particularly well educated. Edouard Jacottet studied at Neuchâtel, Tübingen and Göttingen before entering the mission field in Lesotho. In 1920 he was offered the first Chair in Bantu languages at the University of the Witwatersrand. The second, Henri-Alexandre Junod, studied in Neuchâtel, Basel and Berlin before working in southern Mozambique and the northern Transvaal. In South Africa Junod's pioneering work contributed to the establishment of anthropology as a university discipline.

Coming from a country without colonies, these missionaries were drawn to anthropology out of a desire to understand, rather than to govern, the societies to which they had been called by their vocation. Skills of observation and description developed by missionaries from Neuchâtel were partly built on a Prussian intellectual heritage in the canton that emphasized the importance of philology and the natural sciences (cf. Harries 1998, 2000). But conventions of representation developed at home also framed what they chose to write about in Africa (cf. Harries 1997). In particular, they carried to Africa the European images, themes and attitudes employed to describe the Alps as a primitive wilderness. This was an untamed environment in which Europeans found both freedom and fear, as well as a population that seemed to represent an earlier, more authentic stage of human development. The missionaries who left Neuchâtel for Africa were familiar with this image of domestic primitiveness and were, I would suggest, well equipped to describe its variant in Africa.

This chapter examines the ways in which the discovery and domestication of African society was preceded and informed by a similar process in the mountain wilderness of Switzerland. Early Swiss missionaries projected their fears and hopes onto Africa in much the same way that as a previous generation had projected sentiments onto the Alps. In this sense, the narrative strategies used to describe and explain African society were rooted in, and ultimately formed a part of, the civilizing mission at home.

Dorinda Outram has remarked on this process in the wider context of the eighteenth century when enlightened intellectuals approached the rural population of Europe 'in a way which reminds us of the way missionaries in the following century would regard indigenous peoples. They saw peasants buried in incomprehensible folk superstitions, irrational traditions and religious loyalties' (Outram 1995: 29). Outram's intellectuals defined their commitment to understanding and progress through their rejection of this old-fashioned world built on fantasy and fabrication. In the mountains of Switzerland and France, villagers continued to cling to pre-Enlightenment beliefs and practices well into the nineteenth century. Swiss evangelists serving mountain communities in the High Alps felt engaged in the same civilizing mission as their colleagues in Africa. Throughout the nineteenth century, townspeople observed and recorded the cultural practices of Alpine villagers in ways that measured their superior knowledge and prodigious material achievements. This self-imagery provided the bourgeoisie with the confidence, often seen as a duty, to assimilate a local 'culture' into a universal, modern 'civilization' (Braudel 1981: 101).

Yet simultaneously, this urban intelligentsia, its society severely shaken by industrialization, imbued mountain communities with a series of pre-capitalist virtues proclaimed to be typically Swiss. In this manner the urban bourgeoisie employed the image of an 'internal other' to celebrate both the progress and patriotism achieved under its tuition, as well as to define itself as a social entity. Reformist critics, on the other hand, used the same imagery to reflect on the ills of capitalist society and to propose a return to more simple values and sturdy traditions. Claude Reichler has drawn our attention to this process in an Alpine Switzerland where European visitors, without straying far from home, discovered a space 'destined to receive and preserve the projections and representations of a world that Enlightenment societies were seeing disappear' (Reichler 1996: 244).

While proponents and protagonists argued over the form of the new industrial order developing in nineteenth-century Switzerland, both employed the imagery of Alpine communities to construct a nation dominated by the values and practices of the enlightened bourgeoisie (Guichonnet 1980: 198–202, 211–213; Reichler 1996: 252–253). When these mountain communities were transformed at the end of the nineteenth century, a new social yardstick had to be located against which the Swiss could measure themselves and their achievements. This was accomplished partly by invoking the memory of the Alpine village in art, exhibitions, festivals and regional literature; but it was also attained by introducing the Swiss to other primitive communities elsewhere in the world.

Swiss missionary anthropologists had at their command a positive image of primitive communities that could be used to instill their moribund culture with new life while, at the same time, incorporating African societies into a familiar system of explanation. Both Alpine and African worlds were populated by uncomplicated, small-scale societies that seemed to reflect a primitive past of communitarian values, firm social hierarchies and authentic traditions. The disappearance of the old, Alpine ways haunted the Swiss in Africa where they were determined to salvage a picture of local communities before they, too, were submerged by an invading civilization that reduced cultural diversity to a uniform modernity, and that encouraged a feckless disregard for traditional values, rights and duties. Yet here lies an arresting contradiction. For just as European intellectuals portrayed Africa and the Alps as repositories in which to situate comforting traditions and a reassuring morality, they also condemned the customs, superstitions and irrational beliefs that restricted individualism and development.

This paper has two objectives. First, it highlights Neuchâtel's importance in the emergence of anthropology as a discipline. Second, it unravels the contradictory imagery of Africa and the Alps developed by Swiss commentators. I start by investigating the notion of primitiveness in Switzerland, then turn to the ways in which men like Junod and Jacottet employed this idea to understand their surroundings in Africa. The final section attempts to show how they resolved their need to find tradition and development, stasis and progress, in the representation of Alpine and African worlds.

A wild and ignorant people

During the religious revival that swept across Europe in the wake of the Napoleonic wars, Swiss evangelists initially focused their attention on the poor and unlettered of their own region. Missionaries were particularly drawn to the High Alps of neighboring France where a 'wild' and 'ignorant' people lived in a primitive manner clearly reminiscent of far-off savages in Africa (Bost 1841: 46–47, 1843: 145–147, also 134, 142, 145–146, 178).

Félix Neff and Ami Bost believed their work amongst the uncivilized people of the High Alps resembled that of missionaries in Africa and other corners of their world. Like their colleagues overseas, they were drawn to exotic locations where the sentiments of Christian revivalism and Romanticism overlapped. Individualism, mystery, emotion, zeal and dark spiritual torment could be expressed in areas uncorrupted by the contrived and frivolous materialism of the towns. The deferential attitudes of European peasants seemed little different from the uncorrupted simplicity of obliging blacks that missionaries read about in popular novels, the tracts of the anti-slavery movement, and a gathering tide of Sunday school literature. This led missionaries to conceive of isolated parts of the world, whether in Africa or Europe, as areas in which they could draw up a new civilization unfettered by urban and industrial corruption (Robert 1961: 358). In the High Alps of France, Swiss missionaries considered their congregants to be less depraved than the rich inhabitants of the plains (Bost 1843: 139). And they labored in the hope of replicating the successes of other missionaries in areas like Sierra Leone and Tahiti (Bost 1843: 145, 204, 178).

Yet, despite the deep suspicion with which they viewed the civilization of the plains, the missionaries were apostles of a controlled modernism. Neff considered 'the work of an evangelist in [the Freyssinières] valley' to be 'greatly similar to that of a missionary in uncivilized countries; his whole time must be given up to it' (Bost 1843: 218). Consequently, they spent long hours teaching small bands of students to read, in French, in ways that showed understanding and emotion and that defied the rote learning of oral societies. They then erected schools where students acquired a knowledge of writing, lost their 'detestable accent and pronunciation', and were introduced to grammar 'of which they have not the least idea' (Bost 1843: 243, also 208–209, 215). The missionaries also attempted to impart to their mountain congregants their knowledge of field irrigation, crop cultivation, building maintenance and hygiene (Bost 1843: 213–215).

This message was carried to North America when Bost's colleagues in the Swiss canton of Vaud established a mission to the Sioux in the 1830s. 'Evangelization must be accompanied by civilization', wrote the mission committee in Lausanne; and missionaries were instructed to avoid the 'degenerate' Indians in St Peter and civilize the nomadic Sioux by tying them to the soil (Grandjean 1917: 25, 28). The Vaudois historian Juste Olivier believed that this pastoral mode of production condemned the mountain people of his country to an early stage of human evolution (Olivier 1837 (v.1): 14, 24, 34). Needless to say, the cultural arrogance behind this idea affronted many potential converts (Favre 1908: 18–32).

The role of churchmen as agents of both Christianity and civilization has a long history in Switzerland. In the late eighteenth century roving evangelists and educated clergymen stranded in rural outposts found in the study of nature both an intellectual challenge and a diversion from a humdrum existence. Sharp differences of soil, temperature and vegetation, often on the same mountain, provided the collector with a rich variety of environments in which to practice his pastime. Membership of learned associations, often based on the collecting of specimens to be sorted by urban experts, became a means of retaining contact with the high culture of the towns. Stern Calvinist ministers propagated the collecting of plants, insects and rocks as a way to displace frivolous, even pagan village pastimes with an activity considered disciplined, edifying and utilitarian. Collecting also took the pastor into the fields where his knowledge of science allowed him to act as a secular, as well as spiritual, advisor to his parishioners. But the overriding reason for this clerical enthusiasm for collecting and classifying was the glorification of God's handiwork: the demonstration that the rich diversity of nature could be reduced to visible patterns and systems that could only be explained in terms of divine inspiration.

By uncovering the natural order of the earth and the living organisms that inhabited it, these savants were able to exercise a symbolic dominance over the environment. They (re)ordered the perception of nature in a way that made it entirely familiar to their generation. By cataloging and classifying plants, animals and minerals according to 'modern' criteria, or by collecting meteorological statistics, they reinforced their vision of the world and convinced themselves of their ability to understand it. This confidence was supported by the many learned societies, established in the early nineteenth century, through which findings were popularized in scientific journals, museum exhibitions, botanical gardens and herbaria. Membership of these societies, and the opportunity to advertise talents appreciated by the growing commercial and industrial elite, gave intellectuals the cultural and social capital needed to enter the governing classes (Rambert 1876: 8–9). The intellectual filing system developed by men of science and letters tamed the chaos of the world and reduced the terror of the unknown.

[205]

This heroic role could lead a romantic like Rousseau, when in a climber's hut in the Alps 'unknown to the whole universe', to regard himself 'as almost another Columbus' (Rousseau 1933 [1782]: 725).

Collectors shared the self-imagery of the intrepid explorer. Using a discursive technique immediately recognizable to historians of Africa, for example, Albrecht von Haller, the epitome of the Swiss man of science and letters, believed himself to be the first person to have 'penetrated' into several 'lost valleys' of Switzerland (Secrétan 1876: 604). Horace-Benedict de Saussure regarded the Chamonix valley as 'a new world, a sort of earthly paradise locked within a ring of mountains by a benevolent divinity' (de Saussure 2002: 67; see also Reichler and Ruffieux 1998: 284). Townsmen who ventured into the Alps compounded their heroic imagery of exploration through military metaphors describing the region as an 'impenetrable redoubt' whose 'ramparts' and 'fortifications' were manned by pine 'soldiers' (Murith 1810: 14; Rousseau 1933: 724). Romanticism also infused the Alpine landscape with a gothic sensibility; for wild and dark precipices, deep ravines and torrential rivers separated the valleys and broke the mountain terrain. The collector who scoured these regions in search of rare specimens found himself in a silent, lonely world in which his humble footpaths and narrow bridges seemed to be overwhelmed by the forces of nature. To enter this forbidding, melancholic space, the man of science had to 'drive, push' his way, 'penetrate' or undertake almost military 'incursions' (Murith 1810: 13, 31, 39; Durand and Pittier 1882: 6; Rousseau 1933: 724–725).

Alpine peaks held a special appeal for those who saw their conquest as a testing ground for masculinity and as a symbol of man's domination over the land. It was to test his capacities as an explorer that Alexander von Humboldt journeyed to the Alps before tackling the peaks of South America. For a climber like Emile Javelle, scaling an Alpine peak was the equivalent of crossing an unexplored Australian desert (Javelle 1920: 295). This concept of the Alps as a natural fortress capable of withstanding the assaults of modernity led Dean Bridel to situate the authentic, 'real knowledge of the fatherland' in the 'interior' of Switzerland (Vulliemin 1855: 79, 130).

The Alps constituted a pristine wilderness where the purity of nature was beyond the contagion of commerce and modernizing farmers. But Rousseau, H.B. de Saussure and others also viewed the mountains as a geologically primitive world that recalled the very origins of the earth. The Alps provided ineluctable proof of the insignificance of humanity in a chain of time that stretched back eons before the biblical 6000 years. De Saussure conjured up a picture of deep time when he imagined an age in which the sea covered the Alps (de Saussure 2002: 87–88, 166–167). The essayist Eugène Rambert visualized himself transported back through time when he entered the Alps. 'The higher one goes', he wrote in 1865, 'the more one seems to retreat into the past; one is convinced of accomplishing a voyage through time, and that in approaching the summits one is approaching its origins' (Rambert 1888: 117). Rambert saw not just mountains, but millennia of geological movement that had created them; and found in a deep Alpine valley a silence that reminded him of a prehistoric world untroubled by the destruction accompanying human settlement.

This view of the Alps as a primordial environment had a marked impact on how Rambert and others saw the local population. In the Alps, he believed, people lived as they had since time immemorial (Rambert 1888: 87). In this dark and mysterious Alpine environment, men of science and letters came across a mountain population strikingly different from that of the cities built alongside the lakes and rivers of Switzerland. In 1512 Francesco Guicciardini had described the Swiss as 'a savage uncultured people' (Guicciardini 1969: 240). Rambert employed the same term when he described the vestiges of this population in the Alps as 'half-savage', a 'primitive humanity whom civilization has hardly reached' (Rossel 1903: 652). The great climber, the Englishman Edward Whymper went even further when, in the 1860s, he thought the three female occupants of a cluster of isolated mountain chalets so primitive as to 'belong to some missing link that naturalists are looking to discover' (Whymper 1873: 197).

At a time when many Frenchmen believed that Adam had spoken a form of Breton, the regional dialects or patois of these primitive Alpine people seemed to provide access to the thoughts and concerns of pre-Roman Swiss communities. By practicing a form of 'linguistic paleontology' on these 'most original, least altered' language forms, scholars attempted to create a picture of the extinct, primitive societies of western Switzerland (Pictet 1837; Favrat in Bridel 1866: v). For these Romantic nationalists, the patois was both a source of creativity and a repository for the 'soul' or *Volksgeist* of the people (Olivier 1837 (v. 1): 217, 219, 263, 277).

The natural goodness of the human species

Living close to nature was filled with danger. Alpine communities expressed this danger in their fear of the mountains as a place from which violent storms, boulders and murderous avalanches of snow and mud descended into the inhabited valleys. Rock, ice and a thin crust of soil, together with a long list of insalubrious monsters and ghosts allowed only the most hardy to exploit the High Alps. But even as an oppressive environment crushed the lives of people living in the mountains, in the towns people were establishing a new dominion over nature. By the early sixteenth century a hardy band of explorers started to examine the plant and animal life of the mountains. As this new way of seeing developed, many came to view the infinite diversity, and delicate detail, of nature as resounding proof of God's existence.

Townsmen achieved a major cognitive victory over the Alps when in 1729 von Haller published a long epic poem celebrating the mountains as a source of both aesthetic beauty and moral and ethical values. In opposition to those who feared the Alps and rooted civilization in the towns, von Haller and his followers found in the mountains a refreshing physical and spiritual freedom. Rousseau provided society with a means of criticizing the growing corruption of the towns when he described the perfect communalism of the *montagnons* in the Val-de-Travers near Neuchâtel. His disciple, Dean Bridel, found in his parishioners around Chateau d'Oex a gracious absence of 'the love of novelty, nor the need to take the role of an important person; they march behind the torch of the centuries, and not that of changing fashions' (Murith 1810: 15; Vulliemin 1855: 190; Rousseau 1965: 93–96). In the 1770s Jean-André Deluc of Geneva wrote extensively on the customs of the montagnards in his *Lettres philosophiques et morales sur la montagne* (1773). In the mountains 'one learns', he remarked, 'what the real needs of man are reduced to, what he is able to achieve through the force of habit alone; but one especially learns about the gentle calm of the soul in a state of nature far removed from philosophers and the labyrinths of society' (cited in Guichonnet 1980: 208).

H.B. de Saussure combined scientific observation with romantic sensibility. Just as the great geologist subjected the alpine environment to the logic of measurement and classification, he described the 'ancient simplicity and moral purity' of the people of Chamonix; and he praised the readiness with which Alpine communities looked after their orphans, infirm and elderly (de Saussure 1979: 126–127). As Paul Guichonnet has remarked, for men like Saussure, the voyage in the Alps had become a spiritual 'pilgrimage to the sources of humanity' that 'bore witness to the natural goodness of the human species'. Alpine villagers were the homologues of the explorers' noble savages (Guichonnet 1980: 201, 208).

For a new generation the 'freedom of the soul' found in the mountains easily slid into a 'political freedom' that was sufficiently ambiguous to transcend many of the social divisions in the country. By sinking the image of political freedom in a solidly stable natural environment, the French-speaking Swiss invested themselves with a durable, democratic character very different from that of their alter-natively despotic, or violently turbulent, Gallic neighbors. At the heart of what it meant to be Swiss lay the Alpine villager who was noted for his spontaneous, candid, cordial character, his courage and hospi-tality, and a respect for hierarchy rooted in pastoral traditions and the natural democracy of the village *landsgemeinde*. To the Swiss, Alpine man embodied the virtues of patriotism, democracy and freedom in ways that seemed natural and authentic (Rossel 1903: 654; Niederer 1980: 133).

In Neuchâtel Henri Junod, a pastor in the Independent Church and father of the missionary-anthropologist Henri-Alexandre, could shed tears when looking at the natural beauty created by God (Junod 1884: ix). His friend Frédérick Godet, professor of Theology and a leading intellectual figure in the canton, could also be moved to tears when reading a work such as Oswald Heer's monograph *The Primeval World of Switzerland* (Godet 1913: 82, 334). In this natural environment fash-ioned by God, Eugène Rambert saw peasants as 'simple, hospitable and honest' individuals who, because of their 'semi-patriarchal life' and 'sharp imagination' understood the Bible more easily than enlightened compatriots in the towns.

Local superstitions and universal knowledge

The imagery used to describe this Alpine population could be read in various ways. At different times or from different viewpoints, the noble values of constancy and continuity could be perceived as brakes on the forces of change and modernization; freedom could be viewed as a source of disorder; and the natural virtue of the shepherd could be interpreted as the cause of his ignorance. So while Saussure admired the virtues of the Chamonix villagers, he also found their ideas marked by a 'mixture of reason and superstition' (de Saussure 1979: 129). He was charmed by the local idea that ammonites and fossilized molluscs were 'carvings' produced by fairies; and he enjoyed, with equal conde-scension, the gullibility of rural people who believed in the existence of hidden treasures guarded by magic goats high in the mountains (de Saussure 1979: 39–41).

Through his insistence on the irrational nature of these folk beliefs, Saussure distanced himself from locally held ideas and pronounced the superiority of a form of knowledge that he qualified as universal. But the men of science and letters who carried into the Alps the civiliza-tion of the towns had themselves, only recently, abandoned many of these local superstitions. The belief that the Alps, like the sea, harbored mysterious forces had long been held by a broad cross-section of European society. Dragons had been seen or described in detail by the great Alpine botanist and zoologist, Konrad Gessner, by J.J. Scheuchzer, the pioneer of the physical geography of the region, and by Moriz-Anton Kappeler, the author of the first monograph on a summit in the Alps (Guichonnet 1980: 177–178; Boorstin 1983: 427–428). But by the end of the eighteenth century these beliefs were fast disappearing from educated society. As time went by, the debate over their existence polarized communities into polite and popular wings.

At the end of the nineteenth century, travelers remarked that tales of dragons could still be heard in Alpine villages (Javelle 1920: 47). Many old people still held imps, goblins, sprites and gnomes responsible for unusual occurrences; and witchcraft, sorcery and divination continued to challenge the teachings of the Church (Vulliemin 1849: 360–361; Renard 1892: 121–122, 126–128, 132, 261). 'Simple folk' often explained their situation by resorting to legends and fables. Thus while Rambert thought the 'population of the pastures . . . simple, hospitable and honest', he considered them

> dominated by routine, and a degree of indolence in their respect for ancient customs and their lack of enthusiasm for innovation. This calm, uneventful life, this solitude in the depths of the Alps, plunges the soul into a sort of deep peace and quiet; it acts as an opium that, over time, slowly takes effect. (Rambert 1888: 84)

Nor did Rambert have much time for the enterprise and work habits of stock-keepers who had no idea how to improve their pastures and whose occupation was 'hardly work'. Others were similarly dismissive and criticized the ignorance with which these people looked on the surrounding mountain and, even, failed to name the distant peaks. Even when modern theories, such as the notion of an Ice Age, could be traced to local observations, villagers' knowledge was treated condescendingly as somehow quaint. However, educated townspeople quickly conceded that many Alpine peasants had excelled as naturalists able to search out and find rare botanical or zoological specimens. But while pastors, doctors and other local men-on-the-spot, the purchasers of these objects, conceded the natives' 'gift of observing nature', they derided their inability to analyze their findings in a scientific manner (Vulliemin 1855: 133; Rambert 1876: 13, 1889: 156–157).

Godfrey Lunel thought 'the simple fishermen' of Lake Geneva 'ignorant of any notion of natural history'; their heads were filled with 'a mass of strange ideas about fish . . . drawn from fantasy and tradition' (Lunel 1874, v). Lunel and his colleagues thought they were uncovering common truths through their use of clear, distinctive and reasoned ideas. This process of disenchantment was often expressed in terms of the metaphor of light and dark, and as the product of the noble self-sacrifice of the fieldworker. 'Men of letters who have been of most service to the small band of thinking individuals scattered through the world', Voltaire had written in the eighteenth century from the edge of Geneva, 'are the isolated men of letters' (Voltaire 1954: 272). This figure, the lonely savant struggling to bring light to the darkest corners of his country, became almost emblematic in Switzerland (Rousseau 1933: 726). The value placed on the qualities of fieldwork led the Swiss to pioneer the methodology of direct observation in the natural sciences. This talent was quickly applied to the Alpine world where scientific truth was self-evident, it seemed, and could be discovered in the same way as plant or animal species (Rambert 1876: 22).

Men of science and letters took their idea of knowledge into the Alps with missionary zeal, for they believed their studies would lead the popular classes from the bondage of ignorance into a universal, objective system of understanding. In the nineteenth century, the light of civilization brought by books and libraries to dark mountain huts and obscure villages became an important literary motif in Switzerland (Vulliemin 1855: 198; Secrétan 1930: 200). These new ways of thinking relegated local ideas to the position of 'folk beliefs' that, together with linguistic dialects, would disappear under the swell of modernity. By the late nineteenth century intrusive railways and roads were chasing the last goblins from their lairs, and package tours were driving the spirits and elves from their final abodes (Renard 1892: 134–5). But the substitution of the tyranny of knowledge for the tyranny of superstition was accompanied by the establishment of a new, intellectual domination based on the powers of Cartesian logic (Horkheimer and Adorno 1972). In this sense, Emile Javelle certainly regretted the passing of the old ways but at the same time he held 'patriarchal life and the weight of tradition' responsible for the primitive conditions found in the Alps (Javelle 1920: 30, 123). By implication, only enlightened knowledge and the tutelage of men of science and letters could liberate the *montagnards* from their outdated beliefs and practices.

A new world in Africa

By the end of the nineteenth century the patriarchal traditions of the Alpine villages were melting before the advance of railways, tourism, migration and the new forms of knowledge propagated by school and Church. Even the uncorrupted Alpine peaks fell victim to the advance of civilization when, in the summer of 1855 alone, fifteen climbers reached the summit of Mont Blanc. But ecological balance was often fused with social meaning as anthropology elided with botany. Rambert believed that a struggle for survival was taking place on the plains of Switzerland between 'two rival races' of plants: the indigenous and the immigrant (Rambert 1888: 225–257). And he decried the way in which 'civilization hunts down and destroys' these 'plant victims . . . persecuted races . . . whose fate is no different to that of certain human races' (Rambert 1888: 42–43). Read in metaphorical terms, the foreign and cosmopolitan influence of the plains threatened to transform the *génie de lieu*, or distinctive creative spirit produced when people interacted with their environment. For Juste Olivier, this *génie de lieu* was at the centre of a population's 'racial temperament'. For Rambert, civilization threatened the creative energy of the mountain communities of Switzerland with the corrupting materialism and dry logic of the towns. This was an urban world filled with venal corruption that the Church was attempting to save from absinthe and alcohol – as well as from the crime, promiscuity, sexual disease and social alienation associated with industrialization.

For Javelle the Malthusian struggle for survival was most clearly visible in the Alps where village communities were subjected to the forces of rapid change rising from the plains (Javelle 1920: 224, 236). As this world disappeared, intellectuals locked its spirit within a literature filled with nostalgia for an earlier, simpler age. But the energy with which the Swiss attempted to salvage a picture of their lost past seemed increasingly contrived. A more convincing picture of primitiveness, against which the Swiss could measure their shortcoming and assess their achievements, was to be found in Africa.

For Europeans coming from a part of the world that had been ditched, drained and fenced into submission, the African landscape, like the Alps, stood as a relic of an earlier age (Bryce 1899: 7, 29, 55–56; Stafford 1990). When the missionary Henri Berthoud gazed at the Lebombo mountains for the first time in the winter of 1885, he saw them not as an unimpressive range of low mountains separating Mozambique from South Africa, but as a means of measuring the new, boundless time in which his generation was attempting to situate itself. Berthoud described the Lebombos as a prehistoric rampart against the Indian Ocean and he imagined their peaks, in an earlier age, forming a series of islands in a sea reaching to the base of the Drakensberg (Berthoud 1904: 14). Like Horace-Benedict de Saussure in the Alps a century earlier, he saw everywhere on the coastal plain the prolonged action on the land of a sea that had once stretched to the

foot of the Highveld (Berthoud 1904: 15; similarly see Junod 1911: 26).
In 1890 Junod experienced a comparable voyage into the distant past
when he visited a remote grove of palm trees near his mission station
at Rikatla, some 25 kilometers north of Lourenço Marques (Maputo).
It reminded him of 'a pre-Flood palace whose silence we alone trouble',
he wrote, where

> I believed myself in the middle of one of those antediluvian landscapes
> that Oswald Herr [sic. Heer] resurrected in his *Primeval World of
> Switzerland*. These are the same early plants, the same surprising dimen-
> sions, the same abundant growth that is unknown in our climes. One
> would not be surprised to see a few plesiosaurus or icthyosaurus, hanging
> about across the centuries, spring into the fetid marshland. (Junod
> 1892–93)

By the end of the nineteenth century, just as this kind of time
travel died away in the Alps, it became a common image in much
European writing on Africa (see Knox-Shaw 1986: 145). The magnificent fauna and flora of Africa not only created a setting in which the
European mind could resuscitate prehistoric times; it also seemed to
represent a more primitive stage in the development of the world.
When Junod arrived in southeast Africa in 1889, he found himself in
'a completely new environment ... an entirely new world ... full of
surprises and still virgin' (Junod 1896–97: 77–78). It hosted herds of
animals made extinct elsewhere in the world and preserved a
magnificent array of insect species (Distant 1892: 41, 124–125; Bryce
1899: 17).

In this 'ancient' setting, Junod believed the people he studied to
have experienced a certain evolution; but they still lived at roughly
the same level of civilization as the lake-dwellers of Stone-Age
Switzerland (*LSAT* (2): 147–148; 151, 633). By conflating differences of
culture and time, in a way that was common in those days, he was
able to compare the archeological remnants of Stone-Age communities on the banks of Swiss Lakes with those of 'the black in present-
day South Africa' (Junod 1898a: 7–8, 235, 238, 245, 247; *LSAT* (1): 1,
151; *LSAT* (2): 104, 133). See also Sauter 1977: 86–87. In a scholarly
paper published in 1910, he compared a prehistoric grave in Europe
with the burial, performed in December 1908 at Rikatla, of his neigh-
bor Sokis (who had died of tuberculosis, a disease generally associated
with industrialization). 'It is extraordinary, but it is a fact', he concluded, that 'the Bantu of today is almost identical to the Mousterian
of 20,000 years ago' (Junod 1910b: 967). This form of speculation led
him to value African society for the glimpse it gave him of Europe's

lost past. 'When we turn to these primitives to decipher their conception of life and the world, our own ancient history surges up before our eyes', he wrote in 1898. 'These societies explain certain problems afflicting our civilized souls, which are merely grown up versions of their primitive ones. We become more conscious of ourselves and of the mystery of our evolution' (Junod 1898a: 480).

Visiting Africa was like entering Rambert's forgotten Alpine valley. For the Swiss saw in Africa an example of a living society uncontaminated by the disenchantment and conflict caused by wars of religion and the turmoil of industrialization. This led many missionaries to be critical of aspects of imperialism. Europeans not only brought colonial wars and debilitating liquor to Africa; their civilization was afflicted with 'vices', 'curses', 'debasing influences', wrote Junod; and with 'immoral customs that paganism itself had never known, unbridled luxury, sometimes crying injustices and almost everywhere a selfishness without pity' (Junod 1898a: 481; *LSAT* (2): 541). His sister Ruth saw this process of degeneration most clearly in the drunkenness, dancing and fighting that accompanied life at Lourenço Marques in the mid-1880s. 'The paganism that has been in contact with a Christianless civilization', she wrote, 'was worse than that found in isolated areas where Whites had not yet penetrated' (Berthoud-Junod 1887: 323). Henri-Alexandre saw the consequences of uncontrolled contact between a perverted European civilization and a pure, but weak, African culture even more clearly in the mining cities on the Witwatersrand, 'where everything is for sale, everything is valued in terms of money, and where the struggle for existence has become an everyday part of human existence' (Junod 1898a: 485). In the grimly hybrid slums of these industrial centers, tribesmen lost their values and traditions, abandoned their *volksgeist*, and acquired the new diseases and practices that seemed to threaten the very reproduction of their race.

Junod admired the simple needs and genuine values of African villagers. 'Never to put yourself into a state about tomorrow, never to refuse to lend to those who want to borrow, never to amass worldly wealth, to live like birds in the sky and flowers in the field', he wrote appreciatively, 'is much easier in the simplicity of the lovely African kraal, with the system of common ownership of the soil and the limited role of money, than in our cities'. In African villages, people still displayed 'the respect for elders, the sense of family unity, the habit of mutual help, the readiness to share food with others' (*LSAT* (1): 9, 539; (2): 614).

The African villager lived in the autarchy Rousseau had found in the Val-de-Travers a century earlier. 'At little cost', wrote Junod he obtains from nature whatever he requires to satisfy his very restricted material needs. . . . He is perhaps happier in the simplicity of his primitive life, with his diet of vegetable foods, his simple costume and his longer leisure time than us, his superiors, taken by the impetuous current of our civilization with our industry and our strikes, with our slave-like existence, sometimes, our splendid comfort and our ever growing needs! (Junod 1898a: 114)

Europeans not only found in the culture of African peoples aspects of their civilization that had been destroyed by the values associated with unbridled economic growth, materialism and rationalism. Africa also echoed the sense of liberty found in the Alps and duplicated the creativity of its population.

For many Swiss, European civilization was stale, moribund and weighed down by custom and tradition. Europe was burdened by the dissension and doubt caused by religious strife, materialism, class struggle and a militant nationalism. These problems were compounded by the fatal undermining of the moral leadership of the Church by the secular state. The result was everywhere to be seen in the absinthe-ravaged and alcohol-dependent populations of Neuchâtel; in the uprooting and breakdown of the family, and the threat posed to its reproduction by prostitution, the spread of venereal disease, homosexuality and even masturbation. European civilization had become 'depraved and unscrupulous', wrote Henri-Alexandre Junod, for 'the curses of civilization far exceed its blessings' (LSAT (1): 10; (2): 629).

Africa presented a contrast to this grim picture. The continent was untrammeled by the constraints of a degenerate civilization. Instead, it was a place of cultural experimentation where instinct and the soul triumphed over intellectual conformity, and creativity burst through the bonds of logic. For those missionaries who refused to see the devil's hand behind the natives' cultural practices, Africans had a good deal to teach Europeans. Their creative forms were the product of the uncontaminated soul of an individual people (LSAT (1):9; (2): 225; Junod 1898a: 481). In Africa, Europeans could study the origins of language through a careful application of their linguistic paleontology (Junod 1896: 2; LSAT (2): 166). They could also find in African oral literature, or folklore, vivid expressions of the soul and morality of different tribal peoples (Junod 1898b: 514. See also Theal 1886). 'Imagination overflows' in Thonga folklore, wrote Junod of this early magical realism, 'it completely submerges all reason . . . from this perspective certain tales are stupefying. It beats all moderation'. African music and art also brought new and dynamic aspects to European cultural forms (Junod 1898a: 231, 252; LSAT (2): 125, 211, 215, 218–219, 221–222). But perhaps most importantly, Africans were unencumbered by the skepticism of a material age and, like Rambert's Alpine villagers, were able to embrace Christianity in a way that was no longer possible for most Europeans. 'From various perspectives', wrote Junod in 1898

> it is easier for them to take at face value various aspects of Christianity, for example the precepts of the Sermon on the Mount, than it is for us, Europeans of the nineteenth century, whose existence is so complicated. (1898a: 485)

The Mission believed that, on the basis of its experience in Europe, it could build a Christian community in Africa capable of revitalizing the universal Church (Anonymous 1896: 3–4; Berthoud 1896: 20, 140; Junod 1898a: 403; Grandjean 1917: 2, 28, 41).

Salvage anthropology

The idealized, Arcadian image of an Africa from which Europeans could learn about their abandoned values and forgotten virtues had to be finely balanced by the picture of a continent in need of Christian salvation. So the respect for hierarchy and community found in African society was tempered by criticism of the despotism that cramped the creative energies of African individuals (Junod 1898a: 246; *LSAT* (1): 271; (2): 150). The continent's isolation from Europe was responsible for the freedom and originality of African civilization; but it also accounted for the ignorance and superstition that pervaded African life. Above all, Africans had lost their original, monotheistic beliefs and, in exchange, had acquired a profusion of inconsequential cults (Junod 1898a: 403). 'The black is not always as happy as is thought', Junod had to caution Sunday school monitors, for 'the African village, which could be a little paradise, is often rendered a hell by the profusion of sin' (Junod 1922: 4–5).

The form of anthropology developed by Junod, Jacottet and Perregaux sought to salvage a picture of Europe's lost values and traditions from the study of present-day African communities (E. Perregaux 1906: 312; *LSAT* (1): 7). To achieve this they had to represent Africans as members of a pure, pre-contact society. But this was patently impossible without a good deal of literary improvisation. For the Gold Coast had a centuries-old experience of contact with both Muslim and Christian worlds; and by the 1880s Southern Africa was in the throes of an industrial revolution occasioned by the discovery of diamonds and gold. In their attempt to capture the image of a secure, harmonious African world governed by simple values and everyday traditions, the missionaries divided their work into scientific and religious texts. While they stuffed the missionary journals with observations on the dark practices of tribal Africans and the threat posed to their existence by an invasive capitalism, they placed their scientific observations in specialist journals. One searches in vain in these works for references to the tens of thousands of Basothos and Mozambicans employed in the South African mines; no reference is made to colonial policies, particularly head taxes and forced labor, that had shattering consequences for the family; nor did the authors take account of the impact on society of new consumer trends, particularly guns and alcohol. Most blatantly absent from their scientific work were the missionaries themselves, together with their converts and their creed. Photographs too, were carefully composed, cropped, juxtaposed, titled, and even changed, in order to create a visible and realistic picture of a pristine, pre-contact African society. This form of salvage anthropology amounted to a genre of representation that segregated Africans in a space and time that was as artificial as the Swiss village at national and international exhibitions.

In Swiss cities and villages, a timelessly pre-capitalist vision of the Alps was salvaged by vigorous styles of literature and painting, and by extensive museum collections. The African and Alpine salvage traditions came together grotesquely in exhibitions that featured implements and artifacts manufactured in both regions. The Swiss Mission's collection of African artifacts, housed in a makeshift museum in the Theological College in Lausanne, was displayed on numerous occasions, starting in 1883, at cantonal and national exhibitions (Anonymous 1883; Büchler 1970). The organizers of these events were concerned to present a vivid and realistic picture of various aspects of life in Africa in a way that would appeal to supporters of the Mission. At the National exhibition of 1896 in Geneva, the freedom of the Alps was linked to that of Africa by ranging an idealized, pre-industrial Swiss village alongside an equally idealized African structure. But the verisimilitude of the displays, and their juxtaposition with manufactures of modern European industry, served to reinforce European perceptions of Africans as simple and backward (Froidevaux 2002). The self-respect and pride of the Swiss as a nation grew when over two million visitors passed through the Hall of Machines at the exhibition. The admiration with which they gazed on their achievements and progress mounted as they contrasted the power of their turbines, flywheels and presses with the simple industries and manufactures on display in the 'Negro', and nearby 'Swiss', villages. Spectators were led at these exhibitions to compare a visibly pre-capitalist Switzerland with an assembled image of modern Africa. The path of progress, and the route to perfectibility, was laid out before their eyes as they passed from the primitive African structure to the sturdy Swiss village before, finally, entering the Hall of Machines (Crettaz and Michaelis-Germanier 1982–83; Crettaz and Détraz 1983: 39–40; Arlettaz and Pauchard 1991: 16, 58).

Junod also drew frequent comparisons between aspects of life in Africa and Europe. But while exhibitions constructed a tangible ladder of evolution on the basis of this comparison, the missionary was more concerned to highlight the role of the Church. The culture of 'tribesmen' in Africa, he pointed out, was comparable with that of 'the peasantry or less cultivated portion of the town population' in Switzerland (Junod 1920: 84; Germond 1967: 526). 'In those parts of Europe where education is less widespread,' superstition 'still marked the basic mentality.' Many uneducated Europeans still practiced elements of animism and magic. In the industrial city of La Chaud de Fonds, Junod had seen the instruments used by a witch to cast a spell on her enemy (Junod 1898a: 246, 1910a: 622, 1920: 84; LSAT (2): 345–346, n1). 'In all civilized countries', wrote Junod, the culture of 'the peasantry or the less cultivated portion of the town population' could still be compared with that found in Africa (Junod 1907: 143). In some cases, such as in the field of botanical knowledge, he considered African ideas more evolved, and rational, than those of European peasants and workers (Harries 2000: 23–24, 32–33).

Through this form of analogy, Junod suggested that the poor of Europe were vestiges of a primitive past, almost savages in a civilized society. This idea was of widespread currency. Emile Zola, for instance, wrote about the urban poor with enormous compassion; but he considered them a sort of 'race apart', trapped by the oppressive forces of milieu, alcohol and, especially, biological inheritance. The base instincts of this class were inadequately repressed by the controls of civilization and had the potential to surge to the surface at any moment. This had happened most recently during the Paris Commune, when the mindless savagery of the poor had exploded in an orgy of violence. For many Europeans, these 'barbarians in our midst' seemed to present civilization with the threat of destruction (Sue 1843; Chevalier 1958: 162, 510–511; Edwards 1971: 340–341; Brown 1995: 346–357; Bullard 2000). Many expected the Church to exercise a civilizing influence over these savages at home that was little different from the role assigned to missionaries in Africa (Thorne 1999).

Conclusion

In Switzerland, as elsewhere in the world, the outlines of modernity were defined against a primitive other. In the wilderness areas of the Alps the Swiss had discovered their own primitive world. Out of the relationship that emerged between the townsmen of the plains and their primitive cousins in the Alps, the Swiss developed a vocabulary of empire. When missionaries from Neuchâtel established themselves in various parts of Africa at the end of the nineteenth century, they employed the words, images and rhetoric of this literary genre to describe the continent. The facility with which missionaries elided the primitive worlds of Africa and Europe soon spread beyond their profession. When Arnold van Gennep accepted the first Chair in Anthropology at the University of Neuchâtel in 1912, he considered the study of Alpine communities a legitimate alternative to expensive fieldwork amongst the more primitive peoples of Africa, Tibet or New Guinea (van Gennep 1980: 91).

The missionaries from Neuchâtel took to Africa, alongside their established way of describing a primitive environment and its occupants, their own concerns with modernity and its consequences. In the field to which they had been called by their vocation, they found themselves living alongside the 'less evolved' or 'primitive' peoples that van Gennep would regard as the prime target of his discipline. In Switzerland it was possible to find the remnants of the material culture of prehistoric peoples; but in Africa the beliefs and practices of those people could be examined at first hand. This allowed missionary intellectuals to fill in the monstrous gap in time, opened by the geological discoveries, which separated the Act of Creation from the beginning of History. It also allowed the missionaries to conjure up the picture of a natural social order in which the beliefs and values of a lost European past could be (re)discovered. At the same time, the picture of primitive African communities provided both a glimpse of the dark savagery from which Europeans had escaped; and outlined the pathway to perfectibility (for a modern example, see Trevor-Roper 1965; 9).

This picture of Africa became particularly important to the Swiss at the end of the nineteenth century when the Alpine wilderness, which harbored the last redoubts of domestic primitivism, fell to the forces of modernity. Many Swiss then looked to Africa, and other corners of their world, to provide the yardstick with which to measure their achievements and draw lessons from their failures. As they gazed on the Dark Continent, Europeans were made aware of the progressive evolution experienced by their society under the tuition of an enlightened elite. When missionaries drew an analogy between tribal Africans and the poor and dangerous classes at home, they implicitly underlined the incomplete nature of the civilizing mission in Europe. By comparing the popular classes in their country with the younger and immature members of primitive humanity in Africa, the Church gave notice of its paternal obligations and of its position at the summit of progress.

Both African and Alpine communities had the gift of observation; but neither community was able to systematize or explain its discoveries. Hence men of science and letters in Africa, like their homologues in the Alps, were duty-bound to free primitive communities from the shackles of ignorance and obscurantism. A combination of religion and science had delivered most of Switzerland from magic; and the same could be achieved in Africa if the natives submitted themselves to a controlled modernity that combined the light of reason with the truth of Christianity (Junod 1920: 84). The Church and its clergy were capable of protecting and redeeming Africans and of lifting them from darkness. But equally importantly an enlightened Church, strengthened and revitalized in the testing-ground of the mission field, had the duty and capacity to play a central role in the guidance and tutelage of the population of western Switzerland.

References

Anonymous. 1896. *Evangélisation des païens au sud-est de l'Afrique par les églises libres de la Suisse romande*. Genève: Exposition Nationale Suisse.

Arlettaz, Gérald, and Pauchard, Pierre. 1991. *Les Suisses dans le miroir: les expositions nationales suisses*. Lausanne: Payot.

Berthoud, Henri. 1904. 'Deux problèmes hydrographiques du pays de Gaza'. *BSNG* XV.

Berthoud, Paul. 1896. *Les Nègres Gouamba; ou, les vingt premières années de la Mission romande*. Lausanne: Conseil de la Mission romande.

Berthoud-Junod, Ruth. 1887. Letter in *Bulletin de la mission suisse romande* 72:323.

Boorstin, Daniel J. 1983. *The Discoverers*. New York: Random House.

Bost, Ami. 1841. *Visite dans la portion des Hautes-Alpes de France qui fut le champ des travaux de Félix Neff*. Geneva: Impr. Ch. Grauz.

Bost, Ami. 1843. *Letters and biography of Félix Neff, protestant missionary in Switzerland, the department of Isère and the High Alps*. Translated by M.A. Wyatt. London: R.B. Seeley and W. Burnside.

Braudel, Fernand. 1981. *The Structures of Everyday Life*. New York: Harper & Row.

Bridel, Dean. 1866 [1845]. *Glossaire du Patois de la Suisse romande*. Lausanne: G. Bridel.

Brown, Frederick. 1995. *Zola: A Life*. New York: Farrar, Strauss, Giroux.

Bryce, James. 1899. *Impressions of South Africa*. 3rd edn. London: MacMillan and Co.

Bullard, Alice. 2000. *Exile to Paradise: Savagery and Civilization in Paris and the South Pacific, 1790–1900*. Stanford: Stanford University Press.

Chevalier, Louis. 1958. *Classes laborieuses et classes dangereuses à Paris pendant la première moitié du XIXe siècle*. Paris: Plon.

Crettaz, Bernard, and Détraz, Christine. 1983. *Suisse, mon beau village: regards sur l'exposition nationale de 1896*. Genève: Le Musée.

Crettaz, Bernard and Michaelis-Germanier, Juliette. 1982–83. 'Une suisse miniature ou les grandeurs de la petitesse'. *Bulletin annuel du Musée d'éthnographie de la Ville de Genève* 25/26:63–185.

Distant, William Lucas. 1892. *A Naturalist in the Transvaal*. London: R.H. Porter.

Durand, Théophile and Pittier, Henri. 1882. *Catalogue de la flore Vaudoise*. Lausanne: Libraire Rouge.

Edwards, Stuart. 1971. *The Paris Commune, 1871*. London: Eyre and Spottiswoode.

Favre, Edouard. 1908. *François Coillard: enfance et jeunesse, 1834–1861*. Paris: Société des missions évangéliques.

van Gennep, Arnold. 1980. *Coutumes et croyances populaires en France*. Paris: Chemin vert.

Germond, Robert C. 1967. *Chronicles of Basutoland: a Running Commentary on the Events of the Years 1830–1902*. Morija: Morija Sesuto Book Depot.

Godet, Philippe Ernest. 1913. *Frédéric Godet: 1812–1900: D'après sa correspondance et d'autres documents inédits*. Neuchâtel: Attinger.

Grandjean, Arthur. 1917. *La Mission Romande*. Lausanne: Georges Bridel.

Guicciardini, Francesco. 1969. *The history of Italy*. Translated and edited by S. Alexander. New York: MacMillan.

Guichonnet, Paul. 1980. 'L'Homme devant les Alpes'. In P. Guichonnet (ed.). *Histoire et civilisation des Alpes. Vol. II, Destin Humain*. Toulouse: Privat, pp. 169–246.

Harries, Patrick. 1997. 'Under Alpine Eyes: Constructing Landscape and Society in Late Pre-colonial South-east Africa'. *Paideuma* 43:171–191.

Harries, Patrick. 1998. 'Missionary Endeavour and the Politics of Identity in Switzerland'. In 'L'héritage missionnaire en perspective: approches croisées'. Special edition of *Le Fait Missionnaire* 6. Lausanne: Le Fait Missionaire, pp. 39–69.

Harries, Patrick. 2000. 'Field Sciences in Scientific Fields: Entomology, Botany and the Early Anthropological Monograph in the Work of H.-A. Junod'. In S. Dubow (ed.). *Science and society in southern Africa*. Manchester: Manchester University Press, pp. 11–41.

Horkheimer, Max and Adorno, Theodor. 1972. *Dialectic of Enlightenment*. New York: Herder and Herder.

Javelle, Emile. 1920. *Souvenirs d'un Alpiniste*. Lausanne: Payot.

Junod, Henri. 1884. *Sermons*. Neuchâtel: A G. Berthoud.

Junod, Henri Alexandre. 1892–93. 'Correspondences: De Rikatla à Marakpuène, 23 novembre 1891'. *BSNG* VI:318–327.

Junod, Henri Alexandre. 1896–97. 'Le climat de la baie de Delagoa'. *Bulletin de la société neuchâteloise des sciences naturelles*.

Junod, Henri-Alexandre. 1898a. 'Les Ba-Ronga'. *BSNG* 10:1–500.

Junod, Henri-Alexandre. 1898b. 'Edouard Jacottet, *Contes populaires des Bassoutos*'; book review. *BSNG* X:514.

Junod, Henri-Alexandre. 1907. 'The Best Means of Preserving the Traditions and Customs of the Various South African Native Races'. *Reports of the South African Association of Science*:141–159.

Junod, Henri-Alexandre. 1910a. 'Sorcellerie d'Afrique et sorcellerie d'Europe: étude d'ethnographie comparée'. *Foi et Vie* 13:616-624.

Junod, Henri-Alexandre. 1910b. 'Deux enterrements à 20,000 and de distance'. *Anthropos* V:964–967.

Junod, Henri-Alexandre. 1911. *Zidji; étude de moeurs sud-africaines*. Saint-Blaise: Foyer Solidariste.

Junod, Henri Alexandre. 1920. 'The Magic Conception of Nature Amongst Bantus'. *South African Journal of Science* XVII:76–85.

Junod, Henri-Alexandre. 1922. 'La biographie d'Elias Libombo, jadis connu sous le nom de Spoon'. *Causeries sur l'Afrique à l'usage des cercles d'étude missionnaire pour enfants des écoles du Dimanche, des Unions Cadettes et des familles*, 2nd edn. Lausanne: pp. 10–12.

Junod, Henri-Alexandre. 1927. *Life of a South African Tribe*. 2 vols London: MacMillan.

Knox-Shaw, Peter. 1986. *The Explorer in English Fiction*. New York: St. Martin's Press.

Lunel, Godefroy. 1874. *Histoire naturelle des poissons du Bassin du Léman*. Genève: H. Georg.

Murith, Laurent Joseph. 1810. *Le guide du botaniste qui voyage dans le Valais*. Lausanne: H. Vincent.

Olivier, Juste. 1837. *Le Canton de Vaud; sa vie son histoire. II vol.* Lausanne: Librairie de Marc Dulcoux.

Outram, Dorinda. 1995. *The Enlightenment*. Cambridge: Cambridge University Press.

Perregaux, Henri. 1906. *Edmond Perregaux missionaire: d'après sa correspondence 1868–1905*. Neuchâtel: Delachaux.

Rambert, Eugène. 1876. *La Société vaudoise des sciences naturelles: sa fondation et son développement*. Lausanne: F. Rouge.

Rambert, Eugène. 1888. *Etudes d'histoire naturelle*. Lausanne: F. Rouge.

Rambert, Eugène. 1889. *Récits et Croquis*, 2nd edn. Lausanne: F. Rouge.

Reichler, Claude. 1996. 'La bibliothèque des voyageurs'. In R. Francillon (ed.). *Histoire de la littérature en Suisse Romande. I, Du Moyen Age à 1815*. Lausanne: Editions Payot, pp. 243–254.

Reichler, Claude and Ruffieux, Roland (eds). 1998. *Le voyage en Suisse: anthologie des voyageurs français et européens de la Renaissance au XXe siècle*. Paris: Laffont.

Renard, Georges. 1892. *Autour des Alpes*. Lausanne: F. Payot.

Robert, Daniel. 1961. *Les églises réformées en France (1800–1830)*. Paris: Presses universitaires de France.

Rossel, Virgile. 1903. *Histoire littéraire de la Suisse romande*. Neuchâtel: F. Zahn.

Rousseau, Jean-Jacques. 1933 [1782]. *Rêveries du promeneur solitaire*. Texet établi et annoté par Louis-Martin Chauffer. Paris: La Pléiade, 1933.

Rousseau, Jean-Jacques. 1965 [1758]. *Lettre à M. d'Alembert sur les spectacles*. Paris: Garnier.

Stafford, R.A. 1990. 'Annexing the Landscapes of the Past: British Imperial Geology in the Nineteenth Century'. In J.M. MacKenzie (ed.). *Imperialism and the Natural World*. Manchester: Manchester University Press.

de Saussure, Horace-Bénédict. 1979 [1852]. *Premières ascensions au Mont-Blanc 1774–1787*. Abridged edition, with introduction by R. Canac. Paris: F. Maspero.

Secrétan, Charles. 1876. 'Albert de Haller'. In Secrétan (ed.) *Galerie Suisse: Biographies Nationales*. Lausanne: Bridel.

Secrétan, Charles. 1930. 'Savants et chercheurs'. In D. Baud-Bovy, et al. (eds). *La Vie Romantique au Pays Romand*. Lausanne: Freudweiler-Spiro, pp. 189–202.

Sue, Eugène. 1843. *Les mystères de Paris*. Paris: C. Gosselin.

Theal, George McCall. 1886. *Kaffir folk-lore*. London: S. Sonnenschein, Le Bas & Lowrey.

Thorne, Susan. 1999. *Congregational Missions and the Making of an Imperial Culture in Nineteenth-Century England*. Stanford: Stanford University Press.

Voltaire, François-Marie Arouet de. 1954 [1765]. Introduced and Annotated by Julien Benda. *Dictionnaire philosophique*. Paris: Garnier.

Vulliemin, L. 1849. *Tableau du canton de Vaud*. Lausanne: F. Weber.

Vulliemin, L. 1855. *Le Doyen Bridel: essai biographique*. Lausanne: Bridel.

Whymper, Edward. 1873. *Escalades dans les Alpes de 1860 à 1869*. Translated from English by A. Joanne. Paris: Hachette.

Abbreviations

BSNG   *Bulletin de la société neuchâteloise de géographie*
BSSNN *Bulletin de la société des sciences naturelles de Neuchâtel*
LSAT   Junod 1927. *Life of a South African tribe.*

CHAPTER EIGHT

Colonial anthropologies and the primordial imagination in equatorial Africa

John M. Cinnamon

Scholars have frequently complained about the paucity of ethno-graphic and historical sources on equatorial Africa, but even a cursory review of the published literature on the anthropologies and histories of the region would require a lengthy tome. Already by 1914, colonial administrator Georges Bruel published a bibliography on French Equa-torial Africa that cited over 7,000 titles (Bruel 1914). This chapter traces a narrow path through this forest of nineteenth- and later twen-tieth-century sources by following a set of key themes – centering on the construction of 'Fang' identity, history, mobility and crisis – that run through accounts by colonial ethnographers, professional anthro-pologists and postcolonial Gabonese intellectuals.

In the years following the 1843 establishment of Libreville as a French naval *comptoir*, Fang (also referred to in the literature as Fan, Mfans, Pangwe, Pahouin) marched onto the pages of European travel accounts as an exceptional race of hearty, rustic, migrating 'cannibals'. Thus, very early a sort of Fang exceptionalism emerged in European representations of equatorial Africa. The more polished, 'effete', coastal 'tribes', despite their 'civilized veneer', had ironically been degraded through sustained exposure to European debauchery and civ-ilization; they would, it was thought, eventually die out. The unadul-terated, 'invading' Fang might, on the other hand, be harnessed as yeoman farmers and laborers necessary for the *mise en valuer* of colo-nial Gabon. Even today, the long seaward march of the Fang (by some accounts all the way from Egypt) is thought to have been halted only by the counter-invasion of an even more powerful tribe – the French (see Pourtier 1989: 27).

The term 'exceptionalism', used advisedly here,[1] refers to an atti-tude running through the colonial literature and later appropriated by Fang-speaking intellectuals, that the Fang were equatorial Africa's chosen people, whose supposed unique attributes would serve to build Gabon. In a recent survey of the Gabonese colonial library, historian Florence Bernault reviews what she calls 'the myth of Fang invasions'. As she puts it, 'European texts present the Fang as *an exceptional race*, quasi monotheist, intelligent and vigorous, possessing elaborate technical and historical knowledge'. In nineteenth-century writings, Fang 'warriors', 'cannibals', and 'idealized savages', were compared to the coastal Mpongwe, themselves represented as skillful 'Europeanized auxiliaries' but also as 'degenerate and suspect' (2003: 175, 180, 182).[2] Writing at the end of the colonial period, Alexandre and Binet (1958: 88) noted that not only 'Fang-Boulou-Beti' but also their colonizers indulged in Fang exceptionalism: 'Like most known peoples, the Pahouins have a very high and flattering opinion of themselves; what is more curious, is that this opinion is broadly shared by foreign observers . . .'

At issue here is not whether the Fang were actually more exceptional than other equatorial African peoples. Indeed, Jane Guyer and Samuel Eno Belinga (1995) have argued that due to their grand capacities of imagination and invention, the peoples of the entire West Central African region, from Cameroon to Angola, were exceptional. The aim here is to trace Fang exceptionalism through the ethnographic record. As Byron E. Shafer suggests, exceptionalism is an 'empirical phenomenon', observable when it motivates public opinion, policy, behavior, or in this case, ethnographic representations. 'The accuracy or inaccuracy, the truth or falsity, or the propositions allegedly constituting this exceptionalism are not important' (Shafer 1999: 446).

Fang exceptionalism dates back at least to the apical ancestor of Gabonese fieldworkers, Paul Du Chaillu (1861), who published his *Explorations and Adventures in Equatorial Africa* in both English and French; almost all subsequent fieldworkers have had to contend with Du Chaillu's legacy. Fang exceptionalism has continued to inform twentieth-century Fang ethnography and auto-ethnography. In order to trace the genealogy of a Fang exceptionalism that arose in the mid-nineteenth century to inform colonial and postcolonial ethnographic imaginaries, I focus here on the work of four key ethnographers: explorer and adventurer Du Chaillu, Spiritain missionary Henri Trilles, and professional anthropologists Georges Balandier and James Fernandez. In a concluding section, I turn briefly to the Mvet epic to illustrate how themes that preoccupied colonial-era ethnographers for a century have been appropriated and reconfigured in Fang auto-ethnography. The goal is to illustrate how, in specific ways, colonial anthropology has both inherited and constructed its object over time.

While all four ethnographers examined here both contended with and contributed to the elaboration of Fang exceptionalism and more broadly to a Western canon of Gabonese ethnography, each nonetheless broke in significant ways from his predecessors: Du Chaillu was the first European to travel extensively inland and to publish accounts of his travels. Of 'mixed' parentage, he also lacked the pedigree of other 'noble' explorers. Trilles was reviled by many of his missionary brethren and was eventually sent home from Gabon, but also had scholarly pretensions, constituting himself as an expert on Fang and pygmies. Balandier, a Frenchman who first visited Africa in the late 1940s, examined Fang exceptionalism in light of the ruptures of the colonial situation. Fernandez, originally from Chicago, met both Balandier and postwar Gabonese intellectuals, but established his identity as a Fang ethnographer within the institutional context of the American academy. His writings bear the marked imprint of the Boasian tradition of cultural anthropology.

From this discussion of colonial anthropology emerges a number of questions that animate representations of culture and history in the region, including those put forth by Gabonese themselves. How is it, for example, that supposedly static, bounded societies came to be characterized by their migratory zeal? How, conversely, did the colonial situation make societies already characterized by fluidity, instability, and fragmentation more volatile? How, in response to colonial crises, did Gabonese intellectuals and leaders come to reconfigure and re-imagine tradition as a means of embracing colonial modernity? Such questions continue to fuel the postcolonial primordial imagination.

To address these recurring representations of boundedness, migration, volatility, colonial crisis, and the modernity of tradition, I explore two related themes in colonial and postcolonial anthropology of former French Equatorial Africa. By now, the first theme is widely acknowledged: nineteenth- and twentieth-century explorers, missionaries and anthropologists created and disseminated a tribal paradigm, which was reconfigured by Africans themselves. Today, critiques of the tribal paradigm challenge functionalist notions of spatial and temporal fixity. James Ferguson summarizes this familiar critique:

Classical social anthropology in Africa, of course, was dominated by what has been called the 'tribe study,' the detailed, holistic ethnographic account of 'a society' (or a community, or an ethnic group – sometimes it was not altogether clear which). Most often this was in a functionalist vein, and usually ... in a way that made unwarranted assumptions about isolation, cohesion, and systemic equilibrium. (Ferguson 1999: 25)

Although the tribal paradigm evolved in the context of nineteenth-century nationalism, evolutionism, and the civilizing mission, it is, as Ferguson notes, most often linked with functionalism, which 'represented the natural condition of society as static, not dynamic' (Kuklick 1991: 267). The critique of the tribal paradigm and its playing down of history or spatial mobility may be overstated; in any event, it only partly applies to the Fang ethnography of Balandier and Fernandez, both of whom devoted considerable attention to precolonial and colonial population movements, the impact of colonialism, and the creative revitalization of tradition.[3]

The second theme examined here both derives and departs from the first. Nineteenth-century explorers and missionaries in equatorial Africa were interested in questions of origins, history and migration of the specific tribes they helped to delineate; these interests subsequently preoccupied both academic historians and anthropologists and Africans themselves. As historian Jan Vansina (1983: 75) puts it, oral traditions of equatorial Africans 'deal mainly with migrations and origins, partly because Europeans did not record other data, partly because this aspect dominates the traditions themselves'.[4] Central African ethnographies thus present a curious counter-example to the standard portrait of twentieth-century Africanist anthropology as 'structural functionalist' – at least to a point. In part because of the challenges of *longue-durée* historical reconstruction, anthropologists and historians of the region have nonetheless been tempted to project functionalist models of working societies into the distant past.[5]

These apparently stable societies were then confronted by what Balandier (1982 [1955]) labeled 'the colonial situation'. According to Balandier, this was a complex 'total social phenomenon' that linked colonizing and colonized societies in an ongoing situation of conflict, adaptation and crisis. While reluctant to reduce the colonial situation to a list of attributes, Balandier enumerated what he saw as its most salient features:

> domination imposed by a foreign minority . . . in the name of a racial (or ethnic) and cultural superiority dogmatically affirmed, on a materially inferior autochthonous majority; between radically heterogeneous societies: a civilization of mechanization, with a powerful economy, of rapid rhythm and of Christian origin imposing itself on non-mechanized civilizations, of backward economy, slow rhythm and radically 'non-Christian'; the antagonistic character of relations existing between these two societies is explained by . . . the necessity, to maintain domination,

to resort not only to 'force', but also to a system of pseudo-justifications and of stereotypical behaviors, etc. (Balandier 1982 [1955]: 34–35)

However, there remains an unresolved contradiction in both Balandier and Fernandez. Each wrote about how colonialism disrupted working social systems, but each also suggests that there existed a high degree of precolonial disorder and social volatility. More recently, Jane Guyer and Samuel Eno-Belinga (1995: 118) have pointed to precolonial social processes of *social composition*, by which they mean the fluid, dynamic, contingent, 'even anarchic' coalescence of 'networks and collectivities of shifting shape and spatial reach'. To what extent do these tensions in late colonial and postcolonial anthropology derive from earlier ethnographic representations?

Taken together, the four Fang ethnographers examined here bracket the colonial period in Gabon. In spite of the controversies they aroused, Du Chaillu's accounts, based on his travels in 1855–59 and 1863–65, and Trilles' copious Fang ethnographies, have exerted a lasting impact on the ethnographic imagination. Balandier and Fernandez undertook their fieldwork after World War II during a period of economic recovery and relative political liberalization that preceded Gabonese independence in 1960. Both ethnographers grappled with the legacy of earlier colonial ethnography as Gabonese themselves have struggled with the colonial and postcolonial situation. To illustrate the ongoing impact of colonial anthropology on the postcolonial ethnographic imagination in Gabon, I end this chapter by examining briefly the commentaries of the Mvet epic as an example of auto-ethnography.

Du Chaillu and Fang ethnography

An examination of Paul Belloni Du Chaillu's ethnographic writings reveals that they drew on already circulating representations by French naval officers and American missionaries that juxtaposed coastal and interior peoples.[6] In this sense, he too inherited certain preoccupations from his predecessors. For Gabon, however, he stands as the apical ancestor of both francophone and anglophone popular and scholarly ethnographic traditions.[7] His *Explorations and Adventures in Equatorial Africa*, published in English (1861) and French (1863), recounted his travels in the northern and southern Gabonese interior, including his face-to-face encounters with gorillas, chimpanzees, and Fang. Achieving almost immediate popularity and even notoriety, his writings have served for over a century to shape perceptions of tribal identities and character.

Du Chaillu's ancestry is a matter of some speculation. He was born in 1831 (or 1835) in Paris or Réunion to a French *commerçant* father and possibly a 'mulatto' or Italian mother. In the 1840s his father relocated to Libreville, shortly after the French navy had established a presence there. Du Chaillu lived there from 1848 to 1852, during which time he came under the influence of American missionaries, including John Leighton Wilson and William Walker (Du Chaillu 1861: 4, 22, 89; see Wilson 1856). From 1852 to 1855, Du Chaillu studied natural history in Philadelphia, taught French in New York State, and learned that his first-hand knowledge of Africa was of considerable interest to Americans. 'His one marketable achievement when he first arrived in New York City as a man of twenty-one was his African experience' (Bucher 1979: 29). After his return to Africa in 1855, Du Chaillu explored the Gabonese hinterland from 1856 to 1859, studying fauna, flora, geography and people. I focus here primarily on his travels inland from the Muni River to the Monts de Cristal, where he met 'the cannibal Fans'. Du Chaillu returned to Gabon from 1863 to 1865, but traveled in the south (Du Chaillu 1867).

Du Chaillu's Africans were profoundly other. In his narrative, Africans readily acknowledged the vast superiority of European civilization, Christianity, and 'the wisdom and goodness of God'. Moreover, they admitted the iniquity of their ways, but responded by irrationally sinking 'back into every superstitious or cruel custom . . . at the first excitement', arguing that whites were superior, rich, and 'spirits', and therefore, did 'not need all the fetishes and idols we have' (Du Chaillu 1861: 255). Du Chaillu's Fang, firmly anchored in the tribal paradigm, emerged as noble savages and cannibals who, once tamed by Christian civilization, would become peaceful farmers and manufacturers, 'going to their contented daily tasks' (Du Chaillu 1861: 57). In his initial meeting, he immediately gained a favorable impression:

> These fellows . . . are real unmistakable cannibals. And they were, by long odds, the most remarkable people I had thus far seen in Africa. They were much lighter in shade than any of the coast tribes, strong, tall, well made, and evidently active; and they seemed to me to have a more intelligent look than is usual to the African unacquainted with white men. (Du Chaillu 1861: 67)

Du Chaillu noted that 'all the Fans, when asked whence they came, pointed to the north-east'. He also noted their inextricable movement westward to the coast (Du Chaillu 1861: 89–90). The Fan belonged, 'I should think, to a different race from the coast natives, or indeed any tribes I have seen before' (Du Chaillu 1861: 68). Writers who followed

Du Chaillu would strive to explain this perceived difference. In Du Chaillu's eyes, Fans stood out through their enthusiastic cannibalism. He described piles of human bones in the village, the sale of the dead to neighbors, a woman carrying a piece of human thigh, and his own horror at eating from their cooking pots or being cooked in them himself. '[S]ymptoms of cannibalism stare me in the face wherever I go, and I can no longer doubt . . . In fact, the Fans seem regular ghouls, only they practice their horrid custom unblushingly and in open day, and have no shame about it.' But at the same time, 'They are the finest, bravest looking set of negroes I have seen in the interior, and eating human flesh seems to agree with them . . .' (Du Chaillu 1861: 89).

Du Chaillu's Fans were also 'an unusually warlike tribe', but possessed few guns. After a detailed description of the Fan armory – cross-bows with iron-tipped poison arrows, war axes, knives, tomahawks, spears and shields – he wrote of his impressions upon meeting a group of warriors:

> It was a grand sight to see so many stalwart, martial, fierce-looking fellows, fully armed and ready for any desperate foray, gathered in one assemblage. Finer-looking men I never saw; and I could well believe them brave, did not the completeness of their armory prove that war is a favorite pastime with them. In fact, they are dreaded by all their neighbors, and, if they were only animated by a spirit of conquest, would soon make short work of the tribes between them and the coast. (Du Chaillu 1861: 80)

To the east were other warlike, cannibal tribes, armed with poisoned arrows whose names he was unable to learn. Du Chaillu cited low trade provisions, fears of poison arrows, and above all the fear of falling sick among them, thereby tempting 'their great penchant for human flesh', and reluctantly turned back toward the coast (Du Chaillu 1861: 95).

In the early 1860s, Du Chaillu's accounts of gorillas and Fang cannibalism in public lectures and *Explorations and Adventures in Equatorial Africa* created a sensation in American cities, as well as London and Paris, but the work did not go unchallenged. Du Chaillu's 'mixed' pedigree also seems to have raised doubts in the class- and race-conscious scientific community (McCook 1996: 179). The American Winwoode Reade (1864) and even Richard Burton (1863, 1876) were dispatched to Gabon to verify Du Chaillu's accounts; both sent back mixed reviews. Mary Louise Pratt (1992: 208–213) cites Du Chaillu's explorations and adventures in a discussion of 'Hyphenated White Men and the Critique from Within'. In Pratt's eyes, the hybrid Du Chaillu imitated, satirized and demystified the imperial surveys of his

British contemporaries, such as Burton and John Speke. This suggests that while he made standard appeals for the civilizing mission and founded what would become orthodox Fang studies, Du Chaillu both challenged and was marginalized by the conventions of Victorian anthropology.

By the 1890s, another unorthodox traveler, Mary Kingsley, came to consider herself Du Chaillu's 'immediate successor' (Kingsley 1897: 369–370). Such intertextuality contributed to the lasting influence of Du Chaillu's Fang ethnography, an influence that remains strong to the present. In the 1970s, historian K. David Patterson concluded, 'His material on coastal groups is excellent in quality and rich in detail; his information on interior groups is valued by such authorities as [Gabonese scholar] Abbé Walker and [French Geographer] Giles Sautter'; 'despite the cannibal stories', French ethnographer and linguist Pierre Alexandre called Du Chaillu 'an "exact and rigorous" observer' on many topics and repeatedly cites his material (Patterson 1974: 665).

Trilles and the Nilistic imagination

At the end of the nineteenth century, Du Chaillu's Fang exceptionalism was taken up and amplified by French Spiritain missionary and ethnographer Henri Trilles. Together, their ethnography has exercised formative and lasting influence on representations of Fang expansionism, migratory zeal, cannibalism and aggression while reinforcing the tribal paradigm. Whereas Du Chaillu indicated that the Fang had come from the northeast, Trilles went further in adopting the Hamitic hypothesis, which situated Fang origins in the Nile Valley. Trilles, in turn, set the stage for Balandier and Fernandez, who had to consider not only mid-century anthropological theory and the ethnographic situation 'on the ground', but also the legacy of previous ethnography, some of which had been re-appropriated and transformed by Fang speakers themselves.

Trilles lived in Gabon in three extended visits between 1893 and 1907. He made several long stays in Gabon's heavily forested interior and wrote profusely of his experiences and the peoples he encountered. His writings combined ethnographic and geographical description, extensive citation of published sources, missionary anecdote, and highly imaginative representations of Fang and 'pygmies'. Even during his lifetime, Trilles gained renown for plagiarism, shameless invention of data and fantastic flights of fancy. In a biographical notice, Berger (1977: 730) observed that Trilles was 'gifted with multiple talents', but was also 'victim of a wild imagination and an almost unhealthy

sensibility'. He has nonetheless exercised immense influence over subsequent ethnographic knowledge production, particularly through his
copious Fang ethnography (Trilles, n.d., 1898, 1900, 1912a,b, 1920,
1931). At issue here is not the truth or falsehood of Trilles' ethnographic observations, but his role, through fieldwork and scholarship,
in the elaboration of a Fang historical imagination.[8]

Trilles' participation in the 1899 Lesieur–Trilles expedition in Rio
Muni, Northern French Congo, and Kamerun provides rich geographic
and ethnographic description of the interior. His account contains
information on politics, the ivory and rubber trade, population movements, conflict, hunting and agriculture, religious practices, relations
with 'pygmy' and Dzem peoples, and the implantation of concession-
ary companies and colonizers. He noted, for example, the multiple
trade routes that linked the interior regions to the coastal trading fac-
tories. At the same time, he lamented the fact that much of the rubber
and ivory flowing out of French Congo went not to the French but to
the Germans (Trilles 1931: 67). Trilles observed a landscape in motion,
in which people closer to the coast ventured inland and people from
the interior carried their rubber and ivory coastward. 'From far away,
traders, especially the sons of chiefs, pass through here, . . . and for
payment, undertake to carry away ivory, and later, to bring back merchandise that they purchased on the coast' (1931: 56, 61).

Of more spectacular and lasting influence than his descriptive
ethnography were his speculations on Fang origins, gastronomy, and
exceptionalism. In *Chez les Fang* (Trilles 1912a: 14), Trilles wrote
simply, 'the Fang belong incontestably to the Bantu race, . . . but also,
the Fang is the least Bantu of all the Bantus'. Already in 1898, Trilles
depicted the Fang as a tribe of migrating cannibals that had swept
across Africa from Upper Egypt (or the Upper Nile) and that was literally devouring its way through the Gabonese rainforest. 'Where do
the Fang come from!' he writes. 'Schweinfurth links them to the Mom-
buttus, the Dinkas, the Nyamnyam or Sandelis, people living . . . in
the basin of the Upper Nile, an affluent of the Bahr-el-Ghazal, in other
words in Upper Egypt, not far from Ethiopia. This region seems the
most probable. It is certain that many habits are similar, those for
example of filing the teeth in points, and the sacrifice of human
victims in order to have bloody feasts' (Trilles 1898: 68). Trilles portrayed Fang migration strategies as follows:

Three, four or five Fang' families one day leave the tribe, moving forward
to ask for hospitality in a foreign tribe. Through fear, or through habit-
ual custom, this is accorded them. Next to the other houses, at one end
of the village, they raise, in the space of a few hours, a new roof.

[233]

All goes as in the past: the immigrants live as good neighbors, remaining at a certain distance, avoiding disagreements. And one day, a man has disappeared; they look for traces of him. In the lead, more zealous than anyone else, are our Fang. Vain efforts – the man is nowhere to be found. The next day arrives the turn of another, then another, then of yet another.

Out in the forest, here and there beneath the bows, you might find a few tibias, some femurs, silent witnesses to a horrible feast.

But who?

The forest remains mute and the tall trees do not unveil their secret.

But the tribe is distraught. Only one course of action remains to be taken: to flee, to abandon its fields, its ancient domain. It leaves, and the Fang, a sardonic smile upon his lips, watches it depart. The tribe goes further on, but there it will find other Fang families. One day, the men are powerless to defend a female population that has become too numerous for them. In a razzia, they succumb; women and children become the prey of the ravisher; a tribe has disappeared and, more numerous, stronger than ever, the Fang take up anew the march ahead. In the strict sense, as in the wide sense, this is the incorporation of the foreigner. (Trilles 1898: 53)

In this lurid passage Trilles summarized what he saw as the heart of Fang-ness: a strategy of predatory expansion via ingestion. By the time he penned his words, such accounts had circulated among Europeans and had filled published reports for more than half a century. Trilles wrote of constant movement, consumption of weaker 'tribes', tactics of 'ravishers', and the relentless 'march ahead'. In just a few paragraphs, he classified and characterized a people and ascribed to them their essence and raison d'être. Trilles' writings and their legacy both reflected colonial discourse and played a central role in the production and reproduction of ethnic identity. His views continue to influence subsequent generations of scholars a century later. As recently as the mid-1980s, Gabonese historian Nicolas Métégué-N'nah (1984) still felt obliged to argue that nineteenth-century Fang-speakers had not practiced widespread anthropophagy. Yet Trilles' emphasis on Nilotic origins and long-distance migrations remains a fixture of the oral tradition and contemporary historiography (see for example Aubame 2002; Minko Mve 2003: 30–36).

Nonetheless, Trilles had his detractors even during his own lifetime. As early as 1913, German ethnologist Günter Tessmann referred to Trilles as 'the most fecund, but also the most annoying author', whose 'innumerable exaggerations' and 'prejudices . . . completely falsify his presentation of Pahouin culture. . . . His goal is exclusively to show to what point the life, morals, and especially religion of these "poor" Negroes are abominable, corrupted, and contemptible' (Tessmann 1991 [1913]: 171–172). Tessmann did not, however, entirely reject the Hamitic hypothesis espoused by Trilles: 'An important sequence of the history of this people' might have taken place in the Bahr-el-Ghazal region (in present-day Sudan), but such conclusions could only be reached if and when Fang migration history had been 'scientifically constituted' (Tessmann 1991: 182).[9]

Trilles' missionary brethren within the Spiritain order challenged his reliability even more harshly. Fellow missionary-ethnographer Maurice Briault, for example, argued that Trilles' alleged fifteen-year stay *chez les Fang* amounted to nine at most, and that the 'twenty years of life among the pygmies of Gabon . . . [could] be reduced to only one or two brief encounters' (Briault n.d.). Briault accused Trilles of numerous inventions: 'water tigers', 'woman-fish with smooth hair', and a forged pygmy vocabulary based on 'Nilotic roots that he then altered further'. According to Briault, Trilles had claimed that pygmies ('negritos') could walk across the treetops as if on a lawn and that he himself had been carried from tree to tree on the shoulders of a pygmy (Trilles 1932).

After he had burned all his bridges in Africa, Trilles was sent back to Europe in 1907, where he became a 'vagabond' (*gyrovague*),[10] acting 'outside all control, giving conferences, writing articles and making new books, assembling old articles, mixing apologetics and ethnography, sometimes borrowing from other authors . . . all without shame' (Briault n.d.). Trilles' innumerable 'gratuitous inventions', continued Briault, 'lead to formal public contradictions, and humiliations to make him completely lose face . . . [But] he only sees salvation in making matters even worse'.[11]

In spite of these pointed attacks on Trilles' ethnographic authority, and his eventual exclusion from both scientific and missionary communities, Trilles still exercised formative and lasting influence. One might reject or ignore his claims of Fang gastronomic cannibalism while embracing his thesis of Egyptian or Nile Valley origins, a thesis that continues to enjoy considerable popularity among Gabonese and Cameroonian intellectuals. Even the great Senegalese scholar Cheikh Anta Diop (1974: 179, 200), who argued so eloquently for the Egyptian origins of African (and European) civilization, cited Trilles as a source of evidence.[12] In the 1990s, Trilles (via Diop) continued to influence Gabonese students at the Centre Cheikh Anta Diop at Omar Bongo University in Libreville directed by Professor Pierre Biyogo.[13] Indeed all Fang ethnographers, including Balandier and Fernandez, have had to grapple with his legacy.

From colonial ethnography to the anthropology of the colonial situation

Georges Balandier entered the Gabonese field in 1949, more than a half-century after Trilles; by the time James Fernandez left Gabon in 1960, more than a century had elapsed since Du Chaillu's travels in the Monts de Crystal. Although both Balandier and Fernandez were thoroughly grounded in mid-twentieth century anthropology,[14] their rich Fang ethnography bears the stamp of a regional ethnographic tradition profoundly marked by Du Chaillu and Trilles. This tradition, based on the tribal paradigm, long-distance Fang migration, and Fang exceptionalism, was evident in missionary and administrative accounts, which in turn shaped academic and auto-ethnography.

Balandier and Fernandez carried out their investigations of social and cultural change against the backdrop of the colonial situation. Their work was marked by both the well-developed tradition of 'Fang studies' and the specific moment of Gabonese late colonial cultural effervescence. Indeed by the 1950s, Fang-speakers themselves had come to sound more and more like Trilles. They had embraced migration and spatially distant origins as a matter of ethnic identity and pride. Migration narratives drew on Biblical, European and Fang knowledge that had passed back and forth over the years between oral and written traditions in ways that both camouflaged and revealed social and historical processes of their production.

It is within this context that Balandier and Fernandez constructed their ethnographic object and then inserted that object into history. Both relied heavily on a relatively abundant body of primary sources, including Du Chaillu, Trilles and colonial reports. Balandier in particular made extensive use of the colonial archives. He wrote: 'The high colonial administration ... had a certain awareness of its responsibility [for the 'intractable crisis' faced by village populations in Congo and Gabon]. It wanted to understand and permitted me access to sources of information until then reserved to its exclusive use. I completed a systematic perusal of the archives, then dispersed in diverse places' (Balandier 1977: 230).

Following World War II, Balandier worked under Michel Leiris at the Musée de l'Homme in Paris. From 1946 to 1952, he worked with the Institut Français d'Afrique Noire in Senegal, Mauritania, Guinea (Conakry), and Congo (Brazzaville). During this time, Balandier undertook ethnographic and sociological studies of Senegalese fishermen, Gabonese villagers and urban Africans in colonial Brazzaville. In his attempt to theorize social change under colonization, he departed from the then dominant synchronic perspectives of structural-functionalism. In a seminal 1951 article, 'La situation coloniale, approche théorique', Balandier laid out an approach that treated the colonial situation as a complex, total social phenomenon, which linked colonizing and colonized societies in an ongoing dynamic of conflict, adaptation, and crisis.[15] His studies of colonial Africa mirrored the post-World War II ethnographic present, in which Africans sought greater autonomy and access to the benefits of modernity. At the same time his focus on history, power relations, conflict and crisis prefigured the more recent anthropology of colonialism.

In 1948, after having spent several years in West Africa, Balandier was assigned to Brazzaville to open a department of social sciences at the Institut d'Etudes Centrafricaines. There he began studies of social and cultural change in Brazzaville and among Kongo-speakers and, the following year, among Gabonese Fang. He wanted to compare Kongo society, 'with its long history, hierarchies, former kingdoms, and inequalities' to the 'more egalitarian', less territorially rooted Fang, 'who gave form to their modernizing initiatives in the framework of a recomposition movement of tribes and clans' (Balandier 1997: 280). On the one hand, this comparative study reproduced the classic dichotomy between centralized and acephalous societies put forth in *African Political Systems*.[16] On the other, the focus on 'foreign impositions', 'subterranean autonomy', 'religious innovation', 'the birth of peasant nationalism', and the 'critique of the colonial situation' differed sharply from studies by 'the classic ethnologists [who] only had curiosity for the ... authentic' (Balandier 1977: 231–232).[17]

It is difficult to separate Balandier's conceptions of Fang identity from his ideas about history, because his primary goal was to study the evolution of Fang social organization under the colonial situation. Yet in order to explain social dislocation, it was necessary to posit a previous social cohesion. This is evident in Balandier's choice of chapter titles in *Sociologie actuelle de l'Afrique noire*. The long chapter on 'Fang society' precedes the chapter on 'Fang crises'. At the center of Balandier's notion of precolonial Fang society lies a tension that he himself recognized – stable social institutions characterized by instability, volatility and displacement. Due in large measure to the assumed rapidity with which the Fang had migrated across Africa, precolonial Fang had suffered from 'a poor fixation to the land', weak village communities, and a 'complex entanglement of clans' (Balandier 1950: 99). Paradoxically, precolonial ethnic cohesion was characterized by 'multiple fragmentations'. Moreover, in spite of the disruptions of their migration history and the colonial crisis, the Fang had emerged as a coherent society with a firm sense of their present and past.

Fang crisis was part of the larger colonial situation in postwar Gabon and Congo (Brazzaville), where once again precolonial instability had been ruptured by colonialism. The late colonial Gabon of Balandier's *Ambiguous Africa* (Balandier 1966 [1957]) was one in which forest peoples were overwhelmed by both hyperabundant nature and the colonial situation. 'Too few roads', wrote Balandier, 'and bad ones, span regions which are inadequately populated. Too much water and too many forests create frequent impasses. The [African] human groups seemed disturbed, isolated, withdrawn' (1966: 152–153). In the Ogooué River town of Lambaréné – a nineteenth-century trading and administrative post where Fang-speakers and southern Gabon populations met, and the site of Albert Schweitzer's hospital[18] – Balandier discerned that 'civilizations have been corroded and people debilitated in less than a century by contact with our economic, administrative and religious imperatives' (1966: 146).[19] Along the Ogooué, French memories of nineteenth-century explorer Savorgnan de Brazza clashed with the postwar 'face of poverty and the destruction of traditional cultures', 'sinister resignation', 'miserable villages', 'shores abandoned by hope', and 'devastation of forests, societies, and men' (1966: 18). Had nature, underpopulation, and dispersal – in short, the forest itself – hampered social cohesion all along or had a fragile social order foundered upon the rocks of colonization? At the same time, precolonial 'particularism', 'zones of isolation', 'large vacuums of population' and 'instability' actually may have served during 'periods of crises' provoked by the slave trade, colonial implantation, and labor recruitment, to protect these 'tribes whose social structure is capable of breaking down without being destroyed' (1966: 155–156).

Balandier grappled with the historical tensions between an idealized precolonial social order, with its attendant pre-contact dispersion and fragmentation, and the disruptive impact of colonial regimes of power. In his ambiguous Gabon, the very components of the clan system had disintegrated beneath the crushing weight of the colonial situation. One sign was the 'weakening (or almost disappearance) of the distinctions between tribes and clans, the fragmentation, the dispersion and the semi-autonomy of these diverse groups, [leading] to a confusion' (Balandier 1982 [1955]: 80). Social disorder was so extensive and traditions 'so altered in Gabon, that the relations between clan fragments are poorly known' (Balandier 1982 [1955]: 237). Postwar Fang aspired to a segmentary stability that would nonetheless enable them to embrace late colonial modernity. A clan reunification movement that had begun in Southern Cameroon in the 1940s (or earlier) and spread into northern Gabon, attempted 'to reestablish the former cohesion of the Fan group' while seeking the benefits of late colonial modernity

(Balandier 1949: 24; 1966: 158–159, 166). Balandier was of course aware that such cohesion may never have existed, but referred rather to 'an idealized past', of 'tribal fraternity, common origin, consanguinity and "religious" respect for tribal unity' (1966: 161). The clan reunification movement he described sought to revive the tribe 'after a long period of decline', thereby imposing 'an abnormal unity by traditional criteria' (1966: 161, 166).

One senses that Balandier was profoundly marked by his Central African fieldwork and ethnographic experiences of the 'predatory economy' (Balandier 1997: 282), social disintegration and colonial crisis, but also by the 'ingeniousness and know-how, . . . multiple inventions, . . . and skillful bricolage' (Balandier 1977: 228–229), especially of the Fang and Kongo peoples among whom he worked. As he put it, 'Everything moved, decomposed and was recomposed, underwent experimentation, leading to the appearance of problems and originality, [and] provoking unforeseen effects and refusals' (1977: 229). Many of these same preoccupations have continued to inform Balandier's later work on the social dynamics, disorder, mazes, and systems of modernity and hypermodernity (Balandier 1988, 1994, 2001b). As he himself concluded, 'When I left Equatorial Africa in 1952, I disposed of both copious materials to elaborate and a method of interpretation' (Balandier 1997: 290).

James Fernandez arrived in Gabon in 1958, a decade after Balandier and two years before Gabonese independence. He had studied anthropology and African Studies at Northwestern University under Melville Herskovits, a founder of African Studies in the United States. Fernandez left Gabon in summer 1960, just prior to independence, and has never returned. Nonetheless, while turning to fieldwork in South Africa, West Africa and, since the early 1970s, Spain, he has written abundantly on the Fang, most notably on their religious imagination. In his monumental ethnography, *Bwiti* (Fernandez 1982), Fernandez situated his own ethnography in at least three overlapping fields: 1) the Malinowskian ethnographic tradition, 2) the richness of local practices, and 3) the written tradition of colonial ethnography. He wrote, 'To me the best work in anthropology has been done, to speak only of a generation or age grade now passed on, by Malinowski, Ruth Benedict, E.E. Evans-Pritchard, Marcel Griaule, and Clyde Kluckhohn. It is not so much the theoretical perspectives of these works, . . . but rather their embeddedness in local idiom, their skillful presentation of local points of view that impresses' (Fernandez 1982: xx). Fernandez's point runs counter to that of much of the critique of anthropology literature, first in his unabashed admiration for anthropological ancestors, and second, in his claim for the embeddedness of this earlier ethnography

[239]

in 'local idiom', a phrase that has perhaps fallen out of fashion in the age of globalization.

Fernandez was acutely aware of the legacy of earlier Fang ethnographers, including Du Chaillu, Trilles and Tessmann. Du Chaillu, in spite of the fact that his writings were 'simply a little decorated in spots', had 'made Africa come alive' in nineteenth-century Western minds, and had exercised 'lingering influence' on the ethnographic imagination (Fernandez 1982: 33–34). By the 1860s, 'attitudes and beliefs about the Fang were well crystallized. Few visitors and explorers [and later, anthropologists?] were able to escape them entirely, though each new visitor gave . . . his particular emphasis' (p. 35). In a discussion of his own ethnographic encounter, Fernandez tantalizingly referred to the distinct agendas of Tessmann and Trilles: 'It is clear that the meanings assigned by the first Fang ethnographer, Gunter Tessmann, emerged out of his particular interaction and dialogue with the Fang. The meanings he assigned were significantly different from those assigned by Father Trilles and by other missionaries' (Fernandez 1982: 5).[20] Later, he pointed ironically to Trilles' pride in his grasp of Fang 'figures of speech – or what Trilles called "la métaphore juste" '. 'But naturally', Fernandez continues, 'such subtle matters were often misinterpreted or counter-productive' (p. 282). Here, Fernandez appeared to dismiss, in Malinowskian fashion, an amateur missionary ethnographer. Nonetheless, Fernandez duly recognized elsewhere that Trilles and his missionary colleagues had shaped the ways Fang themselves represented their heritage, especially the genealogical tradition: 'The custom of tracing genealogies back to God may owe something to Trilles (and other missionaries), who invented his own genealogy and following the biblical model, traced it triumphantly back to God' (p. 78n; see Trilles 1912a: 5–6).

If Balandier was influenced by British political anthropology and the followers of Gluckman, Fernandez has drawn more heavily on symbolic anthropology, the 'play of tropes in culture', and religious movements. Nonetheless, the two overlapped on many points, including their basic conceptions of Fang identity. Like Balandier, Fernandez emphasized the dynamic tension between cohesion and dispersion in precolonial society. In a 1970 article, he summarized 'the classic Fang social organization', which 'consisted of dispersed clans – patrilineally related, exogamous social units of common ancestry – which were, probably because of the dispersal process of rapid migration, scattered about in small villages and not at all represented in an integral area of clan lands' (Fernandez 1970: 431). Following Balandier and a long line of predecessors, Fernandez situated Fang origins outside the equatorial rainforest. He posited that 'though they speak a neo-Bantu language, it is true that the Fang are originally a Sudanic people of savannah origin'. Moreover, he concluded, 'the Fang still do not feel fully at home in the forest' (Fernandez 1970: 432). This feeling of displacement and clan dispersal, compounded by the frustrations of colonization, motivated the Fang to participate in the clan reunification movement and to reconstruct an 'equatorial pleasure dome' through the Bwiti religion.

In *Bwiti*, Fernandez dropped the definite article before the Fang ethnonym, indicating a certain uneasiness with the tribal paradigm: '[W]e shall avoid speaking of *the* Fang doing, saying, or believing such and such. Rather, when the custom is fairly widespread among them we shall say Fang say, Fang do' (Fernandez 1982: 12). He nonetheless illustrated the ongoing influence of Fang exceptionalism by calling nineteenth-century Fang 'the terror of autochthonous peoples' (1982: 51). As he saw it, their notoriety arose in part from flattering European depictions of their ability to colonize rainforest landscapes, which contributed to a 'lively sense of superiority' over other Gabonese groups (Fernandez 1982: 51). Fernandez questioned, however, Balandier's early (1949) characterization of migrating Fang as '*conquérants en disponibilité*'' (i.e., conquerors left unemployed by colonization). Fang 'migration was more a flight from some greater power – variously symbolized – than a conquest toward some objective' (1982: 52). Fernandez's point here was to nuance representations of Fang superiority, not to question the notion of long-distance migration. Fang, Fernandez concluded, 'were aggressive, but not truly warlike' (1982: 51).

Like Balandier, Fernandez suggested a more coherent precolonial social order: the apparent decline of such grouping concepts as tribe and clan had led to a 'sense of uncertainty and confusion about the social order and [one's] place in it' (Fernandez 1982: 97–98). Instead of making concrete claims about the past, however, Fernandez emphasized feelings. Former social unity was experienced as a common feeling of dispersal:

> Terminological evidence that clan organization was formerly greater, coupled with present ambiguities about the application of terms, convinced many that their social affairs were in a vestigial state. [This created] a feeling of being a scattered people and of needing to reunite and reorganize. (Fernandez 1982: 87)

At the same time, Fernandez cautioned against the reification of bygone 'social grouping concepts' – especially the major Fang 'tribal' divisions. The study of genealogical histories showed how volatile and difficult to define such groups were. 'Tribes', he concluded, were not 'composed of separate sets of clans. . . . Most clans, due to the turmoil of Fang migration, were widely dispersed and represented in the various tribes' (1982: 84).

This permeability of 'tribal divisions' suggests a precolonial historical ethnography characterized by population movements, long-distance inter-ethnic alliances and highly flexible social groups, inconsistent with the tribal paradigm. The genealogical histories to which Fernandez referred contained social memory and were therefore indicators (however partial) of historical relationships that involve a constant mediation of power, identities, roles and obligations (Vansina 1990). When we step outside the constraints of the tribal paradigm, Balandier's contradictory portrayal of a coherent yet deeply fragmented past begins to make sense. Fernandez's critique of the reification of 'tribal divisions' can be extended to the idealized coherence of Fangness itself. In the northern Gabon forest, social actors have long used genealogical knowledge to express, create and conceal ever-shifting local, regional, and even inter-ethnic identities (Cinnamon 2005). In the past, the genealogical idiom provided a flexible framework in which a wide variety of social actors could define power relations, inclusion and exclusion, rights and duties, and individual and group identities. It is thus hardly surprising that local intellectuals turned to genealogies and 'clan traditions' during the clan reunification movement of the 1940s and 1950s, when Balandier and Fernandez were undertaking their research. As Balandier (1997: 286) noted, the 'founding myths of the clan regroupments went from fragments of Fang mythology to fragments of Biblical inspiration'. The legacy of the clan reunification movement continued to inform the oral and written traditions I encountered in the field at the end of the 1980s, which have also filtered into performances and written versions of the Mvet epic.

The Mvet epic as auto-ethnography

The Mvet (or Mvett) epic is chanted by Fang-, Bulu-, and Bëti-speaking artists in villages and cultural festivals of northern Gabon, southern Cameroon and Rio Muni. The epic narrative centers on cosmic and apocalyptic warfare between two imaginary races of giants: a race of mortals from the land of Okü, and a race of immortals from the land of Engong. The immortals, who have discovered the medicine of life, cannot be killed and so always win. Published versions exemplify Fang auto-ethnography and illustrate the legacy of colonial ethnography, but are not merely a derivative discourse.[21] The epic and especially commentaries by Gabonese and Cameroonian intellectuals address both primordial and modern themes in Fang studies: origins,

[242]

migrations, exceptionalism, power, colonialism, nationalism and, in the 1990s, opposition politics (see Assoumou Ndoutoume 1993). Narratives of Fang origins, migrations and identity in the epic both parallel and depart from the preoccupations of colonial anthropology. Rather than using Fang exceptionalism as an ideology that converted Fang-speakers into colonial auxiliaries, auto-ethnographers used it to claim greater independence and political power.

The epic itself expresses, in extreme form, the violence and dislocation of the colonial situation. It also exemplifies the creativity, 'multiple inventions', and 'skillful bricolage' referred to by Balandier above.[22] It first appeared in serialized form in the review *Réalités Gabonaises*, which began publication in April 1959, 'the hour of our national construction', while Fernandez was in the field. The written text thus served as a cultural production and representation of the very milieu that Fernandez was studying. The review editor and author of the serialized Mvet, Ndong Ndoutoume Philippe, who 'played the Mvett on paper' (Ndong Ndoutoume 1975: 68–71), translated the Fang epic into the colonial language, French, thereby making a regional or ethnic epic available for the construction of a national literary identity.

The richness, extravagance and hyperbole of the Mvet have led to extravagant claims by students of the genre. According to Cameroonian scholar Eno Belinga (1978: 39), 'the mvet is a veritable encyclopedia, divided into several categories, of which the most important are ... physics, psychology, cosmogony, theogeny, and social organization'. Engonga Bikoro (1987: 105–106) argued that the cosmology enunciated in the Mvet represented 'the Fang conception of the world, of life, and the Supreme Being'. In her view, the Mvet expressed 'the quasi-totality of the culture of this people'. Ndong Ndoutoume (1993: 31), called this epic genre ' "total art": a fusion of speech (*parole*) and music, poetry, literature, pedagogy, psychology, philosophy, sociology, cosmogony, spirituality, in two words *Fang Culture*.' Mvet artists in southern Cameroon told French ethnographer Pascal Boyer that the Mvet was *mam mese* or 'all things'. Boyer (1988) complained that the epic was so complicated and paradoxical, so filled with 'mysterious barricades' and 'traps of thought', that it confounded all interpretation. One might argue, however, that the very fluidity and ambiguity of the Mvet, reconfigured (or 're-bricolaged') at each telling, does not preclude interpretation; rather its multiple narratives invite various readings by both tellers and listeners. One of these readings faithfully reproduces the narrative of Egyptian origin so eloquently expressed by Trilles.

Ndong Ndoutoume (1975, 1983, 1993), Marc Ropivia (1981, 1989) and Fernandez (1982) have all posited that the Mvet developed, historically or mystically, in response to the 'Fang migrations'. In the introduction to the 1970 version of the epic Ndong wrote 'The Fang descended, according to the stories and accounts of our elders, from the banks of the Nile, from which they were chased by the Mvélé or Bassa' (Ndong Ndoutoume 1983: 16). During their flight, mythico-historical ancestor Oyono Ada Ngone awoke from a dream to invent the Mvet instrument and 'began to recount the epics of the imaginary warrior people that he baptized the "people of Engong" or people of Iron. These epics excited the Fang. They hurled themselves into the peoples of the southwest with the violence of the Mvet heroes, pil-laging, sacking all in their passage.' Ndong's migration narrative ended with the familiar segmentation and settlement of the extant cultural-linguistic groups in their current habitats (Ndong Ndoutoume 1983: 16–18).

The imagined epics served to mold 'the bellicose spirit of the Fang' and to give them the courage to affront the 'uncountable difficulties' of the migrations and the 'Obane' wars.[23] The 'fictional' epic cycle, produced by what Fernandez (1982) called the 'vision experience' of Oyono Ada Ngone, was set against the historical narrative of the migration across Africa. As argued above, the theory of migrations from Upper Egypt, widespread today among 'Beti-Bulu-Fang' speakers, was introduced by nineteenth-century European missionaries and pro-ponents of 'degradation theory', including Trilles. These histories were later confirmed when literate Fang-speakers discovered their own history in the genealogies and stories of the Old Testament. Migration narratives continue to play a central role in oral traditions; claims of Egyptian origins grew increasingly important in late colonial Gabon, when Ndong Ndoutoume first began to write the Mvet.

In the 1980s, Geographer Marc Ropivia sought to interpret the Mvet as the key means by which the Fang, 'a people without writing', had been able to preserve their 'veritable history' through time and across space (Ropivia 1981: 46–47). He argued that an attentive reading of the epic revealed the primitive habitat, the migration to the west, and the current *oekoumène* in the Gabon-Congo space (Ropivia 1981: 49). Relying on morpho-semantic analysis of Ndong's French-language ver-sions, Ropivia traced Fang origins to the Nile (1981: 50). This is the territory of the mortals of Okü (the country of the north). Citing a dif-ferent passage, he situated the country of the ancestors of the Immor-tals to the east, in the land of the rising sun, on the shores of the Lake of Life (*Atok Ening*). This Lake of Life could only be Lake Victoria, Africa's 'inland sea'. Ensuing analysis led Ropivia to conclude that Fang were among the first metal-workers in sub-Saharan Africa, that they had practiced copper metallurgy on the western shores of Lake

Victoria during a period of great antiquity, and that overpopulation prompted their westward migrations (1989: 324–333). Like aspects of the writing of Trilles, this version of history, which underlined Fang uniqueness and prestigious origins, has been immensely appealing to certain Fang and Bëti intellectuals.

Conclusion

In 1856, as Du Chaillu was setting out for his explorations of the Gabonese interior, missionary John Leighton Wilson wrote that the Fang (or Pangwes as he called them) were 'a very remarkable people; among savages, I do not know that I ever met men of nobler or more imposing bearing'. Once 'the truths of the Gospel are made known to them' in their own language, 'they will show as much susceptibility to it as any other people' (Wilson 1856: 300–301). Here, Wilson weighed in with an early expression of a Fang exceptionalism that would be amplified and widely disseminated by Du Chaillu, Trilles and their academic and auto-ethnographer successors. As this chapter has sought to argue, some of the main contours of Fang studies date back to the very beginnings of the colonial period, a full century before Balandier, Fernandez and others professionalized Fang anthropology. Wilson's hopes for the salutary impact of the Gospel also prefigure the colonial situation, or the 'colonization of consciousness' (Comaroff and Comaroff 1991), a situation that inevitably escaped colonial control. Gabonese intellectuals, while attentive to European power and representations, have frequently sought to draw on colonial ethnography in the creation of their own expressions of Fang exceptionalism.

The genealogy of colonial anthropology and of postcolonial auto-ethnography leads back to the initial field encounters and ethnographic writings explored here, and to the enduring discourses they begat. Current critiques have tended to emphasize the power relations inherent in the face-to-face fieldwork encounter, the predicaments of outsiders' claims of ethnographic authority, or the sins of our anthropologist forefathers: Malinowski, Evans-Pritchard and Griaule. Such critiques, while vital in the academy, have had somewhat less relevance to equatorial African ethnography than the enduring legacy of nineteenth-century representations.

Notes

1 Although used to refer to the notion that a thing, people, or nation is exceptional in relation to others, the term has frequently been applied to the US. See Lipset 1996 and Shaffer 1999.

2 According to Bernault (2003: 173n, 181, 186), representations of Fang as 'invading hordes' fueled colonial projects of control, domination, fixing of populations, and exploitation. Later, the image of Fang as 'devourers of the nation' has justified their relative marginalization and 'political failures' in postcolonial Gabon. As argued here, Fang themselves have repeatedly re-appropriated aspects of these myths to bolster their own sense of exceptionalism.

3 Referring to the postwar years he spent in Central Africa and Brazzaville, Balandier himself (1977: 228–229) reiterates the critique: 'my predecessors or my colleagues had practiced or still practiced the standard inquiry corresponding to a vision that erases all relief and all movement.' Balandier's work on Central Africa draws on the Rhodes-Livingstone Institute and 'Manchester School' anthropologists who formed around Max Gluckman.

4 Vansina does not explain just why equatorial Africans, and the European scholars who studied them, have found questions of origins and migration so compelling, but such emphasis has long shaped ethnographic accounts of the region.

5 Vansina himself, seeking an alternative to the ahistorical model based on segmentary lineages and clans, elaborated a model of equatorial African societies based on big man competition and flexible spatial units (the house, village, and district) that formed the backbone of what he termed the 'Equatorial African Tradition': a tradition that persisted for over 2,000 years until irredeemably shattered by twentieth-century colonialism (Vansina 1990). Along similar lines, Balandier (1977: 232), drawing on colonial documents, also traces 'a rapidly generalized degradation' of the Fang social edifice to the interwar years.

6 Fernandez (1982: 34) noted, 'In fact, much of what Du Chaillu says could be an elaboration of what was said in the 1840s by other Americans.'

7 On the anglophone side, his line has passed through Richard Burton (1863, 1876), Mary Kingsley (1897), the American Presbyterian missionary Robert Nassau (1904), Trader Horn (1928), and later Fernandez, Chamberlin (1978) and Gray (2002). On the more prolific francophone side, Du Chaillu's intellectual descendants include the explorer Brazza (1966), the missionary Trilles, the administrator Largeau (who published a 'pahouine encyclopedia' in 1901), R. Avelot (1905), Pierre Alexandre (1965), and Balandier. More recently, geographer Roland Pourtier (1989) draws extensively from Du Chaillu in his two-volume historical geography of Gabon. To these names it is necessary to add an increasing number of Gabonese and Cameroonian intellectuals who extend this genealogy. Patterson (1974), Bucher (1979), and McCook (1996) have discussed historical and scientific implications of Du Chaillu's legacy. The European fascination with Du Chaillu continues. In summer 2004, I participated in a French-funded multidisciplinary project in southern Gabon that sought to retrace the itinerary of Du Chaillu's travels in southern Gabon.

8 My goal here has been to assess the ongoing impact of a handful of major figures in 'Fang' historical ethnography rather than to answer the question of Fang origins and migrations once and for all. There is a large literature on this question dating at least back to Trilles. For relatively recent syntheses, see Alexandre (1965), Laburthe-Tolra (1981), Vansina (1990: 130–137), and Bernault (2003). These sources, using a variety of written, oral, and linguistic evidence, trace the origins of 'Beti-Bulu-Fang' or 'Sanaga-Ntem' speakers to the Oubangui River valley in present-day Central African Republic or to the Sanaga River valley in Cameroon instead of the Nile Valley.

9 Although partially translated into English by the Human Relations Area Files (and cited by Fernandez (1982), Jane Guyer, and Cameroonian archeologist Joseph-Marie Essomba), Tessmann's Die Pangwe has had more limited influence on Fang ethnography, probably because he wrote in German. Laburthe-Tolra's partial 1991 French translation should make his important ethnography more accessible to francophone researchers. I have been particularly impressed by Tessmann's detailed descriptions and illustrations of early twentieth-century material culture.

10 A term that referred during the monastic era to 'monks who spent their life roaming from province to province, cell to cell, only staying for three or four days in the same place, and living from alms'. Anon. 1966. *Emile Littré Diction-naire de la langue française. Tome 4.* Edition intégrale, p. 358. Paris: Gallimard/ Hachette.

11 Handwritten notes in Briault n.d.

12 Diop (1974: 200) writes, 'In an article published in the *Encyclopédie de la France d'outre-mer* (December 1951, pp. 347–348), Pédrals reports that Father Trilles, after making a series of contacts, is convinced that the Fang had some contact with Chris-tian Ethiopia during their ancient migration. This is a people who, as we noted earlier, still had not reached the coast during the nineteenth century in its north-east-southwest trek.'

13 In a work on the Egyptian sources of Knowledge, Biyogo (2000: 191n.) refers in passing to the work of Trilles in a brief discussion of the 'genetic kinship' between Fang and ancient Egyptians.

14 Balandier read widely in French and English, paying particular attention to the writ-ings of Max Gluckman and the Rhodes-Livingstone Institute/Manchester School on social change, urbanization and industrialization in British Central Africa. Fernan-dez, more than Balandier, shows the influence of American cultural anthropology.

15 This article was revised as the first chapter of *Sociologie actuelle de l'Afrique noire* (1982) [1955]. It was recently republished in a thematic edition of *Cahiers Interna-tionaux de Sociologie* that emerged from a 2001 conference on 'the colonial situa-tion' held at New York University (Balandier 2001a). In an overview and critique of colonial studies, historian Frederick Cooper (2005: 33–40, 53–55) writes very favorably of Balandier's 'engaged and rigorous' analysis of the colonial situation. Such renewed interest in Balandier's path-breaking colonial studies suggests his ongoing relevance.

16 In this volume, which became a sort of administrators' handbook in British colonial Africa, only chapters by Max Gluckman on the Zulu and Audrey Richards on the Bemba addressed the period of European rule (Fortes and Evans-Pritchard 1940).

17 Balandier distinguishes himself from his anthropological forebears and con-temporaries by his attention to change and movement. He writes: '[M]y predeces-sors or my colleagues had practiced or still practiced the standard inquiry corresponding to a vision that erases all relief and all movement' (Balandier 1977: 228).

18 Balandier (1977: 76) describes Schweitzer unflatteringly as 'an autocratic and soli-tary sovereign'.

19 Here Balandier echoes the familiar nineteenth-century lament that coastal popula-tions had been corrupted by their contact with European traders' debauchery and merchandise.

20 See Laburthe-Tolra and Falgayrettes-Leveau (1991) for a discussion of Tessmann's sometimes heavy-handed ethnographic methods. I do not mean to imply here that we return from the field without having assigned our own particular meanings based on our own interactions and dialogues. Nonetheless, the field we encounter is, in part, a product of previous ethnographic encounters.

21 Mary Louise Pratt (1992) and others have used the term 'auto-ethnography' to refer to texts in which colonial and postcolonial subjects represent themselves using the 'colonizers' own terms'. Pels and Salemink (1994, 1999) argue for a critical view of auto-ethnography, which they view as a self-objectifying, derivative discourse.

22 Jane Guyer (1996) writing more generally of equatorial Africa, refers to a 'tradition of invention'.

23 Here Ndong conflated migration and *obane*. Obane is usually glossed as 'a period of generalized warfare'. Such widespread social disruption would have been linked to population movements.

References

Alexandre, Pierre. 1965. 'Proto-histoire du groupe beti-bulu-fang: essai de synthèse provisoire'. *Cahier d'Etudes Africaines* 5:503–560.

Alexandre, Pierre and Binet Jacques. 1958. *Le Groupe dit Pahouin (Fang-Boulou-Beti)*. Paris: Presses Universitaires de France.

Assoumou Ndoutoume, Daniel. 1993. *Du Mvett. L'orage. Processus de démocratisation conté par un diseur du Mvett*. Paris: Harmattan.

Aubame, Jean-Marie. 2002. *Les Beti du Gabon et d'ailleurs. Tome 1: Sites, parcours et structures*. Paris: Harmattan.

Avelot, R. 1905. 'Recherches sur l'histoire des migrations dans le bassin de l'Ogooué et la région littorale adjacent'. *Bulletin de géographie historique et descriptive* 20:357–412.

Balandier, Georges. 1949. 'Les "Fan" du Gabon: des conquérants en disponibilité'. *Tropiques* 44:23–26.

Balandier, Georges. 1950. 'Aspects de l'évolution social chez les Fang du Gabon'. *Cahiers internationaux de sociologie* 9:76–106.

Balandier, Georges. 1966 [1957]. *Ambiguous Africa: Cultures in Collision*. Translated from the French by H. Weaver. New York: Meridian.

Balandier, Georges. 1977. *Histoire d'autres*. Paris: Stock.

Balandier, Georges. 1982 [1955]. *Sociologie actuelle de l'Afrique Noire: Dynamique sociale en Afrique Centrale* (4ᵉ ed.). Paris: Presses Universitaires de France.

Balandier, Georges. 1988. *Le désordre: Éloge du movement*. Paris: Fayard.

Balandier, Georges. 1994. *Le dédale: Pour en finir avec le XXe siècle*. Paris: Fayard.

Balandier, Georges. 1997. *Conjugaisons*. Paris: Fayard.

Balandier, Georges. 2001a [1951]. 'La Situation Coloniale: Approche théorique'. *Cahiers Internationaux de Sociologie* CX Nouvelle Série: 9–29.

Balandier, Georges. 2001b. *Le grand système*. Paris: Fayard.

Berger, Augustin. 1977. 'Henri Trilles (1866–1949)'. In *Hommes et Destins (Dictionnaire biographique d'Outre-Mer)*, Nouvelle série 5, tome 2. Paris: Académie des Sciences d'outre-mer, pp. 729–731.

Bernault, Florence. 2003. 'Dévoreurs de la nation: le mythe des invasions fang au Gabon'. In C. Coquery Vidrovitch, Odile Georg, Issiaka Mande; and Faranirina Rajaonah (eds). *Etre étranger et migrant en Afrique au XXe siècle: Enjeux indentitaires et modes d'insertion. Vol. I: Politiques migratoires et constructions des identités*. Paris: Harmattan, pp. 169–187.

Biyogo, Grégoire. 2000. *Aux sources égyptienne du savoir. Tome 1. Généalogie et enjeux de la pensée de Cheikh Anti Diop*. Yaoundé: Editions MENAIBUC.

Boyer, Pascal. 1988. *Barricades mystérieuse & pièges à pensée: Introduction à l'analyse des épopées fang*. Paris: Société d'ethnologie.

Brazza, Pierre Savorgnan de. 1966. *Brazza explorateur, l'Ogooué, 1875–1879*. H. Brunschwig, with J. Glénisson, M.-A. Ménier, G. Sautter and R. Sillans (eds). Paris: Mouton.

Briault, Reverend Père Maurice n.d. 'Notes sur le P. Trilles. Cas du Père Trilles et de son ouvrage chez les pygmées'. Congrégration du Saint Esprit. Archives Générales. Chevilly-Larue, France. 631.A 2D12. 1 à 3.

Bruel, Georges. 1914. *Bibliographie de l'Afrique Equatoriale Française*. Paris: Larose.

Bucher, Henry H. 1979. 'Canonization by Repetition: Paul Du Chaillu in Historiography'. *Revue française d'Histoire d'Outre-Mer* LXVI:15–32.

Burton, Richard. 1863. 'A Day amongst the Fans'. *Anthropological Review* 1:43–54.

Burton, Richard. 1876. *Two Trips to Gorilla Land and the Cataracts of the Congo*. London: S. Low, Marston, Low, and Searle.

Chamberlin, Christopher. 1978. 'The Migration of the Fang into Central Gabon in the Nineteenth Century: A New Interpretation'. *International Journal of African Historical Studies* 11:429–456.

Cinnamon, John M. 2005. 'Mobility, Genealogical Memory, and Constructions of Social Space in Northern Gabon'. In A.M. Howard and R.M. Shain (eds). *The Spatial Factor in African History: The Relationship of the Social, Material, and Perceptual*. Leiden: Brill, pp. 177–219.

Comaroff, Jean and Comaroff, John. 1991. *Of Revelation and Revolution: Christianity, Colonialism, and Consciousness in South Africa, Vol. 1*. Chicago: University of Chicago Press.

Cooper, Frederick. 2005. *Colonialism in Question: Theory, Knowledge, History*. Berkeley: University of California Press.

Diop, Cheikh Anta. 1974. *The African Origin of Civilization: Myth or Reality*. Chicago: Lawrence Hill Books.

Du Chaillu, Paul Belloni. 1861. *Explorations & Adventures in Equatorial Africa*. London: John Murray. Revised and Enlarged French edition 1863. *Voyages et aventures dans l'Afrique équatoriale*. Paris: Michel Lévy Frères.

Du Chaillu, Paul Belloni. 1867. *A journey to Ashango-Land: and further penetration into equatorial Africa*. London: J. Murray. French edition 1868. *L'Afrique sauvage: Nouvelles excursions au pays des Ashangos*. Paris: Michel Lévy Frères.

Engonga Bikoro, Blandine. 1987. 'Cosmologie bantu: Origine de la vie, du monde et de Dieu chez les Fang'. *Muntu* 6:105–119.

Eno Belinga, M.S. 1978. *L'épopée camerounaise-mvet: Moneblum ou l'homme bleu*. Yaoundé: CEPER.

Ferguson, James. 1999. *Expectations of Modernity: Myths and Meanings of Urban Life on the Zambian Copperbelt*. Berkeley: University of California Press.

Fernandez, James W. 1970. 'The Affirmation of Things Past: Alar Ayong and Bwiti as Movements of Protest in Central and Northern Gabon'. In R. Rotberg and A. Mazrui (eds). *Protest and Power in Black Africa*. New York: Oxford University Press, pp. 427–457.

Fernandez, James W. 1982. *Bwiti: An Ethnography of the Religious Imagination in Africa*. Princeton: Princeton University Press.

Fortes, Meyer and Evans-Pritchard, E.E. (eds). 1940. *African Political Systems*. London: KPI/International African Institute.

Gray, Christopher J. 2002. *Colonial Rule and Crisis in Equatorial Africa: Southern Gabon, c. 1850–1940*. Rochester, N.Y.: University of Rochester Press.

Guyer, Jane and Eno Belinga, Samuel M. 1995. 'Wealth in People as Wealth in Knowledge: Accumulation and Composition in Equatorial Africa'. *Journal of African History* 36:91–120.

Guyer, Jane I. 1996. 'Traditions of Invention in Equatorial Africa'. *African Studies Review* 39:1–28.

Horn, Trader. 1928. *Trader Horn; Being the Life and Works of Alfred Aloysius Horn*. E. Lewis (ed.). New York, Simon and Schuster.

Kingsley, Mary. 1897. *Travels in West Africa: Congo Français, Corisco and Cameroons*. New York: Macmillan.

Kuklick, Henrika. 1991. *The Savage Within: The Social History of British Social Anthropology, 1885–1945*. Cambridge: Cambridge University Press.

Laburthe-Tolra, Philippe. 1981. *Les seigneurs de la forêt*. Paris: Editions de la Sorbonne.

Laburthe-Tolra, Philippe and Falgayrettes-Leveau, Ch. 1991. *Fang*. Paris: Musée Dapper.

Lipset, Seymour Martin. 1996. *American Exceptionalism: A Double-edged Sword*. New York: W.W. Norton.

McCook, Stuart. 1996. ' "It May Be Truth, but It Is Not Evidence": Paul du Chaillu and the Legitimation of Evidence in the Field Sciences'. *Osiris* 2nd series 11:177–197.

Métégué-N'nah, Nicolas. 1984. *Lumière sur points d'ombre: contribution à la connaissance de la société gabonaise*. Langres, France: Imp. Guéniot.

Minko Mve, Bernadin. 2003. *Gabon entre tradition et post-modernité: Dynamique des structures d'accueil Fang*. Paris: Harmattan.

Nassau, Robert Hamill. 1904. *Fetichism in West Africa; forty years' observation of native customs and superstitions*. London: Duckworth.

Ndong Ndoutoume, Philippe. 1975. *Le Mvett: Livre II*. Paris: Présence africaine.

Ndong Ndoutoume, Philippe. 1983 [1970]. *Le Mvett: Epopée fang*. Paris: Présence africaine/ACCT.

Ndong Ndoutoume, Philippe. 1993. *Le Mvett: L'homme, la mort et l'immortalité*. Paris: Harmattan.

Patterson, David, K. 1974. 'Paul B. Du Chaillu and the Exploration of Gabon, 1855–1865'. *The International Journal of African Historical Studies* VII:647–667.

Pels, Peter and Salemink, Oscar. 1994. 'Introduction: Five Theses on Ethnography as Colonial Practice'. *History and Anthropology* 8:1–34.

Pels, Peter and Salemink, Oscar. 1999. 'Introduction'. In P. Pels and O. Salemink (eds). *Colonial Subjects: Essays on the Practical History of Anthropology*. Ann Arbor: University of Michigan Press, pp. 1–45.

Pourtier, Roland. 1989. *Le Gabon. Tome 1: Éspace-historicité-société. Tome 2: État et développement*. Paris: Harmattan.

Pratt, Mary Louise. 1992. *Imperial Eyes: Travel Writing and Transculturation*. London: Routledge.

Reade, William Winwood. 1864. *Savage Africa: Being the Narrative of a Tour in Equatorial, South-Western, and North-Western Africa*. New York: Harper.

Ropivia, Marc. 1981. 'Les Fang dans les Grands Lacs et la Vallée du Nil: Esquisse d'une géographie historique à partir du Mvett'. *Présence Africaine* 120:46–58.

Ropivia, Marc. 1989. 'Mvett et Bantuistique: la métallurgie du cuivre come critère de Bantuité et son incidence sur les hypothèses migratoires connues'. In T. Obenga (ed.). *Les peuples bantu: migrations, expansion et indentité culturelle. Libreville 1–6 Avril 1985, Tome II*. Paris: Harmattan, pp. 317–335.

Shafer, Byron E. 1999. 'American Exceptionalism'. *Annual Review of Political Science* 2:1, 445–463.

Tessmann, Günter. 1991 [1913]. *Les Pahouins. Monographie ethnologique d'une tribu d'Afrique de l'Ouest* (Extraits)'. In P. Laburthe-Tolra and Ch. Falgayrettes-Leveau. *Fang*. Paris: Musée Dapper, pp. 167–312.

Trilles, Henri. 1898 'Chez les Fang: leurs moeurs, leur langue, leur réligion'. *Les Missions Catholiques* 30.

Trilles, Henri. 1900. *Dans les rivières de Monda (Gabon)*. Lille: Desclée de Brouwer, Société Saint-Augustin.

Trilles, Henri. 1912a. *Chez les Fang, ou Quinze années de séjour au Congo français*. Lille: Société Saint-Augustin. Desclée, De Brouwer.

Trilles, Henri. 1912b. *Le totémisme chez les Fân*. Münster: Aschendorff.

Trilles, Henri. 1920. *Deux ans de voyage dans le Congo nord: ancien contesté franco-allemand-espanol*. Bruges: Desclée, De Brouwer & cie.

Trilles, Henri. 1931. *Mille lieues dans l'inconnu en pleine forêt équatoriale chez les Fang anthropophages*. Paris: D. de Brouwer.

Trilles, Henri. 1932. *Les Pygmées de la forêt équatoriale, cours professé à l'Institut catholique de Paris*. Paris: Bloud & Gay.

Vansina, Jan. 1983. 'The Peoples of the Forest'. In D. Birmingham and P. Martin (eds). *History of Central Africa, Vol. 1*. London: Longman, pp. 75–117.

Vansina, Jan. 1990. *Paths in the Rainforests: Toward a History of the Political Tradition in Equatorial Africa*. Madison: University of Wisconsin Press.

Wilson, John Leighton. 1856. *Western Africa: Its History, Its Conditions, and Prospects*. New York: Harper.

CHAPTER NINE

Colonial medical anthropology and the making of the central African infertility belt

Nancy Rose Hunt

Even a cursory search for possible 'origins' of medical anthropology leads immediately to the medical doctor and experimental psychologist W.H.R. Rivers and his *Religion, Magic, and Medicine* of 1924. Rivers is credited with many things: inventing the genealogical method, welcoming Freud's notion of the unconscious into anthropology, studying nerve regeneration, and pioneering the method of participant observation through the notion of a singularly gifted witness. His interests in psychology and anthropology also led him to work with shell shock victims during World War I (Kuklick 1991, 1996, 1998). Less known is Rivers' intervention into Melanesian depopulation discourse. He downplayed the pathological role of venereal disease while psychologizing – *and politicizing* – the problem. In a lecture to doctors and public health specialists on 'The Dying-Out of Native Races' in 1918, Rivers quoted natives as saying, 'Why should we bring children into the world only to work for the white man?' Such melancholy and defeatism, he explained, was part of what lay behind 'racial suicide' in the Pacific. So was conscious voluntary restriction of birth through induced abortion. Indeed, the colonial-induced psychological problem was more consequential than the 'trivial' effect of sterility from venereal disease. The problem, Rivers insisted, had nothing to do with any 'original decadence' of these people. Rather 'the cause of the dying out of a whole people' amounted to the colonial 'production of native decadence'. In particular, 'unintelligent and undiscriminating action towards native institutions' had meant that 'the people were deprived of nearly all that gave interest to their lives'. What was missing was 'zest'. Not only had people been deprived of their native customs (especially head-hunting), but colonial labor conditions meant that their lives lacked economic intrigue, too. In sum, this expert on the relationship between psychology and anthropology diagnosed the major factor involved in this 'peril' of sterile marriages as 'psychical' (Rivers 1920: 109–110, 1922: 43), while pointing to the *colonial production* of the problem.

Such ideas did not disappear, even if the politics of Rivers' position often became lost, as the psychic became naturalized. Such ideas keep reappearing in equatorial Africa in the interwar and postwar periods, where Belgian and French colonial officials, missionaries and doctors worried about the psychological consequences of colonialism on birth rates and the fecundity of women. Outcries about depopulation and race suicide were not limited to equatorial Africa, of course. Topoi of degeneration and sterility had been kindling demographic disquiet in Europe for decades, and these anxieties were easily transposed and refigured as they moved echo-like between national and imperial registers and situations.

Infertility scares emerged in several African locations perceived to have low birth rates, and colonial anxieties were expressed in a language of depopulation and degeneration, sterility and extinction. They kept alive concern for vanishing races and species,[1] while using language reminiscent of representations of degeneration and the degenerate in European culture (Pick 1989; Brantlinger 2003). There was frequent recourse to a causal logic that assumed that low fertility combined a conscious and willed aspect (that is, in the form of self-aborting women) with a psychological or neurasthenic one related to the 'shock' of life under colonialism. A parallel to shell shock was not an idle metaphor. Shock became a household word in a globalizing lexicon during the World War I, and the trauma of war would have been exactly the comparison at work in W.H.R. Rivers' thinking when he first formulated his ideas about the psychic effects of colonial conditions on native 'zest'.

Most historians have found that the effects of labor migration on social reproduction and the control of women drove such demographic scares, which usually translated into anti-venereal disease campaigns (Summers 1991; Vaughan 1992; Callahan 1997; Wallace 1998; Jochelson 2001). Thus, for the most part, these have been histories of moral panic and sexually transmitted diseases (STDs), often in contexts where a tropical skin disease (treponemal yaws) was mistaken for venereal disease (Larsson 1991: 97, 103–105; Vaughan 1991). Given the overwhelmingly anglophone orientation of this historical literature, the work of Anne Retel-Laurentin has tended to be neglected, as has francophone equatorial Africa in general. Indeed, areas where childlessness pressed in on colonial imaginations as an urgent problem have hardly been considered.[2] This paper compares two equatorial situations where birth rates were low, and where there were childless women who wished to be mothers, as well as those unable to become pregnant again or carry pregnancies successfully to term – among 'the Mongo' in the Belgian Congo's Tshuapa District, and among the Nzakara in French Ubangi-Shari (a province of French Equatorial Africa, now the Central African Republic).[3] Unlike most of the British African colonial situations treated by historians, the Mongo and Nzakara fertility crises were in zones where discourses of moral panic cannot simply be seen with historical hindsight as excited misreadings of yaws rather than as venereal syphilis (Vaughan 1992). Rather, in these two parts of the Belgian and French Africa, infertility was not just an imaginary problem in the first half of the twentieth century.

Complex identifications and transferences were embedded in all such colonial infertility scares, whether the imaginary corresponded to social or biological reality or not. Statistical enumerative and interventionist practices – whether professional or amateur, official or unofficial – appeared and developed in relation to them, while some colonial figures were caught up in the moral panics that ensued. If voyeurism motivated some, humanitarian benevolence and scientific intrigue were also involved. If some investigators were professional experts, many were not. All observed, and most counted and reckoned with variations and probabilities. In anglophone Africa, these investigators included missionary anthropologists, district officers, colonial medical service and mining company doctors, and Native Authority chiefs (Callahan 1997), as well as missionary doctors (Larsson 1991; Summers 1991; Vaughan 1992) and settlers (Wallace 1998).

In the two equatorial cases considered here, although the realms of metaphor and language corresponded to some actual childless women and couples, these scares were no less forms of moral panic among European colonials and their African 'middles' (native intermediaries, experts, translators; see Hunt 1999). Indeed, there was a 'global circulation' of such 'ethnographic commonplaces of colonial intelligence' (Pels and Salemink 1999a: 23): racial suicide, dying races, empty villages and self-aborting women. Native women induced their own abortions; detribalized women avoided maternity; and the psychological shocks of colonialism and modernity vitiated the desire to procreate. So the logic went. And this global circulation was not unrelated to *national* and *nationalist* concerns with the birth rate, degeneration, and modern women at home (see Hunt 1999, 2002b).

This essay urges for studying anthropological practice within colonial situations in a capacious way that questions the distinction between the guild of academic anthropologists and other less schooled and credentialed practitioners. By comparing the ethnographic practice of a professional anthropological fieldworker in French Equatorial Africa with the ethnographic practices by practical persons on the spot in the Belgian Congo – missionaries, doctor, and a private colonist with time, ideas and experience on his hands – it works to 'unsettle the comfortable boundary of professionalism' within anthropology and focuses on 'practical relationships among observers and observed' in the field (Pels and Salemink 1999a).

Moving between Belgian and French Africa, this essay also takes up the reason to think about differences and convergences between ethnographic and statistical representation that Talal Asad (1984) posed rather elusively some time ago. Asad elaborated the contrast between the ethnographic and the statistical as one between the experiential and interpretative, on the one hand, and the enumerative, practical and interventionist, on the other. He was careful to not suggest that the ethnographic is benign, even though he associated the statistical with Western hegemony and forms of knowledge production intent on changing colonial and postcolonial worlds in relation to notions of modernity and progress. By clarifying the difference between these two modes of knowledge as centering on interventionist intent and capacity for comparative and de-territorialized analysis, Asad implicitly critiques the purifying, territorially bounded and anti-comparative tendency of the ethnographic. How are we to imagine the territorial microcosms that anthropologists study as incommensurable, he seems to ask, without doing so in a purified way that empties out the contaminations of history, politics – in a word, colonialism?

Asad's intervention also calls into question experience as the central foundation of anthropological knowledge. Of course, the privileging of ethnographic fieldwork has its own vexed history, and Asad (1984) has not been the only one to point to the kinds of natural science backgrounds of many early anthropologists who thought of experience less in terms of 'a notion of subjective vision and "empathy"' than in terms of experimentation within a laboratory. Still, the idea of the lone fieldworker has prevailed since the time of W.H.R. Rivers in British anthropology, and as we will see it became commonplace in French and Belgian professional anthropological practice after World War II.

By taking up an analysis of anthropological practice in two colonial situations where there was a sense of urgency about solving a social and medical problem, we enter into a revealing juncture in the history of anthropology – the splitting off of an 'applied' subfield called medical anthropology.[4] No subfield of anthropology has become easier to denigrate as complicit and atheoretical, as practical in insidious ways. Yet where did this subfield come from historically? How did its practitioners – both professional field anthropologists and other professionals and amateurs on the spot – produce knowledge? When did they work from experience-based observations, and when did they deploy more enumerative, interventionist, and governmental forms of knowledge? In sum, how did various forms of colonial eugenics or biopower produce this split-off, 'applied' and apparently lesser other?

Anthropology remains riddled by a hierarchy between the pure and the applied. Asad's elusive point is that the distinction is exaggerated and reified. A history of (medical) anthropological practice in two different colonial equatorial situations – one French, one Belgian – cannot be a purified history of professionally trained anthropologists alone. Rather, this paper contrasts the infertility work of two iconoclastic persons who combined experiential and enumerative approaches – one a Belgian *colon* (independent colonial resident) with a small plantation in the Belgian Congo, Charles Lodewyckx, one a French professional doctor and anthropologist working in French Ubangi-Shari, Anne Retel-Laurentin. The comparison enables an analysis not only of differences in French and Belgian colonial spheres of professional anthropology, but of an important realm of colonial governmentality: medical and eugenic reckoning and practice.

Flemish missionaries, an independent planter, and 'zest'

A file of letters between a francophone Belgian planter and a distinguished Flemish scholar-priest begin to tell a history of a campaign to re-inspire fertility among a 'dying race' of Congolese subjects, alternately called the Nkundo or Mongo of the Equateur region.[5] Not at all reluctant to investigate Congolese women's sexual hygiene habits, this planter with formal pharmaceutical training and experience in botanical specimen collecting, Charles Lodewyckx, began a crusade in 1946 to alter their enema and post-coital douching practices while keeping a count of births and pregnancies that suggested a rising birth rate. Colonial officials, doctors, demographers and gynecological specialists, as well as Congolese men and women, also became concerned about reduced fertility from the 1930s through independence in 1960. Lodewyckx's argument was distinctive, however, and he was the only *colon* to play a visible role. The birth rate was falling not because Mongo women did not want children, he contended, but because of 'unconscious neo-Malthusian practices'. These women were not willfully aborting fetuses, but accidentally preventing conception and provoking miscarriages through douching and enemas.

A 1931 report on labor resources in the region first touched off the outpouring of official, scientific and missionary concern about these 'lands without people'. Compulsory cultivation requirements and attempts to institutionalize a 'modern', regimented plantation economy in the 1930s were also working to pauperize the Congolese of this region (Nelson 1994). If labor issues lurked in the background, so too did colonial concerns about psychic trauma.[6] Depopulation mania peaked near the close of World War II, when the effects of the doubling of forced labor requirements to 120 days a year as part of the Congolese allied war effort became visible and acute.

Lodewyckx's campaign began among overworked, exhausted people in 1946, and culminated in the nearby city of Coquilhatville ten years later. He toured the countryside in a van purchased with native welfare funds, and increasingly communicated to Congolese through government-controlled communications media of the 1950s. When he passed through Coquilhatville, he would 'speak once or twice by microphone' with his voice broadcast via the three loudspeakers mounted in the African township: 'each time a crowd of attentive listeners crowd[ed] around these' (Lodewyckx 1949: 81). He held over 200 meetings in 1950 drawing some 12,000 listeners, and 159 meetings in 1951 attended by 15,000 people (Ghilain 1953). He also visited the capital city of Leopoldville where, with permission of the colonial information service, he aired his views on a Lingala-language radio show (Lodewyckx 1949).[7]

Colonial Africa knew other campaigners who gathered Africans together to view 'striking pictures' of the bodily consequences of venereal disease (Larsson 1991). Yet explicit images of venereal disease were not part of Lodewyckx's approach. Rather, conversations and lectures about sex and intimate hygiene practices constituted his method. He noted in 1948: 'I must say that up to now my views . . . have encountered less of an audience among Whites than among Blacks.'[8] Some Europeans were suspicious, perhaps scandalized too, while most doctors were focusing on gonorrhea, malnutrition, or psychic and endocrinological causes, not on indigenous forms of gynecology and maintaining bodily flow.

Lodewyckx's explicit language and prurient theme disturbed the local Belgian Catholic missionaries. Their Flemish national orientation colored their careers, as they became pioneering and prominent Mongo linguists, folklorists and nationalists. Jan Vansina (1994: 33) once commented about his years in the Belgian Congo: 'I was far too much of a Kuba nationalist and reacted to the local situation as a Flemish nationalist would at home'. As Flemish-language advocates located in the Congo, Fathers Gustaaf Hulstaert and Edmond Boelaert became colonial 'indigenists'. They founded the bilingual (French-Flemish) journal Aequatoria, dedicated to Africanist research and featuring African language texts and translations (Vinck 1987), and devoted their careers to preserving, recording and extending the use of the Lomongo language. Their publishing projects included Bible translations, a dictionary and grammars, as well as large collections of Mongo oral traditions, poetry and song. One of Lodewyckx's main interlocutors was Father Hulstaert, who fashioned himself as an anthropologist and linguist, while actively collecting and publishing demographic reports. Hulstaert was uncomfortable about the planter's unrefined language, but did not discourage his campaign among people who seemed to have lost the will to procreate. Indeed, he edited Lodewyckx's manuscripts while ensuring that the planter's promising statistics appeared in print in *Aequatoria*.

Boelaert (1945) could be a feisty and ironic colonial critic. 'Depopulation through colonisation?' was the title of one of his articles, where his logic resembled that of Rivers' on the colonial production of zestless Melanesian natives. While officials continued to report on depopulation in some Mongo districts in the 1950s, Boelaert insisted that the causes included the colonial political economy, its labor requirements and migration effects, all of which made 'life . . . more and more untenable' (Boelaert 1955). Mongo national sentiments underlay 'indigenist' missionary interest in Lodewyckx's campaign to save these Nkundo people who were, in Hulstaert and Boelaert's Flemish eyes, Lomongo-speaking members of the Mongo race. These Flemish linguist purists were troubled, therefore, by the fact that this francophone planter was crusading in the crude, colonial-invented vernacular of Lingala. Lodewyckx also tended to ramble; and he mixed men and women together for his explicit lessons. Nor was Hulstaert convinced that post-coital douching was a recent rather than an 'ancestral' routine, though over time he viewed Lodewyckx's campaign to alter practices that bordered on contraception positively. Not only did he publish three of the planter's four published articles in *Aequatoria*, Hulstaert also promoted the planter's crusade in his own writings (Lodewyckx 1948a,b, 1950, 1951).[9]

Relations between Lodewyckx as an ethnographic observer and the observed are difficult to trace. As Lodewyckx told the story, he began by talking to some of his plantation workers and their wives about douching and enema practices and then organized meetings where he dispensed advice about how to ensure pregnancies and births. Some Congolese gave him gifts as his truck passed, and others attributed the birth of a baby to his advice. He became a local hero of sorts, at least among some aspiring *évolué* men. Yet he soon combined that part of his knowledge that came from experience and listening with another enumerative kind, and this register was how Hulstaert guided his representation in colonial print. Lodewyckx counted births and pregnancies and ordered this knowledge in numerical tables. This harder language of statistics helped him get official backing. His advice-giving sessions – or were they lurid sex talks? – did not please all colonials, even if they drew crowds. Eventually the colonial authorities agreed to give him some funding for his campaign's motor vehicle because, at the very least, this campaign seemed to promote the kind of pro-fertility ambience that was needed in this plantation district, seemingly suffering from a partially psychic inability to reproduce.

For Boelaert and Hulstaert, two of many Flemish priests working in the Congo, if the Mongo were a dying people, their language, oral tradition and folklore were also threatened with extinction. The Mongo were a race and a nation, whose people, language and soul needed to be saved.[10] For Belgian colonial authorities, the Congo was *the empire*, and it was important to make it a well-engineered 'model colony'. Belgians did not dither when it came to progress and development. Having the best medical infrastructure on the continent was part of the spectacle and practice of Belgian colonial humanitarianism. Such an infrastructure, especially as it developed in the post-World War II period, meant that the entire colony became a laboratory.

Within this laboratory, some areas received special attention. From the 1930s, Belgian colonial doctors understood that gonorrhea and other STDs were likely part of the Mongo low birth rate problem. And almost as soon as penicillin existed, it began to be distributed – and not only for yaws, but for STDs. In addition, perhaps the most sophisticated infertility clinic in Africa opened its doors in the early 1950s at Befale, not far from where Lodewyckx ran his campaign. Even at Befale, however, psychic factors continued to weigh in as part of bio-medical reasoning. Dr Robert Allard completed plenty of gynecological examinations, performed gynecological surgery and dispensed antibiotics, but he also tested Mongo women's desire for modernity as a possible sterility-producing psychological factor. Allard modified a psychological projective test, the *Congo T.A.T.*, for his own purposes. Whereas the psychologist André Ombredane (1969) showed a series of images to Congolese informants and asked them to tell a story in relation to each one, Allard asked each of three groups of women patients, pre-categorized by gynecological condition in relation to fertility, to choose their preferences among six images. He pre-coded three of these images as corresponding to projections of desiring 'maternity' and three as desiring 'sterility'. Whereas, the images signifying a wish for 'maternity' consisted of household utensils, a mother with her children, and a mother nursing a baby, those signifying a wish for sterility showed a woman drinking beer, an *évolué* man doing 'non-traditional' work, and a bicycle! While admitting that his was an imperfect test and never dismissing gonorrhea and infection as epidemiological factors, Allard's findings led him to conclude that psychosomatic dynamics, especially 'the wish for modernist emancipation from the responsibilities of maternity, at least among young subjects', played a role in Mongo infertility (Allard 1956).

Professional academic anthropology was weak in Belgium and the Congo, in comparison with the more robust scientific operations of demography, medicine and gynecology in this colony. Anthropological practice within Belgium and its colonies had long been closely linked to exploratory travel and collecting (Schildkrout and Keim 1998; Fabian 2000), missionary scholarship and everyday governmentality, with considerable space within and beyond these realms for amateur activity. Travelers and colonial agents wielded ethnographic questionnaires from the Congo Free State days. Authoring ethnographic texts on beliefs, migrations and genealogies intensified as the practical imperatives of organizing native units into manageable sizes became a major aspect of territorial administration from 1920 on. It was not until after World War II that anthropological practice became detached from territorial administration, missionary scholarship and museum collecting and classification.

A canny history of Belgian and Congolese anthropological practice will need to track two dimensions: a history of collecting and classifying ethnographic objects as this became centralized within the colonial museum founded on the outskirts of Brussels in 1910 (Couttenier 2003; cf. Zimmerman 2001); and the humanist, hermeneutic tradition followed by self-trained missionaries, many of whom followed the Catholic *Anthropos* tradition of Wilhelm Schmitt (Mudimbe 1988; Vellut 2001). Poised between these two traditions is the fascinating Flemish figure of Frans Olbrechts, whose career moved between professional anthropological training and fieldwork in America and public exhibits of Congolese 'primitive art' in Belgium.

Olbrechts studied under Boas at Columbia University as a Committee for the Relief of Belgians Education Foundation fellow in the 1920s, followed by serious field research among native Americans in 1926–29. When he returned to Belgium, he combined ethnographic museum work at the Royal Museum of Art and History (not the colonial museum at Tervuren) with teaching courses in 'primitive art' at the University of Ghent. He organized major public exhibits in Antwerp and other venues that celebrated and classified Congolese art according to formal stylistic analysis as a way to critique the ethnographic exhibits at Tervuren, which he considered hopelessly old-fashioned. By 1947, Olbrechts was the director of the royal colonial museum at Tervuren, and during his ten years there he had its immense ethnographic collections inventoried and promoted the first professional anthropological fieldwork in the Congo. As the driving force behind the human sciences section of the Belgian organization the Institute for Scientific Research in Central Africa (IRSAC), Olbrechts sent his own and other students for anthropological training in London and Paris and then to the Congo for fieldwork. Daniel Biebuyck, Jacques Macquet, Jan Vansina and Luc de Heusch were among this first generation of IRSAC-funded anthropologists who undertook the first professional anthropological projects in the Congo working in a fieldwork tradition (Vansina 1994; Petridis 2001). Some anthropologists combined Olbrecht's interests in African objects that they defined as art with work in social anthropology, especially his student Daniel Biebuyck, whose approach was one of 'one tribe, one art, one society' (Vansina in Arnaut and Vanhee 2001).

None of the postwar generation of professional Belgian anthropologists did fieldwork with an 'applied' orientation, although there was a brief juncture when the idea of sending someone to do fieldwork among the Mongo arose. Olbrechts advised Biebuyck while he was studying in London that he would 'probably be sent to the Boende region among the Bakutu and Ekota to study the cultural implications of the denatality problem among the Mongo', but several months later, in 1949, Olbrechts changed his mind: 'Mongo studies were out of the question – I was grateful for this as I felt that the Mongo at that time were already too "touched"' (Biebuyck 2001: 111).

This decision was in keeping with the general direction of this first generation of professional anthropological fieldworkers. Their work was more aligned with the arts, oral tradition, myth and history than with contemporary social change or problems of nutrition, health or acculturation.[11] In contrast, in the mid-1950s in Paris and French Equatorial Africa, Georges Balandier was ambivalent about 'applied anthropology', but he was teaching courses in it and was involved in a Gabonese development project concerning depopulation (Balandier and Pauvert 1952; Balandier 1955).[12]

An important consequence was that someone like Lodewyckx had freedom during the same postwar years to produce ethnographic knowledge about local hygiene and enema practices among the Mongo. Projective psychological tests also emerged, if briefly, in relation to medical interventions in the Mongo infertility crisis. Lodewyckx was hardly representative of anything. Still, one must appreciate the extraordinary space that existed for this enthusiastic dilettante with his pharmaceutical background. He was able to move between the experiential and the statistical while producing colonial knowledge that held a special value at a time when psychological theories about the 'shock' of cultural contact permeated this colonial field.

After dinner in Bangui

If one goes north from the Tshuapa and Ruki areas of Congo's Equateur, crossing the Congo and Ubangi rivers, one arrives among the Nzakara-speaking peoples of Central African Republic. From this region hailed the chief critic of Hulstaert and Lodewyckx's writings on Mongo infertility, Anne Retel-Laurentin – a French medical doctor with professional training in ethnology.

Retel-Laurentin first went to Central Africa as a doctor in 1953, working for a diamond mining company in Gabon.[13] She planned to devote her life to medicine, but an automobile accident while in Gabon left her with a disabled arm and unable to work as a full-time doctor. She took up professional training in ethnology instead.[14] When she undertook research in Ubangi-Shari in 1958, she joined a sociological project initiated in 1954 by French historian Eric de Dampierre and Belgian sociologist Pierre Clément (Retel-Laurentin 1986: 5, n1). Clément did a thorough archival study of census figures and official and medical interpretations of it (Clément 1957). Retel-Laurentin, too, worked in the colonial archives and saw history as part of her project. And she became an historian of marriage and the exchange of women before completing her extraordinary analysis of the social epidemiology of Nzakara subfertility (Retel-Laurentin 1974a, 1979). When she first went to Bangassou in 1958, she discovered that 'miscarriages, until now not known, played a major role in the appearance of feminine sterility'. To understand why, she developed a method that linked 'conjugal, demographic, and pathological events', obtaining significant results by 1966 (Retel-Laurentin 1979: 7–8).

In 1978, Retel-Laurentin published a memoir about her experiences as an outsider, medical doctor, anthropologist and white colonial lady in Ubangi-Shari, the AEF province that became Central African Republic (CAR). She intercut her memoirs about her fieldwork among the Nzakara with a colonial dinner scene in the capital city of Bangui. French colonial officials quizzed her about her research, as domestic servants circled the table with wine. This sumptuous dinner where French colonial men blamed Nzakara infertility on their lazy men and loose, self-aborting women was not incidental, but rather an integral part of the social field she went to study (Retel-Laurentin 1978: 118–124). AEF officials also asked her about the 'serious' Belgian research on abortifacients among the Mongo. Retel-Laurentin scoffed at this 'thesis of voluntarily sterile women' and wondered whether

Father Hulstaert knew 'how people make children' (Retel-Laurentin 1978: 121). Later, in her synthetic work on the venereal nature of African infertility, she expressed outrage at the manner that Belgian Catholics misread the epidemiology of sterility as a psychological consequence of colonialism. Indeed, there was such a large and peculiar literature on Mongo infertility that Retel-Laurentin wrote a special case study critiquing it. She used the claims of Charles Lodewyckx, Gustav Hulstaert and others commenting on the Mongo situation to attack the excesses of neurasthenic theories about 'dying races' (Retel-Laurentin 1974a).

Retel-Laurentin's own writings reveal the colonial context in which she worked and the kinds of ethnographic occasions she co-produced. She stayed in village huts, slept on camp beds, befriended her research team, turned her home into a clinic and laughed with informants, whether women patients, their husbands or diviners. Retel-Laurentin also made friends, collected life stories and tales, and allowed herself to be seen as a doctor-savior figure who helped women become pregnant. It is not clear how fluent she was in the Nzakara language, nor how long her sojourns were during her eight years of research among the Nzakara. But several of her scientific texts evoke the intimate relations she had with the women whose bodies, social relations and life histories she had come to Ubangi-Shari to understand. In her case, ethnography bordered closely on experience, observation and an empathic approach to suffering.

She lived in villages with a small group of Nzakara interpreters and nurse assistants, and her interviews with women allowed her to

> discover their conjugal and family lives. We cared for people at their homes. We questioned notables, customary judges and diviners ... Periodically observing these groups allowed me to control objectively for the development of phenomena as disparate as the persistence of gynecological lesions or the conjugal and residential mobility of households. Besides, on an individual level, if certain women whom I interviewed between 1958 and 1966 remained strangers for me, others let me take part in their joys, difficulties, or regrets. During medical exams, couples talked about their difficulties in getting along in daily and sexual life. I compared their discussions to those I listened to during divorce and adultery proceedings, consultations with diviners, religious ceremonies. Such an approach was not only important in the analysis of possible causes of *dénatalité*, but also in discovering the importance of miscarriages and sterility in Nzakara life (Retel-Laurentin 1979: 8–9).

Retel-Laurentin once remarked to the French anthropologist Jean Rouch, when he teased her about her 'dying race' topic, that she had not chosen her own subject (Retel-Laurentin 1979). It is not clear who

[263]

did. Denise Paulme trained her, and Retel-Laurentin dedicated her comparative study on sorcery 'of the belly' and 'negritude' to her. Paulme outlived her student and posthumously helped publish the Nzakara stories (Retel-Laurentin 1974b; Retel-Laurentin 1986). Georges Balandier's influence is present in Retel-Laurentin's work. Indeed, the more politically engaged style of post-World War II, dynamic sociology[15] is evident in her methodology and frequent criticisms of colonialism. We perhaps cannot find a better example than Anne Retel-Laurentin of a French anthropologist who combined and exemplified so much: systematic, sociological data collection *à la* Balandier; archival research in keeping with her Ubangian colleagues, Clément and de Dampierre; and nuanced fieldwork and life history collection among women and oracles *à la* Evans-Pritchard, Phyllis Kaberry, and *Baba of Karo*. To these, she added ethnographic experiments with literary form *à la* Leiris.[16]

What made Retel-Laurentin unique was her subtle understanding of emic physiology as epistemology. At the same time, she did not reject biology: she found out who was sick and who was not, who became better and due to what circumstances. So, we could say, Dr Retel-Laurentin healed. She certainly dispensed some pharmaceuticals. But she also followed her patients to diviners and oracles. She used this rich interweaving of knowledges to undertake an anthropology of the body, to understand how miscarriages, prolonged labor in childbirth, infant mortality, and adultery confessions were integral parts of a widespread African epistemology based in a view of the belly as the site of diagnostic, alimentary sorcery techniques. This physiology rested not only on the opposition of being well- or ill-fed, digesting or vomiting food, but on a wealth of procreative and miscarriage-related metaphors, as in a full and pregnant belly as opposed to one that expelled a tiny, bloody lizard of a pregnancy. Thus, this doctor-turned-anthropologist of infertility, of the body and 'sorcery of the belly', simultaneously pursued clinical (biological) and ethnographic research among the Nzakara, as she sought to resolve 'the mystery' surrounding *dénatalité* among these Ubangian neighbors of the Azande.

In a 1963 UNESCO guide to Africanists, Retel-Laurentin indicated her professional identity as 'ethnologist' and her vocation as 'ethnological doctor in black Africa'. She was born in 1925, received her medical degree in 1953 from the University of Paris, followed by a certificate in tropical medicine from the Ecole de Médecine in Paris, and a diploma in ethnology and anthropology in 1955 from the University of Paris. Her interests are listed as: 'biological, statistical research in African countries; socio-ethnological studies among the Nzakara; change in the status of women in relationship to social development;

studies on magic'. She worked as a researcher at the Centre National des Recherches Scientifiques (CNRS) and undertook a health status study for Senegal's Ministry of Development. She also made a film called 'Le culte des ancêtres' (UNESCO 1963). By 1974, she had directed several projects in Ivory Coast, Mali, Senegal and Upper Volta, as well as CAR, and was the author of a 'thèse de 3ème cycle', a 'thèse de Doctorat ès-lettres', as well as numerous articles and two films.[17]

Retel-Laurentin was hardly representative of French ethnological training and practice in post-World War II Africa. A doctor and a feminist, she was a pioneering figure in the emerging field of the anthropology of illness within France, one of the few at the time willing to call herself a medical anthropologist. Indeed, when she organized a small conference on health and the human sciences in Paris in 1980, she punctuated the phrase 'medical anthropology' with a question mark (Retel-Laurentin 1983). Still, if she embraced the biological to point to STDs as a pathological cause of infertility, we should not forget that her first Nzakara work was on oracles and ordeals, a decidedly ethnomedical topic.

Also a feminist ethnologist, she twice joined female colleagues in joint publications. The first time was in 1960, when she and five other women anthropologists contributed essays for Denise Paulme's pioneering collection on African women. Retel-Laurentin's contribution is a remarkable set of life stories of five Nzakara women, representing different social classes and generations, in which she appears as doctor and ethnographer ([Retel-]Laurentin 1963). The other time was with La Natte et le Manguier, a collection of fieldwork memoirs written with Ariane Deluz and Colette Le Cour Grandmaison, fellow French feminist anthropologists of Africa (Retel-Laurentin 1978).

Her early death from breast cancer interrupted her translation work of sixty Nzakara tales that she had recorded on tape twenty-five years earlier (Retel-Laurentin 1986). Retel-Laurentin (1987) also helped organize a major medical anthropology conference, the proceedings for which were published posthumously. Cahier d'Études Africaines dedicated a large part of one issue to her and her work, including a bibliography (Biraben 1987; Hurault 1987). Since then her work has been largely neglected. How medical anthropology is elided in the important Dictionnaire de l'ethnologie et de l'anthropologie (Pierre Bonté et al. 2000) – figuring there only under maladie and thérapeutique – suggests that her work was not in keeping with those who sought to protect the subfield from anything reminiscent of American applied tendencies, safeguarding it as the anthropology of illness (Walter 1981–82; Augé 1986; Augé and Herzlich 1986).

This subdued reception of the work of the first French doctor-turned-ethnologist suggests the strength of the ambivalence toward the biomedical in French ethnology (Walter 1981–82), even though such misgivings have proved much less tenable since AIDS.[18] Indeed, AIDS, genocide and war-related rape from the late 1980s in Africa has led to a new wave of research on affliction, gender and the body, and medical anthropology has gained greater legitimacy as a social science in France and the francophone world (Fassin 1992; Dozon and Vidal 1995; Vidal 1996; and Becker et al. 1999). Perhaps the time has come to sympathetically reconsider the full corpus of Retel-Laurentin's Nzakara work.

Her biography is compelling indeed, as I learned in 2002 when I had the honor of interviewing her widower, the sociologist Jacques Retel, at his home in Paris. I learned on this occasion that Retel-Laurentin was a highly gifted and unconventional woman of multiple talents and indefatigable energy. She had an excellent musical ear, playing the piano until her car accident in Gabon, which left her in chronic pain for the rest of her life. She had wanted to be an architect when she was young, but her architect father insisted that such a career would not work for a woman. Her actively religious family was from the strongly Catholic and rebellious region of Vendée. Her eldest brother Jean was a doctor who ran an important hospital. Two of her brothers became priests. René Laurentin became a prolific and pre-eminent Marian theologian and historian with over 100 books to his name, many of them exploring Marian apparitions and other sources of popular Catholicism. André was more unconventional, an architect who spent time as a priest in a leftist order working with manual workers before it was denounced by Rome, at which time he became part of an artistic milieu in and around Montparnasse. Her older sister became a popular and maternalist feminist counterpoint to Simone de Beauvoir. Ménie Grégoire was a journalist, novelist and radio personality who first emerged within the French public sphere with articles in *Elle* and other women's magazines and a 1965 book called *Le métier de femme*.

By then, Anne had launched her own career as doctor and ethnologist, though one might say she had her own Marian beginnings, entering a convent when young; she left, however, after her brother André visited her there, saw her thinned and sickly, and encouraged her to leave. Even after choosing medicine, then tropical medicine, then ethno-medicine and the medical anthropology of infertility, what mattered to Anne was not science, but suffering, according to Jacques Retel. A visit to Albert Schweitzer's mission soon after her arrival in Gabon left her deeply disappointed. She had expected to be meeting a kindred doctor and musician also from a theological background, but she did not like the way he handled people, especially women.

Retel-Laurentin tended to keep it a secret within Parisian academic circles that her sister was Ménie Grégoire, the controversial French radio celebrity whose first name became a household word in all of France and francophone Europe as the first and immensely popular practitioner of what intellectuals denigrated as *psychiatrie sauvage*. From 1967 through 1981, Grégoire provoked public controversy while carefully steering the sexual revolution among the lower middle classes with her confessional radio talk show that aired every after-noon on Luxembourg's RTL station. She gave therapeutic advice to her mostly women callers, who spoke on the air about their problems – sexual, marital and otherwise; and received letters from thousands of listeners about their own experiences with contraception, abortion, battering, homosexuality, masturbation, marital loneliness, and the like (Cardon 1995; Gauthier 1999).

Retel-Laurentin's own life moved from a possible missionary direc-tion to one that was also therapeutic and feminist, and also in a decid-edly maternalist sense, focused as it was on female suffering arising from an inability to bear children.[19] If nothing else, this biographical interlude suggests that future historians of African anthropology might do more to consider the role of Catholicism – whether arrived at through upbringing or conversion – in drawing the likes of Evans-Pritchard, Victor Turner, Mary Douglas, Anne Retel-Laurentin, Johannes Fabian and René Devisch to the study of sorcery and ritual, spirit possession and indigenous therapeutics, and pollution and the body in Central Africa.[20]

Contrasts

This paper compared two colonial locations of ethnographic practice where low birth rates and infertility were problems. The contrast of the Belgian Congo and French Ubangi-Shari confirms Rita Headrick's (1994) argument that French doctors in equatorial Africa had reason to envy the Congo's well-developed public health care system; whereas the vision and capacity to deploy professional anthropologists to inves-tigate the complexities of a puzzle like widespread sterility were clearly better developed on the French side.

The practical observers of this paper's comparison could not be more different. One was an amateur, private investigator, who learned about local sexual hygiene and enema habits and allied himself to a Flemish scholar-priest keen to document the fertility problem in demographic terms. The other was a professional doctor and ethnologist who inves-

[267]

tigated infertility as a medical and social problem linked to untreated venereal disease, associated miscarriages, and sorcery accusations. (This contrast was not exclusive though, as other practical observers from the Mongo situation were also introduced: not only Hulstaert and Boelaert, but also infertility specialist Robert Allard.)

If the contrasts resided primarily in the observers and their texts, the analysis also embraced the sites of ethnographic occasions. In each case, though in quite different ways, infertility scares produced colonial gynecological 'clinics'. In the case of the Nzakara, Retel-Laurentin's research implied and produced clinical situations. She performed blood tests and pelvic exams, while testing for rickets and goiter and distributing antibiotics. In the case of the Mongo, the infertility scare led to the opening of a special infertility clinic, at a remove from the area where Lodewyckx campaigned. Dr Allard would have been better financed than Retel-Laurentin and able to undertake complete clinical and gynecological examinations including vaginal smears, tubal insufflations, radioscopies and uterine biopsies as well as gynecological surgery (Allard 1955; Romaniuk 1968).

Still, the frameworks within which these two doctors worked varied considerably. Retel-Laurentin not only functioned as a biomedical specialist; her observations extended to homes and oracles, the places where women sought social diagnoses and help with the social sequelae of miscarriages and infertility. No comparable ethnographic work was done among the Mongo. The psychological paradigm continued to fascinate and motivate research in the Mongo region, especially in an era when psychosomatic research on sterility was attracting attention in international infertility circles.[21] Even in Befale, where Belgian doctors understood the relationships among venereal disease, frequent miscarriages and sterility, the chief gynecological researcher continued diagnosing psychosomatic factors that contributed to infertility.

If 'the clinic' is not defined narrowly, as the biomedical domain of doctors and patients, it is possible to view Lodewyckx as an amateur medical anthropologist whose questions about menstrual and sexual hygiene were not far removed from the kinds of queries that intrigue more recent applied anthropologists working on AIDS in Africa. Indeed, his queries resemble the 'Knowledge, Attitude, Practice' (KAP) surveys of the late 1980s and 1990s concerning e.g. 'dry and tight' vaginal astringents (e.g., Vincke 1991; Brown et al. 1993). Retel-Laurentin's work, however, remains a model involving both sustained ethnographic and biological data collection, and insisting that care – that is, biomedical treatment – remain relevant and feasible. Care (if not empathy) also came into play at Allard's clinic in the Congo, as well as in STDs treatment in many hospitals in the colony through state and parastatal funding.

Retel-Laurentin infuriated colonial doctors in Ubangi-Shari and she outraged French officials and military doctors by insisting on living among these apparently promiscuous people, whose women were thought to willfully abort (Retel-Laurentin 1978). Lodewyckx's social distance from his subjects was greater, though he reveled in being viewed as 'the white doctor of Likili', understanding that this local nickname placed him more in the category of healer and prophet than Western medical doctor. While Retel-Laurentin directly attacked psychological theories, Lodewyckx's campaign consistently gathered its momentum from them. Such contrasts, unfortunately, do not permit an appreciation of the quality of Retel-Laurentin's work, nor the unusual amount of space that was available for Lodewyckx's unorthodox, eccentric campaign. This space was political and performative, but the amount of narrative pleasure that he and others found in his texts and drama should not be underestimated.

Neither Retel-Laurentin nor Lodewyckx blamed African women for not producing enough babies. Each espoused theories that ran counter to dominant explanations that focused on racial neurasthenia, the psychic shock of colonialism and the immoralities of aborting women. The affection that emerged between Retel-Laurentin and her informants (and patients) and between Lodewyckx and his native interlocutors and audiences may have been related to this novel, non-incriminating narrative of 'we-know-you-want-babies'.

Colonial doctors like Allard and his French counterpart, Lotte (1953), as well as a range of individuals who practiced demography, were observers whose biopolitical projects ultimately served modern governmentality. Lodewyckx's practical relationships side-stepped these verticalities; his ethnographic occasions seem to have been horizontal performances of tactical negotiation and exchange, though he relied on the encouragement and convocations of local chiefs. In contrast, Allard was more restricted to vertical encounters of disciplinary observation and discipline.[22] Retel-Laurentin combined both styles. She did much one-on-one life history collection and patient care, yet also benefited from the fact that the Nzakara were accustomed to lining up in rows for colonial medical census work.

Retel-Laurentin was asking extremely important questions by asking about the histories of accumulative polygyny, the circulation of women, and colonial forms of sex work, as she was by thinking about how infertility intensified distrust and sorcery accusations. But her anthropological training had her thinking more about social relations than it did about objects and their circulation. Lodewyckx was a maverick figure in part because he was thinking about local biologies and local technologies, about intimate cleansing and de-blocking practices and the quick trade in imported enema devices.

We can not fully know if Lodewyckx's message about douching less after sex and avoiding enemas during pregnancy mattered or changed many women's practices, but penicillin *was* there on the Belgian side and not just to cure yaws. The Belgians knew that they had an STD problem, penicillin flowed almost as soon as it was available, and the birth rate began to rise. One irony of the demographic construction of the 'Central African infertility belt' is that Retel-Laurentin's pioneering ethnographic work into the semantics and social implications of infertility has been effaced. But the comparison in this paper suggests something else: if professional anthropology focused on sustained fieldwork experience and open to practical problems was more developed on the French side, perhaps due to Balandier's felicitous sociological influence, the Belgians were by far the more gifted social engineers who were busy actually investing in medical infrastructure and research in the troubled equatorial realm that lay within their prosperous, modernizing 'model colony'.

A vexed field, a problematic belt

What might a proper history of the vexed field of medical anthropology look like? This chapter suggests that, at least for Africa, an excellent place to begin is with scientific practice in relation to colonial situations where eugenic and labor anxieties about 'dying races' and infertility flourished.

Histories of medical anthropology are typically cursory and instrumentalist, starting with W.H.R. Rivers and perhaps Evans-Pritchard and then jumping to applied anthropology, sanitation, health and development in the post-World War II period (e.g. Loudon 1976; Foster and Anderson 1978). When a more complex history along the lines suggested here is written, pre-AIDs and post-AIDS periods may seem appropriate. But such a periodization alone will not take account of the way a political consciousness of the vexed history of anthropology's colonial complicities has shaped the kinds of theoretical and political – indeed practical – questions about 'progress', governmentality, statistics and social interventionism that has been shaping the best work in the field. One emphasis of the 1990s, by Veena Das, Michael Lambek, Pamela Reynolds and Arthur Kleinman, among others, on violence, embodiment and social suffering remains critical of the domain of medical anthropology narrowly defined. Another important new critical edge has been the substantial wave of work on

[270]

women, reproduction and the body, initiated by Emily Martin, Rayna Rapp, Margaret Lock and Janice Boddy, etc., much of it influenced by Foucault's ideas about medicine and biopower. Such a history also will need to trace with greater detail how the semantic and semiotic orientation within French corporeal anthropology has been transformed by the urgencies of AIDS.

Still, work that combines sustained ethnography and demography, semantics and biology remains rare, and perhaps we should not be surprised that some of the best work on AIDS and biosociality in Africa is being done by those with training both in medicine and anthropology (Nguyen 2001). Retel-Laurentin's work suggests that combining enumerative, clinical and experiential forms of knowledge can be a productive way of simultaneously understanding biomedical and socially embedded etiologies of illness.

It is not only in the francophone world that ambivalence toward the postwar, American-dominated field of applied medical anthropology is evident. The anglophone field of 'health and healing' studies, pioneered by Steven Feierman, John Janzen and Murray Last in the 1970s, has also tried to steer a course that would hold on to the hallmarks of Africanist anthropological work, namely Evans-Pritchard and Victor Turner, while skirting the depoliticized and instrumentalist work of much applied medical anthropology. The issue of childlessness within fertility-associated cults of affliction has remained largely figurative and metaphorical, however, rather than grounded, as Anita Spring (1978) once suggested it should be, in an 'epidemiology of spirit possession'.[23] Given the anglocentrism of this literature, Retel-Laurentin's work has been overlooked along with most of francophone equatorial Africa. While childlessness has been discounted by historians intent on showing the groundlessness of moral panics, areas where childlessness was clearly problematic are only beginning to receive attention.

A new subfield of medical anthropology has emerged in recent years, focused on issues of infertility and reproductive disruption, though it risks further distorting the already distorted demographic notion of a Central African belt of infertility, partially by not carefully reading the full oeuvre of the distinctive and ground-breaking medical anthropologist, Anne Retel-Laurentin (Inhorn and van Balen 2002; Hunt 2005). This paper concerned two sites where low birth rates, STDs and childlessness flourished in colonial equatorial Africa. Each led to outcries about 'dying races' and depopulation and to particular densities of scientific and anthropological practice. If anthropologists have rediscovered sexuality in the era of AIDS (Adams and Pigg 2005), and historians have begun writing histories of STDs in Africa

(Setel et al. 1999), demographers have had free reign to write a history of population disasters in early colonial Africa. And they have inscribed as fact a geographical space known as the 'Central African infertility belt'.[24]

Statistics have effects, and one effect of the demographic numbers that emerged from the Belgian Congo and Ubangi-Shari was that the Mongo and the Nzakara became pivotal to this demographic invention of a belt of low fertility, a scientific set of facts that still shapes the way population and infertility are understood in Africa, despite the discontinuity in statistics from these regions (Romaniuk 1968; Belsey 1976; and Caldwell and Caldwell 1983). My point is not to dispute this statistical construction, but to interrogate the historical trajectory and causal logic implicit within its insistence on a common *territory* and thus implicitly on *nature*.

Was there a common local biology at work in these two colonial situations of childlessness that can be explained by the equatorial environment that they had in common? If so, it remains to be hypothesized and proved. Over and over again, colonials returned to the word 'mystery' because STDs did not seem to explain fully what was going on. The puzzle may remain, but trying to unpack it will not be helped either through demographers' maps or through hypothetical diagrams proposing a causal chain from Leopoldian-era rape to STDs to sterility (Voas 1981). Historical and demographic facts from the Belgian equatorial situation have became conflated with a venereal epidemiological logic based more on research in Retel-Laurentin's French equatorial setting, while the idea of treating yaws with antibiotics has become the major demographic explanation for the increase in female fertility in Central Africa.[25] The result is a large, unified and homogenized cartographic space, visually graspable, aligned with facile preconceptions about tropical nature, though simplifying and flattening histories of conquest, violence and gender that were dissimilar in more complicated ways than such maps allow.

Conclusion

To think of Lodewyckx as an 'anthropologist' and compare him to Retel-Laurentin is an audacious move, though it has been a productive one for the purposes of this paper – to draw attention to the diverse ways that colonial medical and anthropological knowledge merged the experiential with the interventionist. Retel-Laurentin effectively combined the interpretative with the practical, and at moments – when colonial and postcolonial authorities refused to listen to her epidemiological logic and the need for the massive use of antibiotics to manage

STDs – one senses that she could even become a touch shrill. Regardless, her work challenged anthropologists of her era who imagined a pure world of interpretative fieldwork experience, uncontaminated by the practical and the historical, including Western biological vocabulary, pharmaceuticals and enumerative practices. Lodewyckx's background as a pharmacist and botanical specimen collector perhaps oriented him toward speculation and new hypotheses, and he began testing the latter through conversations, observations, and counting pregnancies and births. It is not clear how empathetic he was, but the idea of a laboratory experiment was there, as was the scientific thrill that comes with feeling like one has made an important discovery.

In the post-World War II period, the academic distinction between the experiential and the enumerative increasingly became one between the pure and the applied, while one of the major subfields that mixed the two in the name of transformation, development and health was the vexed subfield of medical anthropology. The contrast offered here challenges the simplicity of thinking in terms of a pure–applied, experiential–enumerative, qualitative–quantitative hierarchy, while demonstrating that histories of colonial medical anthropological practice will require a capacious definition of this field science, whose practitioners embraced professionals and amateurs; officials, academics, and private persons; doctors, missionaries, credentialed anthropologists, and even *colons*. It also has shown that the practice of professional anthropological field work in the Belgian Congo came very late and was disassociated from applied questions of health and population, whereas many other actors in Belgium and the Congo – missionaries, officials, explorers, collectors, museologists – produced anthropological knowledge about Congolese peoples, objects and practices. Such a fluid situation meant that there was plenty of room for a relative amateur like Charles Lodewyckx to produce ethnographic knowledge about intimate hygiene practice.

Notes

1 On the history of literary expressions of the myth of vanishing races, pre- and post-Darwin, see Stafford 1994. The idea that birth control might lead to the extinction of desirable races was part of population and eugenic discourses in the 1930s; e.g., see Holmes 1932.

2 There are exceptions; see Headrick 1994; Cordell 1993. A new and very interesting literature on fertility anxieties is appearing, including areas where infertility is not a major problem; see Feldman-Salvesburg 1999. In contrast, see too Kielmann 1998; and the Africanist essays in Inhorn and van Balen 2002.

3 The strongest evidence for this among the Nzakara is Retel-Laurentin (1974a), and for the Mongo that of demographer Romaniuk (1968); also Voas 1981; White et al. 2001.

4 This juncture, interestingly, is not so different from the kind of social and governmental urgency of the 1840s that sought new, non-experiential forms of knowledge
to understand contemporary, newly industrialized society, through new kinds of
pragmatic, enumerative practices that led to social surveys and statistics; Asad
1984.

5 The Nkundo were one of multiple groups lumped under a single ethnic name,
the Mongo, by colonial administrators and missionaries. Colonial maps of the
Mongo expanded over time to cover almost a third of all Congolese territory.
Vansina explains the colonial use of a single ethnic name, Mongo, for most of the
societies of the central Congo basin (cuvette) from the fact that all these related
languages had proto-Mongo roots (Vansina 1987). The infertility scare among
'the Mongo' was concentrated in the northwestern region, among the Nkundo
although also found in the Boende and Befale area among other Lomongo-speaking
groups. I alternate between the terms Mongo and Nkundo, in keeping with
colonial usage.

6 Harms 1983; Boelaert 1952; Voas 1981; and most recently in a popular version,
Hochschild 1998. Although mortality from sleeping sickness was drastic in some
areas, the figures are notoriously unreliable and easily exaggerated.

7 See also Lodewyckx to Gustaaf Hulstaert, 1 October 1949, Fonds Hulstaert, Centre
Aequatoria, Bamanya, Congo Democratic Republic.

8 Lodewyckx, 'Note sur la dénatalité', 23 April 1948, Fonds Hulstaert, Centre Aequatoria, Bamanya.

9 See also Gustaaf Hulstaert to Charles Lodewyckx, 8 May 1956, Fonds Hulstaert,
Centre Aequatoria, Bamanya.

10 I explore their Flamingant national sentiments in much greater depth in Hunt
2002b; see also Meeuwis 1999.

11 The number of Belgian psychologists was not insignificant, however, as a UNESCO
(1963) guide on post-World War II Africanists suggests. Among Belgians, there were
also sixteen economists; thirteen sociologists; seven psychologists; five linguists;
five jurists; four political scientists; four educators; three demographers; one management sciences specialist; one historian/librarian; one technical advisor; one
human geographer and ecologist; and one missionary priest with no other professional identification. Six were born between 1887 and 1909; seventeen in the 1910s;
thirty-five in the 1920s; and fourteen in the 1930s. See UNESCO 1963. Luc de
Heusch was the only Belgian anthropologist to receive an entry in the Dictionnaire
de l'ethnologie et de l'anthropologie (Bonté et al. 2000). Biebuyck and Vansina
passed through University College London for training in fieldwork and theory.
Only Luc de Heusch went to Paris for training, with Marcel Griaule and Claude
Lévi-Strauss (Vansina 1987; de Heusch 2001).

12 Something called 'applied anthropology' did emerge in the Belgian Congo by the
late 1950s, but it originated in disciplines other than anthropology and was related
largely to issues of industrialization, urban sociology and acculturation, never to
medicine, nutrition and social obstetrics in the Belgian Congo. See Nicaise 1960,
who ignores the work of Jean-Paul Lebeuf (1957). For a perspective on how little
Belgian medical anthropologists have continued in this applied sanitary direction,
see Devisch and Sebahire 1991; also Hunt 2002a.

13 From the book jacket of Retel-Laurentin 1979.

14 Untaped interview with Jacques Retel, Paris, 29 June 2002.

15 For excellent reviews of this approach, see various entries related to the work of
Balandier in Bonté et al. 2000. See also Balandier 1960.

16 I am thinking of the extraordinarily modernist and self-reflexive ethnography by
Michel Leiris (1934), never translated into English.

17 The first thesis likely resulted in Oracles et ordalies (Retel-Laurentin 1969), the
second in her Un pays à la dérive (1979).

18 See Becker et al. 1999. On the contrast between anglophone and francophone
contributions to this major French-sponsored AIDS conference, see Hunt
1997.

[274]

19 I am deeply indebted to Jacques Retel for generously sharing his memories of his wife with me on this occasion, and I hope that I have done justice to their delicate nature with my summary here. On this occasion, I learned from photographs that Retel-Laurentin was a woman of striking beauty. I also learned that her life was marked by a series of things that went wrong and sometimes involved conflict: the loss of the use of her arm, followed by a long court case with the mining company over insurance and surgery in the United States; an invitation to help plan a major medical research institute in Gabon after oil was discovered there, for which she did an enormous amount of work before it was taken from her; her sudden expulsion from Central African Republic under Bokassa, due to a jealous Senegalese doctor who did not want her around; her subsequent infertility work in Burkina Faso, which was seriously damaged when lab technicians did not preserve the individualized nature of her blood samples, aggregating the STD data instead, thus seriously under-cutting the value of her corresponding personal reproductive histories; the threat of theft of much of her infertility data by some World Health Organization people that prompted her to quickly assemble her synthetic book on infertility (1974a); and various problems in the academic world of CNRS in Paris. Anne's childhood dream of being an architect was given new life during her marriage, when she turned an old factory building into their country home, a design success that made its way into the pages of an architectural magazine. She died of breast cancer in 1983, just days after the first major medical anthropology conference in France, which Retel-Laurentin (1987) helped organize. She was the proud mother of two children. Her circle of French feminist ethnologist friends was extremely important to her, and the sense of joyful solidarity when they gathered in the Retel home to celebrate the completion of her major work for CNRS was intense and palpable. Much of Retel-Laurentin's quantitative data no longer exists, though her library resides in the Fonds Retel-Laurentin at the Musée de l'Homme, and Jacques Retel still had much of her Nzakara material, including field notebooks, extensive photographs, and two ethno-graphic films in his possession in 2002, and was willing to consider sharing them with me on another occasion. Untaped interview with Jacques Retel, Paris, 29 June 2002. Retel's present wife, Marie-Paule Ferry, an Africanist ethnologist who knew Retel-Laurentin and her academic world, was present as well. I left the Retel home convinced that Retel-Laurentin's life and her work among the Nzakara is worthy of a book-length study. May these notes inspire someone to move in that direction. I am also grateful to Doris Bonnet for her recollections, generous help, and a lovely dinner at her home, also in June 2002, when I was able to meet other women anthro-pologists who had known and loved Retel-Laurentin.

20 I owe this insight to my marvelous colleague Webb Keane; see, for example, Fardon 1999. I would only add that it is not at all clear that the first generation of IRSAC Belgian social anthropologists was similarly motivated (they may have been Catholic, but ritual was not their big thing). Indeed, it would seem more important to not lose track of one of the major intellectual and aesthetic challenges to Catholi-cism in Belgium, surrealism, and the way that the latter combined with struc-turalist anthropology in the careers of both Claude Lévi-Strauss and his follower Luc de Heusch, the IRSAC-funded ethnographic filmmaker and structuralist anthropologist of Central African myth (Lévi-Strauss and Eribon 1990; and de Heusch 1998, 2001).

21 See the first volumes of the American journal *Fertility and Sterility*.

22 I borrow the vocabulary of vertical and horizontal here from Pels and Salemink 1999a.

23 Interestingly, only *zar* and *bori* have produced a book on 'women's medicine'; see Lewis, Al-Safi, and Hurreiz 1991.

24 First discussed in Romaniuk 1968, and coined as such in Caldwell and Caldwell 1983.

25 We can see this clearly in the most recent and excellent review of this literature, White et al. 2001, which documents the rise of fertility since the widespread use of penicillin in the 1950s.

References

Adams, Vincanne and Pigg, Stacy Leigh (eds). 2005. *Sex in Development: Science, Sexuality, and Morality in Global Perspective*. Durham: Duke University Press.

Allard, Robert. 1955. 'Contribution gynécologique à l'étude de la stérilité chez les Mongo de Befale'. *Annales de la Société Belge de la Médecine Tropicale* 35:631–648.

Allard, Robert. 1956. 'Essai d'évaluation des facteurs de sterilité chez les Mongo de Befale'. Examen B, Institut de Médecine Tropicale, Antwerp, 1956:55–56.

Arnaut, Karel and Vanhee, Hein. 2001. 'History Facing the Present: An Interview with Jan Vansina'. Available at http://www.h-net.org/~africa/africaforum/VansinaInterview.htm

Asad, Talal. 1984. 'Ethnographic Representation, Statistics and Modern Power'. *Social Research* 61:55–88.

Augé, Marc. 1986. 'L'anthropologie de la maladie'. *L'Homme* 26:81–90.

Augé, Marc and Herzlich, Claudine (eds). 1986. *Le sens du mal*. Paris: Editions des Archives Contemporaines.

Balandier, Georges. 1955. *L'anthropologie appliquée aux problèmes des pays sous-développés*. Université de Paris, Institut d'Etudes Politiques, 3 vols Paris: Les cours de Droit.

Balandier, Georges. 1960. 'The French Tradition of African Research'. *Human Organization* 19/3:108–111.

Balandier, Georges and Pauvert, Jean-Claude. 1952. *Les villages gabonais: Aspects démographiques . . . Projets de modernization*. Mémoires de l'Institut d'Etudes Centrafricaine. Brazzaville: Institut d'Etudes Centrafricaine.

Becker, Charles, Dozon, Jean-Pierre, Obbo, Christine and Touré, Mouriba (eds). 1999. *Vivre et penser le sida en Afrique/Experiencing and Understanding AIDS in Africa*. Paris: Codesria, IRD, Karthala.

Belsey, Mark A. 1976. 'The Epidemiology of Infertility: A Review with Particular Reference to Sub-Saharan Africa'. *Bulletin of the World Health Organization* 54:319–341.

Biebuyck, Daniel P. 2001. 'Olbrechts and the Beginnings of Professional Anthropology in Belgium'. In C. Petridis (ed.). *Frans M. Olbrechts, 1899–1958: In Search of Art in Africa*. Antwerp: Antwerp Ethnographic Museum, pp. 102–114.

Biraben, Jean-Noel. 1987. 'Anne Retel-Laurentin et les Nzakara'. *Cahiers d'études africaines* 27:187–197.

Boelaert, Edmond. 1945. 'Ontvolking door kolonizatie?'. *Aequatoria* 8:92–94.

Boelaert, Edmond. 1952. 'Ntange'. *Aequatoria* 15:58–62, 96–100.

Boelaert, Edmond. 1955. 'Dernières données sur la démographie mongo'. *Zaire* 9:741–743.

Bonté, Pierre and Izard, Michel. 2000. *Dictionnaire de l'ethnologie et de l'anthropologie*. Paris: Quadridge/PUF.

Brantlinger, Patrick. 2003. *Dark Vanishings: Discourse on the Extinction of Primitive Races, 1800–1930*. Ithaca: Cornell University Press.

Brown, Judith E., Okako, Bibi Ayowa and Brown, Richard C. 1993. 'Dry and Tight: Sexual Practices and Potential AIDS Risk in Zaïre'. *Social Science and Medicine* 37:989–994.

Caldwell, John C. and Caldwell, Pat. 1983. 'The Demographic Evidence for the Incidence and Cause of Abnormally Low Fertility in Tropical Africa'. *World Health Statistics Quarterly* 36:2–34.

Callahan, Brian. 1997. '"Veni, Vd, Vici"? Reassessing the Ila Syphilis Epidemic, 1900–1963'. *Journal of Southern African Studies* 23/3:421–440.

Cardon, Dominique. 1995. '"Chère Menie . . . "': Emotions et engagements de l'auditeur de Menie Grégoire'. Réseaux no. 70 CNET, Available at http://www.enssib.fr/autres-sites/reseaux-cnet/70/resume70.html

Clément, Pierre. 1957. *Contribution à l'étude démographique des populations du M'Bomou (Oubangyu-Chari, A.E.F.)*. Paris: Office de la Recherche Scientifique et Technique Outre-Mer.

Cordell, Dennis D. 1993. 'Où sont tous les enfants? La faible fécondité en Centrafrique'. In D.D. Cordell and J.W. Gregory (eds). *Populations, reproduction, sociétés: perspectives et enjeux de démographie sociale*. Montreal: Presses de l'Université de Montréal, pp. 257–282.

Couttenier, Maarten. 2003. 'Antropologie en het museum: Tervuren en het ontwerp van zelf en andere in een Belgische burgerlijke ideologie, 1882–1925'. Catholic University of Louvain: Unpublished Ph.D.

Devisch, Renaat and Sebahire, Mbonyinkebe. 1991. 'Systèmes de soins de santé traditionnels en Afrique centrale: un regard d'anthropologie médicale'. In P.G. Janssens, M. Kivits and J. Vuylsteke (eds). *Analecta de réalisations médicales en Afrique centrale, 1885–1985*. Brussels: Fondation Roi Baudouin, pp. 43–59.

Dozon, Jean-Pierre and Vidal, Laurent. 1995. *Les sciences sociales face au Sida: cas africains autour de l'exemple Ivoirien*. Paris: ORSTOM.

Fabian, Johannes. 2000. *Out of Our Minds: Reason and Madness in the Exploration in Central Africa*. Berkeley: University of California Press.

Fardon, Richard. 1999. *Mary Douglas: An Intellectual Biography*. London: Routledge.

Fassin, Didier. 1992. *Pouvoir et maladie en Afrique: anthropologie sociale dans la banlieue de Dakar*. Paris: Presses Universitaires de France.

Feldman-Salvesburg, Pamela. 1999. *Plundered Kitchens, Empty Wombs: Threatened Reproduction and Identity in the Cameroon Grassfields*. Ann Arbor: University of Michigan Press.

Foster, George M. and Anderson, Barbara Gallatin. 1978. *Medical Anthropology*. New York: John Wiley.

Gauthier, Marie-Véronique. 1999. *Le cœur et le corps: du masculin dans les années soixante: des hommes écrivent à Menie Grégoire*. Paris: Imago.

Ghilain, Jean. 1953. 'La dénatalité dans l'Ethnie Mongo'. *Bulletin des séances de l'Institut Royal Colonial Belge* 24:863–871.

Harms, Robert. 1983. 'The World ABIR Made: The Maringa-Lopori Basin, 1885–1903'. *African Economic History* 12:125–139.

Headrick, Rita. 1994. *Colonialism, Health, and Illness in French Equatorial Africa, 1885–1935*. Atlanta: African Studies Association Press.

de Heusch, Luc. 1998. *Mémoire, mon beau navire: les vacances d'un ethnologue*. Arles: Actes Sud.

de Heusch, Luc. 2001. 'Epilogue'. In C. Petridis (ed.). *Frans M. Olbrechts, 1899–1958: In Search of Art in Africa*. Antwerp: Antwerp Ethnographic Museum, pp. 289–295.

Hochschild, Adam. 1998. *King Leopold's Ghost: a Story of Greed, Terror, and Heroism in Colonial Africa*. Boston: Houghton Mifflin.

Holmes, S.J. 1932. 'Will Birth Control Lead to Extinction?'. *Scientific Monthly* 34:247–251.

Hunt, Nancy Rose. 1997. 'Condoms, Confessors, Conferences: Among AIDS Derivatives in Africa'. *ii: the Journal of the International Institute* 4:15–17.

Hunt, Nancy Rose. 1999. *A Colonial Lexicon: Of Birth Ritual, Medicalization, and Mobility in the Congo*. Durham: Duke University Press.

Hunt, Nancy Rose. 2002a. 'New Anthropological Perspectives for Historians?'. *Journal of African History* 43:145–148.

Hunt, Nancy Rose. 2002b. *Rewriting the Soul in Colonial Congo: Flemish Missionaries and Infertility*. Oretelius-lezing, University of Antwerp, 26 April 2002. Wassenaar: NIAS.

Hunt, Nancy Rose. 2005. 'Empty Wombs and Fertility's Fires in New Africanist Writing'. *Africa*, 75:421–435.

Hurault, Jean J. 1987. 'Un ouvrage méconnu: "Infécondité en Afrique noire" d'Anne Retel-Laurentin'. *Cahiers d'études africaines* 27:177–185.

Inhorn, Marcia C. and van Balen, Frank (eds). 2002. *Infertility around the globe: new thinking on childlessness, gender, and reproductive technologies*. Berkeley: University of California Press.

Jochelson, Karen. 2001. *The Colour of Disease: Syphilis and Racism in South Africa*. New York: Palgrave.

Kielmann, Karina. 1998. 'Barren Ground: Contesting Identities of Infertile Women in Pemba, Tanzania'. In M. Lock and P.A. Kaufert (eds). *Pragmatic Women and Body Politics*. Cambridge: Cambridge University Press, pp. 127–163.

Kuklick, Henrika. 1991. *The Savage Within: The Social History of British Anthropology, 1885–1945*. Cambridge: Cambridge University Press.

Kuklick, Henrika. 1996. 'Islands in the Pacific: Darwinian Biogeography and British Anthropology'. *American Ethnologist* 23:611–638.

Kuklick, Henrika. 1998. 'Fieldworkers and Physiologists'. In A. Herle and S. Rouse (eds). *Cambridge and the Torres Strait: Centenary Essays on the 1898 Anthropological Expedition*. Cambridge: Cambridge University Press, pp. 157–180.

Larsson, Birgitta. 1991. *Conversion to Greater Freedom? Women, Church and Social Change in North-Western Tanzania under Colonial Rule*. Uppsala: Uppsala Universitet.

Lebeuf, Jean-Paul. 1957. *L'application de l'ethnologie à l'assistance sanitaire*. Brussels: Institut de Sociologie Solvay.

Leiris, Michel. 1934. *L'Afrique phantôme*. Paris: Gallimard.

Lévi-Strauss, Claude and Didier Eribon. 1990. *De près et de loin*. Paris: Editions Odile Jacob.

Lewis, I.M., Al-Safi, Ahmed and Hurreiz, Sayyid (eds). 1991. *Women's Medicine: The Zar-Bori Cult in Africa and Beyond*. Edinburgh: Edinburgh University Press.

Lodewyckx, Charles. 1948a. 'Démographie: La dénatalité chez les Nkundo'. *Zaire* 2:915–921.

Lodewyckx, Charles. 1948b. 'Est-il possible de relever la natalité Nkundo?'. *Aequatoria* 11/1:1–5.

Lodewyckx, Charles. 1949. 'Sur la dénatalité Nkundo'. *Aequatoria* 12:77–81.

Lodewyckx, Charles. 1950. 'La dénatalité Nkundo: L'expérience Bunianga'. *Bulletin du CEPSI* 13:66–81.

Lodewyckx, Charles. 1951. 'Encore la dénatalité Nkundo'. *Aequatoria* 14:131–135.

Lotte, A.-J. 1953. 'Aperçu sur la situation démographique de l'A.E.F.'. *Médecine Tropicale* 13:304–319.

Loudon, J.B. 1976. *Social Anthropology and Medicine*. London: Academic Press.

Meeuwis, Michael. 1999. 'Flemish Nationalism in the Belgian Congo versus Zairian Anti-Imperialism: Continuity and Discontinuity in Language Ideological Debates', pp. 381–423 in Jan Blommaert (ed.). *Language Ideological Debates*. Berlin: Mouton de Gruyter.

Mudimbe, V.Y. 1988. *The Invention of Africa: Gnosis, Philosophy, and the Order of Knowledge*. Bloomington: Indiana University Press.

Nelson, Samuel Henry. 1994. *Colonialism in the Congo Basin, 1880–1940*. Athens, Ohio: Ohio University Center for International Studies.

Nguyen, Vinh-Kim. 2001. 'Epidemics, interzones and biosocial change: retroviruses and biologies of globalisation in West Africa'. McGill University: Unpublished Ph.D.

Nicaise, Joseph. 1960. 'Applied Anthropology in the Congo and Ruanda-Urundi'. *Human Organization* 19/3:112–117.

Ombredane, André. 1969. *L'exploration de la mentalité des noirs: Le Congo T.A.T.* Paris: Presses Universitaires de France.

Pels, Peter and Salemink, Oscar. 1999a. 'Introduction: Locating the Colonial Subjects of Anthropology'. In P. Pels and O. Salemink (eds). *Colonial Subjects: Essays on the Practical History of Anthropology*. Ann Arbor: University of Michigan Press, pp. 1–52.

Pels, Peter and Salemink, Oscar (eds). 1999b. *Colonial Subjects: Essays on the Practical History of Anthropology*. Ann Arbor: University of Michigan Press.

Petridis, Constantine (ed.). 2001. *Frans M. Olbrechts, 1899–1958: In Search of Art in Africa*. Antwerp: Antwerp Ethnographic Museum.

Pick, Daniel. 1989. *Faces of Degeneration: A European Disorder, c. 1848–c. 1918*. Cambridge: Cambridge University Press.

[Retel-]Laurentin, Anne. 1963. 'Nzakara Women'. In D. Paulme (ed.). *Women of Tropical Africa*. London: Routledge & Kegan Paul, pp. 121–178.

Retel-Laurentin, Anne. 1969. *Oracles et ordalies chez les Nzakara*. Paris: Ecole Des Hautes Etudes En Sciences Sociales.

Retel-Laurentin, Anne. 1974a. *Infécondité en Afrique noire: Maladies et conséquences sociales*. Paris: Masson.

Retel-Laurentin, Anne. 1974b. *Sorcellerie et ordalies. L'épreuve du poison en Afrique Noire, essai sur le concept de négritude*. Paris: Editions Anthropos.

Retel-Laurentin, Anne. 1978. 'Les soleils de l'ombre'. In A. Retel-Laurentin, A. Deluz and C. Le Cour Grandmaison (eds). *La natte et le manguier*. Paris: Mercure de France, pp. 85–183.

Retel-Laurentin, Anne. 1979. *Un pays à la dérive. Une société en régression démographique. Les Nzakara de l'est centrafricain*. Paris: Editions Universitaires, Jean-Pierre Delarge.

Retel-Laurentin, Anne (ed.). 1983. *Une anthropologie médicale en France? Exposés et débats de la Table ronde 'Santé et sciences humaines', C.N.R.S., mars 1980*. Paris: Editions du CNRS.

Retel-Laurentin, Anne. 1986. *Contes du pays nzakara (Centrafrique)*. Paris: Editions Karthala.

Retel-Laurentin, Anne (coordinator). 1987. *Etiologie et perception de la maladie dans les sociétés modernes et traditionelles*. Paris: L'Harmattan.

Rivers, W.H.R. 1920. 'The Dying-Out of Native Races'. *The Lancet* 3/1/1920:42–44 and 10/1/1920:109–111.

Rivers, W.H.R. (ed.) 1922. *Essays on the Depopulation of Melanesia*. Cambridge: Cambridge University Press.

Romaniuk, Anatole. 1968. 'Infertility in Tropical Africa'. In J.C. Caldwell and C. Okonjo (eds). *The Population of Tropical Africa*. London: Longmans, pp. 212–224.

Schildkrout, Enid, and Keim, Curtis A. (eds). 1998. *The Scramble for Art in Central Africa*. New York: Cambridge University Press.

Setel, Philip, Lewis, Milton James, and Lyons, Maryinez (eds). 1999. *Histories of sexually transmitted diseases and HIV/AIDS in Sub-Saharan Africa*. Westport, Conn.: Greenwood Press.

Spring, Anita. 1978. 'Epidemiology of Spirit Possession among the Luvale of Zambia'. In J. Hoch-Smith and A. Spring (eds). *Women in Ritual and Symbolic Roles*. New York: Plenum Press, pp. 165–190.

Stafford, Fiona J. 1994. *The Last of the Race: The Growth of a Myth from Milton to Darwin*. Oxford: Oxford University Press.

Summers, Carol. 1991. 'Intimate Colonialism: The Imperial Production of Reproduction in Uganda, 1907–1925'. *Signs* 16/4:787–807.

UNESCO. 1963. *Social Scientists Specializing in African Studies/Africanistes spécialistes de sciences sociales*. Paris: Mouton.

Vansina, Jan. 1987. 'Vers une histoire des sociétés Mongo'. *Annales Aequatoria* 8:9–57.

Vansina, Jan. 1994. *Living with Africa*. Madison: University of Wisconsin Press.

Vaughan, Megan. 1991. *Curing Their Ills: Colonial Power and African Illness*. Stanford: Stanford University Press.

Vaughan, Megan. 1992. 'Syphilis in Colonial East and Central Africa: The Social Construction of an Epidemic'. In T. Ranger and P. Slack (eds). *Epidemics and Ideas: Essays on the Historical Perception of Pestilence*. Cambridge: Cambridge University Press, pp. 269–302.

Vellut, Jean-Luc. 2001. 'L'Afrique dans les horizons de l'Université Catholique de Louvain'. In J. Roegiers and I. Vandevivere (eds). *Leuven/Louvain-la-Neuve. Aller retour*. Leuven: Leuven University Press, pp. 205–223.

Vidal, Laurent. 1996. *Le silence et le sens: essai d'anthropologie du sida en Afrique*. Paris: Anthropos.

Vinck, Honoré. 1987. 'Le Centre Aequatoria de Bamanya: Cinquante ans de recherches africanistes'. *Zaire-Afrique* 212:79–102.

Vincke, Edouard. 1991. 'Liquides sexuels féminins et rapports sociaux en Afrique centrale'. *Anthropologies et Sociétés* 15:167–187.

Voas, David. 1981. 'Subfertility and Disruption in the Congo Basin'. *African Historical Demography, volume II*. Edinburgh: Centre of African Studies, University of Edinburgh, pp. 777–799.

Wallace, Marion. 1998. '"A Person is Never Angry for Nothing": Women, VD, and Windhoek'. In P. Hayes, J. Silvester, M. Wallace and W. Hartmann (eds). *Namibia under South African Rule: Mobility and Containment, 1915–46*. Oxford: James Currey, pp. 77–94.

White, Richard G., Zaba, Basia, J. Ties Boerma and Blacker, John. 2001. 'Modelling the Dramatic Decline of Primary Infertility in sub-Saharan Africa'. In J. Ties Boerma and Z. Mgalla (eds). *Women and Infertility in Sub-Saharan Africa: A Multi-disciplinary Perspective*. Amsterdam: Royal Tropical Institute, pp. 117–148.

Zimmerman, Andrew. 2001. *Anthropology and Antihumanism in Imperial Germany*. Chicago: University of Chicago Press.

PART IV

Colonial states, applied ethnography, and policy

The scripts of Alberto Pollera, an Italian officer in colonial Eritrea: administration, ethnography, and gender*

Barbara Sòrgoni

Italian colonialism lasted some fifty years, from 1890 to 1941 and involved Eritrea, then Libya and Somalia, and from 1935, Ethiopia. In 1936 Eritrea, Somalia and Ethiopia were united to form the so-called Empire of Italian Oriental Africa (AOI).[1] Italian academic anthropology of this era was largely of the 'bones, bodies and behavior' variety (Stocking 1988) which assumed that a study of human bodies allowed one to make inferences about the behavior and psychological features of various races, and their level of civilization.[2] Until the 1940s, like early British efforts, academic anthropology in Italy displayed a 'historical and often speculative approach, that was primarily concerned with reconstructing the past of mankind' (Stauder 1993: 410). Given this concern with bones and its largely 'armchair' mode, it has been argued that no academic social anthropology existed in Italy until the end of World War II, and thus that the links between the discipline and colonialism were irrelevant in the Italian case (Lanternari 1974; Grottanelli 1977). Mainstream Italian scholarship has consequently assumed that academic anthropologists were not concerned with colonial issues and that no other form of ethnographic production (e.g. missionary or administrative ethnographies) existed or was worth studying. Yet certain professional anthropologists, most of whom did not travel to the colonies themselves, were concerned with issues raised by the colonial process and the racial classification of the new subjects, and wrote extensively on this topic (Sòrgoni 1998).

This chapter focuses on non-academic ethnographies produced during Italian colonial rule in Eritrea. It challenges the assumption that pre-professional ethnographies are irrelevant in the Italian case, since a consistent corpus of ethnographic documentation was indeed produced by travelers, missionaries and colonial officers from the outset of Italian colonial expansion. Colonial ethnographic studies were carried out mostly as a means of 'better' policing the new subjects, thus pointing to existing links between colonialism and anthropology, which still need to be thoroughly acknowledged and explored.[3]

This issue has been discussed in other colonial settings. Pels and Salemink (1994: 4) argue that Malinowski's introduction to *Argonauts of the Western Pacific* is an attempt to claim professional anthropologists' exclusive authority in representing the other, 'through a tactical denigration of both missionary and administrative ethnographies'. As scientific discourses gained authority and legitimacy, defining their boundaries through processes of inclusion and exclusion (Foucault 1971), anthropology built its own origin myth by expelling from its realm those 'practical men' who did not fit into the new disciplinary paradigm (Stocking 1983). Clearly, by distinguishing professional anthropologists from their non-professional predecessors, much disciplinary history has systematically neglected the pre-professional fieldwork phase, thereby obscuring both the links between anthropology and colonial practice, and the continuity between different ethnographic genres (Pratt 1985; Dirks 1992). Pels and Salemink therefore call for an 'essential move in the study of the history of anthropology . . . the dialectical one of accounting for the extra-academic and extra-disciplinary influences on the constitution of the discipline' (1994: 3), stressing the importance of the préterrain, the 'local colonial milieu' in which ethnographers' work was located and where professional anthropologists encountered local ethnographic strategies and traditions. They also show how 'administrative ethnography could create fertile ground for the relativist and functionalist theories of academic discourse' (1994: 14). This allows them to uncover a homology between colonial and academic discursive patterns, and to argue that theoretical innovations in academic anthropology (such as ethnographic holism, relativism and functionalism) are products of colonial practice, which can be found embryonically in preceding local ethnographic traditions.

The production by administrative ethnographers of static, homogeneous and separate ethnic identities is an issue that has also been explored in French colonial Africa, where both ethnographers and colonial administrators fashioned ethnic identities as discontinuous entities. Far from being mutually exclusive, these two concepts often overlapped. Amselle showed them rooted in 'ethnographic reason' – a classifying, separating and ordering operation – within the colonial practice of administrators-cum-ethnographers, and saw ethnographic comparative stances as stemming from the colonial milieu (Amselle 1990; Amselle and Sibeud 1998).

Within the Italian colonial context, the anthropological division of labor consisted of field collection of 'manners and customs' mostly by colonial officers with no specific training, relying almost exclusively upon administration questionnaires that focused on issues like land rights, crime and punishment. Indeed, throughout most of the Italian colonial era, colonial officials never received any training in the languages, rights or customs they would encounter in the colonies. Occasionally they were asked to gather data on behalf of metropolitan anthropologists. While the latter often expressed their gratitude towards these non-professional ethnographers for their collecting efforts (e.g. Loria 1912: 75; Corso 1916: 180), they firmly believed that they alone were entitled to transform what they viewed as raw data into sound interpretations. The men in the field were referred to as 'science's labor force' (Società di Studi Geografici e Coloniali 1907: 15). This division of labor also points to a peculiarity in the Italian case. Unlike other colonial contexts, until after World War II professional anthropologists in Italy usually derived their data largely from such 'amateur' texts. Furthermore, during the 1920s and 1930s – when British and French social anthropology was being professionalized – Italy was still largely concerned with physical anthropology. The advent of the Fascist regime reinforced this trend, as it was mostly interested in the classification, and separation, of different 'biological' races. One consequence was that an Italian cultural anthropology, clearly distinguished from physical anthropology and the related professionalization of fieldwork practice, only evolved in the late 1940s and, given the loss of its colonial empire, concentrated on internal folklore studies.[4]

This chapter analyzes early Italian colonial experience and its ethnographic production by focusing on Alberto Pollera, an Italian colonial officer who became a self-made ethnographer, living almost his entire adult life in Eritrea and Ethiopia. I focus on his early ethnographic works produced between 1902 and 1922 concerning aspects of the so-called customary laws: local justice in the western lowlands and the highlands of Eritrea, domestic and private customs, and the way Pollera defined 'tradition' while acting as colonial civil judge. His ethnographic knowledge evolved over time and reciprocally influenced his administrative practice. These two aspects – ethnographic and administrative practice – can be related to aspects of his private life as well. Pollera's complex personality, and the strategies he used to describe, police, or experience colonial subjects differed according to the various contexts in which he acted.

Ethnography and administration

Alberto Pollera was born in 1873 in Lucca (Tuscany) to an upper-class family. In 1894 he volunteered for military service in the newly founded colony of Eritrea, remaining in northeast Africa for the rest of his life. In this regard, his life is exceptional as very few Italians actually settled in the colony until the 1930s.[5] In 1903 he joined the civil colonial administration and was appointed first resident (commissioner) of the Gash Setit area, in the southwestern lowlands. Pollera lived in Barentu for six years, with his partner Unesc Araia Capte – a young woman from Axum, Ethiopia – and their two sons. In 1909 he was appointed commissioner of the Seraye region in the Eritrean highlands where he met Chidan Menelik, a young Tigrinya-speaking Eritrean woman from Seraye, who was to be his partner for the rest of his life. When he met Chidan, Pollera terminated his relationship with Unesc, but continued to provide for her subsistence until his own death. He legitimized and provided for the subsistence and education of the three children born to Unesc and the three children born later to Chidan. This behavior was atypical since the vast majority of Italians who fathered children with local women neither legitimized nor supported them.[6]

In 1917 Pollera was appointed 'Royal Commercial Agent' in Ethiopia and lived in Dessie and Adwa until 1928 with Chidan and their two younger children, and in Gonder until 1932 as Italian consul. On the eve of the Italian conquest of Ethiopia, after spending a few months in Adwa to set up the civil administration, he returned to Asmara where he was to remain until his death in 1939, responsible for the Government library and serving as private counselor to the governor of Eritrea, Giuseppe Daodiace. A few days before Pollera's death he married Chidan Menelik, as a protest against the Fascist law (R.D.L. 17.11.1938-XVII, n. 1728) that prohibited marriage between the 'Italian race' and any other 'race'.

Pollera wrote one of his first ethnographic notes in 1903, shortly after he was appointed resident in the Gash Setit area, in response to a circular requesting information about the most common local crimes and the traditional customary penalties adopted. This information was required for impending promulgation of the colonial civil and penal codes, which would establish which customary norms were to be preserved or suppressed by the colonial power. Thus, as Pels and Salemink wrote, 'ethnography, embedded in an administrative practice, was a legalist act' and the 'synecdoche that was most probably dominant in understanding social wholes in the political field was what Europeans perceived as "customary law"' (1994: 11–12). Pollera responded, listing crimes and penalties and suggesting appropriate political action. Two issues, he opined, required earnest intervention: denunciation and arrest. The Kunama, he explained, did not denounce or arrest someone charged with a crime because of 'the strong solidarity existing among members of the same community', and he urged firm reaction, either by punishing the whole village or by setting a price on the offender's head.[7]

Comparing this early note to his first published monograph, *I Baria e i Cunama* (Pollera 1913a), one can see how Pollera developed his ethnographic skills and how his growing familiarity with the local context was reflected in his administrative practice. Pels has argued concerning Tanganyika that British administrators often had high professional standards, a quality that academics denied during their drive to professionalize anthropology. This raises questions concerning 'the social differences expressed in the discourse of academics as compared to "practical" ethnographers' (Pels 2000). In this regard, the Italian case was clearly different, as Italian academics remained interested largely in physical anthropology and gave only marginal attention to social issues. Consider, for example, how Nello Puccioni, a prominent anthropologist, used Pollera's monograph *I Baria e i Cunama* (Pollera 1913a). While the monograph is entirely devoted to historical and social aspects, Puccioni (1915) only focused on the short Appendix that provided Kunama physical measurements. Indeed, for some years Italian academics simply ignored the ethnological data and interpretations Pollera provided, while discussing extensively the little anthropometric data he had collected. It was only in 1937 that Puccioni wrote a monograph on Somali social customs and in the introduction presented his work as 'the brother' of Pollera's books (Puccioni 1937: viii).

In *I Baria e i Cunama* Pollera wrote that after many years spent among the Kunama he was finally persuaded that a direct adoption of Italian justice and penal sanctions could not fit with radically different customs. He further argued that the use of firm and severe methods did not take into account that 'any custom, however barbarian it may be, is always rooted in the historical necessity of a specific context' (Pollera 1913a: 159). Given this proto-functionalist view, Pollera adopted a different administrative strategy, abandoning those penalties he had previously suggested, including imprisonment, since he pointed out that jail as an institution did not exist among the natives, and they would thus suffer greatly from incarceration. More generally prison could corrupt individuals, while justice purportedly rehabilitated

(Pollera 1913b: 19). On the other hand, his new strategy was rooted in local realities. 'Crimes', such as ritual killing of an enemy by young Kunama men before getting married, a practice Italian colonial justice could not tolerate, was in his opinion, a functional strategy adopted by the group to survive and protect itself against protracted and continuous external assaults from neighboring groups. Rather than resorting to severe punishments, he argued that Italian colonialism should concentrate on a long-term policy based on pacifying the area and thus eliminating the very function of those killings.

Conjointly Pollera deployed a new tactic, replacing punishment with 'persuasion'. Pollera found that the harsh punishments he had imposed earlier to stem ritual killings had proved useless: the custom was still flourishing, but was now performed secretly, suggesting to Pollera that 'tradition' could not be suppressed with a violent external intervention, but rather had to be transformed from the inside. Marta Pollera recalled:

> My father tried to show them that this [ritual killing] was not right, while other customs could be preserved. This is how he behaved: he told them 'if someone comes to you and tries to kill you, would you like that? You would not. So why should you do this to other persons?'. This is the type of argument he used with them. He tried to reason assuming their own mentality, and showing them where they were wrong.[8]

This persuasive strategy is confirmed by an event which Pollera regarded as highly important. In March 1909 he organized a solemn oath for various Kunama chiefs, which was staged under his direction at the sacred stone of Betcom, in accordance with what he imagined to be the traditional mode, and legitimized by the presence of the colonial governor in person. Pollera prepared a speech in the local language and tried to replicate the traditional oath: the chiefs were to swear in the name of local divinities Anna, Adum and Aua, with the traditional penalty for perjury being applicable (Pollera 1913a: 253–254). He thus sought to appropriate and manipulate a local institution – the oath – and the expressive modes in which it was performed, and to use them to modify local customs to suit colonial administrative needs. His strategy, and the way in which he explained it to his daughter, suggests a highly paternalistic attitude, which condemned the use of colonial violence. He strongly believed in, and supported, the so-called civilizing mission of colonial conquest, which in his practice amounted to a 'teaching' attitude and a parallel perception of the colonial subjects as lesser beings who needed Europeans in order to evolve. By conflating violence with the use of physical force, he did not see that violence and racism were embedded in the very concept of 'civilizing mission', as well as in every colonial encounter (Mbembe 2000).

Not only did the prolonged field experience change how Pollera administered justice, but it also changed his mode of ethnographic understanding. In 1902 he wrote his first ethnographic note on the Kunama, probably in response to the continuous urgings of the first civil governor, Ferdinando Martini, for officers to write about the people under their jurisdiction (Martini 1913). While he later made an effort to learn the local language, in this particular case he resorted to interpreters for the collection of data. A covering memorandum described the methods used. He had interviewed local chiefs on 'intimate and domestic issues' in order to have access to their 'manners, customs and traditions' and had documented only those customs which were validated by more than one informant and which he had personally witnessed.[9]

This methodological explanation is noteworthy because, two years later, the geographer and geologist Olinto Marinelli emphasized the need to compile special instructions specifically tailored to enable colonial officers and officials to carry out scientifically valid research (Marinelli 1905). This led to the 1907 publication of the *Istruzioni per lo studio della Colonia Eritrea* ('Instruction for the study of the Eritrean colony'), that stemmed from the colonial congress held in Asmara in 1905, attended by Italian professional anthropologists.[10] The *Istruzioni*, written by the most prominent Italian anthropologists, suggested that officers collect only that information shared by various informants and directly verified by the researcher, thus validating Pollera's stance.

The 1902 notes presented a structure similar to his 1913 monograph: both had sections devoted to the ethnic origin and history of the local population, its language, religion, political structure, domestic and family life, economic structure and concluded with remarks, offering policy guidelines that called for the valorization of local customs, which, in his opinion, 'cannot be eradicated' but had to be slowly modified or even preserved, given their function within the local context.[11] What differs between the two papers is not only greater details, but that customs or institutions which in the early notes were merely presented as exotic traits 'of a people so far behind us in the civilization ladder', are viewed in the monograph in historical terms. This stemmed largely from Pollera's increased familiarity with the Kunama after six years of residence, and partly from his participation in the 1905 colonial conference, where he had his first contact with professional anthropologists. A clear example of his interpretive shift is found in his analysis of the Kunama language. In the notes, he described the linguistic structure as 'very simple' – an error derived from the fact that Pollera never understood that it was a tone language – and this in turn he took as a demonstration of Kunama's primitive and childish psychology, which by nature was unable to evolve.

In contrast, the later monograph tried to explain rather than simply judge, thus shifting the emphasis from biology to history. Kunama history was tragic; they had endured continuous assaults from neighboring groups who had destroyed villages and enslaved and killed villagers. In Pollera's opinion this explained their assumed backwardness: rather than being biologically unable to evolve, Kunama had had no historical chance to do so (Pollera 1913a: 245).

Clearly, Pollera was justifying colonialism on the grounds that it would enforce those peaceful conditions under which Kunama could evolve. At the same time, he never questioned their purported primitiveness, and his text – for decades the only ethnographic monograph devoted to that group – contributed to a stereotyped and racist image of the Kunama as the most primitive group of the colony.[12] While using an evolutionary paradigm, Pollera's attempt to understand local customs against a historical background allowed him to shift from mere description and statement of otherness and incommensurability to a tentative interpretation of difference. In his view, Italian citizens in the mainland held 'imagined dreams of a fantastic environment' about the colony, which even postulated the existence of cannibalism. His ethnographic effort – as he repeated in the preface of each publication – was to replace those fantasies with knowledge and understanding, because to 'comprehend allows us also to partially justify barbarianism' (Pollera 1913a: 2). To understand meant attributing function to these customs that superficially appeared to others as savage. In this sense his proto-functionalism is related to proto-relativism since different contexts justify different (even apparently barbaric) customs.

Pollera juxtaposed visions of 'barbarianism' with an embryonic form of relativism in other papers as well. In one case, a 1905 article on Kunama beekeeping, he suggested that, in some situations, local knowledge was more effective than that imposed by the 'superior' colonizers. Their practices were not as 'irrational' as they first appeared. Kunama, he explained, used to push away bees from their hives with torches, absent-mindedly dropping sparks that set their fields on fire:

> One day I tried very hard to persuade the elders about the damages that their carelessness caused, and pointed to the herds grazing in the green fields nearby, a true vision of peace and prosperity; then I pointed to faraway hills, black and burnt, which signalled sadness and hunger. I hoped my feelings could be perfectly shared by my audience, when sud-

denly an old man said to me: 'from those black hills, no locusts will come this year'. So I shut up, pondering which of the two disgraces was worse. (Pollera 1905: 559)

Gender and the definition of tradition

During the nineteenth and early twentieth centuries, legal features, in the form of customary norms, were a core issue in both administrative and ethnographic practice; they were also a central theme in Pollera's activities. While stationed at Adi Ugri, the 1908 *Ordinamento della giustizia nella colonia Eritrea* ('Judicial system of the Eritrean colony') was promulgated, establishing four levels of jurisdiction. In civil suits where no Italian citizens were involved, the local population was first to resort to their village chief; if no agreement was reached, they turned to the district chief and, if again no solution was found, to the Italian commissioner who could ultimately ask the governor to take a final decision. As commissioner of the Seraye region, Pollera was therefore also acting as civil judge. The *Ordinamento* required that colonial officers submit annual reports to the administration on civil sentences, so that local customs could be documented and used by future officers for enhanced administration. The plan was unsuccessful because officials neglected to provide the central administration with such reports, despite repeated requests.[13]

Given this lacuna, Pollera felt the need to write a detailed report on Seraye customs. In a covering letter to governor Salvago Raggi he explained:

> What I describe in these pages is not new: local legal and procedural traditions were shaped through centuries. Mothers transmitted them to their babies through breastfeeding; the following generations completed and refined them. Each of our Abyssinian subject is skilled on the issue. But we, the civilized and educated masters, ignore these laws, which were never written down, were rarely and only partially documented by explorers and travelers, and which nobody, to my knowledge, cared to report in a clear and complete way. Yet, since we are supposed to administer justice, we should apply them. This is why I thought it useful to gather information on this subject.[14]

At the 1905 Asmara colonial conference attended by Pollera, the anthropologist Lamberto Loria had already lamented this lack of knowledge and argued that the concept of race superiority, if wrongly applied, always led to abuses, and called for a deeper knowledge of local customs since 'even ideas about propriety and honesty, concepts about good and evil change according to different populations' (Rossetti 1906: 124). Pollera's monograph *I Baria e i Cunama* shows that he had been

[293]

partly influenced by the methodological suggestions expressed in the *Istruzioni* (Società di Studi Geografici e Coloniali 1907). But it also shows some independence derived from his own experience and interests. For example, the *Istruzioni* suggested that physical features of the people be the first priority of any scientific ethnography, with social customs following, almost as if derived from the first. Pollera inverts this and relegates physical data to a final, short appendix. Culture or customs, he held, were derived pre-eminently from history and context rather than biology. When, shortly after, he turned his interest to the Abyssinians, he concentrated entirely on social aspects and completely neglected anthropometry.

In 1913 the Colonial Office published Pollera's report on Abyssinian justice in the colonial monographic series. *L'Ordinamento della giustizia e la procedura indigena in Etiopia e in Eritrea* ('Indigenous justice and procedure system in Ethiopia and Eritrea') focused on the Tigrinya-speaking people of the Seraye highlands where Pollera lived for ten years. Pollera justified his effort: 'in the Abyssinian countries we occupy, the indigenous judicial organization is fundamentally good, and we must accept and preserve it since there is no real reason to replace it with our own law' (Pollera 1913b: 83–84). He had no doubt that the spirit of Italian law was 'naturally superior', but considered indigenous procedure able to guarantee respect of local customs. He thus described various local legal institutions, as well as penalties. The colonial government had modified the latter, he reported, when they applied too harsh corporal punishments, and substituted it with imprisonment despite the fact that prisons did not exist in the area.

Pollera stressed the need to replace common sense with what he termed 'real knowledge' of local customs, derived from interviewing and listening to the natives. Dialogue with the natives, he suggested, should replace superficial stereotypes and common sense. Explicitly addressing his colleagues, he reminded them that Abyssinians were 'by nature willing to speak . . . therefore it is necessary to patiently listen to them' in order to avoid partiality and arbitrariness (Pollera 1913b: 55). His own method as recalled by his elder son, Giovanni, was to move restlessly about the region verifying each dispute on the spot: 'his office was often a tent or, following local manners, under the shade of a huge sycamore'.[15]

Pollera's text on legal aspects was published in the same year as *I Baria e i Cunama*, but the two scripts differ in relation to literary and rhetorical strategies. The latter monograph, which was actually completed in 1909, focused on groups that were poorly known to colonial officials. In contrast to travelers like James Bruce, Werner Munzinger or the scholar Carlo Conti Rossini, who had only briefly visited the region, Pollera actually remained in the area for some years and this gave his book greater authority. Influenced by evolutionary beliefs, he assumed that, being 'matriarchal' (i.e. matrilineal) and 'egalitarian' (i.e. segmentary) societies, and darker in color than the 'superior' Hamites (i.e. the Abyssinians), Kunama were necessarily inferior. But he was also influenced by a local belief and failed to question the stereotyped image conveyed by Abyssinians and Habab – who regarded the Kunama as potential slaves – thus enjoying what Legesse later termed 'vicarious ethnocentrism' (Legesse 1973: 276). It was this perception of inferiority which accounts for Pollera's literary strategy. Viewing Kunama as a separate but internally homogeneous entity, a well-defined tribe different and separated from all other groups because of its uniqueness and primitiveness, he believed he could describe each aspect of their society in a single book. Their social structure appeared so simple that a single monograph was deemed sufficient to summarize the main aspects of the whole society. By contrast, 'Abyssinians' were perceived popularly and in administrative practice and scientific literature as more complex and more advanced societies. Anthropological classification placed them among the 'superior barbarians', halfway between primitives and civilized groups (Mochi 1900: 92).[16] Consistent with this perception, Pollera did not produce a single book to describe them, opting instead for a series of ethnographic papers, each dealing with a specific aspect of their social structure. In this sense, in relation to the people of the highlands, he adopted a holistic view in which a single social aspect was treated as synecdoche, as a part standing for the whole. This points again to the problematic relationship and reciprocal influences between 'practical men' and academics. It is difficult to assess whether something he had read shaped his new strategy; his library was rather diverse, comprising mostly travel accounts or diaries, historical books, chronicles and ancient manuscripts in a variety of languages, as well as unpublished officials' reports. But he does appear to have been particularly influenced by Conti Rossini, one of the few scholars to have spent some time in the colony. In many ways Pollera's case might be compared to that of Maurice Delafosse, a more famous administrator/ethnographer (Amselle and Sibeud 1998); yet, in contrast to the latter, he never belonged to learned societies. It is true that at death he was lauded as 'one of the most important Italian Africanists' who 'left no issue unexplored in relation to juridical, historical, social and religious aspects of Eritrean and Ethiopian populations' (respectively, La Nazione, 8.8.1939; Rivista delle colonie 10.1939). But because of the hierarchical division of labor within the discipline, Pollera's work was rarely acknowledged by academics.

In relation to other colonial contexts, it has been argued that different literary strategies were called for, depending on varying perceptions of local societies, which in turn were derived from operations of racial classification and ordering. These varied literary strategies also reflected different administrative practices. Amselle (1990) has pointed out that ethnic invention was the outcome of the joint efforts of ethnographers and colonial administrators. Indeed, with his ethnographic and administrative practice Pollera contributed to the strengthening of different ethnic identities for the people of the western lowlands and those of the highlands. Confronted with what were perceived and represented as radically different groups, the colonial government adopted different administrative policies, which, in turn, contributed to the essentialization of ethnic differences. For example, for the 'egalitarian' Kunama the government imposed a chieftainship, while in 'feudal' Abyssinian society it sought to abolish the threatening authority and power of district chiefs by strictly controlling their actions.

Pollera's last work on Seraye is a book *La Donna in Etiopia* ('The woman in Ethiopia' 1922). At that time no professional Italian anthropologist had extensively addressed a similar topic, and when they did, they referred to the 'Female Sex' in its totality, with no specification of time or space (Puccini 1980). Pollera was aware of the peculiarity of his selected topic, since he felt the need to repeatedly justify his choice in a letter to the governor:

> From the very beginning of my not short colonial life, I happened to hear in the natives' chats, the words *resti, sabaiti, carci* (land, woman, money); I would even say that almost any discussion I heard mentioned at least one of these words. When, at a later stage, I performed my duty as colonial judge, I was surprised to notice that almost in any suit land, woman or money were directly or indirectly involved in the dispute.[17]

The practice of listening carefully to the natives, which he had advocated in his earlier reports, led Pollera to select research topics by focusing on what local people considered important. Applying this criterion, he decided to also write about land and monetary issues (Pollera 1913c, 1916).

Pollera gave another reason for his new book. He noted that: 'to examine [the Ethiopian woman] allows us to have access to domestic institutions of the indigenous Christian population, with its origin, its characters, its values and its faults.'[18] To obtain access to women's spheres of intervention and action, Pollera could rely upon his partner Chidan, who lived with him, and he always acknowledged her invaluable support, interpretations and explanations.

It is likely that local women of the district turned to Chidan to intercede with him in disputes concerning them, so that she probably had access to insider stories behind public stances. Yet it was mostly as civil judge that Pollera examined local inhabitants and posed specific questions concerning traditional dispute management techniques and social issues. Pollera himself was aware of the opportunity (and power) his role granted him:

> Each new case offered me the opportunity to penetrate the indigenous mentality and soul, in order to discover, in the way they feel and act, their reasons. During these enquiries, my mind was crowded with the question 'why?' . . . to which I got no other answer apart from: 'because our fathers did so'. Yet, little by little, what seemed obscure started to be clearer and the questions found an answer through a logical consequence of facts or contexts.[19]

The refrain 'because our fathers did so', Pollera believed was only a first reaction which should not be taken literally. On the contrary, the judicial debate allowed him to 'penetrate' a deeper level of meaning and reach a definition of 'true' tradition. The issue around the definition of tradition – more specifically, who defines what as traditional and for which purpose – has been frequently addressed in anthropological literature. Amselle suggests this linguistic exchange reinforces field-researchers in their belief about the presumed strength of tradition, simultaneously consolidating the power of native elders (Amselle 1990). In contrast to this belief, Amselle proposes a vision of tradition which is continuously contested and negotiated.

Pollera's efforts to reach a deeper level of meaning shows that he believed that a true and solid tradition existed, and that it was best expressed by the elders. This had immediate practical, and painful, effects. In his 1922 monograph Pollera wrote about the local way to denounce rape: in the indigenous legal system, he explained, a sworn statement on the part of the woman is sufficient to charge the offender, even in those cases in which the woman could have called for help, but did not. A woman did not need to prove she had been raped since her statement was sufficient to prosecute the offender. Yet, when in 1910 Pollera acted as judge in a rape case, things went differently. As usual, he asked three local notables for advice; two of them agreed that a simple statement on the woman's part was sufficient to charge the offender to compensate the woman, yet the third dissented: '[if we accept this] then all women who dislike us [men] will simply swear in order to get a compensation from us; it is not right that a woman simply swear . . . she must show the proof.'[20]

While the three notables revealed the contested nature of tradition, Pollera did not question his own assumptions about local customs and decided, in the end, that the 'true' tradition was the one expressed by the majority of the elders. This case also shows how, in the colonial context, male notables and elders could forge new traditions that reinforced their own authority and limited the power and rights of other marginal subjects (women, in this case). Moreover, the opinion of the third notable matched the images of class and gender hierarchies then shared by most Italians. It is not clear how the case concluded but it is clear that the sentence introduced a new and ambiguous factor, which reflected both the third notable's stance and Italian visions of justice. While Pollera accepted the woman's statement as proof, he granted the same right to the defendant, who was allowed to swear his innocence, thus challenging the woman's assertion.

The public and the private

In *The woman in Ethiopia* (1922) Pollera devoted the last chapter to a discussion of intimate relationships between Italian men and Eritrean and Ethiopian women. He insisted that inter-racial unions were inevitable and natural in a colonial context, given a lack of European women. Italian men had a natural desire to form a family and have a partner, 'even a colored one' (Pollera 1922: 76). He criticized the fact that many Italians 'easily have concubines, but abandon them when children are born, thus provoking not only the resentment of these unfortunate mothers, but also of their relatives and families ... Once abandoned, [she] falls easily and quickly into poverty' (Pollera 1922: 79). He also agreed that Italian fathers should be allowed to legitimize the children born from these unions without being obliged to marry the mother (a condition set by the Italian civil code), because such a marriage 'would rightly repel anybody [i.e. the Italian men] given the huge gap of civilization' between colonizers and colonized (Pollera 1922: 82).

These statements are ambiguous and partly contradict Pollera's own behavior. On the one hand, Pollera condemned Italian men who abandoned their local partners, but he proposed no preventive measure. It appears that Pollera was more concerned about the children born from such unions than about the fate of the women involved. Yet, when he ended his own relationship with his first partner he continued supporting her for the rest of his life. Pollera seems to consider inappropriate both concubinage and marriage between citizens and subjects, yet he lived with an Eritrean woman for most of his life, and married her shortly before dying. In his will, he wrote that he would have married Chidan much earlier 'if only so many difficulties had not arisen'.[21]

These difficulties included the formal and informal social control exerted by the colonial sector, and the Royal Decrees of 1909 and 1914 which explicitly prohibited colonial officers from cohabiting with local women, and implicitly from marrying them. Such officers would be forcibly retired and repatriated (R.D. 19.9.1909 n. 839, R.D. 10.12.1914 n. 16). To understand these contradictory opinions one should note that Pollera was writing for a governmental publication and was a colonial official. He probably agreed with the general colonial belief that, in most cases, the presumed civilization gap between colonizers and colonized made such unions inappropriate. Yet, his own opinion was less simplistic; while he never doubted Kunama inferiority, his position was much more ambiguous concerning Abyssinians, and there is much evidence in his numerous scripts that he did not see much difference between 'us' and 'them'.

Undoubtedly, he also knew that taking a polemical stance against an official decree placed him and his family at risk. Repatriation would have made it virtually impossible for him to take care of his six children, whom he was 'so proud of'. As he repeatedly wrote his elder son, he kept working long after retirement in order for all of them (including the daughter) to complete high school in Italy, and if possible to attend university, as two did.

Pollera also knew that concubinage in the colony, though illegal, was widely practiced and to a certain extent even tolerated. From the 1920s onward, the sex ratio among the Italians was becoming more balanced and inter-racial relationships were tolerated locally, both because they were becoming less frequent and because a racial hierarchy was by then firmly entrenched: a few intimate relationships were not seen as threatening to white supremacy (Barrera 2002b).[22] Yet Pollera also knew that his behavior was closely observed by the colonial government, which from the outset sought to secure 'white prestige' through segregation. Especially in the early years much colonial literature stigmatized acts as mundane as the local partner of an Italian dressing in European clothes, or if she had a servant provided by her partner, or appeared with him in public. Governor Martini, and his successor, tolerated concubinage as long as it was kept private (Barrera 2002b). It was this lifestyle that Pollera and Chidan adopted. Daughter Marta Pollera recalled that her father never asked Chidan to adopt Western clothes or hair fashion, nor did she appear in public with Pollera. Marta pointed out that such a relationship could survive only when relegated to the private sphere. Only when Pollera and Chidan were living in Gonder, at a time when Ethiopia was still independent, did he publicly introduce Chidan as his wife. In this situation he was the only white man in the town, and far from the control of both government and Italian colonial society.[23]

Pollera's life history and private behavior towards his partner and children partly contradict his public opinions, revealing that his beliefs about an incommensurable gap between colonizers and colonized could be undermined by emotional involvement. Intimate or sexual relationships *per se* did not lead to the suppression of power and racial hierarchies (Sòrgoni 1998; Barrera 2002b). In other colonial contexts, Stoler (1991: 86) argued that 'miscegenation signaled neither the presence nor the absence of racial discrimination'. As Bastide (1961: 10) put it: 'it is in the love-making of partners of different color . . . in those privileged instants which seem to destroy race' that 'racialism' insinuates. Such micro-level analysis helps uncover problematic colonial interrelationships between citizens and subjects, and how the colonizers' community was far from homogeneous (Stoler 1989). It also points to the strict control exerted by colonial authority and society on both citizens' and subjects' private lives, showing how the same subject might adopt different strategies and express different opinions depending on social context.

Pollera never publicly opposed the dispositions outlawing interracial concubinage or marriage. In 1937 governor Guzzoni issued a new decree condemning those colonial officers who still had local concubines or tolerated such relationships amongst subordinates, and threatened them with severe punishments.[24] Shortly thereafter the law invoked punishments of up to five years imprisonment for Italian citizens convicted of having local concubines. At the same time minister for Italian Africa, Alessandro Lessona, announced that 'legitimating and adoption of children born from the union between citizens and subjects must be forbidden'.[25]

It was only against this new disposition that Pollera reacted, by publicly opposing it. In 1937 he wrote a long *memoire*, probably addressed to Lessona, which contained a point by point rebuttal of official doctrine on the supposed inferiority and racial degeneration of mixed offspring (*meticci* in the colonial lexicon), as propounded in contemporary Italian anthropological, medical and genetic literature. Pollera agreed, however, that Italian women's sexuality needed to be strictly controlled and that they should be forbidden to marry colonial subjects. He also agreed with a partial restriction on unions between Italian men and colonial women, although he repeated that such phenomena were natural and inevitable; indeed he also suggested that children born from such unions were equal to 'full blood' Italian ones, since he believed that children inherited most of their characteristics from the father. Precisely because in the colony all Italo-Eritrean children had Italian fathers, to suggest they were inferior was in his opinion simply an insult, and a claim that could not be proved. Historian Luigi Goglia notes the many concessions to Fascist racial policy on Pollera's part and suggests that while Pollera lacked the political power to openly oppose the dictatorship, he also appreciated the regime for its strong interest in colonial policy, which previous liberal governments had lacked (1985: 1072–1073).

To disprove pseudo-scientific theses about *meticci*'s alleged inferiority, Pollera resorted to various arguments: that they inherited their physical and psychological traits from their Italian fathers; that crossing with Abyssinians brought no racial degeneration since they were 'Semites like us'; that morality depended not on genetics but on the environment in which one was brought up. These arguments could no longer be defended under the dictatorship. The regime's strong interest in natality and maternity led scientists to assign to white women a new role as defendants of racial purity, thus asserting that genes were inherited from the mothers (whose sexuality was strictly controlled). Moreover, the new racist doctrine separated Hamites and Semites from the Aryan race to which Italians were said to belong; at the same time somatic, psychological and cultural differences were grounded in biology. Thus, affirming that children inherit from their fathers, that 'we' (Italians) are like the Semites (Abyssinians and Jews), and that individual differences derive from the environment rather than from genes – three widely held theses less than a decade before – was now equated with being outside the Fascist scientific and political paradigm (Sòrgoni 2002). Pollera did not realize that he was using arguments that were being literally banned in the mainland with the dramatic changes brought on by the consolidation of the regime and the new empire taking place in the same period. Pollera, who had adhered to Fascism in the early 1920s, was now taken by surprise by the new racial laws against *meticci*. He went so far as to argue that colonial subjects had been wrongly deprived of access to Italian citizenship on the basis of their skin color:

> Color-phobia, or the common habit to judge all natives on the basis of this wrong evaluation, unfortunately also shared by educated people, damages us and our colonial action much more than the opposite behavior of those who, better understanding the natives' soul, were too often and unfairly accused of going native. (Goglia 1985: 1083)

The last sentence is an autobiographical and polemical note, since Pollera himself had been repeatedly accused of 'going native'.

In December 1938 Pollera wrote a new letter, this time addressing it to Mussolini in person. The text, hand-written and much shorter than the document, has a more private style and tries to reach Mussolini by touching on personal issues. Pollera turned to him because, he wrote, he could understand his anguish: 'You, *Duce*, are also a father!' He recalled that he, Pollera, had lost a son (Giorgio) in the Italo-Ethiopian war because, like all colonial fathers, he had taught his '*meticci* children to love their fatherland' and added: 'we do not want, oh *Duce* . . . to regret we encouraged them to sacrifice their own life in the name of a fatherland which now repudiates them'. The letter had some effect, since the private secretary for the Minister for Italian Africa, Meregazzi, sent Pollera's letter to Mussolini with a note, adding that 'what the officer Pollera affirms is not all wrong' and that those Italo-Eritrean children who had already been legitimized by their fathers should not lose their Italian citizenship.[26] This point was later affirmed by the 1940 law against *meticci* (L.13.5.1940 n.822), the last colonial racial law.

A few months after the letter to Mussolini, Pollera again expressed his opposition to the racial laws, by marrying Chidan. It is therefore not clear why, despite his courageous defense of the juridical status of Italo-Eritrean children, Pollera never opposed those racist laws which outlawed inter-racial marriage. In this regard, and long before Fascist racial laws, no single voice strongly opposed the discriminatory treatment of colonial subjects. The rhetoric about the racial prestige of the colonizer, which an intimate relationship with the 'indigenous element' would have threatened, was from the start promoted, defended, or tacitly accepted by the whole colonial white community. Within this framework, Pollera's opposition to a law that discriminated against mixed-race children, and his marriage to Chidan, were somehow exceptional. But what he publicly expressed in relation to inter-racial intimate relationships was in line with the colonial policy of separation between citizens and subjects.

Conclusion

This analysis of Alberto Pollera's written legacy addressed two broader issues: the types of links existing among colonial ethnographies, administrative practices and professional anthropologies on the one hand; and the creation processes of discontinuous ethnic identities on the part of administrators-cum-ethnographers on the other. These two lines of investigation, which have been developed in the study of other colonial contexts, have proven fruitful when applied also to the Italian case.

By concentrating on the literary and rhetorical strategies Pollera adopted, it is possible to highlight how his ethnographic knowledge and descriptive style were reflected in administrative practices. When comparing two groups (Kunama and Abyssinians, for instance), Pollera adopted different literary models, which in turn essentialized their alleged differences, reinforcing the separation between the two groups and justifying divergent administrative practices. At the same time, as his ethnographic knowledge deepened thanks to his growing familiarity with a given group, the policy guidelines he suggested and adopted also changed accordingly.

Finally, by reading Pollera's texts set against his private life, both his articulated personality and the complex nature of colonial ethnographic scripts emerge. Common sense, current stereotypes, normative stances and the author's own research findings and personal experience are all juxtaposed in the same work, often contradicting one another, and thus revealing the hybrid nature of his colonial texts. Moreover, a closer look at selected examples of Pollera's private behavior confirms not only that white communities in the colonies were not homogeneous, but also that the same individual could express contradictory positions according to the changing context in which he was to act.

Notes

*   This chapter draws from an extensive research on Pollera's life, ethnographic scripts and administrative policy (Sòrgoni 2001), and is also based on the study of his private archive. For this opportunity I would like to thank Marta, Pier Angelo and Albertina Pollera.
1   Italy had just become a nation-state when it started its program of colonial expansion, seen by the monarchy and the military elite as a means to gain prestige vis-à-vis other European powers. The country was then characterized by consistent economic depression and uneven development; in this respect, Gramsci defined Italian colonialism as a 'passional, oratorial colonialism, without any economic or financial basis' (Gramsci 1975: 2018, vol. III), which served to side-track internal problems such as the landless peasants' claims for land.
2   For English works on the early history of Italian anthropology, see Taylor 1987, 1988; Gilman 1992 on Lombroso's theories about African women; and Sòrgoni 2003.
3   So far, only a few studies have analyzed similar issues: see Dore 1980, 1982; Solinas 1988; Sòrgoni 1998; Surdich 1979, 1982.
4   On anthropological trends until the early 1900s, and disciplinary constraints during Fascism, see the various contributions in Clemente et al. 1985; on Italian folklore studies see Cirese 1973; for English works on Italian contemporary anthropology see Saunders 1984, 1993.
5   Until 1896 about 60,000 Italian soldiers were sent to Eritrea, but only about 200 actually remained for more than a few years (Labanca 1990: 96). According to the censuses, Italians in Eritrea numbered 2,333 (of which 482 were women) in 1904;

2,410 in 1913; and 4,188 in 1931. At this date, the Eritrean population numbered 596,000 (Castellano 1948).

6   Barrera 1996, Sòrgoni 1998. In 1931 there were about 2,400 Italian men in Eritrea and about 1,000 Italo-Eritrean children, half of whom had been abandoned by the father (Barrera 2002a).

7   A. Pollera, Residenza del Gasc e Setit, 'Oggetto: Taglie e Multe consuetudinarie', 21.6.1903, private archive.

8   My interview with Marta Pollera, April 1998.

9   A. Pollera, 'Appunti', 1902, private archive.

10 The Instruction's ethnographic questionnaire is published in *Società di Studi Geografici e Coloniali* 1907. Colonial officers usually relied either on a questionnaire prepared by the colonial government (Sòrgoni 1998) or, later, on those prepared in Italy by academicians (Puccini 1998). There is now evidence that a German questionnaire, prepared by the distinguished jurist Albert Hermann Post, was also translated into Italian and circulated in the colony (Guazzini 2000).

11 A. Pollera, 'Appunti', 1902, private archive.

12 At a seminar on Italian colonialism (*Generi Coloniali*, Rome 27–28 October 2000) the late Alexander Naty reported how the myth of colonial peace, reinforced by Pollera, is still largely acknowledged by the elders.

13 Archivio Storico Diplomatico Ministero Affari Esteri (ASDMAE), *Archivio Eritrea* (AE), b. 42, f. 'Giurisprudenza coloniale eritrea 1908–1919'.

14 Letter from A. Pollera, Seraye Regional Commissar, to H.E. the Governor, Adi Ugri 15 March 1913, private archive.

15 G. Pollera 'Alla memoria di Alberto Pollera', unpublished script, n.d., private archive.

16 It should be remembered that evolutionary theories, anthropological interest in the political structure of non-Western societies and modern colonialism are coeval. Also, the opposition between centralized and acephalous societies as corresponding to that between civilized and barbaric societies, long outlived evolutionary theories. See Lewellen 1983 for a history of anthropoloigcal classification of different political systems.

17 A. Pollera, letter to the governor, Adi Ugri 1 January 1917, handwritten, private archive.

18 Ibid., note 15.

19 Ibid., note 15.

20 Commissariato Regionale del Seraè, oggetto: 'Reclamo Selebà Andetzian', 8.9.1910, ASDMAE, *AE*, b. 568, f. 'Selebà Andetzian'. See Chanock 1982 for a similar case in British colonies.

21 Repertorio n. 1890. Raccolta n. 764 'Pubblicazione di testamento olografo', 2.8.1939, private archive.

22 This situation changed drastically after the conquest of Ethiopia in 1936, when the number of colonial subjects increased from a few hundred thousand to some nine million, and the Europeans increased from about 4,000 in 1931 to over 67,000 in 1938.

23 My interview with Marta Pollera, December 2000. In his autobiography, the emperor Haile Selassie (1976) wrote that Pollera introduced Chidan as his wife, but she was only a local prostitute. He believed Pollera responsible for the 1930 Ras Gugsa Olie rebellion against his authority, and this might explain his dismissal of her as a prostitute. But Haile Selassie had known Pollera quite well since 1916 – when he was still Ras Tafari – and it is highly unlikely that he did not know that, by 1930, Pollera and Chidan had been living together for 20 years.

24 Governo dell'Eritrea, Asmara 24.9.1936, ASDMAE, *MAI D.G.AA.PP.* b. 83 f. 241.

25 Quoted in Teruzzi 1939: 70.

26 Respectively A. Pollera to Mussolini, Asmara 10.12.1938; Meregazzi to Mussolini Roma, 8.1.1939, Meregazzi to Pollera, Roma 8.1.1939, in ASDMAE, ASMAI, Gab. 88/XI/V.

References

Amselle, Jean-Loup. 1990. *Logiques métisses: Anthropologie de l'identité en Afrique et ailleurs*. Paris: Éditions Payot.

Amselle, Jean-Loup and Sibeud, Emmanuelle. 1998. 'Introduction. Maurice Delafosse face à l'histoire et à l'anthropologie'. In J.-L. Amselle and E. Sibeud (eds). *Maurice Delafosse – Entre orientalisme et ethnographie: l'itinéraire d'un africaniste (1870–1926)*. Paris: Maisonneuve & Larose, pp. 9–18.

Barrera, Giulia. 1996. 'Dangerous Liaisons: Colonial Concubinage in Eritrea (1890–1941)'. PAS Working Papers 1. Northwestern University. Program of African Studies. Evanston, Ill.

Barrera, Giulia. 2002a. 'Patrilinearità, razza e identità: l'educazione degli Italo-Eritrei durante il colonialismo Italiano (1885–1934)'. *Quaderni Storici* 109:21–53.

Barrera, Giulia. 2002b. 'Colonial Affaires: Italian Men, Eritrean Women and the Construction of Racial Hierarchies in Colonial Eritrea (1885–1941)'. Northwestern University: Unpublished Ph.D.

Bastide, Roger. 1961. 'Dusky Venus, Black Apollo'. *Race* 3:10–18.

Castellano, Vittorio. 1948. 'Sguardo alla demografia della popolazione italiana dell'Eritrea, dal 1882 al 1923. Le rilevazioni della popolazione fino al censimento del 1921'. *Rivista italiana di demografia e statistica* II:127–142.

Chanock, Martin. 1982. 'Making Customary Law: Men, Women and Courts in Colonial Northern Rhodesia'. In M.J. Hay and M. Wright (eds). *African Women and the Law: Historical Perspectives*. Boston: Boston University Press, pp. 53–67.

Cirese, Alberto Mario. 1973. *Cultura egemonica e culture subalterne*. Palermo: Palumbo.

Clemente, Pietro, Leone, Alba Rosa, Puccini, Sandra, Rossetti, Carlo and Solinas, Pier Giorgio. 1985. *L'Antropologia italiana: Un secolo di storia*. Roma-Bari: Laterza.

Corso, Raffaele. 1916. 'L'etnografia scienza politica e coloniale'. *Rivista Coloniale* 3–4:178–189.

Dirks, Nicholas B. 1992. 'Introduction: Culture and Colonialism'. In N.B. Dirks (ed.). *Colonialism and Culture*. Ann Arbor: University of Michigan Press, pp. 1–23.

Dore, Gianni. 1980. 'Antropologia e colonialismo italiano. Rassegna di studi di questo dopoguerra'. *La Ricerca Folklorica* 1:129–132.

Dore, Gianni. 1982. 'Guerra d'Etiopia e ideologia coloniale nella testimonianza orale di reduci sardi'. *Movimento operaio e socialista* V:475–487.

Foucault, Michel. 1971. *L'ordre du discours*. Paris: Gallimard.

Gilman, Sander L. 1992. 'Black Bodies, White Bodies: toward an Iconography of Female Sexuality in Late Nineteenth Century Art, Medicine and Literature'. In J. Donald and A. Rattansi. (eds). *'Race', Culture & Difference*. London: Sage, pp. 171–197.

Goglia, Luigi. 1985. 'Una diversa politica razziale coloniale in un documento inedito di Alberto Pollera del 1937'. *Storia Contemporanea* XVI:1071–1091.

Gramsci, Antonio. 1975. *Quaderni del carcere*. Torino: Einaudi.

Grottanelli, Vinigi. 1977. 'Ethnology and/or Cultural Anthropology in Italy'. *Current Anthropology* 18:493–614.

Guazzini, Francesca. 2000. 'Un documento inedito di etnografia giuridica. Esperimenti di catalogazione degli usi nella colonia Eritrea'. Siena: Facoltà di Giurisprudenza, Facoltà di Scienze Politiche, University of Siena.

Haile Selassie. 1976. *My Life and Ethiopia's Progress, 1892–1937*. E. Ullendorf (ed.). London: Oxford University Press.

Labanca, Nicola. 1990. 'Coscritti in colonia: Appunti in tema di percezione dell'Africa e scrittura popolare'. *Materiali di lavoro* 1–2:93–115.

Lanternari, Vittorio. 1974. 'Le nuove scienze umane in Italia. Genesi e sviluppi'. In V. Lanternari (ed.). *Antropologia e imperialismo e altri saggi*. Torino: Einaudi, pp. 321–348.

Legesse, Asmarom. 1973. *Gada: Three Approaches to the Study of African Society*. New York: The Free Press.

Lewellen, Ted. 1983. *Political Anthropology*. South Hadley: Bergin & Garvey.

Loria, Lamberto. 1912. 'L'etnografia strumento di politica interna e coloniale'. *Lares* I:73–79.

Marinelli, Olinto. 1905. 'Sulla convenienza di compilare formularii per la raccolta di notizie e di materiali giovevoli alla conoscenza delle lontane regioni nelle quali dimorano o si recano di frequente i nostri connazionali'. *Atti del V Congresso Geografico Italiano* (Napoli 6–11 aprile 1904), 2 vol. Napoli: Tocco e Salvietti, pp. 240–251.

Martini, Ferdinando. 1913. *Relazione sulla colonia Eritrea del R. Commissario civile deputato Ferdinando Martini, per gli esercizi 1902–1907, presentata dal ministro delle colonie (Bertolini) nella seduta del 14 giugno 1913*. Atti Parlamentari, Legislatura XXIII, Sessione 1909–1912, 4 vol. Roma: Camera dei Deputati.

Mbembe, Achille. 2000. *On the Postcolony*. Berkeley: University of California Press.

Mochi, Aldobrandino. 1900. 'Gli oggetti etnografici delle popolazioni etiopiche'. *Archivio per l'Antropologia e l'Etnografia*:87–173.

Pels, Peter. 2000. 'A Localising Science: Publicity, Secrecy and the Professionalization of Tanganyikan Anthropology, 1925–1961'. Paper presented at the conference 'Anthropology and Africa: A Cross-colonial investigation', 10–12 March 2000, University of Oxford.

Pels, Peter and Salemink, Oscar. 1994. 'Introduction: Five Theses on Ethnography as Colonial Practice'. *History and Anthropology* 8:1–34.

Pollera, Alberto. 1913a. *I Baria e i Cunama*. Roma: Reale Società Geografica.

Pollera, Alberto. 1913b. *L'ordinamento della giustizia e la procedura indigena in Etiopia e in Eritrea*. Roma: Ministero delle Colonie.

Pollera, Alberto. 1913c. *Il regime della proprietà terriera in Etiopia e nella Colonia Eritrea*. Roma: Ministero delle Colonie.

Pollera, Alberto. 1905. 'L'apicoltura nei Baza'. *Bollettino Agricolo e Commerciale della Colonia Eritrea* III:556–559.

Pollera, Alberto. 1916. 'Il Tallero di Maria Teresa nella circolazione monetaria della colonia Eritrea e problemi che ne derivano'. *Rivista Coloniale* XI:505–520.

Pollera, Alberto. 1922. *La donna in Etiopia*. Roma: Ministero delle Colonie.

Pratt, Mary Louise. 1985. 'Scratches on the Face of the Country, or: What Mr. Barrow Saw in the Land of the Bushmen'. *Critical Inquiry* 12:119–143.

Puccini, Sandra. 1980. 'Antropologia positivista e femminismo: Teorie scientifiche e luoghi comuni nella cultura italiana tra Ottocento e Novecento'. *Itinerari* 3:217–244.

Puccini, Sandra. 1998. *Il corpo, la mente e le passioni*. Roma: CISU.

Puccioni, Nello. 1915. 'Appunti sull'antropometria dei Baria e dei Cunama'. *Rivista di antropologia* XX:1–17.

Puccioni, Nello. 1937. *Le popolazioni indigene della Somalia italiana*. Bologna: Cappelli.

Rossetti, Carlo (ed.). 1906. *Atti del Congresso Coloniale Italiano di Asmara (settembre-ottobre 1905)*. 2 vol. Roma: Tipografia dell'Unione Cooperativa Editrice.

Saunders, George R. 1984. 'Contemporary Italian Cultural Anthropology'. *Annual Review of Anthropology* 13:442–466.

Saunders, George R. 1993. '"Critical Ethnocentrism" and the Ethnology of Ernesto de Martino'. *American Anthropologist* 95:875–893.

Società di Studi Geografici e Coloniali, Società di Antropologia, Etnologia e Psicologia comparata. 1907. *Istruzioni per lo studio della colonia Eritrea*. Firenze: Tipografia Galileiana.

Solinas, Pier Giorgio. 1988. 'Coscienza coloniale e affari indigeni: L'Africa italiana da Ferdinando Martini a Giacomo de Martino'. *La Ricerca Folklorica* 18:41–47.

Sòrgoni, Barbara. 1998. *Parole e Corpi: Antropologia, discorso giuridico e politiche sessuali inter-razziali nella colonia eritrea (1890–1941)*. Napoli: Liguori.

Sòrgoni, Barbara. 2001. *Etnografia e colonialismo: L'Eritrea e l'Etiopia di Alberto Pollera (1873–1939)*. Torino: Bollati Boringhieri.

Sòrgoni, Barbara. 2002. 'Racist Discourses and Practices in the Italian Empire under Fascism'. In R. Grillo and J. Pratt (eds). *The Politics of Recognising Difference: Multiculturalism Italian-Style*. Aldershot: Ashgate, pp. 41–57.

Sòrgoni, Barbara. 2003. 'Italian Anthropology and the Africans: The Early Colonial Period'. In P. Palumbo (ed.). *A Place in the Sun: Africa in Italian Colonial Culture from Post-Unification to the Present*. Berkeley: University of California Press, pp. 62–80.

Stauder, Jack. 1993. 'The "Relevance" of Anthropology to Colonialism and Imperialism'. In S.G. Harding (ed.). *'Racial' Economy of Science: Toward a Democratic Future*. Bloomington/Indianapolis: Ithaca University Press, pp. 408–427.

Stocking, George W. 1983. 'The Ethnographer's Magic: Fieldwork in British Anthropology from Tylor to Malinowski'. In G.W. Stocking (ed.). *Observers Observed: Essays on Ethnographic Fieldwork*. Madison: University of Wisconsin Press, pp. 70–119.

Stocking, George W. 1988. 'Bones, Bodies, Behavior'. In G.W. Stocking (ed.). *Bones, Bodies, Behavior: Essays on Biological Anthropology*. Madison: University of Wisconsin Press, pp. 3–17.

Stoler, Ann Laura. 1989. 'Rethinking Colonial Categories: European Communities and the Boundaries of Rule'. *Comparative Studies in Society and History* 13:134–161.

Stoler, Ann Laura. 1991. 'Carnal Knowledge and Imperial Power'. In M.D. Leonardo (ed.). *Gender at the Crossroads of Knowledge*. Berkeley: University of California Press, pp. 51–101.

Surdich, Francesco. 1979. 'La donna nell'Africa orientale nelle relazioni degli esploratori italiani, 1870–1915'. *Miscellanea di storia delle esplorazioni* IV:191–220.

Surdich, Francesco. (ed.). 1982. *L'esplorazione italiana dell'Africa*. Milano: Il Saggiatore.

Taylor, P.M. 1987. 'Paolo Mantegazza (1831–1910): Reassessing the Florentine School of Anthropology in Pre-Fascist Italy (up to 1925)'. *Antropologia Contemporanea* 10:1–16.

Taylor, P.M. 1988. 'Anthropology and the "Racial Doctrine" in Italy before 1940'. *Antropologia Contemporanea* 11:45–58.

Teruzzi, Alfredo. 1939. 'Lineamenti della legislazione per l'Impero'. *Gli Annali dell'Africa Italiana* II:3.

CHAPTER ELEVEN

Political intelligence, colonial ethnography, and analytical anthropology in the Sudan

Douglas H. Johnson

'Knowledge is power, in Africa and elsewhere', wrote Sir Reginald Wingate in his foreword to the first issue of *Sudan Notes and Records* in 1918 (Wingate 1918: 1). As the head of the Egyptian Army's Military Intelligence department in the lead-up to the Reconquest of the Sudan (1896–99), and as the one who introduced the format of regular consolidated printed intelligence reports for the Sudan both before and after conquest, Wingate knew of what he spoke. In the first years of Wingate's tenure as governor-general the Sudan government was one of a small number of colonial governments in the empire actively to promote anthropological instruction for its staff and the recording and publication of ethnographic information about the people it governed. This symbiotic association between the Sudan government and the discipline of anthropology continued right through the Condominium until the middle of the twentieth century. The research of some of the significant personalities of early and mid-twentieth century British Social Anthropology – Seligman, Evans-Pritchard, Nadel and Lienhardt – was supported by the Sudan government, which also subsidized the publication of several ethnographies,[1] including most of Evans-Pritchard's monographs.[2] With the appearance of *Sudan Notes and Records* administrators, educators and missionaries, along with professional scholars, were given a semi-official outlet in which to record ethnographic data of various sorts.

The general thrust of the critique of anthropology's early patronage by such colonial governments as the Sudan is that the anthropological project was inevitably directed by colonial objectives.[3] According to the Sudanese anthropologist Abdel Ghaffar Mohammed Ahmed, social anthropology, more than any other human science – [had] a major role in introducing to the administration the people of the colonies and in showing ways by which their social system could be controlled and hence exploited ... The Sudan case shows that the indirect role of anthropologists – whether they were aware of it or not – was great; and that the reactions towards the subject are based on findings filling a large number of files in the Sudan Government Archives. (Ahmed 1973: 264, 269)

A more nuanced interpretation of anthropology's relationship with colonial governments has been presented by Wendy James, an anthropologist of northeast Africa, who has suggested that social anthropology in the interwar period often developed as a critique of colonial authority (James 1973: 69). With specific reference to the Sudan this critique was to be found less in the factual reporting of anthropological journal articles, and more in the ethnographic monographs which Evans-Pritchard published from the 1930s to the 1950s. The interests of colonial administration in the Sudan encouraged an 'investigative mode' of ethnographic enquiry, focusing on 'crops and herds, settlement types, chiefs' names and their subjects' opinions'. This concern for factuality had a lasting impact on the social anthropology of the Sudan, concerned as it has been ever since with investigating what are 'seen as the realities of the human condition in that country'. But in 'deliberately seeking fresh perspectives from participant observation and adducing evidence from as yet untapped sources' Evans-Pritchard developed the analytical monograph, each of his having 'an intellectual theme, posing a series of questions and marshalling evidence to answer them'. One aspect which distinguishes all of Evans-Pritchard's monographic writing is its dissection of authority. From this emerged the 'critical tradition of Sudanese ethnography' (James 1990: 97–98, 113–114).

I would like to examine these contrasting propositions further, especially looking at the type of factual ethnographic reporting as it emerged from the government files to which Ahmed refers, and was transformed into modern social anthropology. I will look particularly at the role of the *Sudan Intelligence Report* (*SIR*) and *Sudan Notes and Records* (*SNR*) as media for ethnographic writing and documentation. Both publications were unique in British Africa: *SIR* was the continuation of the Egyptian Army Intelligence department's pre-Reconquest series of printed reports which monitored political, military and economic events in the Mahdist state and other parts of Egypt's former colony of the Sudan. *SNR* was a pioneering semi-scholarly journal. In the range of its subjects it was more comprehensive than the *Nigerian Field Notes* (which concentrated on natural history), and it was the inspiration for later publications in other territories, such as the

Uganda Journal and *Tanganyika Notes and Records*. As was common with many early twentieth-century metropolitan scientific or specialist journals, such as the *Journal of the Royal Anthropological Institute (JRAI)*, the *Geographical Journal*, the *Journal of the African Society* (later *Journal of the Royal African Society*) and *Africa*, a number of its early contributors were serving officers and administrators in Britain's empire. But in the case of *SIR* and *SNR* the connection was more direct, as both drew on the same reservoir of official reports for publication.

While a comparison of these two different publications certainly demonstrates that administrative objectives did try to direct anthropological enquiry, a reciprocal argument can also be made: that colonial perspectives were affected by their embrace of anthropology. There was a difference between the purely utilitarian approach to ethnographic data of the administrators and that of the anthropologist. As anthropological writing became more and more the product of professionals, so the anthropological output of administrators, too, began to conform more to these new standards. The case of the Sudan illustrates that just as there was no single colonial agendum for anthropology which held true throughout the empire, so there could be different agenda within a single territory.

The ethnographic basis of administration in the Sudan

The administration of the Sudan in 1899 was governed by the legal fact that the Sudan was an Egyptian colony, but Egypt itself was under British occupation. The Anglo-Egyptian Agreement of 1899 established British control of the administration of the Sudan, and the first effective administrative force in the country was the Egyptian army, also under British control. Administrative policy grew out of military practice, and the new Sudan administration chose to govern through those it considered its natural allies: the rural leaders who had been deposed or supplanted by the Mahdists during the theocratic rule of the Mahdist state (1881–98). Throughout the eleven-year period between Britain's evacuation of the Sudan and the commencement of the Reconquest (1885–96), the Egyptian Army Intelligence department maintained and expanded active contact with the growing number of dissidents in the Mahdist state, and even entered into correspondence with former allies and subjects of Egypt as far away as the Nile-Congo watershed; the results of these contacts were often published for confidential circulation in the *Intelligence Report, Egypt (IRE)* series (1892–98). When the advance up the Nile began in 1896 the Anglo-Egyptian forces were assisted by numerous anti-Mahdist sheikhs and tribesmen. Following the reoccupation of the country the new administration discovered that years of *jihad*, forced migration and famine had disrupted pre-1881 settlement patterns in many parts of the country. It therefore set about reconstructing the ante-bellum political institutions of the countryside and reinstate the ruling families. To this end the ethnography of nineteenth-century travelers was mined for information for the recreation of tribal structures,[4] though this was soon supplemented and finally supplanted by data gathered through the field reports of military and administrative officers on the ground.

From an early stage, therefore, the higher levels of government advocated, if they did not yet fully practice, what later became known as Native Administration, popularized by Lord Lugard in Nigeria as Indirect Rule. The director of Education in the Sudan, James Currie, set out in a memo to the governor-general, Sir Reginald Wingate, as early as 1901 what the Sudan government perceived as the main differences distinguishing it from the type of colonial rule then being adopted in southern Africa. In commenting on the prospectus of the African Society, founded in honour of Mary Kingsley, Currie wrote:

> I take the late Miss Kingsley to stand for much the same kind of Imperialism as Lord Cromer and yourself, an advocate for the improvement of the native along the lines of his own institutions, and his own customs and regulations, as opposed to what John Morley calls, the 'hasty insertion of the iron ramrod of modern commercialism among half-developed peoples'.[5]

This statement of the ideal of Native Administration is surprising enough for its early date, but what is perhaps more significant from the point of view of the development of anthropological research in the Sudan is that it was made by an educator. The Education department took an early lead in promoting ethnographic knowledge in the Sudan. Members of the department took an active role in writing about the antiquities, races and languages of the Sudan (a special interest of Currie's deputy and successor, J.W. Crowfoot, the father of Nobel laureate Dorothy Hodgkin). Of more practical value was the department's support for the Wellcome Tropical Research Laboratories in Khartoum, and its advocacy of anthropological training for probationary administrators.

The Wellcome Tropical Research Laboratories were attached to Gordon Memorial College as a section of the Education department. Because much of its early research focused on insect-borne diseases, many of its specialists were entomologists, and its first two published research reports dealt entirely with mosquitoes and other noxious insects.[6] The introduction of any research of 'ethnographic' value came through the reports of medics in their examination of indigenous healing practices and ideas about disease, but this was the work mainly of army doctors, with no pretension to contributing to the larger enquiry of anthropology.[7]

The specific concerns of administration – whether civil or medical – provided a wealth of field data but little overall interpretation. Crowfoot's contribution on the ethnology of the Sudan, in Count Gleichen's first official survey of the country following the Reconquest (Gleichen 1905), drew on the theories of German ethnologists and linguists for its classifications of racial groups and language families. But this was far from satisfactory, and he was critical of ' "arm-chair savants" who base great theories upon stray skulls, fragmentary vocabularies, chance studies of natives touring about Europe "on show" ' (Crowfoot 1905: 318).

In many parts of the Sudan, Crowfoot felt, the objects of material culture were already well described. Among the pagan tribes of the South, he argued in 1907, 'the work that remains – the further penetration into their religion, their more intimate customs, their psychology, their inter-relations, – all these require years of patient work under conditions of great difficulty, for the climate is unhealthy, the people are shy, and their dialects legion . . . research among them must be carried out by men who can "think black" ' (Crowfoot 1909: 169–170). The close connection between medicine and anthropology in Britain at this time, however, meant that any professionally qualified ethnographic researchers would come to the field from a medical background. The person chosen to fill in the ethnographic map of those regions undescribed by nineteenth-century travellers was an Edinburgh medical doctor, A. MacTier Pirrie. His expedition was far from successful. Quite apart from his unexpected death on return to Scotland, his collection and notes (published posthumously by his Edinburgh colleagues) consisted almost entirely of researches on material culture and physical types (Vallance 1908; Waterston 1908). While the Sudan government wanted a shortcut to understanding native thinking, the anthropologists at this time were more interested in measuring the primitive cranium than in penetrating the primitive mind.

The Sudan government in 1908 recommitted itself to the support of anthropological work in two ways. The first was to hire Charles Seligman, veteran of the Torres Straits Expedition, and his wife Brenda, for an expedition to the Upper Nile in 1910, ultimately with the hope that they would be able to coordinate anthropological research in the Sudan. The second was to introduce a component of anthropological education to the training of probationary civilian recruits to Sudan government service. Currie justified both of these initiatives on the

[313]

grounds of practical utility. In the case he presented to the Financial Secretary for the hiring of the Seligmans he dismissed any 'urgent political necessity' for supporting the study of 'racial affinities' or 'primitive arts and crafts' in the Sudan. Rather, he focused on anthropology as 'the study of laws and of organisation':

> we can never hope to educate or even govern people without understanding something of the way in which their minds work, of the meanings and association which words and custom convey, and the sanctions they recognise and the acts they reprobate. (Currie 1909: 161–162)

These were broadly the same benefits he hoped would come from including anthropological instruction in the probationary year of administrative recruits. Again he argued the value of practical utility. It was in the non-Muslim areas, particularly in the 'unhealthy districts' of the south with their high turnover of staff, that officials were needed

> who can rapidly familiarise themselves with the structure of primitive forms of society, so far that they can appreciate the relative importance of native laws and customs, and understand the way in which people round them are thinking and are therefore likely to act.

> There can be little doubt that much time will be saved to officials, many errors avoided, and much value added to their reports and observations, if they could start with some foundation of knowledge. (Currie 1909: 160–161)

This experiment in anthropological training was first tried in Oxford, where, providentially, all three of the probationary recruits for 1908 had studied as undergraduates (taking degrees in Lit. Hum. and Classics). In addition to their courses in Arabic and law, they attended eight special lectures on the ethnology of the Sudan by the University Reader in Egyptology (F. Ll. Griffith), eight special lectures on comparative technology by the curator of the Pitt Rivers Museum (H. Balfour), and eight special lectures on primitive social institutions by the secretary of the Anthropological Committee (R.R. Marett) (Currie 1909: 160).[8] The following year the Sudan service recruits from Cambridge were also taught a far less ambitious course of anthropology by Professor A.C. Haddon. Not all of those who attended his course came away convinced of the general utility of anthropology. One year, probationers ceased to attend his lectures when they found he had mislaid his Sudan notes and lectured exclusively on New Guinea instead.[9] Other prewar Oxford probationers found their course nearly as casual,[10] so one should not make too much of the Education department's early optimistic assessment. Virtually no civilian recruits were taken during World War I, and in the 1920s probationary training switched to London University, with little or no time for anthropology. In the 1930s Sudan service recruits were sent to Oxford to attend the Tropical African Services Course set up for Colonial Office recruits. This, too, included some anthropology, but it seems to have left little impression on those Sudan officials who took it (see Robertson 1974: 4; Bell 1983: 16).

The laudable sentiments attached to the arguments in favor of anthropological courses must be seen in the context of the rest of the probationers' training. Arabic language, law, tropical hygiene and first aid also appeared on the curriculum. In order to stay on or advance in the service a recruit had to pass exams in the first two subjects; tropical hygiene and first aid could save a life – their own or someone else's. In this respect anthropology was an optional extra: neither one's life nor one's career depended on it. And despite the arguments of Currie, none of the prewar recruits who received anthropological instruction at Oxford and Cambridge were sent immediately to those areas needing men who could 'think black'. Military skills were still required in the administration of the southern Sudan, where soldier-administrators predominated until the early 1930s.

In the prewar period the first generation of Sudan administrators used skills other than ethnographic to collect and assess indigenous information. In the all-important issue of land rights throughout the northern Sudan, administrators attempted to reconstruct not only pre-Mahdist, but pre-Turco-Egyptian patterns of ownership, rights and use. For this they relied on judicial skills, using the English Common Law concern for precedent to sift through oral testimony and surviving Arabic documentation (Spaulding 1979: 329–330). The results of their investigations might later be considered ethnographic, but this skill from probationary training in law was of such obvious and immediate utility that no special pleading was needed in its favor.

The Sudan Intelligence Report *as a source of ethnographic information*

Dissemination of ethnographic information was as important as gathering it, but despite the director of Education's acknowledgement of this need in 1909 (Currie 1909: 162–163), there was no regular scholarly forum for such dissemination in the Sudan for most of the first two decades of the Condominium. The Wellcome Research Laboratories reports were infrequent and ended in 1911. The only ethnographic article published there outside of the realm of physical or medical anthropology was Seligman's first account of the Shilluk divine king (Seligman 1911). But one place where ethnographic data regularly appeared was *SIR*.

SIR was the continuation of Wingate's *IRE*, the original format of which consisted of a brief summary of events, followed by appendices of selected verbatim reports or correspondence. Following the Reconquest the reports dealt with a wide variety of information relating to the condition of the country and the establishment of administration. In the years before World War I the appendices constituted the largest section of the reports, the monthly summaries often being no longer than two or three pages. The volume of appendices was already declining before the War, but dropped off sharply during it with the recall of so many administrators to their regiments. They never regained prewar levels in the 1920s, and were finally discontinued altogether after 1925.[11]

Because the *SIR* was compiled from reports sent to Khartoum, which were then printed for circulation, the political intelligence they contained was not urgent. These reports were distributed to all departments and provincial headquarters, where they formed a record of events and a source of reference data on the whole of the Sudan (and on some neighboring territories). As the years wore on this seems to have been their main use. Provincial, and even some district, headquarters kept whole sets of *SIR* on file, and administrators consulted them for background information on their own provinces or districts. This helps to explain the wide selection of types of reports that appeared between 1899 and 1914, written by both military and civil staff of the Sudan government, as well as some non-officials.

The majority of the appendices were purely administrative: diaries of punitive patrols, reports of raids, route reports, road, river and railway surveys, inspection tours, trade returns, notes on illicit trade and potential economic resources, the cost and use of different types of pack animals, medical reports on human and animal diseases, diplomatic correspondence, boundary commissions, and the occasional government proclamation. Some reports of political intelligence, such as general notes on new territories, lists of tribes, sections, sheikhs, sultans and chiefs, by their very nature contained ethnographic data, in so far as they attempted to record the political and social organization of different peoples. But imbedded in the longer, more detailed reports of administrative patrols was material which, for the same reason, would now be classed as ethnographic, and which Evans-Pritchard later described as containing 'interesting, often shrewd, observations' (Evans-Pritchard 1940: 1). Not all of the observations recorded were on strictly political matters. The first reference to the

Nuer myth of the cow and the calf (as told by a Dinka), which Evans-Pritchard later cited, appeared in a 1907 report (Struvé 1907, cited in Evans-Pritchard 1940: 125–126).

Religion in the Sudan was a political issue. Egypt having been expelled in the 1880s by a religious revolt, the new Sudan government was alive to the subversive potential of any ecstatic, prophetic millennial figure or movement (Johnson 1994: 23–29). It is partly for this reason that many of the *SIR* appendices reported on religious customs and leaders, both Muslim and pagan. But quite apart from the surveillance of potentially dangerous Mahdis and witchdoctors, there was the beginning of an attempt at some systematic description of religious beliefs as a whole and of customary law. Two *SIR* reports were, in fact, later reprinted as straight ethnography in the *JRAI*: S.L. Cummins, 'Sub-tribes of the Bahr-el-Ghazal Dinka', *JRAI* 34 (1904) (which appeared in *SIR* 100 (November 1902), App. B), and H. O'Sullivan, 'Dinka laws and customs', *JRAI* 40 (1910) (*SIR* 162 (January 1908), App. D). Just the same, the tone and content of the 'Religion and Customs of the . . .' reports were little different from nineteenth-century travel writing. They were not obviously informed by any wider ethnographic reading in African or 'primitive' religions. The government was still far from getting men who could 'think black'.

By 1908 a more scholarly tone began to appear in some of the *SIR* appendices, a point Currie remarked on with some pride (Currie 1909: 162–163). Dr Pirrie's only report on the Burun had been published in 1907 (Pirrie 1907). Harold MacMichael, a Junior Inspector in Kordofan, varied his district tour reports with a reconstructed tribal history, combining first-hand field reporting with reference to other published sources (MacMichael 1908). MacMichael was an early civilian recruit, coming with a first-class Classics degree from Cambridge in 1905. He was too early to have been exposed to the ethnographic lectures later required of Oxbridge probationers, and his points of academic reference were not the grand theories of armchair anthropologists, but the texts of classical geographers and historians. Thus we find Herodotus, Strabo and Diodorus Siculus footnoted in Kordofan. In this MacMichael was following the style established by such Egyptologists as Wallace Budge (another of his sources), who attempted to make connections between the sparse references found in ancient texts and modern excavations and observations.

MacMichael also began publishing in *JRAI*. Some articles, such as 'Rock pictures in Kordofan', *JRAI* 39 (1909), originated from purely scholarly interest. But others were re-worked from his *SIR* appendices. 'Notes on the ethnology of the Kababish tribe, 30 March 1909', *SIR* 178 (May 1909), App B was transformed into 'The Kabábísh. Some remarks on the ethnology of a Sudan Arab tribe', *JRAI* 40 (1910). 'Ethnography and history of the Zagháwa', *SIR* 194 (September 1910), App A and 'Note on J. Meidob' *SIR* 200 (March 1911), App B became 'The Zaghwa and the people of Gebel Mídób', *JRAI* 42 (1912). Ten of MacMichael's reports on Kordofan appeared as *SIR* appendices between 1908 and 1911. These formed the core of his first book, *The tribes of northern and central Kordofan*, five chapters being based directly on the appendices, and many of the other chapters incorporating information from the other reports. MacMichael cited and acknowledged his *JRAI* publications, but not his *SIR* reports. He alluded to them obliquely in a disclaimer, stating that the materials from which the book was composed did not show 'the solidarity which is an essential qualification of a scientifically historical work'. As a contribution to ethnology he further pleaded 'that I am a mere tyro with no expert knowledge of the science whatever' (MacMichael 1912: v).

The fact that the origins of *The Tribes of Northern and Central Kordofan* lay in administrative reports does not detract from its place in the development of Sudanese ethnography. Rather, it helps to explain why Sudanese ethnography developed along such strictly empirical, local-level lines, and why the ethnography of the northern, Muslim Sudan proceeded along historical, Orientalist lines. But if these reports of MacMichael's crossed over from administration to scholarship, it was because they were reports of a certain kind, being broadly descriptive of peoples and districts, or attempting to reconstruct the history of political structures and migration. Other reports by MacMichael did not fall into this category. As political officer to the Darfur Campaign in 1916, when the independent sultan of Darfur was overthrown and his sultanate annexed to the Sudan, MacMichael produced other types of political intelligence: personality reports of enemies and potential friends, maps from oral testimony (Gillan 1939: 8). These were not the sorts of reports which would have been considered for transfer to scholarly publication, and not even of general confidential circulation outside the provincial and central governments. Nor, for that matter, was this the sort of information that the government felt it needed an anthropologist to gather for them. This was the standard fare of administrative reporting.

The foundation of Sudan Notes and Records

Reports selected for publication in *SIR* came from many administrative levels. The government was then far more centralized under the authority of the governor-general than it later became. Reports by army officers and civil inspectors were either sent directly to the governor-general (who was also the commander-in-chief of the Egyptian army), or forwarded through senior officers, provincial governors and department heads. It was the intelligence department's duty to collate these reports and select those for distribution through *SIR*, but neither the reporters, nor their reports, were part of the intelligence department. Since many of the same personnel were later involved in editing *SNR*, it was natural to adapt this selection process for the new journal.

The idea for a journal devoted to the Sudan originated with the former director of Surveys, Lt. Colonel the Hon. Milo Talbot, R.E., during his return service to the Sudan as a representative of the British Army Intelligence Service during World War I. It was taken up by Crowfoot, now director of Education, who formed a committee under his chairmanship, and brought out the first volume in 1918.[12] The first committee for *SNR* was heavily dominated by the Education department, not only through Crowfoot and S. Hillelson, a lecturer at Gordon Memorial College, but through many of the staff at the Wellcome Tropical Research Laboratories. Other central government departments represented were the civil secretary's office, the Survey department, and the Intelligence department (in the person of the assistant director, later director). MacMichael, a rising star and then sub-governor of Darfur, was included as the most scholarly member of the service. The chairmanship of the committee passed to MacMichael after he became civil secretary in 1926. From that time until 1946 the civil secretary was the automatic chairman of the committee, and the majority of the committee members came from the sub-departments in his expanded office.[13]

The range of articles in the new journal was far broader, naturally, than the administrative reports of *SIR* (which was still publishing its appendices), including antiquities, linguistics and natural history along with history, memoirs and ethnography. The ethnographic and linguistic research of missionaries and educators now found a regular outlet (which it had not in *SIR*), but the bulk of this early ethnography was still produced by administrators. Not only that, but some of it was reprinted from *SIR*, with or without acknowledgement. Between 1918 and 1922 at least eight articles were reprinted or extracted from *SIR*.[14] This was not mere padding out. It was, instead, fulfilling one of the original purposes of the journal, as suggested by Wingate (by then high commissioner for Egypt) in his foreword to the first number when he specifically urged the study of 'the superstitions and the folk-lore of primitive tribesmen' as subjects which 'apart from their anthropological and ethnological values, are of importance as contributing to that sympathetic comprehension of the people and their mentality which is so essential to a successful administrator' (Wingate 1918: 1–2).

SIR as a source of such articles soon dried up. The number of reports printed there had been declining in any case before *SNR* appeared and stopped altogether in 1925. But the members of the committee (the director of Intelligence and the civil secretary) had access to the same source of materials which fed *SIR* – the accumulated provincial and departmental reports which came into their offices. A few of the earliest such articles were either verbatim reports sent to the civil secretary, or extracts from them.[15] Other reports provided copy simultaneously for *SIR* (now *Sudan Monthly Intelligence Report*, or *SMIR*) and *SNR*. Captain Fergusson's first account of the Nyuong Nuer in 1921 was edited to provide an appendix for *SMIR* and an article for *SNR*.[16] In the next year Major R.H. Walsh published on the same area of eastern Equatoria in both *SMIR* and *SNR* (Walsh 1922a,b,c). A more curious case was the article on 'The religious confraternities of the Sudan', written by C.A. Willis, the director of Intelligence, published in *SNR* at the end of 1921, but issued by the Intelligence department as a 'confidential' pamphlet, dated February 1922 (Willis 1921, 1922). The steady diversion of administrative reports with an ethnographic content into *SNR* from the early 1920s coincided with a noticeable decline in the ethnographic value of *SMIR* (Evans-Pritchard 1940: 1).

With the restructuring of central government in Khartoum following the assassination of the governor-general and the army mutiny in 1924, the intelligence department was absorbed into an expanded Civil Secretariat under MacMichael. One of his reforms was to establish a single filing system for the administration throughout the country, where reports and correspondence were filed under uniform numbered subject categories: 1 (Administration), 36 (Intelligence), 57 (Reports), 66 (Tribal), etc. In the civil secretary's department (Civsec) and the Intelligence sub-department (Dakhlia) subject category 112 was 'Anthropological & Historical Records'. These files contained collections of reports deemed to be of anthropological or historical interest copied from old intelligence files or new correspondence originally filed under other subjects.

Officials within the civil secretary's office now decided which administrative reports would be designated as having sufficient 'ethnographic' value to be included in *SNR*. Each major group of people in the Sudan (and many lesser ones as well) had their own 112 file or set of files. Out of these files papers which had obviously never been intended for publication now found their way into *SNR*, modified to conform to a standard of ethnographic writing. Thus, for instance, a short tour report on the Meban written in 1935 was published as a note in *SNR* in 1936, but only after the district commissioner's caustic comments about the behavior of the local police in shooting dead the followers of a local prophet had been excised.[17]

The way in which a highly political report could be transformed into 'ethnography' by inclusion in *SNR* is illustrated by the publication history of another article written by Willis, this time as governor of Upper Nile Province, on 'The Cult of Deng' (Willis 1928). As head of the Intelligence department Willis was discredited for failing to anticipate the White Flag mutiny of Sudanese troops in Khartoum in 1924, following the assassination of the governor-general, Sir Lee Stack, in Cairo. He was moved sideways out of Khartoum and into the governorship of Upper Nile Province, then a remote and unimportant southern province. There he was instrumental in precipitating a rebellion amongst the Nuer, which he attributed to the machinations of witchdoctors (Johnson 1994: chapters 5 & 6). Unlike the White Flag mutiny, this rising was preceded by Willis's predictions of rebellion, which were accompanied by requests that the governor-general devolve to Willis some of his own executive authority to enable the governor to deal quickly with the conspiracy of witchdoctors. Unconvinced by the request, or the evidence of conspiracy, Khartoum demanded further information. This was fulfilled by Willis's report on the 'cult of Deng', outlining the subversive nature of a variety of witchdoctors operating among the Nuer. It was, in effect, a White Paper, but it failed in its purpose; for both the governor-general and the civil secretary remained unconvinced of the governor's argument, and denied him the extra executive powers he craved. But, perhaps in compensation, the civil secretary's office then published the report as an ethnographic article in *SNR* (Johnson 1985).

Professional anthropologists and ethnographic investigation

Willis's 'The cult of Deng' was a travesty of ethnography, but indirectly it helped to stimulate the further professionalization of anthropological research and reporting in the Sudan. Unconvinced by Willis's marshaling of the ethnographic facts, MacMichael, now civil secretary, minuted to the governor-general:

> I believe the fact of the matter is that to obtain an understanding of the recesses of the savage mind one must either be a savage or a very highly trained anthropologist of wide technical knowledge on the one hand and of a broad human sympathy on the other. At present we fall between the two stools. (MacMichael to Sir John Maffey, quoted in Johnson 1985: 144–145)

[321]

Anthropology was no longer being seen as something which could be crammed into an administrator's probationary training to make him 'think black', but as an altogether more complex subject requiring its own specialisms. Charles Seligman had continued his field visits to the Sudan throughout part of the period of World War I, but he never freed himself from the use of government interpreters and other government intermediaries. In the mid-1920s he was no longer able to continue his journeys to the Sudan and urged the Sudan government to employ his student, Evans-Pritchard, in his stead. The government at that time had no particular project for Evans-Pritchard to undertake, other than to travel to the Sudan-Ethiopian border and finish the tribal survey begun, but never finished, by Pirrie before the war. He was then more or less given leave to travel south and study the first large tribe he came across that struck his fancy. Evans-Pritchard chose the Azande, a group of people about whom quite a lot was known, and who were governed by a British district commissioner who had been fluent in the language for many years. There were some in Khartoum who felt that little of practical value would come out of this choice. The need to divine the recesses of the Nuer mind altered Evans-Pritchard's direction, as the Sudan government – MacMichael in particular – instructed him very much against his will to switch from the Azande to the Nuer. This was the first time the Sudan government employed an anthropologist to conduct research which was anticipated to have a direct benefit to administration.

This is not the place to go into Evans-Pritchard's relationship with the administration of the Sudan during his Nuer research, other than to repeat that it had very ambiguous results from the point of view of administration (see Johnson 1982). His research experience with the Nuer led him to question the practical utility of anthropology to administration. In two successive years at Margery Perham's Oxford University Summer School on Colonial Administration (1937–8), he cautioned young colonial administrators, brought together from various parts of the empire, against having overly high expectations about anthropology's benefits. Anthropologists could gather facts which administrators did not have the training, time or opportunity to do. But the mere collecting of data would not automatically benefit governments, as 'the data collected by anthropologists is often irrelevant to administrative problems, or cannot be used in administration or, where it is relevant and can be used, its use would be contrary to policy'. In the end, the interests of anthropologists and administrators were different, as, first and foremost, 'anthropologists are men of science interested in establishing uniformities and interdependencies. It is this first duty to seek for laws and not to aid administration.' It is as 'a disseminator of facts through books', rather than as a government servant, that the anthropologist could have an educative effect on administrators and, indirectly, 'humanize policy' (Evans-Pritchard 1937: 87–89). In the case of the administration of the southern Sudan, he pointed to the recent history of coercion which was the foundation of administration. As a result 'the moral relations between natives and Government provide the most fundamental of administrative problems, for the natives have to integrate into their social system a political organization that has no moral value for them'. If the Sudan government was to make good its intention of basing administration on native institutions, 'one must first know the nature of these institutions. If rule is to be through native chiefs, one must first know what constitutes a chief. If law is to be native law, one must first codify it and discover its guiding principles' (Evans-Pritchard 1938: 75–77).

The gap between anthropology and administration, then, was wide, but there could be communication between the two. In the end the anthropologist resisted being restricted by administration in the types of questions to study or the types of data to gather. If the administrator was to make effective use of anthropological data, it could only come through some exposure to anthropological writing and teaching. This was far from making him 'think black' – but the demands of administration prevented that anyway.

The professionalization of ethnographic reporting

Part of the contact and dialogue between anthropologists and administrators in the Sudan took place through the pages of SNR. And here Evans-Pritchard did have an impact, both direct and indirect. There had been some disappointment with the publications of Seligman. His massive Pagan Tribes of the Nilotic Sudan (Seligman 1932) was taking years to compile, and was based increasingly on questionnaires filled in by administrators and missionaries in the field. MacMichael had this in mind when he commented on 'the danger to which one is always liable in dealing with the scientific expert, viz: that he will sink the practical in the recondite and lapse into over-elaboration'.[18] One condition of Evans-Pritchard's original grant from the Sudan government was 'that he should give the Sudan Government, within a reasonable time, a report of his studies in a form suitable for use of administrative officials'.[19] These he provided, not in confidential reports, but in his survey articles published in SNR (e.g. Evans-Pritchard 1927, 1928, 1929). His very first published piece was in SNR in 1927, and he continued publishing articles there until 1969, a few years before his death in 1973. His total output of articles (excluding notes, reviews and correspondence) amounted to approximately a sixth of all ethnographic articles published in *SNR* from 1918 to 1969. For the period 1927–55, he accounted for about twenty percent of all ethnographic articles; rising to thirty-five percent in the immediate post-independence period of 1956–69.[20]

There was a marked change in the style of ethnographic article published in the journal after the appearance of Evans-Pritchard's first three-part article on the Nuer (Evans-Pritchard 1933, 1934, 1935). Prior to that time administrators had no academic models to follow; in fact their own reports had served as models when reprinted in the *JRAI* or *SNR*. Very occasionally an administrator would bring in a reference to Frazer's *Golden Bough*, but that was about the extent of acknowledging anthropological concerns.[21]

Following the publication of his Nuer articles Evans-Pritchard became much more involved in the vetting of articles for *SNR*, though he was never part of the editorial committee. The civil secretary's office continued to extract reports from its files. But other articles were purpose-written for publication, following more the standard of presentation set by Evans-Pritchard. One of the earliest such article was Ibrahim Bedri's 'Notes on Dinka religious beliefs in their hereditary chiefs and rainmakers', *SNR* 22/1 (1939), which was passed up the chain from district commissioner to governor to assistant civil secretary, causing some surprise that a Muslim northern Sudanese would take such interest in Dinka religion.[22] By the 1940s not only were Sudan administrators beginning to write like anthropologists on subjects such as religion and kinship, they were becoming students of anthropologists: B.A. Lewis and P.P. Howell took further degrees at the Institute of Social Anthropology at Oxford under Evans-Pritchard's supervision.

But it should not be inferred from this that anthropology had become firmly fixed on the curriculum for Sudan administrators. Of some 350 civilians recruited into the administrative service of the Sudan between 1899 and 1952, only five came with an undergraduate qualification in anthropology. Each of these came with Cambridge anthropology tripos: four of the five were recruited in the 1930s, three being recruited in 1938 alone. The subject was still not seen as a skill which defined the ideal recruit. Very few saw it as a subject inviting additional systematic study. In the postwar period only five administrators took further anthropology diplomas or degrees (details from Bell and Dee 1958).

Developments in the writing and teaching of British social anthropology in the 1930s and 1940s did have an influence on the way administrators wrote about the peoples under their charge, but the demands of administration were never far removed. It is instructive to compare briefly some of the major ethnographic writing projects undertaken by administrators in the Sudan. These included the tribal survey of Mongalla Province in the 1930s, the description of the succession rites for the Shilluk kings in the 1940s and 1950s, the manual of Nuer law, and the environmental and ethnographic surveys of the Jonglei investigation team. In these cases one can see clearly how administrators did use the writings of professional anthropologists as a point of reference, but they relied on themselves to undertake ethnographic research and produce ethnographic writing, eschewing the more 'recondite' theories of the professionals.

The compilation of a series of province handbooks had been an unrealized ambition of the Intelligence department before World War I (Johnson 1995: x–xi). In the interwar years L.F. Nalder was the only province governor with the intellectual breadth and stamina successfully to revive the project. His first effort, *The Fung Province Handbook* (c. 1929), existed in mimeographed form only (its ethnographic section was extracted and divided up into numerous Dakhlia 112 files in Khartoum). As governor of Mongalla (later Equatorial) Province he supervised two parallel projects, resulting in one government publication, the *Equatorial Province Handbook*, and one academic publication with the International African Institute, *A Tribal Survey of Mongalla Province* (Nalder (ed.) 1936, 1937). Most of the *Handbook* was derived from unreferenced government sources. Some of the historical summaries were obviously compiled from earlier numbers of *SIR*. The ethnographic, or tribal, sections were also written by administrators, but the bibliography lists only publications in *SNR*, the *JRAI*, and *Africa*, as well as books written by professional anthropologists or linguists (Seligman, Driberg, Westermann). The *Survey* was structured as comparative, descriptive ethnography. It, too, was written entirely by serving administrators and missionaries. 'The framework for anthropological research in Mongalla Province has been laid down by Dr. Seligman', Nalder declared in his preface, 'all subsequent inquiries can only be extensions of his', and there are continued implicit references to his articles and *Pagan Tribes*. The team who compiled the *Survey* were 'all amateurs only, but the book has this merit that the facts have been collected by those with a fluent knowledge of the native languages' (Nalder 1937: iii). There is expressed in both books, then, a recognition that the work of professional anthropologists was providing both a factual and a scholarly standard to which the work of even amateurs must refer and be compared. At the same time there was the confidence that those fluent in local languages and local knowledge could make a contribution to the growing ethnographic literature. And the intention of both the *Handbook* and the *Survey* was purely utilitarian: they were to provide background material for the newcomer to administrative or missionary service in the province.

The myths and rites surrounding the Shilluk king were of particular interest to Seligman, too, for their evidence of a continuation of divine kingship in Africa, and were the subject of his first published article of Sudan ethnography in the Wellcome reports (Seligman 1911). A rapid succession of deaths, burials and installations of Shilluk kings in a ten-year period beginning in 1943 was described in great detail by British administrators and published in *SNR* (Howell and Thompson 1946; Thompson 1948; Howell 1952, 1953). The difference between these articles and the work of Seligman is great. Whereas Seligman relied mainly on local missionaries as his sources of information, the British administrators P.P. Howell and W.P.G. Thompson (both of whom studied under Evans-Pritchard) wrote from direct observation and investigation through the Shilluk language. Their pieces pay close attention to the involvement of different parts of the Shilluk polity in the disposal and election of kings. In fact, their articles became 'how-to' manuals some twenty years later when Kur Fafiti, whose installation ceremony was described in 1953, died in 1974 and the Shilluk had to install his successor. Literate Shilluk used the old *SNR* articles as reference points. Neither Howell nor Thompson were concerned with diffusionist theories of divine kingship. That was left to Evans-Pritchard, who cited their work (and many other *SNR* articles) in his 1948 Frazer Lecture criticizing the theories of Frazer and Seligman (Evans-Pritchard 1962).[23]

The creation of customary courts and the use of customary law was one of the basic principles of native administration in the Sudan. This might have been an area where the government could have commissioned anthropologists to describe a set of customary law (as Evans-Pritchard implied in his colonial summer school lectures), but it was not. Any attempt at writing down or codifying customary law emerged directly from the administrator's legal training and his duty as magistrate supervising customary courts. In 1943 the Nuer district commissioners' meeting decided to embark on a project of producing a manual of Nuer law (Johnson 1986). Their choice of P.P. Howell as the secretary in charge of compiling the manual had very little to do with his having a Cambridge tripos in anthropology; it had much more to do with the fact that he was the youngest and most junior district commissioner at the meeting. Many of his seniors had been serving in Nuer districts since the late 1920s and early 1930s and did not confer expert status on Howell because of his academic background. Howell's own approach to the task, however, was guided very much by his anthropological interests and growing expertise over the next few years. The manual, in its final form (Howell 1954), draws heavily on the work of Evans-Pritchard. This is not surprising, especially as it formed the core of Howell's doctoral thesis, written under Evans-Pritchard's supervision (Howell 1949). But the data on which it is based came out of the administrative and court records of Howell and other district commissioners' legal work, and derives much of its legal theory from common law practice.

The largest engineering project for the southern Sudan proposed by the Condominium government was the Jonglei canal. Its original intention was to increase the flow of Nile water to Egypt, but objections were raised by British administrators in the South as early as the 1920s, based in part on the impact such a canal would have on the livelihood of local peoples. When the canal scheme was revived by the Egyptian Irrigation department in the mid-1930s, it was a Nuer-speaking British administrator, John Winder, who raised objections to the scheme, based on his own surveys in his district. As a result of this Winder (who later become governor of Upper Nile Province) was assigned as political advisor and secretary to the first Jonglei Investigation Team established after the war. In so far as the team included an irrigation engineer, a surveyor and a veterinarian, its report would now be called 'multidisciplinary', but the ethnographic information was gathered by Winder as an administrator, and included reference to administrative reports from *SIR*. A second, more professional team was formed in 1948–54, under the chairmanship of P.P. Howell. The collection of ethnographic information was more systematic, provided mainly by Howell as both an administrator with direct experience in many of the districts concerned, and a trained anthropologist (see Howell et al. (eds) 1988: 33–44).[24] But all members of the team were drawn from existing departments of the Sudan government: external 'experts' were not recruited. This was local expertise provided by the men 'on the spot'.[25]

The relationship between the Sudan government and the discipline of anthropology from the very early years of the century to the end of the Condominium was on the whole friendly, but ambivalent. The Sudan government took an interest in the work of anthropologists, and supported some of their research in semi-official capacities. But administrators were not unanimous in their appreciation of the work of anthropologists. One governor of Equatoria denounced Seligman's depictions of 'typical' Dinka in *Pagan Tribes* as 'a libel on the tribe on the whole'.[26] The deputy governor of Bahr el-Ghazal commented, when informed of Godfrey Lienhardt's impending research on the Dinka, 'I think there are severe limits to which administrative mea-

[327]

sures should be influenced by anthropological theories', and suggested that ethnographic studies were useful mainly to provide background to newcomers.[27] The same official reserved his sharpest criticism for Nadel, who apparently worked very closely with administrators, and complained that his anthropological advice in the Nuba Mountains, 'did not prove of great value'.[28]

On the whole administrators were wary of anthropological theory. We see this in Currie's skeptical comments on 'arm-chair savants'. Evans-Pritchard was commended at the beginning of his work on the Nuer as 'young, keen and unspoilt by theory'.[29] Many administrators found his first series of articles on the Nuer published in SNR useful: they were even summarized and circulated to district offices. But others were disappointed that his subsequent books did not describe all Nuer tribes in the same detail, and in fact relied on administrators for those areas he did not visit.[30] To these readers Evans-Pritchard's books were not the models of analysis they were to become to anthropologists; they were too theoretical.

How true, then, is Abdel Ghaffar Mohammed Ahmed's assertion that anthropologists had 'a major role in introducing to the administration the people of the colonies'? The case of the Sudan would argue the opposite. More often administrators introduced their 'people' to the anthropologists (as MacMichael did with the Kababish to Seligman). The ethnographic reports filling the government archives in Khartoum are written by government officials, not anthropologists. To what extent did the demands of administration direct anthropological enquiry in the Sudan? Political intelligence needed names, numbers and faces – and these could best be provided by the district commissioner on the spot. Anthropologists were both unnecessary and useless in providing the type of political intelligence administrators needed on a daily basis. Anthropologists increasingly did provide reference points for administrators in their own data gathering and reporting. But when it came to providing ethnographic information for administrative purposes, administrators relied on themselves. This very brief survey of administrative ethnographic writing, whether in SIR, SNR or larger reports, confirms the similarities in the investigative and empirical approach marking the work of Evans-Pritchard and his successors, to which Wendy James has already drawn our attention. But the differences are also clear.

Anthropology needed to generalize from particular instances, to identify underlying patterns of thought or social organization which informed action. The strictures of political intelligence were just too narrow to sustain a whole discipline. Had Evans-Pritchard allowed himself to be guided entirely by the mundane needs of administration, we would never have had *Witchcraft, Oracles and Magic among the Azande*, and *The Nuer* would have resembled *A Tribal Survey of Mongalla Province* or volume one of *The Equatorial Nile Project and its Effects in the Anglo-Egyptian Sudan*. In other words they would have been serviceable, factual, descriptive accounts of remote regions, which today are primarily of local interest, though of increasing historical value. However sympathetic or humane the later government reports are, they give little insight into the way people think and behave and have sparked no intellectual engagement or debate within anthropology or any other discipline. The responses of anthropologists, philosophers, theologians and historians to Evans-Pritchard's *Witchcraft, Oracles and Magic*, and *Nuer Religion*, and to Lienhardt's *Divinity and Experience: The Religion of the Dinka* (Lienhardt 1961) – not to mention the reactions of many literate members of the peoples studied – are testimony to how successfully these books engage with their subjects, not as subject peoples to be controlled, nor as exotic 'Others', but as part of the total human community.

Notes

1 The Sudan government gave financial and administrative support to the research of these anthropologists, but none held an official appointment in any government department. All were supervised by the Education department. In the 1950s the independent Sudan government created the short-lived position of 'government anthropologist', and its only holder was Andreas Kronenberg, a German, who published mainly in German.
2 Evans-Pritchard's *Nuer Religion*, published in 1956, the year of the Sudan's independence, was the only one of his major Sudan ethnographies not subsidized. Nadel 1947 and Paul 1956 were both published with grants from the Sudan government (Paul being a former administrator).
3 See especially Faris 1973, Ahmed 1973.
4 See Gleichen 1898. The Egyptian Army Intelligence department's extensive collection of nineteenth-century geographical journals and travel literature later formed the core of the library of the University of Khartoum.
5 James Currie to Wingate, 1 July 1901, Sudan Archive, Durham University (SAD) 271/7/1. Part of the Sudan's perceived uniqueness within the empire rested in it being a territory administered by the Foreign, rather than the Colonial, Office.
6 Balfour 1904 and 1906.
7 The *Third Report* (Balfour 1908) contained four articles on medical practices in the northern Sudan, and the *Fourth report* (Balfour 1911) one article by an R.A.M.C. Captain on medicine in the South.
8 Of the three probationary recruits (A.B.B. Howell, A.W. Skrine and R.K. Winter) only Winter had any subsequent influence on the ethnography of the Sudan. First as assistant civil secretary, secretary for Education and Health, and finally secretary for Education in the 1930s he was responsible for both archeological and anthropological research, including Evans-Pritchard's fieldwork among the Nuer (Bell and Dee 1958: 20).
9 Sarsfield-Hall 1975: 18–19. It is doubtful that the probationers would have learned much from Haddon's Sudan notes (which are deposited in the Cambridge depart-

ment of Anthropology), as they consisted entirely of extracts from the nineteenth-century explorers Schweinfurth and Junker.

10 Sir Angus Gillan, who was part of the 1909 intake, remembered his ethnology course as having very little on the Sudan; it consisted of being shown the exhibits of the Pitt Rivers Museum by the Curator (interview with Sir Angus Gillan, 9 May 1979, Oxford Development Records Project, 'The role of British forces in Africa – The Sudan Defence Force', Rhodes House, Oxford, MSS Afr. S. 1715).

11 The average number of appendices published per year fell from forty-five in 1898–1909, to sixteen in 1910–13, to three in 1914–18, but rose to seven in 1919–25.

12 Sir E. Bonham Carter quoted in 'Editorial notes', *SNR*, 31/1 (1950): 4

13 A number of assistant and deputy civil secretaries sat on the committee, including Hillelson on his transfer to the Intelligence department when it was incorporated into the civil secretary's office. The numbers from the Education department continued to rise, until by 1954, the year of Sudanization of the civil administration, the committee consisted almost entirely of staff from the Education department and the University College of Khartoum.

14 Logan, 'The Beirs', *SNR*, 1/4, 1918 (from Logan, 'Manners and customs of the Beirs', *SIR* 229 (August 1913), App); Major R.F. White, 'Notes on the Turkana tribe', *SNR*, 3/4, 1920 (from R.F. White, 'Further notes on the Turkana patrol, 1918', *SIR* 290 (September 1918), App); 'The Manufacture of Iron by the Juers', *SNR*, 4/1, 1921 (from A.B. Bethell, 'Report on the Jur river', *SIR* 117 (January 1904), App B); 'The reason for the Beir's hatred of the Dinka', *SNR*, 4/1, 1921 (from H.D.E. O'Sullivan, 'Tradition of reason for the Beir hatred of Dinka tribe', in 'Report on the Beir and Berri tribes', *SIR* 134 (September 1905), App C); J.P. Mostyn, 'Some notes on Burun customs and beliefs', *SNR*, 4/4, 1921, (from J.P.L. Mostyn, 'Some notes on Burun customs', *SIR* 255 (October 1915), App A); 'Mongalla Province. Ornaments and arms among the Acholi and their neighbours', *SNR*, 4/4, 1921 (from J. Powell, 'Extracts from the medical report on the Sudan-Uganda boundary rectification commission, including some notes on tribal customs, dress, etc.', *SIR* 227 (June 1913), App); Sagar, J.W., 'Notes on the history, religion and customs of the Nuba', *SNR*, 5, 1922 (from J.W. Sagar, 'Notes on the history, religion, and customs of the Nubas', *SIR* 186 (January 1910), App A); Anon, 'The Ujang tribe', *SNR*, 5/3, 1922 (extract from *SIR* 332 (March 1922), main body of report).

15 See Munro 1918, Somerset 1918, Anon. 1919 (a recent case of cannibalism among the Jur), and Anon. 1920 (a partial transcript of two murder cases from 1913 and 1920 presented by the editors, one of whom, the assistant civil secretary, Corbyn, had presided over the first case).

16 Fergusson's 'History of Nuong Nuer' (National Records Office, Khartoum (NRO), Civsec 1/2/5) appeared in part in *SMIR* (Fergusson 1921a), and a further part in *SNR* the same year (1921b).

17 H.G. Wedderburn-Maxwell, 'The Maban', November 1935, NRO Dakhlia 112/16/105 appeared as 'The Maban of southern Fung', *SNR* 19, 1936.

18 H. MacMichael to Financial Secretary, 10 January 1929, NRO Civsec 112/1/1.

19 Ibid.

20 Evans-Pritchard published twenty-nine articles in all in *SNR*. Using a very broad definition of 'ethnography' (but excluding linguistics and agricultural science), I calculate some 180 ethnographic articles published from 1918 to 1969, of which 66 appeared in 1918–26, 114 in 1927–55, and only 25 in 1956–69 (seven of which were Evans-Pritchard's).

21 See H.C. Jackson 1923. It is worth recording that when Jackson attempted to interpret his encounters with the Nuer prophet Guek Ngundeng according to Frazer's theories, he misunderstood every one of Guek's gestures and statements (Jackson 1954: 164–165, 168).

22 See the correspondence surrounding this article in P.P. Howell's papers, 'Dinka: General Information Vol. II', SAD.

23 Thompson took a diploma in Social Anthropology at Oxford at the time he wrote his articles. It was probably the availability of this new material which inspired Evans-Pritchard to tackle the subject of divine kingship in his Frazer lecture.

24 Winder's field notes are now in SAD. The first team's findings were published in the *First, Second* and *Third Interim Report of the Jonglei Investigation Team* (Khartoum, 1946–48). The final report appeared as the 4-volume Jonglei Investigation Team 1954.

25 The final report did include a section on the Mandari, compiled from notes provided by Jean Buxton, a student of the Institute of Social Anthropology at Oxford (Jonglei Investigation Team 1954, vol. I: 201–206). Jean Buxton had undertaken fieldwork among the Mandari in 1950–52, under the supervision of Godfrey Lienhardt. She was not employed by the Sudan government, but many of her family members were serving in the Sudan in various capacities in education and administration. Paul Howell was her cousin.

26 B.V. Marwood, governor Equatoria to the secretary, Anthropological Board, 17 April 1947, Southern Records Office (SRO) EP 104.A.3.

27 T.R.H. Owen, deputy governor, Bahr el Ghazal Area to governor Equatoria, 10 March 1947, SRO EP 104.A.3.

28 T.R.H. Owen, 'Sudan Days', 1960/61, ms in SAD and Rhodes House. A critique of Nadel's collaboration with administration is found in Faris 1973.

29 Comment by A.G. Pawson, governor of Upper Nile Province, in R.K. Winter to civil secretary, 21 November 1933, NRO Civsec 112/1/3.

30 See for instance the maps of the Jikany and Gaawar reprinted in *The Nuer* (Evans-Pritchard 1940: 58, 60, 233), provided by the district commissioners C.L. Armstrong and B.A. Lewis.

References

Ahmed, Abdel Ghaffar M. 1973. 'Some Remarks from the Third World on Anthropology and Colonialism: the Sudan'. In T. Asad (ed.). *Anthropology & the Colonial Encounter*. London: Ithaca Press, pp. 259–270.

Anon. 1919. 'Cannibalism (extract from Bahr el Ghazal Province diary for 1919)'. *SNR* 2/4:309.

Anon. 1920. 'Two Murder Trials in Kordofan'. *SNR* 3/4:245–259.

Balfour, Andrew (ed.). 1904. *First Report of the Wellcome Tropical Research Laboratories at the Gordon Memorial College*. Khartoum & London: Bailliere, Tindall & Cox for the Education department, Sudan government.

Balfour, Andrew (ed.). 1906. *Second Report of the Wellcome Tropical Research Laboratories at the Gordon Memorial College*. Khartoum & London: Bailliere, Tindall & Cox for the Education department, Sudan government.

Balfour, Andrew (ed.). 1908. *Third Report of the Wellcome Tropical Research Laboratories at the Gordon Memorial College*. Khartoum & London: Bailliere, Tindall & Cox for the Education department, Sudan government.

Balfour, Andrew (ed.). 1911. *Fourth Report of the Wellcome Tropical Research Laboratories at the Gordon Memorial College*. Khartoum & London: Bailliere, Tindall & Cox for the Education department, Sudan government.

Bell, Gawain. 1983. *Shadows on the Sand*. London: C. Hurst.

Bell, Gawain and Dee, B.D. 1958. *Sudan Political Service 1899–1956*. Oxford: Oxonian Press.

Crowfoot, John Winter. 1905. 'Ethnology of the Sudan'. In E. Gleichen (ed.). *The Anglo-Egyptian Sudan, a Compendium Prepared by Officers of the*

Sudan Government. *Vol. I.* London: Her Majesty's Stationery Office, pp. 317–321.

Crowfoot, John Winter. 1909. 'The Anthropological Fields in the Anglo Egyptian Sudan'. Appendix C to Currie, pp. 169–175.

Currie, James. 1909. 'Annual Report. Education Department'. *Reports on the Finance, Administration and Condition of the Sudan, 1908.* Khartoum: F. Nimr, pp. 147–165.

Evans-Pritchard, Edward Evan. 1927. 'Preliminary Account of the Ingassana Tribe of the Fung Province'. *SNR* 10:69–83.

Evans-Pritchard, Edward Evan. 1928. 'Oracle Magic among the Azande'. *SNR* 11:1–53.

Evans-Pritchard, Edward Evan. 1929. 'The Bongo'. *SNR* 12/1:1–61.

Evans-Pritchard, Edward Evan. 1933. 'The Nuer: Tribe and Clan'. *SNR* 16/1:1–53.

Evans-Pritchard, Edward Evan. 1934. 'The Nuer: Tribe and Clan'. *SNR* 17/1:1–57.

Evans-Pritchard, Edward Evan. 1935. 'The Nuer: Tribe and Clan'. *SNR* 18/1:37–87.

Evans-Pritchard, Edward Evan. 1937. 'Anthropology and Administration'. *Oxford University Summer School on Colonial Administration: St. Hugh's College, 3–17 July 1937.* Oxford: Oxford University Press, pp. 87–89.

Evans-Pritchard, Edward Evan. 1938. 'Administrative Problems in the Southern Sudan'. *Oxford University Summer School on Colonial Administration: Second Session, 27 June–8 July 1938 at Lady Margaret Hall.* Oxford: Oxford University Press, pp. 75–77.

Evans-Pritchard, Edward Evan. 1940. *The Nuer: A Description of the Modes of Livelihood and Political Institutions of a Nilotic People.* Oxford: Clarendon Press.

Evans-Pritchard, Edward Evan. 1956. *Nuer Religion.* Oxford: Clarendon Press.

Evans-Pritchard, Edward Evan. 1962. 'The Divine Kingship of the Shilluk of the Nilotic Sudan'. In E.E. Evans-Pritchard (ed.). *Essays in Social Anthropology.* London: Faber and Faber, pp. 66–86.

Faris, James C. 1973. 'Pax Britannica and the Sudan: S.F. Nadel'. In T. Asad (ed.). *Anthropology & the Colonial Encounter.* London: Ithaca Press, pp. 153–170.

Fergusson, Vere Henry. 1921a. 'Summary of Information on the Nuong Nuer in the Northern Bahr-el-Ghazal Extracted from a Report by Capt. V.H. Fergusson, OBE (the Cameronians) on a Tour in the Nuer Country, February and March 1921'. *SMIR* 323 (June 1921), App A:11–12.

Fergusson, Vere Henry. 1921b. 'The Nuong Nuer'. *SNR* 4/3:§46–§55.

Gillan, J. Angus. 1939. 'Darfur 1916'. *SNR* 22/1:1–25.

Gleichen, Edward Lord [Count]. 1898. *Handbook of the Sudan.* London: Her Majesty's Stationery Office.

Gleichen, Edward, Lord (ed.). 1905. *The Anglo-Egyptian Sudan, a Compendium Prepared by Officers of the Sudan Government. Vol. I.* London: Her Majesty's Stationery Office.

Howell, Paul Philip. 1949. 'A Comparative Study of Customary Law among Cattle Owning Tribes in the Southern Sudan'. Oxford University: Unpublished D.Phil. thesis .

Howell, Paul Philip. 1952. 'The Death and Burial of reth Dak wad Fadiet of the Shilluk'. *SNR* 33:156–164.

Howell, Paul Philip. 1953. 'The Election and Installation of reth Kur wad Fafiti of the Shilluk with an Account of the Final Ceremonies by J.O. Udal'. *SNR* 34:189–203.

Howell, Paul Philip. 1954. *A Manual of Nuer Law*. London: Oxford University Press for the International African Institute.

Howell, Paul Philip, Lock, Michael and Cobb, Stephen (eds). 1988. *The Jonglei Canal: Impact and Opportunity*. Cambridge: Cambridge University Press.

Howell, Paul Philip and Thompson, W.P.G. 1946. 'The Death of a Reth of the Shilluk and the Installation of His Successor'. *SNR* 27:5–85.

Jackson, Henry Cecil. 1923. 'The Nuer of the Upper Nile Province'. *SNR* 6/1 & 2:59–107, 123–189.

Jackson, Henry Cecil. 1954. *Sudan Days and Ways*. London: Macmillan.

James, Wendy. 1973. 'The Anthropologist as Reluctant Imperialist'. In T. Asad (ed.). *Anthropology & the Colonial Encounter*. London: Ithaca Press, pp. 41–69.

James, Wendy. 1990. 'Kings, Commoners, and the Ethnographic Imagination in Sudan and Ethiopia'. In R. Fardon (ed.). *Localizing Strategies: Regional Traditions of Ethnographic Writing*. Edinburgh & Washington DC: Scottish Academic Press & Smithsonian Institution Press, pp. 96–136.

Johnson, Douglas H. 1982. 'Evans-Pritchard, the Nuer and the Sudan Political Service'. *African Affairs* 81/323:231–246.

Johnson, Douglas H. 1985. 'C.A. Willis and the "Cult of Deng": A Falsification of the Ethnographic Record'. *History in Africa* 12:131–150.

Johnson, Douglas H. 1986. 'Judicial Regulation and Administrative Control: Customary Law and the Nuer, 1898–1954'. *Journal of African History* 27/1:59–78.

Johnson, Douglas H. 1994. *Nuer Prophets: A History of Prophecy from the Upper Nile in the Nineteenth and Twentieth Centuries*. Oxford: Clarendon Press.

Johnson, Douglas H. 1995. 'Editor's Preface'. In C.A. Willis (ed.). *The Upper Nile Province Handbook*. Oxford: Oxford University Press for the British Academy, pp. ix–xiii.

Jonglei Investigation Team. 1954. *The Equatorial Nile Project and Its Effects in the Anglo-Egyptian Sudan*. 4 vol. Khartoum: n.p.

Lienhardt, R. Godfrey. 1961. *Divinity and Experience: the Religion of the Dinka*. Oxford: Clarendon Press.

MacMichael, Harold H. 1908. 'Notes on the History of Kordofan before the Egyptian Conquest'. *SIR* 165 (April 1908), App G.:18–27.

MacMichael, Harold H. 1912. *The Tribes of Northern and Central Kordofan*. Cambridge: University Press.

Munro, P. 1918. 'Installation of the King of Shilluks'. *SNR* 1/3:142–152.

Nadel, Siegfried Frederick. 1947. *The Nuba*. London: Oxford University Press.

Nalder, Leonard Fielding (ed.). 1936. *Equatorial Province Handbook. Vol. 1 Mongalla*. Sudan Government Memoranda No. 4. Khartoum: n.p.

Nalder, Leonard Fielding (ed.). 1937. *A Tribal Survey of Mongalla Province by Members of the Province Staff and Church Missionary Society*. London: Oxford University Press for the International African Institute.

Paul, Andrew. 1956. *A History of the Beja Tribes of the Sudan*. Cambridge: Cambridge University Press.

Pirrie, A. MacTier. 1907. 'Report on the Burun Country, May 1907'. *SIR* 155 (June 1907), App A.:4–6.

Robertson, James. 1974. *Transition in Africa: from Direct Rule to Independence*. London: C. Hurst.

Sarsfield-Hall, Edwin Geoffrey. 1975. *From Cork to Khartoum: Memoirs of Southern Ireland and the Anglo-Egyptian Sudan 1886 to 1936*. Kendal: T. Wilson.

Seligman, Charles Gabriel. 1911. 'Cult of Nyakang and the Divine Kings of the Shilluk'. In A. Balfour (ed.). *Fourth Report of the Wellcome Tropical Research Laboratories at the Gordon Memorial College*. Khartoum & London: Bailliere, Tindall & Cox for the Education Department, Sudan government, pp. 216–238.

Seligman, Charles Gabriel. 1932. *Pagan Tribes of the Nilotic Sudan*. London: G. Routledge & Sons.

Somerset, F.R.R. 1918. 'The Lotuko'. *SNR* 1/3:153–159.

Spaulding, Jay. 1979. 'Farmers, Herdsmen and the State in Rainland Sinnar'. *Journal of African History* 20/3:329–347.

Struvé, Kenneth Chetwood Price. 1907. 'Some Points on the Religion of the Nuers and Dinkas, as Set Forth by Deng Agweir, Keeper of the Shrine of Deng Dit at Luang Deng'. *SIR* 151 (March 1907), App A(II):7.

Thompson, W.P.G. 1948. 'Further Notes on the Death of a Reth of the Shilluk 1945'. *SNR* 29/2:151–161.

Vallance, D.J. 1908. 'Notes on Ethnographical Specimens Collected by Dr. A. MacTier Pirrie'. In A. Balfour (ed.). *Third Report of the Wellcome Tropical Research Laboratories at the Gordon Memorial College*. Khartoum & London: Bailliere, Tindall & Cox for the Education Department, Sudan government, pp. 377–384.

Walsh, R.H. 1922a. 'Information Concerning Swahili and Abyssinians Located at Lotelpay, on Lokalian River, Mongalla Province, 1 August 1922'. *SMIR* 337 (August 1922), App A.:6.

Walsh, R.H. 1922b. 'Extracts from Report on the Taposa by Major R.H. Walsh, DSO, MC, Royal Artillery, Dated 1st August, 1922'. *SMIR* 337 (August 1922), App B:6–7.

Walsh, R.H. 1922c. 'The Beri or, More Correctly, Pari'. *SNR* 5/1:47.

Waterston, D. 1908. 'Report upon the Physical Characters of Nilotic Negroid Tribes' In A. Balfour (ed.). *Third Report of the Wellcome Tropical Research Laboratories at the Gordon Memorial College*. Khartoum & London: Bailliere, Tindall & Cox for the Education Department, Sudan government, pp. 325–376.

Willis, Charles Armine. 1921. 'The Religious Confraternities of the Sudan'. *SNR* 4/4:175–194.

Willis, Charles Armine. 1922. *The Religious Confraternities of the Sudan.* Khartoum: Intelligence department, Sudan Government.

Willis, Charles Armine. 1928. 'The Cult of Deng'. *SNR* 11:195–208.

Wingate, Francis Reginald. 1918. 'Foreword'. *SNR* 1/1:1–2.

CHAPTER TWELVE

Colonial ethnology and political rationality in French West Africa

Gary Wilder

In one of his later interviews, Michel Foucault remarked that 'a real science is able to accept even the shameful dirty stories of its beginning' (Foucault 1997b: 132). It was certainly the case that before the 1970s, Anglo-American anthropology was in certain respects unwilling to confront the colonial genealogies of its own privileged categories and canonical works. However, French colonial administrators and ethnologists in the early twentieth century were frank and unapologetic about their mutual implication.[1] Even before African decolonization, professional scholars and colonial intellectuals formulated a critique of this relationship (Leiris 1950; Balandier 1955; Fanon 1956, 1967: 83–108). Given that it was not a secret, the goal of unmasking ethnology as complicit with colonialism would be gratuitous.

The critical history of French ethnology is still in formation (Stocking 1968; Copans 1975, 1979; Williams 1985; Clifford 1988; Gringeri 1990). Some scholars, building upon the self-reflexive turn within disciplinary anthropology have identified the cultural biases of French colonial ethnographies produced within relations of power (Grosz-Ngaté 1988; Van Hoven 1990). Others have sought to recuperate the monographs produced by French administrators as legitimate scientific scholarship that offers a historically specific perspective on African social relations (Wooten 1993). These writings often emphasize colonial ethnographers' interest in individuality, collectivity, and the family, but do not account for that interest in terms of the colonial field in which such studies were produced.

Similarly, a recent collection of essays suggests that the work of Maurice Delafosse prefigured contemporary Africanist research but that he has been marginalized by academic ethnology in an attempt to disavow its colonial origins (Amselle and Sibeud 1998). This dual emphasis on the scientific character of administrative ethnography and the colonial character of academic anthropology has been developed most fully by Emmanuelle Sibeud (1994, 2002). These important interventions allow us to disrupt institutional anthropology's often apolitical self-understanding (Pels and Salemink 1999). Yet they are more concerned with the epistemological status of administrative and scientific discourses than with the colonial projects with which these discourses were entwined.

As an alternative, my account will contribute to a growing literature that explores the nexus between ethnographic knowledge and colonial government in France and West Africa (Harrison 1988; Robinson 1992; L'Estoile 1997, 2000; Conklin 1998a; Amselle 1998a,b). I have organized my essay around the concept of 'political rationality', developed by Michel Foucault (Foucault 1982, 1984, 1988a, 1991, 1997a, 1998, 2003).[2] Although Foucault used it in multiple ways, I treat political rationality as an analytic term that refers to socially and historically specific logics of political practice; or, as Foucault put it, to 'the specific type of rationality the state produced' (Foucault 1981: 242).[3] The term 'political rationality' is thus meant to be more analytically precise than 'rationalization' or 'capitalism' – terms that may encompass quite different state logics. Moreover, Foucault also used 'political rationality' empirically to describe a particular form of modern administration oriented toward population management, socio-economic regulation and social welfare.[4] The concept is therefore useful both for understanding the interconnected relationship between ethnography, as a form of practical science, and native policy as a form of scientific administration, and for appreciating the features of the new welfarism in French West Africa. Instrumental science and scientific administration formed a complex that I am calling colonial ethnology: government policies were informed by and produced ethnographic knowledge just as ethnological science was informed by and produced administrative categories.[5]

In what follows I will explore the circular and mutually reinforcing dynamics between professional anthropology and new technologies of administration that emerged after World War I in France and West Africa. My goal is neither to dismiss anthropology as tainted by colonial history, nor to accuse individual anthropologists of supporting colonial violence. Instead, I would like to analyze the way that ethnology and administration were entwined disciplines that produced knowledge of native societies as objects to be protected and transformed. Local administrators wrote fieldwork monographs that were formative for metropolitan science while new native policies concerned with protecting yet improving indigenous social institutions incorporated the methods and insights of professional ethnologists. Together they created a shared field of colonial ethnology which

[337]

included practical science and scientific government. This essay thus seeks to develop Gérard Leclerc's provocative but undeveloped assertion: 'between the wars, colonial policy . . . can be defined as a scientific policy and anthropology as a political science' (Leclerc 1972: 95).[6]

Practical reason

It was not until the Institut d'Ethnologie was created in 1925 that professional certification became possible for ethnologists within the French university system. Marcel Mauss, Lucien Lèvy-Bruhl and Paul Rivet, from their respective locations in comparative sociology, philosophy and physical anthropology founded a scientific institute that, from its inception, was linked to colonial concerns (Jamin 1984, 1986).[7] According to Lèvy-Bruhl, its first objective was to train not only professional ethnologists, but also 'those living or destined to live in the colonies' including 'future administrators, colonial doctors, and missionaries' (Lévy-Bruhl 1925: 235). He argued that because native populations were the most valuable natural resource in the empire, colonial development [la mise en valeur] would require savants and technicians in addition to capital. Insisting that indigenous languages and religions had to be studied, Lèvy-Bruhl proposed that the Institute provide scientific and technical education to cadres of a colonial Anthropological Service like the one that Britain had created in the Gold Coast (233–234).

The Institute was financially supported by the Ministries of Colonies and Public Education. Mauss hoped the fieldworkers trained by this new research center – such as Alfred Métraux, Jacques Soustelle, Claude Lévi-Strauss, Marcel Griaule, Michel Leiris, Germaine Dieterlen, André Schaeffner and Denise Paulme – could help preserve the indigenous cultures he feared were disappearing after decades of French intervention (Gringeri 1990: 162–171). Lèvy-Bruhl explained that the Institute would send ethnographic study missions, with the collaboration of colonial governors, into the field or would entrust such missions to qualified colonial officials. These teams were 'to collect, classify, and study all sorts of documents and objects concerning past and present civilizations that are in danger of quickly disappearing or being removed by foreign ethnographers . . . instead of being conserved in colonial and metropolitan museums' (1925: 236). The most celebrated and influential of these was the Mission Ethnographique et Linguistique Dakar-Djibouti from 1931 to 1933. Marcel Griaule led a team of researchers across sub-Saharan Africa from east to west to study linguistic forms, transcribe oral testimonies, produce an archive of maps and photographs, and collect material culture, including objets d'art.[8]

Scholarly monographs that came out of these trips, by figures such as Griaule and the missionary-ethnographer Maurice Leenhardt, were published by the Institute, whose 'Travaux et Mémoires' series was to disseminate the new ethnology.[9] These scientific missions also enabled Paul Rivet between 1928 and 1937 to transform the older Musée d'Ethnographie into the modern Musée de l'Homme, which became the repository of ethnographic objects systematically collected by the research teams. Its expansion and reorganization were funded by the Ministry of Colonies and it was formally affiliated with the Institut d'Ethnologie (Rivet and Rivière 1930: 138–148).[10] The new museum would display objects in cultural contexts; it sought to substitute ethnographic understanding for aesthetic appreciation. Separate exhibition halls were devoted to geo-cultural regions 'according to the rules of modern museology' (148).[11] Rivet used the colonial idiom of *la mise en valeur* to describe the museum's will to 'develop [*mettre en valeur*] all its incalculable riches and to render it worthy of the admirable colonial effort of our country' (Rivet and Rivière 1930).

The missions and the museums would thus produce fixed and comprehensive representations of those indigenous societies that colonial administrators sought, as we will see, to protect. This imperative toward definition and classification corresponded to the ethnographic principles outlined by Marcel Mauss in the seminar on method at the Institute that he gave every year from 1926 to 1939 entitled, 'Descriptive Ethnographic Instructions for the Use of Voyagers, Administrators, and Missionaries' (Mauss 1989). Mauss recognized the imperial character of the new ethnology, writing, 'The field of our studies is limited to those societies that people the French colonies and others of the same stage [of development]' (7).[12] He addressed his teaching not only to academic ethnographers, but also to 'administrators and colonials without professional training' (14). He acknowledged the scientific contribution already made by colonial administrators and called on ethnologists to study France's colonial populations more systematically in order to aid the overseas administration (Mauss 1913: 550–51).

Lévy-Bruhl also addressed his work to colonial officials. Michel Leiris, who studied with Mauss in the 1930s, recalls the brochure announcing the Institut d'Ethnologie in which Lèvy-Bruhl explained that ethnology would enable 'more rational and human modes of colonization' (Leiris 1992: 38). In a note to his English reading public Lèvy-Bruhl relates that many 'among those whose official functions or vocations brings them into constant relations with primitives', including 'administrators and missionaries who share their everyday life', wrote to tell him that his books, including *Les fonctions mentales dans les sociétés inférieures* (1910 [English translation 1926]) *La mentalité primitive* (1922), and *L'ame primitive* (1927), had helped them 'comprehend much that had appeared both unintelligible and ridiculous in the way natives reason, and also in their customs, and that their relations with them are accordingly facilitated and improved' (Lèvy-Bruhl 1985: 5).

Building on Durkheim's project, Lévy-Bruhl sought 'to determine . . . the most general laws governing collective representations . . . in the most undeveloped peoples known to us' (15). He presented a critique of 'the English school of anthropology' (including Frazer and Tylor) for positing continuity between savage and civilized forms of thought based on a presumption of the universality of reason. Refusing to treat 'primitive' thinking as logical attempts to produce rational explanations of the world, Lèvy-Bruhl insisted that there existed distinct and irreconcilable modes of thought: 'A definite type of society, with its own institutions and customs, will therefore necessarily have its own mentality' (27–28). Yet despite this apparently pluralistic conception of socially determined mentalities, Lévy-Bruhl identified only two categories into which the diversity of societies could be reduced, primitive and civilized: 'The social milieu which surrounds them differs from ours, and precisely because it is different, the external world they perceive differs from that which we apprehend' (43).[13]

Mauss too remained preoccupied with the Durkheimian question of collective representations (Durkheim and Mauss 1963; Mauss 1979b: 9). Whereas Lévy-Bruhl created a rigid distinction between mystical primitive and rational civilized mentalities, Mauss historicized modes of thinking and insisted on their socially determined character. Rather than restrict collective representations to non-Western societies and make them a function of a general and irreconcilably primitive mentality, Mauss identified them as central features of all societies. Instead of making modern, rational, Europe a norm against which to measure the evolutionary stages of other societies, he sought to make the West one among many. He thus attempted to show the socially and historically specific character of seemingly universal practices (of the body, classification, exchange) and categories (such as the self, the person, the individual) (Mauss 1979a, 1967). Mauss challenged the universalist idea (which he called an Occidental fantasy) that there exists one civilization to which all the peoples of the world must inevitably aspire or conform as well as the particularist idea that any one nation's civilization could be *the* singular civilization to which

others, unworthy of the name, would be incapable or unfit to assimilate (Mauss 1968: 249–252).

Yet there existed an underlying tension between cultural relativism
and social evolutionism in Mauss's ethnology. On the one hand, he
outlined a world composed of separate but equal societies, each of
which was an integrated totality with its own categories, norms and
practices. On the other hand, he qualified that schema by contrasting
primordial family-based societies defined by custom and collectivism
with modern *national* civilizations regulated by law and individualism. (Mauss 1969a,b) His description of the nation captures this
tension:

> the title nation . . . only applies to a small number of historically known
> societies . . . Presently living human societies are far from all being of
> the same nature and rank in their evolution. To consider them as equals
> is an injustice with regard to those for whom civilization and a sense of
> law are fully developed. (1969a: 584)[14]

Mauss thus implied the existence of a historical dynamic that led
peoples from one developmental stage to the next. In other words,
indigenous societies were at once culturally fixed and socially flexible. It was precisely this tension that characterized colonial policy in
French West Africa at the time Mauss was writing.

It is not difficult to link Mauss's ethnological analyses to questions
of government policy. Mauss's concern with reciprocity and social
harmony in so-called archaic societies, especially in *The Gift*, has
often been read as a response to the horror of World War I. In that text
he sought to identify social practices that would ensure peace for his
own fragmented society. However, I would argue that a deeper historical reading can identify Mauss as articulating the new political rationality that began to organize both republican and colonial forms of
government during this time. If Durkheimian sociology was a theoretical formulation of the late nineteenth-century politics of solidarity, then we can also recognize Mauss's ethnology as a theoretical
formulation of early-twentieth century welfare politics (in national
and overseas France). Criticizing the way that the human being in the
modern West had become an 'economic animal' and a 'calculating
machine', Mauss insisted that a public order organized around 'social
insurance, solicitude in mutuality or cooperation' would be preferable
to either feudal paternalism or capitalist income (75, 67). This welfare
logic, impelled largely by the changing relationship between the
French state, economy, and society after World War I, characterized
the new rationality of colonial administration that developed during
the same period (Wilder 1999a).[15] Mauss could be describing interwar

colonial policy when he writes, 'the art of politics should not be independent of sociology, and sociology should not be disinterested in politics' (75).[16]

The Ecole Coloniale, located in Paris, occupied precisely this intermediary domain of practical rationality between science and action. Created in 1887 as part of the Third Republic's attempt to professionalize and rationalize the colonial service, the Ecole would become the place where most administrators posted in Indochina, Africa and Madagascar received their training. By the interwar period, it gathered functionaries, educators and scholars into a community of discussion and debate on the changing character of the colonial project. Administrators moved back and forth between empire and classroom, just as students who graduated to become administrators often returned later as instructors. The personnel were linked to different branches of the colonial service, colonial interest groups, the press, scholarly societies, academic journals and metropolitan universities.[17]

As William Cohen's research has shown, the Ecole Coloniale's early curriculum emphasized legal studies, colonial policy and colonial history. But after World War I, following a series of reforms, the training emphasized knowledge of local cultures and languages as well as the pragmatic challenges facing a bush administrator (Cohen 1971: 40–48). In 1920 a Chair in Dialectics and Customs of French West Africa was created for Maurice Delafosse, who had taught courses at the school in 1909.[18] Georges Hardy, who became director of the Ecole after Delafosse's death in 1926, reorganized it on the model of France's prestigious grands écoles and institutionalized its ethnological focus.[19]

Under Hardy's tenure, the Ecole sought to form broadly educated administrators possessing specialized management skills and ethnological understanding of their assigned regions. He required students to acquire an increasingly wide range of 'general knowledge'. By 1937, entering students were expected to be familiar with sociology and ethnology (Durkeim, Hubert, Mauss, Lèvy-Bruhl, Simiand, Halbwachs, Febvre, Bloch, Frazer), political economy (liberalism, Marxism, Saint Simonism, and the Physiocrats), and literature (Hugo, Balzac, Taine).[20] Hardy's curriculum also emphasized practical and specialized social studies so that future bureaucrats could 'address administrative, financial, economic, and social questions with the same ease and mastery'.[21] In addition to courses on civil, commercial, and constitutional law, as well as Zoological Technology and Colonial Husbandry, Hardy introduced classes on Applied Colonial Psychology and The Duties of Colonial Administration, which he taught.[22]

Through the 1930s, the Ecole also embraced knowledge of native societies as a requirement of colonial government. In 1929 Hardy had recruited the reformist administrator Henri Labouret for a Chair in General Ethnography at the school.[23] Labouret taught courses on African ethnography, history, and languages as well as one explicitly focused on 'colonial ethnology'. He also applied the school's plan to prepare students for concrete colonial realities when he took one with him on a study mission to Senegal and Guinea in 1932 and another to Cameroon two years later. He described these field trips as 'sociology applied to colonialism' whose goal was 'to observe local collectivities practically, to compare them, and to establish a balance sheet of what they lack in order to provide it to them'.[24]

Students at the Ecole were encouraged to take classes at the Institut d'Ethnologie, the Ecole de Langues Orientales and the Institut de Géographie; faculty circulated among these institutions and the Ecole Coloniale.[25] There were lecture series where colonial administrators as well as colonized elites spoke on subjects such as 'Colonial Sociology' and 'The Psychology of Dahomeans'.[26] At a 1932 student assembly attended by Sarraut, then Minister of Colonies, Governor-General Roume summarized the Ecole's pedagogic project whose 'fundamental object' was 'detailed study of the history and geography of our colonies, the habits (*moeurs*), customs, languages of their populations, and the explanation of different methods of colonization practiced in France and abroad' (Roume 1933: 80–81). He also reminded students that this training had policy implications: 'intimate and confident collaboration with native populations, in view of their moral and material development' (Roume 1933).

In sum, the Ecole sought to integrate knowledge of native societies into a practical administrative sociology taught by instructors with primary experience of colonial government. Affiliated with the school during the interwar period was a critical mass of noted reformist administrators, colonial intellectuals and scholars of indigenous societies.[27] When Robert Delavignette became the Ecole's Director in 1937, he maintained its commitment to link practical colonial experience to local knowledge in the service of good government. He informed provincial lycées offering preparatory courses that the school would provide 'an education in applied administrative science, on the one hand, and a knowledge of geography combined with history, ethnology, sociology, and law, on the other'.[28]

In a convocation speech Delavignette signaled the way that the colonial administration had assimilated the lessons of Durkheimian sociology:

[In the colonies] it is a matter of pursuing an exploration that no longer has to do with territories but that extends to societies . . . we have the responsibility of gathering diverse peoples with a spirit that is attentive to their customs, their religions, their modes of work, and their progress, to guide them to a fraternal organization that will be as fertile for them as for us.[29]

As 'society' had became an object of scientific knowledge since the turn of the century, intellectuals and policymakers shifted their attention away from abstract humanity toward concrete populations formed by distinct histories, cultures and societies. By the interwar period, social reform would no longer target universal individuals but would manage particular communities and would require scientific knowledge of the specific 'milieux' that shaped them.[30]

Administrative ethnography

Discussions of practical rationality in the metropolitan academy and the Ecole Coloniale, which linked ethnography to administration, were echoed by policy initiatives in French West Africa. Knowledge production became an explicit priority for overseas officials who promoted a new art of administration dedicated to the informed management of populations. The privileged instrument of this administrative art was 'the tour' through which the administrator engaged local society in order to define natives' needs and care for their interests. Such understanding, it was believed, would allow administrators to maintain social order, promote economic development and improve Africans' welfare.

This art of government required scientific knowledge of native society, or, in Hardy's words, a new 'colonial sociology' (Hardy 1937). After he became Governor-General, Jules Brévié declared that 'the government of natives . . . requires a veritable science of ethnology' and 'the constitution of a colonial political science' (Brévié 1936: 42). But he acknowledged that rather than being disinterested and objective, this 'science must be subordinated to action' and 'apply itself to concrete, living problems' (43). In a remarkable and prescient recognition that ethnological knowledge could not efface its own conditions of production, Delavignette observed 'We drive in an automobile from village to village researching native women's lip-plugs, on a road that the *commandant* had constructed, without asking how he did so and how he organized the road building crews . . . we can no longer separate native society from territorial colonial administration'.[31] Delavignette believed that while administration had to be scientifically informed, it would also have to adapt to specific local conditions. In other words, rather than create invariable principles of native rule, the ethnologically informed colonial science would have to be a *social* science attentive to geo-cultural differences. Brévié suggested that 'science in the service of colonization always leads to man, to the population, to the native milieu . . . The grand colonial science is still definitively a science of man' (Brévié 1936: 43).

As we have seen, ethnology was the emergent human science during this period and native policies became increasingly concerned with questions of indigenous consciousness. Delafosse thought administrators should be 'nativologists' charged with 'knowing [natives'] needs and desires, what they are, what they want to be, and what they can be' (Delafosse 1923: 107). Hardy distinguished himself from Lèvy-Bruhl by arguing that 'there are no longer primitives, only different people' and advocating an 'ethnic psychology' (Hardy 1925). Asserting that 'the entire object of our native policy is . . . to know and to make ourselves known', he proposed producing a 'psychological monograph, the analysis of a clearly determined and situated mentality' for 'each colonial population' (Hardy 1929: 196–198).

Delavignette also implicitly criticized Lèvy-Bruhl when he insisted that 'the native mentality is not a stagnant thing' but something that 'varies by country and by race' (Delavignette 1931: 553, 556). He envisioned 'an administrator who, instead of producing reports, would have as his principal task the observation of his district' and warned that there would be a colonial crisis if the government did not create ethnological research centers: 'peril is imminent if we do not act . . . the great public works, the great products, the great intentions of Greater France all definitely depend on knowledge of native mentalities' (562–563). Delavignette's remarks on 'Knowledge of Native Mentalities in French West Africa' were presented at the 1931 International and Intercolonial Congress on Native Society (hosted by the Ecole Coloniale in conjunction with the International Colonial Exposition), whose objective was to study 'native society in itself and not only as a function of European action'.[32] This conference indicates how, after World War I, colonial governments began to conceptualize African societies as autonomous entities with their own norms, structures and histories. They, rather than indigenous individuals, became objects of ethnological knowledge and fields of administrative action.

Maurice Delafosse was one of the figures to outline this emergent relationship between postwar native policies and native societies. By 1915, when he became a political advisor to the government-general, he had already served for twenty years as an administrator in French West Africa (Clozel 1912; Delafosse 1976).[33] His scientific publications on African languages and society had already earned him a reputation as an ethnological savant. In a 1919 report on the necessity of African social improvement, Delafosse had argued that colonial authority and political order depended on satisfying natives' 'needs' and 'legitimate aspirations'. He added that 'the material development of the [West African] colonies is strictly correlated with the social development of the indigenous population'.[34]

However this was not a straightforward example of modernizing governmentality. Delafosse's point of departure, as he outlined two years later, was a cultural anthropological, or relativist, conception of non-Western societies:

> It seems that we have a clearer and broader notion of the existence, next to and outside of our society, of other societies each of which has, like ours, its own civilization, its own aspirations, its special needs, and no one now dreams of denying these societies, however different they may be from our French society, the right to conserve their civilizations, to realize their aspirations, to provide for their needs, according to the norm of their genius and their temperament. (Delafosse 1921)

He argued that from the moment human beings began living together, they constituted a society with their own forms of social organization and specific social laws. According to his logic, every individual is a member of some society, which led Delafosse to acknowledge 'every society's right to self-determination': 'human societies . . . cannot be eliminated from the surface of the globe simply by the will of another society . . . we cannot reduce them to slavery or impose on them from a distance customs that they reject, that were not made to fit them, the forced adoption of which could kill them' (146).

In order not to violate this principle, Delafosse proposed a colonial policy that would protect *and* improve native society: 'we have contracted the obligation, first, not to destroy these societies, and second, to help them develop and prosper morally and materially' (147). His goal was 'the conservation and reinforcement of these societies and of all their institutions that will contribute to the material, intellectual, and moral development of black societies' (149). As in 1919, he argued that colonial policy would succeed 'only if we are careful to maintain [natives] in a continually growing state of vigor and activity, which is not conceivable for members of a sick or simply weakened society' (147). In short, this concern with African social integrity was not only an ethical imperative, it was a governing strategy.

Delafosse's vision of colonial government also presupposed and envisioned a pragmatic ethnography of local social and political relations. For example, he characterized 'the patriarchal form of the family' as 'the basis of all native West African social and even political institutions'. He explained that 'the principle of familial solidarity is a powerful lever whose existence can singularly facilitate the work that we want to realize'. Likewise, he proposed that clans, secret societies and age groups were indigenous institutions promoting 'solidarity and mutual aid' that could be 'channeled' to promote 'social improvement'.[35]

There was a direct relationship between this dual concern to protect yet develop native societies and his ethnological account of them. Delafosse's scholarship was marked by the same tension I discussed in Mauss between conceptualizing indigenous societies as fixed *and* fluid. For example, he identified 'collectivism' as a trait common to *nègres* in general which determines the social, religious, property, economic and political domains of African life and subsumes the interests of the individual (Delafosse 1927: 38, 40, 51). Yet he also addressed the mutability of African collectivity. He observed that native converts to Islam or Christianity decided to practice an individualism that would lead to 'a disruption of society, beginning with the total disorganization of even family principles' (39, 41). Scientific evaluations and administrative imperatives thus mirrored each other in Delafosse's writing.

Delafosse, who was one of the founders of the Institut d'Ethnologie, served as an important intermediary between colonial-administrative and metropolitan-scientific communities (Delafosse 1976: 375–380). He was also a crucial bridge between pre- and postwar cohorts of administrator-ethnographers. If the earlier group was motivated largely by the anti-slavery campaign, questions of African Islam and legal questions related to property rights, the new generation of reformers was concerned largely with the internal coherence of African ethnicities and social formations (Cohen 1971: 37–101; Sibeud 1994; Amselle and Sibeud 1998). As scholars and administrators, these interwar figures internalized the integrated vision of African geography, ethnology, linguistics, history and civilization that Delafosse elaborated in *Haut-Sénégal-Niger* (Delafosse 1912). On the one hand, this encyclopedic overview synthesized the practical ethnology initiated by Francois-Joseph Clozel in Cote d'Ivoire beginning at the turn of the century (Clozel and Villamur 1902; Villamur and Delafosse 1904).[36] On the other hand, it charted a course for a postwar administrative sensibility most fully realized under Governor-General Brévié.

After graduating from the Ecole Coloniale and serving as Director of Political Affairs in Sudan under Clozel, Brévié collaborated with Delafosse on *Haut-Sénégal-Niger*. In turn, Delafosse wrote the preface for Brévié's own contribution to African ethnology, which he published in 1923 after having been promoted to supervise political affairs for all of French West Africa (Brévié 1923; Labouret 1930c).[37] This 'essay on colonial political psychology' valorized indigenous African religious practices over an imported Islam. Brévié argued that colonial policy should work to preserve authentic African civilizations whose essentially collectivist character he insisted upon throughout the text, in which he cited Lévy-Bruhl approvingly.[38] Brévié's scholarship anticipated his later administrative concerns by integrating ethnography and recommendations for native policy.

Delafosse also served as an example for another interwar reformer, Henri Labouret. After Delafosse's death in 1926, Labouret was chosen to assume his elder colleague's Chair in Soudanese Languages at the Ecole des Langues Orientales. After later becoming an instructor at the Ecole Coloniale, his courses on African history, languages and ethnology had a deep influence on those students who became African administrators between the wars (Cohen 1971: 94–95). Labouret began as a captain in the Colonial Infantry, where he participated in subjugating natives in Cote d'Ivoire in 1911. After being wounded and losing the use of his right arm, he petitioned to join the civilian administration and became a *commandant* in Haute Volta in 1912.[39] Assigned to a supposedly 'difficult' region, his early years were focused on suppressing rebellions among the Lobi people.[40] Labouret was engaged in a 'civilizing' militarism that combined force and administration. He described this population as 'backward, primitive', a group that 'knew no other law than that of the most savage vengeance, they lived in a state of complete anarchy and permanent hostility'. He recounted tours focused on 'the destruction of armed gangs' and 'numerous nocturnal arrests of those involved in blood feuds [*les vengeurs de sang*], rapists and thieves'. But Labouret also added 'at the same time, permanent administrative contact has been made with still rebellious natives, the education of whom has been initiated and pursued'.[41] For him the successful 'submission of natives' included the payment of taxes, increased commercial activity, the recruitment of indigenous soldiers and the disarmament of hostile and 'savage' populations.[42] This military pacification and administrative normalization earned him high performance evaluations.[43]

Despite this personal involvement in direct conquest, Labouret's professional reputation would be based more on his knowledge of native languages and societies than on the suppression of native rebellions. Although turnover among local administrators was rapid, he served an uncharacteristic fourteen years in the same region. This continuity allowed him to study the forms of social organization under his command. Like Delafosse, Labouret was a pragmatic linguist-ethnologist. He had entered the colonial service speaking English,

German and Portuguese, and had studied African languages at the Ecole des Langues Orientales. His linguistic and ethnological competence was praised by the colonial governors under whom he served. They recognized a relationship between his success in restoring peace and prosperity to a recalcitrant region and his deep local knowledge.[44]

In the 1920s, this former military hero came to exemplify the interwar ideal of the culturally informed, politically effective bush administrator who understood the relationship between good government, local knowledge, and native welfare. In 1926 he was appointment as Director of Political Affairs in the Ministry of Colonies, which was interested in his field experience and ethnological expertise.[45] In a telling summary of Labouret's career, the Ministry recast his conquest of the Lobi as 'the methodic action of a fortunate native policy'. The review noted his 'several study missions' and emphasized that 'M. Labouret is also a learned ethnologist, whose work is as renowned in France as abroad'.[46]

By the time he began this second career as a metropolitan bureaucrat, Labouret had indeed become a respected scholar who published monographs on African society, linguistics and colonial politics.[47] He trained future administrators at the Ecole Coloniale to promote a vision of native policy founded upon ethnological competence, the protection of indigenous social organization, and native social welfare. He argued that native policy 'requires an exhaustive study of the society and a skillful adjustment of our methods to the framework of that society ... The enterprise is not only administrative, it is scientific and cannot be improvised' (Labouret 1930b: 133). In an article titled 'Colonial Ethnology', he wrote that administration would depend upon 'the exact understanding of natives' languages, *moeurs*, institutions, manners of living, acting, reacting and thinking', and explained that administrators must be 'linguists, ethnologists, and above all psychologists' (Labouret 1932: 49).

Unlike many interwar reformers engaged in knowledge production, Labouret was oriented more toward questions of objective social structures than subjective native mentalities. He produced an elaborate 'Plan for Regional Monographs' which provided administrators with 'all the elements necessary to understand and guide populations that will be placed under their authority'. This was a comprehensive and highly detailed document that categorized the totality of native society in terms of geographic milieu, history, populations, material technologies, indigenous industries, languages, forms of knowledge, aesthetics, social organization, family practices, kinship systems, economic, political, juridical, and religious organization, and systems of belief. The Plan indicates precisely what kind of information should be gathered in each of these domains and the types of questions to be asked of different social actors (Labouret 1933a).[48] Informed by academic anthropology's concern with the holistic study of society, this text can be read as a French imperial combination of Mauss's *Manuel d'Ethnographie* and the British *Notes and Queries*.[49] Labouret's professional affiliation with academic anthropology at the inception of its 'classical period' was indicated by the scholarly bibliography that he attached to the monograph plan.[50] He warned against relying on the accounts of cultural mediators (servants, youth, native police and soldiers, interpreters) and counseled researchers to learn local languages and live 'alongside tribal society' instead of actually 'sharing the life of the tribe' (1933a: 2–3).

Like Mauss and Delafosse, Labouret's own ethnology was marked by a tension between static and evolutionary understandings of native society. His major monograph, *Les tribus du rameau Lobi*, presents a totalizing representation of a timeless African society fixed by custom. His discussions of Lobi demographics, technology, aesthetics, social and economic organization, law, morality and religion continually remark on the high degree of functional integration among such a seemingly decentralized and disorganized 'tribe' with no formal governing structures or socio-political hierarchy beyond the family (Labouret 1931b).[51] Labouret takes pains to establish the scholarly legitimacy of his monograph and assures the reader that the work is based on rigorous ethnological methods including knowledge of the Lobi language, a long stay in the field, and knowledgable informants (v–viii). Although he conducted research while a local colonial administrator, the text is written with minimal reference to his own colonial location or to the colonial field which structured Lobi social practices.

However, a brief final section, 'Evolution', identifies the intimate relationship between colonial ethnology and governing strategy, between local knowledge and colonial authority. In order to manage the violent and rebellious Lobi, he proposes the 'methodical purging' of select agitators based on extensive local knowledge (495). Once purified, he suggests, indigenous society will naturally evolve as the administration builds roads, promotes market exchange and organizes local political hierarchies. A new municipal spirit, growing economic intercourse and the freer movement of subjects across larger regions, according to Labouret, would then effectively ensure social order and contribute to indigenous evolution. After almost 500 pages of decontextualized ethnography that describes an unchanging social formation, the monograph thus concludes with a vision of comprehensive

African social transformation driven by a program of economic and administrative intervention.

In *Les manding et leur langue*, Labouret focuses on the centrality of the family to this process of social evolution in the French Soudan. He criticizes previous scholarship for focusing on political and military history while neglecting 'the transformation of the family' which he argues is 'the principal element upon which progress in African territories should and must rest' (Labouret 1934: 50). This account addresses the influence that colonial intervention has had on the authority of the *chef de famille*. According to Manding custom, the family head is charged with managing collective property and executing group justice in order to ensure social solidarity and protect the common good. Manding marriages, in this traditional order, had been contracts between two families. This system, Labouret tells us, has been accurately labeled 'communism' (60).

He then recounts the way that in a single generation of French rule this collective family economy was being displaced by 'an already powerful urban economy'. Colonial 'peace and security' allowed for the greater circulation of colonial subjects across colonies where they could acquire 'new ideas' (62). A new class of Soudanese migrant laborers traveling to Togo, Gold Coast, Cote d'Ivoire and Senegal returned to Manding villages and demonstrated their independence, refusing to obey traditional family heads. This 'seasonal proletariat', in Labouret's account, attended school, stimulated social envy, and had sufficient personal savings to pay for marriage ceremonies without needing chiefs to grant them collective property. With the support of colonial administrators who restricted the authority of traditional chiefs generally, as well as colonial courts that recognized individual rights of self-determination contrary to custom, marriage became a contract between individuals. Labouret concludes 'the kinship collectivity upon which we have counted until now is rapidly disintegrating; another group is succeeding it, weaker but more accessible, more flexible and easily educated: the nuclear household [*simple ménage*] . . . the conjugal family' (64).

In this text it is not clear whether Labouret fears or embraces this transformation. In either case, he presents the family as a central index and site of these changes. He identifies social disintegration as an effect of colonial intervention. Finally, he treats this entire process as the object of ethnological inquiry. Labouret indicates the close relationship between scholarship and administration when he refers to this monograph as a 'manual' which synthesizes courses he taught at the Ecole Coloniale and the Ecole des Langues Orientales: 'intended for students about to leave for West Africa, it is designed to be used as instrument for work in the field' (7). This study thus addressed directly the way colonial ethnology and policy informed one another.

As we have seen with Mauss, Delafosse and Labouret, colonial ethnology fixed African masses within their social groups by maintaining that they were subsumed by their cultures, existing in a state of pure collectivity, where myth reigned over reason and the group wholly dominated the individual. Yet colonial ethnologists were also preoccupied with the problem of social transformation caused by French intervention. They believed that indigenous social categories such as clan, collectivity, communal property, and custom were transmuting respectively into nuclear families, individuality, private property, and law. French native policy sought both to prevent and promote these developments.[52]

Scientific administration

These members of the Ecole Coloniale and the administrator-ethnographers that I have discussed belonged to a cohort of reformist administrators whom after World War I elaborated a new logic and strategy of colonial government. As senior administrators, teachers and writers they were able to shape colonial policies, theories of administration and public opinion (Wilder 2005). These reformers expanded on well-established prewar precedents, including the critique of colonial assimilation (as scientifically unsound, administratively ineffective and politically dangerous) and announcements by the government-general that native evolution in Africa should unfold within local social systems. But a number of developments converged after the war that allowed administration in West Africa to be reconceptualized as older currents of colonial politics were reactivated, redirected and combined with each other in novel ways.[53]

Internationally, Wilson's and Lenin's different reason for promoting the rights of colonial peoples to self-determination vitalized a new anti-imperialist sentiment in Europe and its overseas empires (Liauzu 1982). Nationally, a new consciousness of Greater France insisted that colonies were no longer merely a source of manpower, materials and markets but integral parts of the nation itself (Sarraut 1923, Lebovics 1992, Wilder 2001). Politicians and the public also acknowledged France's so-called 'blood-debt' to colonial populations who, in return for their war-time loyalty, were seen to deserve a new deal. By the 1920s, a new generation of modernizers, informed by theories of scientific management, advocated 'administration' and 'welfare' as instruments of comprehensive social management by an activist state allied with both capital and labor (Maier 1970; Kuisel 1981; Donzelot 1984; Rosanvallon 1990).

Within West Africa, by the end of World War I, generations of French policies appeared to have undermined indigenous institutions and created new sources of disorder: demilitarized colonial soldiers reluctant to resume their former village lives, uprooted peasants attracted to growing colonial cities, a nascent urban bourgeoisie eager to play a greater role in municipal politics, and a generation of students who expected employment opportunities and political liberties commensurate with their education (Cohen 1971; Johnson 1971; Conklin 1997). By this time a growing population of colonial immigrants – workers, professionals and students – had also settled in metropolitan France. There, a small but organized community of black activists, accustomed to greater social mobility and civil rights, addressed liberal, communist and nationalist messages to their colonial brethren (Spiegler 1968; Dewitte 1985; Wilder 1999b). These groups posed potential political problems that required novel administrative strategies.

Deracinated peasants, unruly veterans and resentful elites also threatened the West African economy, which depended largely on the productivity of independent cultivators who had to be persuaded to produce export crops (Suret-Canale 1962). Economic growth thus required indigenous populations to remain connected to rural social networks and production systems. However post-World War I policymakers, who saw the empire as an engine of national economic growth, began to promote *la mise en valeur* at precisely the moment when village society, upon which development depended, appeared to be breaking down.

Out of this constellation of circumstances emerged colonial humanism, a new political rationality for the administration of West Africa. Colonial humanism was a governmental logic – entailing strategies, targets, and techniques – organized around three interdependent objectives: political order, economic development, and social welfare. Note that 'humanism', as the term is used here, does not simply refer to reformers' benevolent attitudes toward natives (whether sincere or disingenuous), but to the fact that colonial government became preoccupied with indigenous welfare and sought to manage African societies as dynamic wholes.[54]

A concern with population pervaded administrative discourse in French West Africa through the 1930s. When Jules Brévié became Governor-General, he immediately asserted that 'we could not possibly separate our political action from our social action' (Brévié 1930: 28). He explained, 'the metropole has a direct interest in quickly increasing the number of births and the standard of health of colonial populations, from whom it demands soldiers, workers, products, and rising purchasing power' (Brévié 1936: 20). Brévié linked these social policies directly to an economic project: 'The production of wealth is almost exclusively in native hands. Our economic development and their social progress at this time therefore depends on the constant improvement of their productive faculties' (Brévié 1930: 40). These statements indicate that promoting native welfare was not a *justification for French power* in West Africa (as under the old civilizing mission). It was a new strategy for exercising a specific *form of power* designed to promote economic growth (whether or not this vision was practiced successfully).

The interwar administration thus sought to protect African village life as a precondition for economic development. But it also identified traditional society – characterized as irrational, collectivist, corrupt – as an obstacle to colonial development, which would require rational, autonomous, consuming individuals organized into nuclear families and possessing private property. In other words, colonial humanism was as eager to promote social evolution as it was to protect social structures.

Consistent with his earlier scholarship, Brévié maintained that colonial subjects lived within 'primitive collectivities' that stifled individualism, even as he warned that native societies could 'rapidly disintegrate into the dust of anarchic individualities over whom we have no authority' (Brévié 1930: 16–17, 28). Likewise, Labouret invoked a 'universal tendency toward individualism' to explain the unavoidable native social evolution initiated by French colonialism, yet also commented on 'the fragmentation of indigenous collectivities' that 'is accelerating with impressive speed and would risk being dangerous if it was not directed' (Labouret 1931a: 24, 1933b: 190). Hardy wrote that although the government in West Africa attempted to respect customary social institutions, 'we bring individualism with us, despite ourselves' (Hardy 1931: 616–617). This inexorable shift from collectivity to individuality was both feared and desired, a deliberate goal and unfortunate consequence of French policies.

The governing project in West Africa was grounded upon a constitutive contradiction.[55] Administrators sought to promote socioeconomic individuality without creating legal and political individuals. They dreamed of colonial subjects possessed by rational self-interest, consumerist desires and a productivist ethos, who were nevertheless embedded in indigenous relations of production. These ideal Africans would respect local norms and remain obedient to traditional authority. Yet, unburdened by cultural misconceptions, they would also respond immediately to the colonial state's administrative directives.[56]

Following these competing imperatives, interwar native policies concerned with the welfare of African populations sought both to protect and to transform indigenous social relations.[57] This tension was explored at the 1931 Congress on Native Society, where presentations discussed balancing a need to protect native customs from the malignant social transformations that were produced by the colonial encounter with the need to produce other transformations necessary for African economic, social and moral development. Native society was something to be known but directed; protected yet improved. Colonial ethnology, which linked practical science and scientific administration, was a feature of both poles of this political rationality. These competing ethnological-administrative objectives led to a governmental preoccupation with the African family, which was seen to be the elemental unit of native society and matrix of traditional culture. Policymakers identified the family form as an institution guaranteeing social order, an index of social evolution and an instrument of social engineering.

Family dynamics, for example, were at the center of Delavignette's *Les Paysans Noirs*, published in 1931 when he was working at the Agence Économique, and based on his own field experience. The novel dramatizes a government program to turn a village community into self-contained households of property-owning individuals through the introduction of a peanut oil press. But marriage practices come to figure centrally in this story of economic development. Villagers are persuaded to accept the new machine because it will allow them to cultivate an export crop on their own family farms so that they can make enough money to pay bride-prices and thereby enable their children to marry according to tradition. But after the harvest, we learn, the newly married couples modify indigenous customs by establishing independent households (Delavignette 1931: 256–257). Delavignette thus traces the circular ideal of colonial humanism: modernizing reforms work to increase colonial revenues *and* protect native family institutions, but marriage practices themselves work in turn to modernize village society, which continues, nevertheless, to exist.

Throughout the interwar period, contradictory native policies, family discourses and administrative ethnography became entwined. Consider the prototypically 'public' issue of native chiefs. Governor-General Brévié, like his interwar predecessors, conceded the failure of prewar policies to eliminate indigenous political structures.[58] His policy of restoring authority to native chiefs required detailed ethnographic knowledge not only of indigenous political systems, but also of family lineages, kinship systems and rules governing succession (Brévié 1930: 12, 15, 16, 1931: 42–43, 1935: 27). This information would enable administrators to follow customary practices in their selection of indigenous rulers who would be sufficiently embedded in their communities to possess genuine political legitimacy.

Throughout the 1930s, field administrators reported perpetual struggles between rural populations and the new 'traditional' chiefs supported by the colonial state. Tensions between chiefs and educated elites also flared. The administration believed that such traditional leaders were needed to prevent rural communities from unraveling and to restrain the disorderly elements of a modernizing population. But they also regarded these chiefs as obstacles to colonial development.[59] Reformers argued that local chiefs, and especially their younger heirs, had to be educated and that African political systems had to be changed in order to correspond to evolving social conditions (Brévié 1931: 45–46). Colonial reforms were thus designed to modify indigenous institutions, which could then moderate disruptive social change yet initiate needed social improvements.

The administration also sought to prevent village society from disintegrating by organizing a distinct native justice system that would allow colonial subjects to live in their own communities, regulated by customary civil law.[60] Governor-General Brévié explained to his administrators that this system, which he had inherited, depended upon detailed knowledge of 'native juridical customs, and institutions, especially those concerning the family and property' (Brévié 1935: 63). Corresponding to a decree reforming this system in 1931, Brévié ordered a comprehensive ethnographic survey of West African customs concerning labor, exchange, contracts, property, inheritance, family, marriage and religion; a work of 'classification and coordination' to be carried out by local administrators according to a 'patient, prudent, and scrupulous method' (Brévié 1931: 51, 1935: 63). He also instructed administrators to maintain regional monographs in order to create an archive of local knowledge for their non-juridical activities (Brévié 1935: 17–18). But five years later, despite 123 responses from administrators, a Commission of Codification was unable to synthesize them into coherent manuals of customary law (Maupoil 1939: 26, 40–41).

This outcome was in part due to tensions within the very enterprise. The administration sought to codify customary law without creating native legal codes. On the one hand, colonial reformers wanted to rationalize native justice by objectifying indigenous social norms, forms and practices. On the other hand, colonial reformers opposed codification because they believed it would be impossible to keep up with the rapid transformation of native societies or because fixing codes would impede the evolution of the societies that the administration was encouraging.[61]

Although codification could be read as a policy failure, the administration's pledge to observe customary law (i.e., to study it and to respect it in policymaking) also became an instrument of social regulation. Consider Léon Geismar's *Receuil des coutumes civiles des races du Sénégal* (Geismar 1933). Published to enable judges to respect local practices, it also proposed juridical interventions that would prohibit forced and child marriages, limit bride-wealth payments (so wives could not be 'bought'), and legalize divorce by mutual consent (218–219). He argued that such texts could help judges 'adapt the native to his new form of life' (Geismar 1934: 164). In 1933 the Governor of Senegal told administrators they should use Geismar's legal text to 'guide jurisprudence in a direction that favors the healthy social development of your *administrés*'.[62] This civil law manual thus began as descriptive, became prescriptive, and ended as an instrument to encourage social change. The administration sought to transcribe native customs in order to allow colonial subjects to live within their own indigenous communities. Yet the very practices of ethnographic documentation worked to change those native customs in order to promote social transformations.[63]

The existence of a dual justice system in colonial West Africa created another set of ethnological-administrative problems. Even as the administration worked to fix and separate African society, it also made provisions for exemplary Africans to 'advance to the status of French citizenship'.[64] Interwar discourse on colonial citizenship refracted the government's dual imperative to protect and transform indigenous life. Debates over citizenship also signaled the ways in which the colonial state simultaneously described natives and produced the native as a category. Moreover, colonial citizenship was one of the primary sites for ethnology and scientific administration to work on and through one another. During the interwar period, the African family was implicated in struggles to define or access this ever ambiguous legal status.

Many West Africans who otherwise met the basic criteria for citizenship – proven devotion to French interests, the ability to read and write French, good morals – were rejected because they had not detached themselves sufficiently from the indigenous cultural milieu.[65] In most cases the candidate's family circumstances – polygamy, wives who could not speak French, children who did not attend French schools – were used as proof that he was unsuitable for citizenship. In cases where applicants were granted citizenship, their wives and children usually were not.[66] Officials argued that the 1912 decree defined citizenship as an individual status that could not be conferred automatically upon family members. Article Six of that decree stipulated that wives could only advance to citizenship alongside their husbands if the couple had been married 'under the empire of French law' (which also required registering in the *état civil*). But even cases where couples tried to comply with this regulation were rejected regularly. The West African administration argued that because the civil affairs of colonial subjects were regulated by customary law, it was technically impossible for them to be married under French law. Nor, by definition, could they register their marriages in the French *état civil*, which was reserved for citizens.[67]

It is not surprising that the colonial state deployed legal semantics to restrict citizenship. More remarkable is the fact that family practices became the focal point of a struggle over political rights, which are usually associated with the public sphere.[68] Most administrators did not believe that African women could easily transcend their autochthonous mentality. Unassimilated wives rearing unschooled children in a customary manner were seen to degrade citizenship rights, which they could not exercise responsibly, and undermine indigenous social order. The administration's fear was so deep that it was willing to risk inevitable conflicts that would arise when family members of different citizenship status would have to adjudicate shared civil affairs in separate courts regulated by distinct legal codes.

However there was more at stake here than cultural appearances. The administration recognized that once an African woman obtained citizenship through marriage, all of her subsequent children would be automatic French citizens, whether or not they were assimilated, without having to fulfill the normal requirements for 'advancement'.[69] This would be an unacceptable colonial variant of republican motherhood. The colonial state, in other words, would lose control over political enfranchisement. However, policymakers realized that limiting family citizenship would not resolve this dilemma: once a husband was granted French citizenship it would be perfectly legal for him to (re)marry according to French civil law, register the marriage in the French *état civil*, and even go to court to legally recognize children.[70] In this way, his entire family, including future children, would become citizens, regardless of how 'evolved' they were seen to be.[71]

Debates over family citizenship continued throughout the 1920s in Paris and West Africa. The administration finally introduced measures that increased surveillance over family practices and control over the citizenship process. Following directions from the Minister of Colonies (Sarraut), Brévié introduced new legislation in 1932 that

[358]

revised the 1912 decree, which had insisted that legal status was individual.[72] The new system allowed wives and children to share the new legal status of men who were granted citizenship. But there was a catch: the cultural criteria for 'advancement' were extended to the entire family. The applicant was required to be monogamous, to have registered his marriage and births with the *état civil*, and to provide a French education to his children. If he could not demonstrate that his whole family 'approached [French] civilization through education, lifestyle and social customs', neither he nor they could become citizens.[73] Brévié warned his governors that in order to evolve, a native 'must not be constantly subject, in his own home [foyer] to influences that are directly opposed to the direction in which he is evolving'.[74] The administration also hoped to thereby prevent unassimilated women, children and future progeny from diluting the citizenship pool.

Corollary measures were needed for this system to function properly. First, the administration had to verify the candidate's family circumstances. Since the 1912 decree, Africans had to demonstrate their 'good life and good morals' in order to obtain citizenship.[75] The broader 1932 criteria for family assimilation required local administrators to conduct an investigation of a candidate's household before issuing an official Certificat de Bonne Vie et Moeurs without which citizenship could not be granted.[76] Such a determination would necessarily entail ethnographic inquiry; the *commandant* would evaluate the candidate's home life in terms of an implicit understanding of the difference between African and European domestic norms and practices.[77]

A second instrument of documentation-regulation that complemented the 1932 citizenship decree was the *état civil indigène*. The new citizenship law, like the old one, required Africans to register marriages and births with the *état civil* as a condition of citizenship.[78] But Brévié also resolved the paradox of previous policy that had required candidates to make such declarations in a civil registry that the law prohibited them from using. After sanctioning family citizenship, he also created an official *état civil indigène* which attempted to rationalize a system that had been informally regulated by local bureaucrats.[79] Following his predecessors, he promoted native registries as a way to prevent Africans from manipulating French tribunals in order to obtain citizenship for their children.[80] He also maintained that this new legislation would provide a 'legal basis' for Africans' civil declarations; they would now be regulated by native tribunals and would count for their citizenship applications.[81] The *état civil*, like the native justice system, thus worked to police the boundary between European citizens and African subjects, upon which the colonial order depended.

The administration designed the *état civil* to be a flexible instrument of ethnographic inquiry, political control and social reform. As early as 1915, the Chef du Service Judiciaire in West Africa characterized the *état civil* in terms of bio-politics: 'to assure as perfectly as possible the parentage of every child born on our territory and to identify him in order to follow him during the entire course of his life, to know his life-cycle and to protect his public, private and family interests'.[82] He claimed that including Africans in the *état civil* would 'facilitate surveillance' as well as be indispensable for creating military recruitment rolls, tax lists and police records.[83] In similar terms, Sarraut later supported Brévié's *état civil indigène* on the grounds that it was 'good administration' that would 'enable the methodical classification of declarations and facilitate future research'. He envisioned the creation of a central alphabetized catalogue that would track every individual's civil life (including birth, marriage, death, divorce, children) and serve as the basis for 'judicial decisions . . . the census, fiscal policy, emigration, the health service, military recruitment'.[84] A subsequent report on the *état civil indigene* pronounced that 'very soon the entire population of French West Africa will come to understand the utility and benefits of our work which will have salutary repercussions on . . . the social life of populations, notably regarding the constitution of the family, the observation of demographic movements, the recruitment of native troops, the fixing and collecting of taxes, etc.'.[85]

Brévié's new system reflected the same duality present in his other native policies. Local governors were told that this *état civil indigène* was a tool of 'demographic documentation' designed to record village life as it existed. Yet Dakar reminded them that the *état civil* was 'the only institution that could guarantee the identity of individuals and provide a written basis for the constitution of the family'.[86] Civil registration would also signal that Africans were 'sufficiently emancipated from their ancestral customs' (Brévié 1935: 13). In other words, the collection of information was part of a documentary policy to protect native society at the same time that it sought to transform Africans into modern individuals organized into nuclear families.

Ironically this system, designed to supervise and reform colonial subjects, also became a source of intense governmental anxiety. For years field administrators complained that ordinary Africans refused to register their civil acts with colonial authorities. Many of them did not know about the system and there were not enough field agents to supervise it.[87] In other cases, cultural practices such as polygamy and naming babies eight days after birth, disinclined them to use the registries.[88] Officials debated whether registration should remain voluntary, as Brévié insisted, or whether sanctions should be applied to those who ignored the process, as his agents often suggested.[89]

The administration was even more troubled by the way in which Africans did use the civil registries. Officials complained that they were unaccustomed to bureaucratic procedures and declared false information, listed multiple names for the same child, and borrowed European names.[90] The colonial state was most troubled by the local practice of deliberately making false statements in the *état civil* or before French and native courts. Africans were accused of using such fraudulent methods to obtain citizenship for themselves (by declaring their birth in one of the four communes), for their wives and children (by officially recognizing them after obtaining citizenship) for other people's children (by declaring them as their own), or to evade military recruitment. Dakar railed regularly against colonial courts for their lack of supervision and uninformed decisions. Judges often didn't have the correct names of the Africans on trial. These courts were instructed to conduct field investigations to verify native declarations through family visits, interviewing witnesses to births and deaths, requiring documents proving claims/demanding written proof for claims, and recording the custom by which couples were married.[91]

Designed to rationalize surveillance, restrict citizenship and control fraud, the *état civil indigène* offered Africans an opportunity to manipulate the colonial legal system and bypass the naturalization process altogether. This institution, which documented the civil lives of colonial populations, was a source of ethnographic information. But it was disorganized, loosely regulated and easily manipulated. For it to function at all, administrators had to produce even more ethnography about family norms, marriage practices, kinship rules and local genealogies.[92]

Conclusion

Colonial ethnology privileged African households precisely because family structures were understood by the colonial state to be indices and catalysts for the social transformations that government policies sought to promote and prevent. I am neither claiming that French political or intellectual biases prevented them from truly understanding local cultures nor am I taking a position on the adequacy of representations. Rather, I have tried to identify how ethnologists' (contradictory) characterizations of African social relations and (contradictory) native policies were intrinsically related to, and did not simply influence, one another.

Administrative and scientific imperatives within the French empire were linked dialectically as they constructed African society as fixed yet fluid, ruled by collectivity yet drawn inexorably to individuality. Both were crystallized forms of practical reason or rational government. Together they produced colonial humanism, a doubled and contradictory political rationality, even as they were its products. This political rationality informed government initiatives, administrative ethnography, academic institutions and metropolitan scholarship; it provided the very categories for analysis, debate and policy. Colonial government thus produced terms and data taken up by French ethnology that then shaped administration, which fueled administrative ethnographies that generated metropolitan scholarship ... and vice versa.

Colonial ethnology must thus be understood as a scientific-administrative complex that included scholars, teachers and administrators, inside and outside of government, in the metropole and overseas through which practical science and scientific administration constituted one another, whether deliberately or despite actors' self-understanding.[93] In 1903, Mauss and Durkheim recognized in 'primitive classification' a correspondence between systems of logic and social systems (Durkheim and Mauss 1963). Although their model was crudely mechanical, they could have employed it self-reflexively insofar as interwar anthropologists (and administrators) were engaged in processes of classifying primitives. They would perhaps have been able also to identify the underlying relation between scientific and social categories that characterized their own colonial ethnology.

Notes

1 Interwar British anthropologists were also clear about this connection. See Malinowski 1929 and James 1973.
2 Although Foucault's late work on the state has received considerable attention in recent years, more focus has been placed on the issue of 'governmentality' than on 'political rationality', especially by British scholars who are interested in developing a Foucauldian account of liberalism. See Miller and Rose 1990; Gordon 1991, 2000; Rose and Miller 1992; Barry et al. 1996; Dean 1999; Rose 1999. Insightful discussions of political rationality are presented in Rose and Miller 1992: 178–81 and Dean 1994: 181–187.
3 In Wilder n.d. I develop a fuller critical reading of the methodological, empirical and meta-historical ways in which Foucault uses this term which I then modify in order to exploit its analytic potential.
4 In addition to the Foucault articles that I have cited, see Donzelot 1979; Ewald 1986; Rosanvallon 1990; Procacci; 1993.
5 Precisely these connections are illuminated in Salemink 1991, 1999; Lorcin 1995; Mamdani 1996; Comaroff and Comaroff 1997: 365–404, Schulte Nordholt 1999; Dirks 2001; Steinmetz 2003.

6   In this book Leclerc focuses more on British social anthropology than on French ethnology.

7   For an intellectual history of French ethnology that names but does not explore its relationship with French colonialism, see Richard Gringeri, 'Twilight of the Sun Kings: French Anthropology from Modernism to Postmodernism, 1925–1950' Ph.D. Dissertation, University of California, Berkeley, 1990.

8   For a self-critical first-hand account of this mission, see Leiris 1981. In Jamin 1984 the close relationship between this study mission, the new Musée de l'Homme, colonial institutions and academic ethnology is explored. See also Clifford 1988: 55–91, 165–174.

9   For example, Marcel Griaule's *Jeux Dogons* (1938) and *Masques Dogons* (1938). On Leenhardt, who embodied this relationship between colonialism and the *Institut d'ethnologie*, see Clifford 1982: 138–139, 151–157.

10 On Rivière, who was a close friend of Leiris, see Leiris 1992: 30, Lebovics 1992: 149–156. On the earlier schemas against which the new ethnology defined itself, see Dias 1991.

11 Rivet and Rivière, 'La réorganisation du Musée d'ethnographie du Trocadéro': 148.

12 Mauss's Institute lectures were transcribed by students and later collected in this volume. Mauss distinguished between primitive and archaic societies, the latter being those subject to colonial domination, which he identifies as the proper object of ethnographic observation.

13 He maintained that all primitive societies share a common form of 'pre-logical' thought (mythical and synthetic rather than analytic) wherein things have mystical properties and persons apprehend them in an unmediated fashion through relationships of subjective 'participation' (35–136). It is as if Lévy-Bruhl simply displaced Bergson's epistemology onto so-called primitive societies.

14 He again argues that not all societies are nations on 594.

15 For an interesting discussion of Lévy-Bruhl's *Ethics and Moral Science* (1903) as it relates both to Durkheimian sociology and the Third Republic's moralizing project, see Bullard 2000: 285–290. But Bullard reads Durkheim's cultural relativism (found also in the work of Lévy-Bruhl, Mauss and Leenhardt) as a redemptive alternative to a universalizing Republican racism rather than its particularizing counterpart.

16 He also warns that social science must remain relevant to present concerns and cannot restrict itself to studying 'that which is facile, amusing, curious, bizarre, past, and without danger' in dead or faraway societies.

17 The most comprehensive institutional history of the Ecole Coloniale is provided in Cohen 1971.

18 ANSOM, EC 127/1, Dossier Maurice Delafosse; ANSOM EC 10/4 'Rapports généraux du conseil du perfectionnement', 1927.

19 ANSOM EC 10/4 'Rapports généraux du conseil du perfectionnement', 1930.

20 ANSOM EC 16/5 'Lettre de l'École colonial aux MM. Les Proviseurs des lycées', 9 September 1937.

21 ANSOM EC 10/4 'Rapports généraux du conseil du perfectionnement,' 1930; ANSOM EC 10/4 'Rapports généraux du conseil du perfectionnement', 1934.

22 ANSOM EC Régistre 9 'Procès verbal de la Commission de l'enseignement', 26 June 1930.

23 ANSOM, EC, 129/32, Dossier Henri Labouret. The École des Langues Orientales was another site where ethnology intersected with colonial administration.

24 ANSOM, EC 129/32, Letter from Labouret to the Director of the EC, June 17, 1934, Dossier Labouret. By 1937 Delavignette institutionalized summer field trips (*voyages d'études*) to colonial posts for students at the École. ANSOM, EC 14, Rapport Général au Conseil de Perfectionnement, 1937; ANSOM, EC 15/3, Rapport sur le Fonctionnement de l'École, 1938; ANSOM, EC, Régistre 11, Procès Verbal, Conseil de Perfectionnement, 27 May 1938; ANSOM – EC 37/10, Letter from Réné Barthes, Le Chef de Cabinet du Ministre des Colonies to MM. les Gouverneurs-Généraux de l'AOF, AEF, et M. le Commissiare de la République au Cameroun, 18 July 1937.

25 For example, Labouret and Delafosse also offered courses on ethnography at the Institut d'Ethnologie and students from the Ecole regularly attended classes there. See Gringeri, 1990: 162–167.

26 ANSOM EC 15/3, Rapport sur le Fonctionnement de l'École, 1938. The École was one of the institutions to incorporate native elites into the colonial humanist project. Paul Hazoumé, who would become one of the first African ethnographers as well as a novelist, gave the lecture on Dahomean Psychology. Indochinese intellectuals were also brought in to lecture students of the school. Hamani Diori, who would become a leader of decolonization in Niger, was recruited by Labouret to teach Djerma and Haussa languages at the school in 1938. After the war, Léopold Senghor would also be a language instructor there.

27 These included Delafosse, Hardy, Labouret and Robert Delavignette, as well as high functionaries who had participated in colonial reform debates since the turn of the century (governors-general Olivier, Roume, and Brévié; Albert Duchène, Charles Régismanset and Gaston Joseph), younger progressive West African administrators (Albert Charton, Hubert Deschamps), leading ethnologists affiliated with the Musée de l'Homme and the Institut d'Ethnologie (Paul Rivet, Jacques Soustelle, Maurice Leenhardt), and an influential colonial legal scholar (Henri Solus).

28 ANSOM, EC 16/5, Letter from the École to the Proviseurs des lycées, 9 September 1937.

29 ANSOM, EC 37/4 Robert Delavignette, Allocution, 1937.

30 On the importance of milieu in nineteenth-century social thought and policy, see Rabinow 1989.

31 Delavignette 1946: 31–32. This text was originally published in 1939.

32 *Congrès international et intercolonial de la société indigène, tome II* (1931), Paris: Exposition coloniale international: 5–6.

33 See also 'La Vie de Maurice Delafosse' *Outre-Mer, No. Spécial: Mémorial Maurice Delafosse* (1929), 1 (3): 263–69. On Delafosse's role in the colonial administration's rehabilitation of African political institutions, see Conklin 1997: 177–187.

34 Maurice Delafosse, 'Étude préparatoire d'un programme de measures à prendre en vue d'améliorer la situation des indigènes au double point de vue administrativa et social', May 1919. Reprinted in Michel 1975: 317.

35 Delafosse, 'Étude préparatoire' in Michel 1975: 324. For another ethnographic discussion presented in a welfarist idiom, see Randau 1934. Randau, a colonial administrator, characterizes magic as an African form of *prévoyance* against bad 'luck, probability, risk', in order to 'ensure [assurer] security, prosperity, and health'. This ethnography, he explains, 'contributes to European science . . . because it comes from the surest source.' He introduces Delobsom as both 'a native from Mossi country' and 'a distinguished black, very educated, intelligent, Frenchified, who in Ougadougou occupies an important post in the French administration'.

36 For an overview of Clozel's career, see Conklin 1997: 176–180.

37 ANSOM EE-II 3022/5, Personnel Dossier: Jules Brévié.

38 On the relation between Delafosse's and Brévié's views of African Islam, see Harrison 1988: 144–150.

39 ANSOM EE II 1058/2 Notes confidentielles: Henri Labouret, 1934.

40 ANSOM EE II 1058/2 Letter from Labouret to Minister of Colonies, 1 August 1919.

41 ANSOM EE II 1058/2 Letter from Labouret to Minister of Colonies, 14 November 1918.

42 ANSOM EE II 1058/2 Letter from Labouret to Minister of Colonies, 1 August 1919.

43 ANSOM EE II 1058/2 Notes confidentielles: Henri Labouret, 1934.

44 ANSOM EE II 1058/2 Notes confidentielles: Henri Labouret, 1934, 1922, 1924.

45 ANSOM EE II 1058/2 Notes confidentielles: Henri Labouret, 1934, 1927.

46 ANSOM EE II 1058/2 Notes confidentielles: Henri Labouret, 1934.

47 Labouret participated in scholarly associations such as the International Institute of Ethnography, the International Colonial Institute, and the International Institute of African Languages and Cultures (L'Estoile, this volume). On the Institute and its concern with applied anthropology and colonial administration in Africa, see Kuper

1983: 105–109; Kuklick 1991: 56–57, 207–215; Goody 1995: 7–25. On the role of American foundations in the funding of disciplinary anthropology, Stocking 1992: 178–211.

48 This plan was also included in Labouret 1932.

49 See Stocking 1992: 12–59 and Kuklick 1991: 90.

50 It included Lowie, Rivers, Kroeber, and Malinowski, Cohen (a linguist), the latest 'Notes and Queries,' texts published by the Musée d'Ethnographie, the I.A.I., the Année Sociologique, and courses taught by Mauss at the Ecole des Hautes Études and the Institut d'Ethnologie. On the 1920s as the classical period of anthropology see Stocking 1992: 114–177.

51 This manuscript was edited by Mauss and published in 1931 by the Institut d'Ethnologie when Labouret was a professor at the École Nationale des Langues Orientales Vivantes and the École Coloniale.

52 For a discussion of the way French 'administrator-ethnographers' in West Africa addressed the relationship between individualism and social hierarchy there through a Western optic, see Van Hoven 1990.

53 For general accounts of the reorientation of colonial doctrines or policies after World War I, which are then evaluated in different ways, see Cohen 1971: 84–142; Girardet 1972: 175–199, 253–273; Meynier 1990: 71–209; Roberts 1996: 109–192; and Conklin 1997: 142–245.

54 My conception of 'colonial humanism' thus contrasts directly to the way this term has been used in the historiography by Girardet 1972: 253–68; Cohen 1971: 83, 84–107; and Coquery-Vidrovitch 1990: 259–266.

55 This final section on interwar colonial policy is excerpted from Wilder (2005).

56 This tension between abstracting, universalizing or modernizing policies and concretizing, particularizing and primitivizing policies has been a persistent feature of colonial politics throughout the modern period. See Cohn 1987: 632–682; Chatterjee 1993: 3–34, 200–239; Thomas 1994: 105–142; Mamdani 1996; Comaroff and Comaroff 1997: 365–404. In the French imperial context, see Betts 1961; Cohen 1971: 117; Rabinow 1989; Lebovics 1992; Cooper 1996; Conklin 1997; Dubois 1999.

57 Here I am using 'welfare' to refer to a government rationality, a political logic, and not to a fully formed system in which the state pays social benefits to different categories of citizens. For an account of a 'colonial welfare state' in the latter sense, see Thompson 2000.

58 On the attempts by Ponty, Von Vollenhoven, Merlin and Carde to restore authority to native chiefs, see Buell 1928: 995–998; Labouret 1931a: 33–42; Cohen 1971: 114–119; Conklin 1997: 174–211. For an overview of the native chief system, see Crowder 1978; and Crowder and Ikime, 1978.

59 Rapport politique 1937, Archives de l'AOF 2G 37 (200mi 1782).

60 Governor General Roume organized the first system of justice in French West Africa in 1903 based a principle that would guide policy through the thirties: 'In all cases, native justice will apply local customs in so far as they are not contrary to the principles of French civilization.' The full decree is reprinted in Villamur and Delafosse 1904: 137–172. Subsequent juridical reforms in 1912, 1924 and 1931 maintained this principle. See Decret portant reorganization de la justice indigene en AOF, June 1923, ANSOM 1AP 1645. Brévié's 1931 decree is reprinted in La Justice Indigène en Afrique Occidentale Francaise (1941): 57–72. For an explanation of the administrative organization of West African native justice in the 1920s, see Buell 1928: 1002–1020. For the history of successive juridical reforms beginning in 1903, see Labouret 1930a, 1931c, and Conklin 1997: 86–94.

61 For various positions on codificaton see Girault 1926: 387–388, Solus 1927: 188–196, Labouret 1931a: 65, 70–71, Geismar 1933: 5–11, 1934: 257–266.

62 Quoted in Maupoil 1939: 28–29.

63 On the politics of customary law, see Channock 1985; Mann and Roberts 1991; Cohn 1996: 57–75; Mamdani 1996: 49–61, 109–137; Comaroff and Comaroff 1997: 365–404; Conklin 1997: 86–94, 119–130.

64 This clumsy terminology was a function of African colonial subjects' legal inde-
terminacy. By virtue of the conquest they already possessed French nationality, even
though they enjoyed neither French civil nor political rights. Because they were not
foreigners, they could not be naturalized, but only 'advanced' to citizenship.

65 Décret réglant les conditions d'accession des indigenes de l'AOF à la qualité de
citoyen francais, 25 May 1912, ANSOM 1AP 1638.

66 For rejections of citizenship applications, see dossiers from the Commission
Permanente du Conseil du Gouvernement 1929–1932, ANSOM 1AP 148, 149, 150,
151, 151.

67 For discussion between Paris, Dakar and individual governors on restrictive interpretations of the 1912 decree, see AOF 1AP 23G 9 (200mi 3212).

68 For a political-theoretical account of the constitutive relationship between gender
and families to citizenship and nationality see Stevens 1999.

69 France's 1889 nationality law had presumed that second-generation immigrants
would naturally assimilate French culture (Brubaker 1992). Administrators recognized that in a colonial context, where people regularly inhabited multiple milieux,
legal and cultural identity did not necessarily entail one another.

70 GG AOF, Circulaire: Statut des indigènes de l'AOF, October 8, 1922 and Carde, Nat-
uralisation des indigènes June 1923, both in AOF 23G 9 (200mi 3213).

71 On the gendered politics of family citizenship and nationality in France and the
empire, see Heuer 1999, Camiscioli 1999, Pedersen 1998.

72 Sarraut argued that Dakar's interpretation of the 1912 decree violated its spirit by
making it effectively impossible for any wives or families to meet the citizenship
criteria defined by Article 6. Ministre des Colonies, Sarraut to GG AOF, Interpré-
tation du décret du 25 Mai 1912, July 31, 1922, AOF 23G (200mi 3213). For an
account that interprets the 1932 citizenship reform in terms of 'conservative'
racism in the colonies as well as metropolitan pronatalism, eugenics, and social
hygiene movements, see Conklin 1998b.

73 Accession des indigenes de l'Afrique occidentale francaise aux droits de citoyen
francais, 21 August 1932, *Journal Officiel de la Republique Francaise*, 25 August
1932, 9291.

74 GG Brévié, Circulaire: Accession des indigenes à la qualité de citoyen francais,
January 1933, ANSOM 1AP 1549.

75 Décret réglant les conditions d'accession des indigenes de l'Afrique Occidentale
francaise à la qualité de citoyen francais, 25 May 1912. ANSOM 1AP 1638.

76 Au sujet de la revision des actes réglementant l'accession des indigenes à la qualité
de citoyen francais, August 1931, AOF 23G 8 (200mi 3212), Le GG de l'AOF to M.
le Ministre des Colonies, Refonte des texts relatifs à l'accession des indigenes orig-
inaires de l'AOF à la qualité de citoyens francais, 6 October 1931, AOF 23G8 (200mi
3212), GG de l'AOF Circulaire: Constitution des dossiers de naturalization, 16 April
1932, AOF 23G8 (200mi 3212), GG Brévié, Circulaire: Délivrance de certificates de
bonnes view et moeurs, 15 February 1933, AOF 23G8 (200mi 3212).

77 For pioneering and exemplary analyses on this issue, see Stoler 2002.

78 Accession des indigenes de l'Afrique occidentale francaise aux droits de citoyen
francais, 21 August 1932, *J.O.R.F.* 25 August 1932, 9291.

79 GG Brévié, Arreté: Etat Civil Indigène, 29 May 1933, AOF, 23G 6 (200mi/3210).
Brévié refers to Circulaires from 7 December 1916 and 31 May 1918, that had formerly regulated the native declarations. GG Brévié to Minister of Colonies, 31 April
1932, AOF 23G6 (200mi 3210). Governors-General Clozel and Carde had directed
local administrators to create separate registers for African civil declarations in
order to prevent them from illegally using and abusing the official French *état civil*
where they made false declarations. GG de l'AOF Clozel, Etat civil des indigenes
non citoyens francais, 6 December 1916, AOF 23G 6 (200mi 3210), GG Carde, Lois
du 17 Fevrier 1924, 3 May 1924, AOF 23G6 (200mi 3211).

80 GG de l'AOF, 13 February 1931, AOF 23G 13.

81 Ibid, GG Brévié to Minister of Colonies, 31 April 1932, AOF 23G 6, GG Brévié,
Arreté: Etat Civil Indigène, 29 May 1933, AOF, 23G 6 (200mi/3210).

82 Chef du Service Judiciaire de l'AOF, Jugements Supplétifs d'État Civil, 22 November 1915, AOF 23G 13 (200mi 3218).
83 Ibid.
84 Minister of Colonies to GG AOF, August 23 1932, AOF, 23G 6 (200mi 3210).
85 Rapport sur le fonctionnement de l'État Civil Indigène en AOF en 1934, AOF 23G 6 (200mi 3211).
86 Le GG de l'AOF (Fournier), Circulaire: L'État civil indigène, 2 June 1934, ANSOM 1AP 541.
87 Lt. Gov. Haute Volta, Circulaire: État Civil Indigène, 14 February 1921, AOF, 23G 6 (200mi 3210).
88 Le Maire de Saint-Louis to Lt. Gouv. Sénégal, Etat Civil, 15 July 1921, AOF 23G 13 (200mi 3218).
89 Chef du Service Judiciaire de l'AOF to GG AOF, État Civil, 8 September 1921, Minister of Colonies to GG AOF, État Civil, AOF 23G 6 (200mi 3210).
90 Le Maire de Saint-Louis to Lt. Gouv. Sénégal, Etat Civil, 15 July 1921, AOF 23G 13 (200mi 3218), GG Carde, Circulaire: Abus de nom patronymique, AOF, 30 April 1930 23G 15 (200mi 3219), Minister of Colonies Sarraut, Proposition de loi, francisation de noms, 29 April 1933, AOF 23G 19 (200mi 3221), GG Brévié to Minister of Colonies, Francisation du nom des étrangers et indigenes naturalisés, 11 July 1933, 23G 19 (200mi 3221).
91 Chef du Service Judiciaire AOF, Jugements supplétifs d'état civil, 22 November 1915, AOF 23G 13 (200mi 3218), Directeur des Affaires politiques to Chef du Service Judiciaire, L'État civil indigène, Le Maire de Saint-Louis to Lt. Gouv. Sénégal, Etat Civil, 15 July 1921, AOF 23G 13 (200mi 3218), GG AOF to Chef du Service Judiciaire, Abus des jugements supplétifs en matière d'état civil, 15 February 1922, AOF 23G 13 (200mi 3218), GG Carde, Lois du Fevrier 17, 1924, 3 May 1924, AOF 23G 6 (200mi 3211), Lt. Gouv. Dahomey to GG AOF: Adjovi, 20 August 1926, AOF 23G 9 (200mi 3213), Rapport sur le fonctionnement de l'état civil en AOF 1934, AOF 23G 6 (200mi 3211).
92 For example, Le statut juridique de la femme dans les colonies francaises and Note sure la circulaire du GG relative aux marriages indigènes en AOF (both in ANSOM 1AP 541) and GG de l'AOF De Coppet to Minister of Colonies, June 14, 1938, Minister of Colonies Mandel to GG AOF June 19, 1939, GG AOF Circulaire: Décret sur la mariages indigènes June 24, 1939, Le Governeur du Sénégal to GG AOF, November 29, 1939 (all in AOF 23G 12 (200mi 3218)). The documents relate ethnographic descriptions of African marriages to a government initiative to regulate and transform local marriage practices directly.
93 Compare with 'the tutelary complex' in Donzelot 1979. Pels and Salemink's conception of 'colonial intelligence' also suggests the composite character that I am describing (1999) and Pels 1999. Salemink makes the important point that professional ethnology's increasing independence from colonial government actually increased rather than decreased its political authority (Salemink 1999: 313).

References

Amselle, J.-L. 1998a. 'Maurice Delafosse: un africaniste ambigu'. In J.-L. Amselle and E. Sibeud (eds). *Maurice Delafosse – Entre orientalisme et ethnographie: l'itinéraire d'un africaniste (1870–1926)*. Paris: Maisonneuve et Larose, pp. 122–136.

Amselle, J.-L. 1998b. *Mestizo Logics: Anthropology of Identity in Africa and Elsewhere*. Stanford: Stanford University Press.

Amselle, J.-L. and Sibeud, E. (eds). 1998. *Maurice Delafosse – Entre orientalisme et ethnographie: l'itinéraire d'un africaniste (1870–1926)*. Paris: Maisonneuve et Larose.

Balandier, G. 1955. *Sociologie actuelle de l'Afrique noir: dynamique des changements sociaux en Afrique centrale.* Paris: Presses Universitaires de France.

Barry, A., Osborne, T. and Rose, N. (eds). 1996. *Foucault and Political Reason: Liberalism, Neo-Liberalism and Rationalities of Government.* Chicago: University of Chicago Press.

Betts, R. 1961. *Assimilation and Association in French Colonial Theory, 1890–1914.* New York: Columbia University Press.

Brévié, J. 1923. *L'Islamisme contre 'naturisme' au Soudan francais: Essai de psychologie politique coloniale.* Paris: Ernest Laroux.

Brévié, J. 1930. *Discours prononcé par M. J. Brévié, Goveurneur Général de l'AOF à l'ouverture de la session du Conseil du gouvernement, décembre 1930.* Gorée: Imprimerie du Gouverneur Général.

Brévié, J. 1931. *Discours prononcé par M. J. Brévié, Goveurneur Général de l'AOF à l'ouverture de la session du Conseil du gouvernement, décembre 1931.* Gorée: Imprimerie du Gouverneur Général.

Brévié, J. 1935. *Circulaires de M. le Gouverneur Général Brévié sur la politique indigène et l'administration indigène en Afrique Occidentale Francaise.* Gorée: Imprimerie du Gouvernement Général.

Brévié, J. 1936. *Trois études de M. le gouverneur Brévié.* Gorée: Imprimerie du Gouverneur Général.

Brubaker, R. 1992. *Citizenship and Nationhood in France and Germany.* Cambridge: Harvard University Press.

Buell, R.L. 1928. *The Native Problem in Africa Vol. I.* New York: Macmillan.

Bullard, A. 2000. *Exile to Paradise: Savagery and Civilization in Paris and the South Pacific, 1790–1900.* Stanford: Stanford University Press.

Camiscioli, E. 1999. 'Intermarriage, Independent Nationality, and the Individual Rights of French Women: The Law of 10 August 1927'. *French Politics, Culture, and Society* 17:52–74.

Channock, M. 1985. *Law, Custom, and Social Order: The Colonial Experience in Malawi and Zambia.* Cambridge: Cambridge University Press.

Chatterjee, P. 1993. *The Nation and its Fragments: Colonial and Postcolonial Histories.* Princeton: Princeton University Press.

Clifford, J. 1982. *Person and Myth: Maurice Leenhardt in the Melanesian World.* Durham: Duke University Press.

Clifford, J. 1988. *The Predicament of Culture: Twentieth Century Ethnography, Literature, and Art.* Cambridge: Harvard University Press.

Clozel, G.G. 1912. 'Preface'. In M. Delafosse. *Haut-Sénégal-Niger.* Paris: Larose.

Clozel, F.-J. and Villamur, R. (eds). 1902. *Les coutumes indigènes de la Cote d'Ivoire.* Paris: A. Challamel.

Cohen, W.B. 1971. *Rulers of Empire: The French Colonial Service in Africa.* Stanford: Hoover Institution Press.

Cohn, B.S. 1987. *An Anthropologist among the Historians and Other Essays.* Delhi: Oxford University Press.

Cohn, B.S. 1996. *Colonialism and its Forms of Knowledge: The British in India.* Princeton: Princeton University Press.

Comaroff, J.L. and Comaroff, J. 1997. *Of Revelation and Revolution. Volume 2: The Dialectics of Modernity on a South African Frontier.* Chicago: University of Chicago Press.

Conklin, A. 1997. *A Mission to Civilize: Republican Ideas of Empire in France and West Africa.* Stanford: Stanford University Press.

Conklin, A. 1998a. ' "On a semé la haine": Maurice Delafossse et la politique du Gouvernement general en AOF'. In J.-L. Amselle and E. Sibeud (eds). *Maurice Delafosse – Entre orientalisme et ethnographie: l'itinéraire d'un africaniste (1870–1926).* Paris: Maisonneuve et Larose, pp. 65–77.

Conklin, A. 1998b. 'Redefining "Frenchness": Citizenship, Race Regeneration, and Imperial Motherhood in France and West Africa 1914–40'. In J. Clancy-Smith and F. Gouda (eds). *Domesticating the Empire: Race, Gender, and Family Life in French and Dutch Colonialism.* Charlottesville: University of Virginia Press, pp. 65–83.

Cooper, F. 1996. *Decolonization and African Society: The Labor Question in French and British Africa.* Cambridge: Cambridge University Press.

Copans, J. 1975. *Anthropologie et impérialisme.* Paris: Maspero.

Copans, J. 1979. 'D'un africanisme à l'autre'. *Canadian Journal of African Studies* 13:55–68.

Coquery-Vidrovitch, C. 1990. 'La Colonisation francaise'. In J. Thobie, G. Meynier, C. Coquery-Vidrovitch and C.-R. Ageron (eds). *Histoire de la France coloniale, 1914–1990.* Paris: Armand Colin, pp. 259–266.

Crowder, M. 1978. 'Indirect Rule – French and British Style'. In M. Crowder (ed.). *Colonial West Africa: Collected Essays.* London: Frank Cass, pp. 198–208.

Crowder, M. and Ikime, O. 1978. 'West African Chiefs'. In M. Crowder (ed.). *Colonial West Africa: Collected Essays.* London: Frank Cass, pp. 209–230.

Dean, M. 1994. *Critical and Effective Histories: Foucault's Methods and Historical Sociology.* London: Routledge.

Dean, M. 1999. *Governmentality: Power and Rule in Modern Society.* London: Sage Publications.

Delafosse, M. 1912. *Haut-Sénégal-Niger (Soudan Francais): Séries d'études publiées sous la direction de M. le Gouverneur Clozel.* Paris: Larose.

Delafosse, M. 1921. 'Sur l'orientation nouvelle de la politique indigène dans l'afrique noire'. *Renseignements coloniaux en Afrique francaise* 6:145–153.

Delafosse, M. 1923. *Broussard ou les états d'ame d'un colonial: Suivis de ses propos et opinions.* Paris: Larose.

Delafosse, M. 1927. *Les Nègres.* Paris: Les Éditions Rieder.

Delafosse, L. 1976. *Maurice Delafosse: le Berrichon conquis par l'Afrique.* Paris: Société francaise d'histoire d'outre mer.

Delavignette, R. 1931. 'Connaissances des mentalités indigènes en AOF'. *Congrès international et intercolonial de la société indigène, tome I.* Paris: Exposition coloniale international, pp. 553–566.

Delavignette, R. 1946. *Service africain.* Paris: Gallimard.

Dewitte, P. 1985. *Les mouvements nègres en France, 1919–1939.* Paris: Harmattan.

Dias, N. 1991. *Le musée d'ethnographie du Trocadero: Anthropologie et muséologie en France, 1878–1908*. Paris: Editions du CNRS.

Dirks, N. 2001. *Castes of Mind: Colonialism and the Making of Modern India*. Princeton: Princeton University Press.

Donzelot, J. 1979. *The Policing of Families*. Baltimore: Johns Hopkins University Press.

Donzelot, J. 1984. *L'Invention du social*. Paris: Fayard.

Dubois, L. 1999. ' "The Price of Liberty": Victor Hugues and the Administration of Freedom in Guadeloupe, 1794–1802'. *William and Mary Quarterly* 3rd series, LVI(2):363–392.

Durkheim, E. and Mauss, M. 1963. *Primitive Classification*. Chicago: University of Chicago Press.

Ewald, F. 1986. *L'Etat providence*. Paris: Grasset.

Fanon, F. 1956. 'Racisme et culture'. *Présence Africaine* No. Spéciale: Le Premier Congrès International des Écrivains et Artistes Noirs, pp. 122–131.

Fanon, F. 1967. *Black Skin, White Masks*. New York: Grove Press.

Foucault, M. 1981. 'Omnes et Singulatum: Towards a Criticism of "Political Reason"'. In S. McMurrin (ed.). *The Tanner Lectures on Human Value, Volume 2*. Salt Lake City: University of Utah Press, pp. 223–254.

Foucault, M. 1982. 'The Subject and Power'. In H. Dreyfus and P. Rabinow (eds). *Michel Foucault: Beyond Structuralism and Hermeneutics. With an Afterward by and an Interview with Michel Foucault*. Chicago: University of Chicago Press, pp. 208–226.

Foucault, M. 1984. 'What is Enlightenment?'. In P. Rabinow (ed.). *The Foucault Reader*. New York: Pantheon, pp. 32–50.

Foucault, M. 1988a. 'The Political Technology of Individuals'. In L.H. Martin, H. Gutman and P.H. Hutton (eds). *Technologies of the Self: A Seminar with Michel Foucault*. Amherst: University of Massachusetts Press, pp. 145–162.

Foucault, M. 1991. 'Questions of Method'. In G. Burchell, C. Gordon and P. Miller (eds). *The Foucault Effect: Studies in Governmentality*. Chicago: University of Chicago Press, pp. 73–86.

Foucault, M. 1997a. 'The Courses'. In P. Rabinow (ed.). *Essential Works of Michel Foucault, Volume I: Ethics, Subjectivity and Truth*. New York: The New Press, pp. 223–254.

Foucault, M. 1997b. 'Michel Foucault: An Interview with Stephen Riggins'. In P. Rabinow (ed.). *Essential Works of Michel Foucault, Volume I: Ethics, Subjectivity and Truth*. New York: The New Press, pp. 121–133.

Foucault, M. 1998. 'Structuralism and Post-Structuralism'. In J.D. Faubion (ed.). *Essential Works of Foucault 1954–84, Volume 2: Aesthetics, Method, and Epistemology*. New York: The Free Press, pp. 433–458.

Foucault, M. 2003. *Society Must Be Defended: Lectures at the Collège de France 1975–1976*. New York: Picador.

Geismar, L. 1933. *Receuil des coutumes civil des races du Sénégal*. Saint Louis: Imprimerie du Gouvernement Général.

Geismar, L. 1934. 'L'action gouvernmentale et les coutumes indigènes'. *Outre-Mer* 6:257–266.

POLITICAL RATIONALITY IN FRENCH WEST AFRICA

Girardet, R. 1972. *L'Idée coloniale en France de 1871 à 1962*. Paris: La Table Ronde.

Girault, A. 1926. *Principes de colonisation et de législation coloniale*. Paris: Sirey.

Goody, J. 1995. *The expansive moment: the rise of social anthropology in Britain and Africa, 1918–1970*. New York: Cambridge University Press.

Gordon, C. 1991. 'Governmental Rationality: An Introduction'. In G. Burchell, C. Gordon and P. Miller (eds). *The Foucault Effect: Studies in Governmentality*. Chicago: University of Chicago Press, pp. 1–52.

Gordon, C. 2000. 'Introduction'. In J.D. Faubion (ed.). *Essential Works of Michel Foucault 1954–1984, Volume 3: Power*. New York: Free Press, pp. xi–xli.

Gringeri, R. 1990. 'Twilight of the Sun Kings: French Anthropology from Modernism to Postmodernism, 1925–1950'. University of California, Berkeley: Unpublished Ph.D.

Grosz-Ngaté, M. 1988. 'Power and Knowledge: The Representation of the Mande World in the Works of Park, Caillié, Monteil, and Delafosse'. *Cahiers d'études africaines* XVIII:485–511.

Hardy, G. 1925. 'L'histoire coloniale et psychologie ethnique'. *Revue de l'histoire des colonies francaises* XVIII:161–172.

Hardy, G. 1929. *Nos grands problèmes coloniaux*. Paris: Armand Colin.

Hardy, G. 1931. 'Rapport général'. *Congrès international et intercolonial de la société indigène, tome 1*. Paris: Exposition coloniale internationale, pp. 605–627.

Hardy, G. 1937. 'Sociologie Coloniale'. *Outre-Mer* 9(1):55–62.

Harrison, C. 1988. *France and Islam in West Africa, 1860–1960*. Cambridge: Cambridge University Press.

Heuer, J. 1999. 'Adopted Daughter of the French People: Suzanne Lepeletier and her Father, the National Assembly'. *French Politics, Culture, and Society* 17:31–51.

James, W. 1973. 'The Anthropologist as a Reluctant Imperialist'. In T. Asad (ed.). *Anthropology and the Colonial Encounter*. Atlantic Highlands, NJ: Humanities Press, pp. 41–69.

Jamin, J. 1984. 'Aux origines du musée de l'homme: la mission ethnographique et linguistique Dakar-Djibouti'. *Cahiers ethnologiques: Revue du centre d'études ethnologiques* No. 5:7–86.

Jamin, J. 1986. 'L'ethnographie mode d'inemploi: De quelques rapports de l'ethnologie avec le malaise dans la civilization'. In J. Hainard and R. Kaehr (eds). *Le Mal et la Douleur*. Paris: Musée d'Ethnographie, pp. 45–80.

Johnson, G.W. 1971. *The Emergence of Black Politics in Senegal: The Struggle for Power in the Four Communes, 1900–1920*. Stanford: Stanford University Press.

Kuisel, R. 1981. *Capitalism and the State in Modern France*. Cambridge: Cambridge University Press.

Kuklick, H. 1991. *The Savage Within: The Social History of British Anthropology, 1885–1945*. Cambridge: Cambridge University Press.

[371]

Kuper, A. 1983. *Anthropology and Anthropologists: The Modern British School*. London: Routledge & Kegan Paul.

Labouret, H. 1930a. 'La justice indigène en Afrique Occidentale'. *Outre-Mer* 2:58–64.

Labouret, H. 1930b. 'A la recherche d'une politique coloniale'. *Le Monde Colonial Illustré* 82:133.

Labouret, H. 1930c. 'Le Gouverneur Général Brévié'. *Afrique Francaise*: 531–533.

Labouret, H. 1931a. *A la recherche d'une politique indigène dans l'ouest africain*. Paris: Eds. du Comité de l'Afrique francaise.

Labouret, H. 1931b. *Les tribus du rameau lobi*. Paris: Institut d'Ethnologie.

Labouret, H. 1931c. 'Le respect des coutumes indigènes'. In Institut Colonial International (ed.). *Compte rendu de la XXI session tenus a Paris les 5,6,7,8 mai 1931*. Brussels: Établissements Généraux d'Imprimerie, pp. cxvi–cxlvi.

Labouret, H. 1932. 'Ethnologie coloniale'. *Outre-Mer* 4(1):49.

Labouret, H. 1933a. *Plan de Monographie Régionale*. Paris: Larose.

Labouret, H. 1933b. 'Les siècles obscurs'. *Le monde colonial illustré* 124:186–188.

Labouret, H. 1934. *Les mandingue et leur langue*. Paris: Larose.

La Justice Indigène en Afrique Occidentale Francaise. 1941. Rufisque: Imprimerie du Haut Commisariat.

'La Vie de Maurice Delafosse'. 1929. *Outre-Mer No. Spécial: Mémorial Maurice Delafosse* 1(3):263–269.

Lebovics, H. 1992. *True France: The Wars Over Cultural Identity, 1900–1945*. Ithaca: Cornell University Press.

Leclerc, G. 1972. *Anthropologie et colonialisme: Essai sur l'historie de l'africanisme*. Paris: Fayard.

Leiris, M. 1950. 'L'ethnographe devant le colonialisme'. *Les Temps modernes* 6(5):357–374.

Leiris, M. 1981. *L'Afrique fantome*. Paris: Gallimard.

Leiris, M. 1992. *C'est-à-dire: Entretien avec Sally Price et Jean Jamin*. Paris: Jean-Michel Place.

L'Estoile, B. de. 1997. 'The "Natural Preserve of Anthropologists": Social Anthropology, Scientific Planning, and Development'. *Social Science Information* 36(2):343–376.

L'Estoile, B. de. 2000. 'Science de l'homme et "domination rationelle": Savoir ethnologique et politique indigene en Afrique coloniale francaise'. *Revue de synthèse* 4:292–323.

Lévy-Bruhl, L. 1925. 'L'Institut d'Ethnologie de l'Université de Paris'. *Revue d'ethnographie* 23–24:233–236.

Lèvy-Bruhl, L. 1985. *How Natives Think*. Princeton: Princeton University Press.

Liauzu, C. 1982. *Aux origines des tiers-mondismes: colonisés et anticolonialistes en France, 1919–1939*. Paris: Harmattan.

Lorcin, P. 1995. *Imperial Identities: Stereotyping, Prejudice, and Race in Colonial Algeria*. London and New York: I.B. Tauris.

Maier, C.S. 1970. 'Between Taylorism and Technocracy: European Ideologies and the Vision of Industrial Productivity in the 1920s'. *Journal of Contemporary History* 5(2):27–61.

Malinowski, B. 1929. 'Practical Anthropology'. *Africa* II:22–38.

Mamdani, M. 1996. *Citizen and Subject: Contemporary Africa and the Legacy of Late Colonialism*. Princeton: Princeton University Press.

Mann, K. and Roberts, R. (eds). 1991. *Law in Colonial Africa*. Portsmouth: Heinemann.

Maupoil, B. 1939. 'L'étude des coutumes juridiques de l'AOF', *Coutumiers juridiques de l'Afrique Occidentale Francaise*, Paris: Larose, Publications du Comité d'études historiques et scientifiques de l'Afrique Occidentale Francaise.

Mauss, M. 1913. 'L'ethnographie en France et a l'étranger'. *La Revue de Paris* 20, Pt. 5:550–551.

Mauss, M. 1967. *The Gift: Forms and Functions of Exchange in Archaic Societies*. New York: Norton.

Mauss, M. 1968. 'Les Civilisations: Élements et formes'. In M. Mauss. *Essais de Sociologie*. Paris: Minuit, pp. 249–252.

Mauss, M. 1969a. 'La Nation'. In M. Mauss. *Oeuvres, Vol. 3: Civilisation sociale et divisions de la sociologie*. Paris: Minuit.

Mauss, M. 1969b. 'La Nation et l'Internationalisme'. In M. Mauss. *Oeuvres, Vol. 3: Civilisation sociale et divisions de la sociologie*. Paris: Minuit.

Mauss, M. 1979a. 'A Category of the Human Mind: The Notion of Person, the Notion of "Self"'. In M. Mauss. *Sociology and Psychology*. London: Routledge & Kegan Paul, pp. 57–94.

Mauss, M. 1979b. 'Real and Practical Relations between Psychology and Sociology'. In M. Mauss. *Sociology and Psychology*. London: Routledge & Kegan Paul, pp. 1–33.

Mauss, M. 1989. *Manuel d'ethnographie*. Paris: Payot.

Meynier, G. 1990. 'La France coloniale de 1914 à 1931'. In J. Thobie, G. Meynier, C. Coquery-Vidrovitch and C.-R. Ageron (eds). *Histoire de la France coloniale 1914–1990*. Paris: Armand Colin.

Michel, M. 1975. 'Un programme réformiste en 1919: Maurice Delafosse et la "politique indigene" in AOF'. *Cahiers d'études africaines* XV:313–327.

Miller, P. and Rose, N. 1990. 'Governing Economic Life'. *Economy and Society* 19:1–31.

Pedersen, J.E. 1998. ' "Special Customs": Paternity Suits and Citizenship in France and the Colonies, 1870–1912'. In J. Clancy-Smith and F. Gouda (eds). *Domesticating the Empire: Race, Gender, and Family Life in French and Dutch Colonialism*. Charlottesville: University of Virginia Press, pp. 21–42.

Pels, P. 1999. 'The Rise and Fall of the Indian Aborigines: Orientalism, Anglicism, and the Emergence of an Ethnology of India, 1833–1869'. In P. Pels and O. Salemink (eds). *Colonial Subjects: Essays on the Practical History of Anthropology*. Ann Arbor: The University of Michigan Press, pp. 22–116.

Pels, P. and Salemink, O. 1999. 'Introduction: Locating Colonial Subjects of Anthropology'. In P. Pels and O. Salemink (eds). *Colonial Subjects: Essays on the Practical History of Anthropology*. Ann Arbor: The University of Michigan Press, pp. 1–52.

Procacci, G. 1993. *Gouverner la misère: La Question sociale en France*. Paris: Seuil.

Rabinow, P. 1989. *French Modern: Norms and Forms of the Social Environment*. Cambridge: MIT Press.

Randau, R. 1934. 'Préface'. In D. Delobsom *Les secrets des sorciers noirs*. Paris: Librairie Émile Nourry, pp. 5–28.

Rivet, P. and Rivière, G.-H. 1930. 'La réorganisation du Musée d'ethnographie du Trocadéro'. *Outre-Mer* 2:138–148.

Roberts, R. 1996. *Two Worlds of Cotton: Colonialism and the Regional Economy in the French Soudan, 1800–1946*. Stanford: Stanford University Press.

Robinson, D. 1992. 'Ethnography and Customary Law in Senegal'. *Cahiers d'études africaines* XXXII:221–237.

Rosanvallon, P. 1990. *L'Etat en France de 1789 à nos jours*. Paris: Seuil.

Rose, N. 1999. *Powers of Freedom: Reframing Political Thought*. Cambridge: Cambridge University Press.

Rose, N. and Miller, P. 1992. 'Political Power beyond the State: Some Problematics of Government'. *The British Journal of Sociology* 43:173–205.

Roume, E. 1933. 'Discours de M. Ernst Roume'. *Outre-Mer* 5(1):80–81.

Salemink, O. 1991. 'Mois and Maquis: The Invention and Appropriation of Vietnam's Montagnards from Sabatier to the CIA'. In G.W. Stocking Jr. (ed.). *Colonial Situations: Essays on the Contextualization of Anthropological Knowledge*. Madison: University of Wisconsin Press, pp. 243–284.

Salemink, O. 1999. 'Ethnography as Martial Art: Ethnicizing Vietnam's Montagnards, 1930–1954'. In P. Pels and O. Salemink (eds). *Colonial Subjects: Essays on the Practical History of Anthropology*. Ann Arbor: The University of Michigan Press, pp. 282–325.

Sarraut, A. 1923. *La mise en valeur des colonies francaises*. Paris: Payot.

Schulte Nordholt, H. 1999. 'The Making of Traditional Bali: Colonial Ethnography and Bureaucratic Reproduction'. In P. Pels and O. Salemink (eds). *Colonial Subjects: Essays on the Practical History of Anthropology*. Ann Arbor: The University of Michigan Press, pp. 241–281.

Sibeud, E. 1994. 'La naissance de l'ethnographie africaniste en France avant 1914'. *Cahiers d'études africaines* XXXIV:639–658.

Sibeud, E. 2002. *Une science impériale pour l'Afrique: la construction des savoirs africanistes en France, 1878–1930*. Paris: Éditions de l'École des hautes études en sciences sociales.

Solus, H. 1927. *Traité de la conditions des indigènes in droit privé*. Paris: Sirey.

Spiegler, J. 1968. 'Aspects of Nationalist Thought Among French-Speaking West Africans, 1921–1939'. Oxford University: Unpublished Ph.D.

Steinmetz, G. 2003. '"The Devil's Handwriting": Precolonial Discourse, Ethnographic Acuity, and Cross-Identification in German Colonialism'. *Comparative Studies in Society and History* 45:41–95.

Stevens, J. 1999. *Reproducing the State*. Princeton: Princeton University Press.

Stocking, G.W. 1968. 'French Anthropology in 1800'. In G. Stocking. *Race, Culture, and Evolution: Essays in the History of Anthropology*. New York: The Free Press, pp. 13–41.

Stocking, G.W. 1992. *The Ethnographer's Magic and other Essays in the History of Anthropology*. Madison: University of Wisconsin Press.

Stoler, A.L. 2002. *Carnal Knowledge and Imperial Power: Race and the Intimate in Colonial Rule*. Berkeley: University of California Press.

Suret-Canale, J. 1962. *Afrique noire: l'ère coloniale, 1900–1945*. Paris: Editions Sociales.

Thomas, N. 1994. *Colonialism's Culture: Anthropology, Travel, and Government*. Princeton: Princeton University Press.

Thompson, E. 2000. *Colonial Citizens: Republican Rights, Paternal Privilege, and Gender in French Syria and Lebanon*. New York: Columbia University Press.

Van Hoven, E. 1990. 'Representing Social Hierarchy – Administrators-Ethnographers in the French Sudan: Delafosse, Monteil, and Labouret'. *Cahiers d'études africaines* XXX:179–198.

Villamur, R. and Delafosse, M. 1904. *Les coutumes Agni: Rédigées et codifies*. Paris: Augustin Challamel.

Wilder, G. 1999a. 'The Politics of Failure: Historicizing Popular Front Colonial Policy in French West Africa'. In T. Chafer and A. Sackur (eds). *French Colonial Empire and the Popular Front: Hope and Disillusion*. New York: Saint Martins Press, pp. 33–55.

Wilder, G. 1999b. 'Practicing Citizenship in Imperial France'. In J.L. Comaroff and J. Comaroff (eds). *Civil Society and the Political Imagination in Africa: Critical Perspectives*. Chicago: University of Chicago Press, pp. 44–71.

Wilder, G. 2001. 'Framing Greater France Between the Wars'. *Journal of Historical Sociology* 14:198–225.

Wilder, G. 2005. *The French Imperial Nation-State: Negritude, Colonial Humanism, and Interwar Political Rationality*. Chicago: University of Chicago Press.

Williams, E. 1985. 'Anthropological Institutions in Nineteenth-Century France'. *Isis* 76(3):331–348.

Wooten, S.R. 1993. 'Colonial Administration and the Ethnography of the Family in the French Soudan'. *Cahiers d'études africaines* XXIII:419–446.

INDEX

Note: 'n.' after a page number indicates the number of a note on that page.

EU authorised representative for GPSR:
Easy Access System Europe, Mustamäe tee 50,
10621 Tallinn, Estonia
gpsr.requests@easproject.com